VINE'S
TOPICAL
COMMENTARY

PROPHECY

VINE'S
TOPICAL
COMMENTARY

PROPHECY

W. E. VINE
WITH C. F. HOGG

THOMAS NELSON
Since 1798

Vine's Topical Commentary: Prophecy

Published in Nashville, Tennessee, by Thomas Nelson. Thomas Nelson is a registered trademark of Thomas Nelson, Inc.

Thomas Nelson, Inc., titles may be purchased in bulk for educational, business, fund-raising, or sales promotional use. For information, please e-mail SpecialMarkets@ThomasNelson.com.

Library of Congress Cataloging-in-Publication Info

Names: Vine, W. E. (William Edwy), 1873-1949, author. | Hogg, C. F.
Title: Prophecy / W. E. Vine ; with C.F. Hogg.
Description: Nashville : Thomas Nelson, 2022. | Series: Vine's topical
    commentaries
Identifiers: LCCN 2022008991 (print) | LCCN 2022008992 (ebook) | ISBN
    9780310143567 (paperback) | ISBN 9781418560539 (ebook)
Subjects: LCSH: Prophecy--Christianity. | Prophecy--Christianity--Biblical
    teaching.
Classification: LCC BR115.P8 V56 2022 (print) | LCC BR115.P8 (ebook) |
    DDC 234/.13--dc23/eng/20220407
LC record available at https://lccn.loc.gov/2022008991
LC ebook record available at https://lccn.loc.gov/2022008992

22 23 24 25 26 — 5 4 3 2 1

CONTENTS

Introduction 7

Section 1: Prophecy

Prophetic Utterances 10

Section 2: Prophecies of Messiah

Isaiah 49–57: Prophecies, Promises, Warnings. 16

Isaiah 50 22

Isaiah 51 25

Isaiah 52:1–12 29

Isaiah 52:13–53 32

Isaiah 54 38

Isaiah 55–57 41

The Baptist's Testimony. 48

Section 3: End Times Prophecies

Witnesses to the Second Advent. 52

The Lord's Second Advent , ... 66

The Coming Priest-King 72

The Times Determined 90

The Expectancy of Christ. 93

The Resurrection and the Rapture. 101

The Parousia of the Lord 115

The Judgment Seat of Christ 124

The Epiphany of the Parousia 131

The Final Gentile World-Ruler and His Dominion 141

The Effect of Hope 148

A Synopsis of the Bible Doctrine of the Second Advent. 156

The Church and the Tribulation. 164

The Great Tribulation and the Wrath of God 167

CONTENTS

The Rapture and the Great Tribulation 176
Objections Considered 182
The Coming Revival of the Roman Empire 202
The Everlasting Kingdom 213
The Four Women of the Apocalypse 220
The Sealed Book of the Apocalypse 239

Appendix 250

INTRODUCTION

While many will agree with Vine's insight into the value and meaning of prophecy, this is a subject of varied interpretations. However, even if your own beliefs are different from Vine's, you will appreciate his openness to God's truth and his sense of excitement in seeing God's prophetic will revealed. He is not an extremist, but he conveys a genuine love for the prophetic teaching of Scripture.

—F. F. Bruce

Undoubtedly William Edwy Vine was qualified in many fields. As well as being a theologian and a man of outstanding academic intellect, he had a heart for all humanity that made him a master of communication.

Born in 1873, at the time when C. H. Spurgeon, D. L. Moody and F. B. Meyer were enjoying popularity on both sides of the Atlantic, Vine was brought up in a boarding school owned and governed by his father as its headmaster. This factor was a major contribution to his interest in teaching. At the age of seventeen he was a teacher at his father's school while attending the University College of Wales in preparation for his eventual London University degree, an M.A. in classics.

At the age of twenty-six he spent an Easter vacation at the home of a godly couple, Mr. and Mrs. Baxendale, where he met their daughter Phoebe; a few years later, Vine and Phoebe married. It was a marriage made in heaven. They had five children: Helen, Christine, Edward (O.B.E.), Winifred, and Jeanette. During the time of their engagement, Vine's reputation as a clear Bible expositor was growing. It was not long before he accepted the joint headmastership of the school with his father. In 1904, after his father died, his brother Theodore then became joint headmaster with him.

It was during this time, in conjunction with Mr. C. F. Hogg, that he produced three classic commentaries: 1 and 2 Thessalonians, followed by Galatians. These master works display the full scope of Vine's scholarship.

While Vine was teaching in the school, preparing for his M.A. and writing in-depth commentaries, he also developed a lifetime habit of teaching classes in New Testament Greek grammar. This laid the foundation for his all-time classic work, *An Expository Dictionary of New Testament Words*, and later, *An Expository Dictionary of Old Testament Words*. His Dictionaries are classics—copies are in excess of 3 million worldwide—proof that his scholarship and clarity of expression is as relevant as when first published.

Vine applies a "microscopic" approach to expository teaching—a word approach that takes into consideration every reference to that word in the Bible as well as its use in contemporary and classic Greek. Vine's verse-by-verse exposition reveals a depth of understanding that commentaries many times their size fail to give. He explains the meaning of the key words in each verse and links them with the complete passage.

Introduction

This volume is compiled from the writings on prophecy found in the five-volume series *The Collected Writings of W. E. Vine*. In some cases these articles have been condensed from their original form. They were written in the early years of the twentieth century, and any allusions to "current events" or political-geographical references should be considered in this light. Introductory paragraphs in italic type have been added to assist the reader.

PROPHETIC UTTERANCE

PROPHETIC UTTERANCES

PROPHECY

PROPHETIC UTTERANCES

This first article fitly introduces many key topics about prophecy that will be very beneficial to the reader in better understanding the nature and role of prophecy. The prophets did not obtain a general sense of what they were to say, mastering their subject and expressing it at their will, like a modern-day preacher; their statements were so under divine influence that the forms of expression which their communications took were the outcome of the action of the Holy Ghost. These messages fit into two basic categories: foretelling ("the things that will take place") and forth telling ("the things one needs to change right now").

The mission of the prophet was to speak in the name of the Lord. The message consisted in uttering the mind of God. "With the idea of a prophet there was this necessarily attached, that he spoke, not his own words, but those which he had directly received" (Gesenius' Hebrew Lexicon). Thus when Moses argued his inability to reason with Pharaoh God said, "Aaron thy brother shall be thy prophet" (Exod. 7:1), that is to say, Aaron would utter the word of God on Moses' behalf. The nature of prophecy in this respect applies to all the prophets of Scripture whether in the period covered by the Old Testament or in apostolic times.

"No prophecy is of private interpretation." This is explained, firstly, by the statement that "no prophecy ever came by the will of man." That prophecy was not of private interpretation means, then, that it did not originate in the will of the prophet. On the contrary, secondly, it was given by God; "men spake from God." Then as to the divine action in and through the prophets, "they were moved (lit., borne along) by the Holy Ghost." Accordingly, not only did prophecy not originate in the will of the prophet, but neither did he put his own construction upon the message he was to communicate. Both origin and control lay with God. The prophets did not obtain a general sense of what they were to say, mastering their subject and expressing it at their will; their statements were so under divine influence that the forms of expression which their communications took were the outcome of the action of the Holy Ghost.

EXEMPLIFIED IN BALAAM'S CASE

In this connection the case of Balaam is instructive. Despite his desires to the contrary, the Lord compelled him to declare messages exactly as he gave them. Balaam himself said, "I cannot go beyond the word of the Lord my God, to do less or more" (Num. 22:18), and again, later, "Have I now any power at all to speak anything? the word that God putteth in my mouth, that shall I speak" (22:38). On the next occasion it says, "The Lord put a word in Balaam's mouth, and said, . . ." (23:5). Again, replying to Balak's remonstrance he says, "Must I not take heed to speak that which the Lord putteth in my mouth?" (23:12). The next record is that "the Lord put a word in his mouth, and said, . . ." (v. 16). Finally, when Balak's anger is kindled because of his utterances, Balaam says, "If Balak would give me his house full of silver and gold, I cannot go beyond the word of the Lord, to do either good or bad of mine own mind; but what the Lord speaketh that will I speak" (24:13).

All this shows clearly that the Spirit of God determined, in the case of a prophet, not only the form of his prophecy but the very words. Even if Scripture were silent on the point it would be a perfectly reasonable conclusion that what was thus true of the spoken prophecy was likewise true of the written Scriptures. The statement of the apostle Peter quoted above is authoritative on the subject.

The language of their messages was thus inspired, and if this was true in the case of the spoken words, it was at least equally possible in the case of written words. That it was so with the former is indicated in several passages of Scripture. For instance, concerning the prophesying of the seventy elders with Moses, the narrative states that "When the Spirit rested upon them they prophesied, but they did so no more" (Num. 11:25). That is, the Spirit was speaking by them. They were not simply interpreting a divine message imparted to them. While they were under the power of the Spirit their words were not their own as on ordinary occasions; they were the words of God. Their utterances were not the outcome of their own volition. Not that the prophets were carried into an ecstatic condition of mind, rendering them incapable of entering intelligently into the meaning of their words. They did not speak apart from their understanding though they did not comprehend fully the purpose or complete application of their message.

PREDICTIVE PROPHECY

As to predictive prophecy, the accuracy of Bible predictions affords a striking evidence of its divine inspiration. Many attempts have been made to eliminate as far as possible this predictive element.[1] The whole character of these predictions, however, and especially in regard to Messianic prophecy, presents such "marvelous unity, self-consistency and comprehensiveness" as bears witness against all such efforts. The words of Professor Flint in this respect are worth quoting: "This broad, general fact—this vast and strange correlation of correspondence— cannot be in the least affected by questions of the 'higher criticism' as to the authorship, time, origination and mode of composition of the various books of the Old Testament. . . . Answer all these questions in the way which the boldest and most rationalistic criticism of Germany or Holland ventures to suggest; accept in every properly critical question the conclusions of the most advanced critical schools, and what will follow? Merely this, that those who do so will have, in various respects, to alter their views as to the manner and method in which the ideal of the Messiah's person, work, and kingdom was, point by point, line by

---

1 See "Bible Predictions and the Critics," by the writer. Also Prof. Orr, "The Problem of the Old Testament."

line, evolved and elaborated. There will not, however, be a single Messianic word or sentence, not a single line or feature the fewer in the Old Testament."

DEUTERONOMY 18:18–20

In the divine instructions to Israel concerning the prophets who were to be raised up for them, God said, "I will raise them up a prophet from among their brethren, like unto thee; and I will put My words in his mouth, and he shall speak unto them all that I shall command him. And it shall come to pass, that whosoever will not hearken unto My words which he shall speak in My name, I will require it of him. But the prophet, which shall speak a word presumptuously in My name, which I have not commanded him to speak, or that shall speak in the name of other gods, that same prophet shall die" (Deut. 18:18–20). It will be observed that the Lord speaks of "the words" not as so many statements, but as the separate words which constitute the statements. The utterances were to be given word for word. Obviously a prophet had the power of uttering fresh communications carrying with them the authority of divine law, and which, if put on record, would become part of Holy Scripture. The authority of the written Word is unquestionable with Israel. It was always accepted among the Jews that the appeal to that Word was final.

JEREMIAH 36

A striking passage in Jeremiah which illustrates the divine inspiration of the words of Scripture is the narrative which tells of the roll of the book which the prophet was commissioned to write. "This word came unto Jeremiah from the Lord, saying, Take thee a roll of a book, and write therein *all the words that I have spoken* against Israel, and against Judah, and against all the nations, from the day I spake unto thee, from the days of Josiah even unto this day." The prophet uses Baruch as his amanuensis: "Baruch wrote from the mouth of Jeremiah *all the words of the Lord, which he had spoken unto him*, upon a roll of a book. And Jeremiah commanded Baruch, saying, 'I am shut up; I cannot go unto the house of the Lord: therefore go thou, and read in the roll, which thou hast written from my mouth, *the words of the Lord* in the ears of the people . . .' And Baruch, the son of Neriah, did according to all that Jeremiah the prophet commanded him, reading in the book *the words of the Lord* in the Lord's house" (Jer. 36:2–8).

Nothing could be clearer than this, as confirmation of what has been said above, that while the faculties and intelligent cooperation of a prophet were not ruled out, yet the words he was to record were arranged for by God. In confirmation of this, in verse 10, what has been spoken of as "the words of the Lord" are said to be "the words of Jeremiah." And, further still, there follows in the same chapter the statement by Baruch as to how the writing was produced. In reply to the question asked by the princes, "How didst thou write all these words at his mouth?" he says, "He pronounced all these words unto me with his mouth, and I wrote them with ink in the book" (vv. 17, 18). Thus emphasis throughout the whole passage is laid upon the words. Moreover, this does not refer to what the prophet had just written, it consists of all the prophecies uttered by him up to that time concerning Israel and other nations (see v. 3).

This is substantiated by what Jeremiah says at the very beginning of his prophecies. In stating how the word of the Lord came to him at the first, making known to him that he was to be His messenger, he states that the Lord said to him: "Behold, *I have put My words in thy mouth*; see, I have this day set thee over the nations and over the kingdoms, to pluck up and to break down, and to destroy and to overthrow; to build, and to plant" (chap. 1:9, 10).

After the king had burned the roll, "the word of the Lord came to Jeremiah, saying, Take again another roll, and write in it all the former words that were in the first roll, which Jehoiakim the king of Judah hath burned. . . . Then took Jeremiah another roll, and gave it to Baruch the scribe, the son of Neriah; who wrote therein from the mouth of Jeremiah all the words of the book which Jehoiakim king of Judah had burned in the fire, and there were added besides unto them many like words" (vv. 27–32). Clearly there was to be no deviation in phraseology from the former record; the records of the burnt roll were to be repeated verbatim, though other words were added. The Spirit of God who had been the author in the first case came to the prophet's aid in the rewriting. In view of Peter's testimony that "men spake from God, being moved by the Holy Spirit," we are safe in taking this example of Jeremiah's case as illustrative of the other writings of Scripture.

ZECHARIAH 7:12

Again, when God is speaking to the prophet Zechariah concerning his former messages to the nations He speaks of the Law and "the words which the Lord of Hosts had sent by His Spirit by the hand of the former prophets" (Zech. 7:12). Thus the messages of the prophets were verbally inspired. Compare with this the exhortation of the apostle Peter that his readers "should remember the words which were spoken of before by the holy prophets, and the commandment of the Lord and Savior through your apostles" (2 Pet. 3:2). Jude similarly lays stress upon the words spoken by the apostles (Jude 17).

SECTION

2

PROPHECIES
OF MESSIAH

ISAIAH 49–57: PROPHECIES, PROMISES, WARNINGS

In this large section of Isaiah, we see nine total prophecies given and delineated. In chapter 49, we see the first subject: Jehovah as Servant. This chapter to the end of chapter 57 consists of nine prophecies.

There is a renewed association of Israel as the servant of Jehovah with Christ in the same relation. While Israel is directly addressed in this way in *verse 3* in its restored condition, yet in *verses 5 and 6* the Servant of the Lord is marked as in distinction from the nation itself, and the statement there, **"that thou shouldest be My Servant to raise up the tribes of Jacob, and to restore the preserved of Israel,"** shows that Christ Himself is in view and not here the remnant of the nation. Moreover, *verse 6* is quoted in Acts 13:47 as directly applying to Christ, though there in connection with the Gospel. All this is entirely appropriate, inasmuch as Israel could not in its restored state act as the Lord's servant in the earth apart from identification with Christ Himself as their Messiah on the ground of His sacrificial and redemptive work at Calvary.

Since the evangelization of the Gentiles is in view, the message goes forth, **"Listen, O isles, unto Me; and hearken, ye peoples, from far"** (*v. 1*), that is, the far distant nations (cp. 42:4, 10:12 and see 5:26). The twofold statement, **"the Lord hath called Me from the womb; from the bowels of My mother hath He made mention of My Name,"** is specifically true of the Lord Jesus (see Matt. 1:21). Moreover, it is noticeable that everywhere else where Israel is thus spoken of, the phrase "from the womb" is used without the addition of the word "mother" (51:2 is not an exception).

The Speaker, as the Servant of Jehovah, now applies a simile and a metaphor to Himself as His Agent in this relationship. The Lord has made His mouth **"like a sharp sword,"** hid in the shadow of His hand, just as a sword is kept in the sheath, ready for use at the appointed time for the purpose of overcoming the enemy. He has made Him **"a polished shaft,"** keeping Him close in His quiver, so that in due time He may pierce the heart. That Christ Himself is in view and that the time is yet future is indicated in chapter 11:4 and 30:30–33 (cp. Hos. 6:5 and Heb. 4:12). The latter passage, together with these, and Revelation 1:16, show how closely identified are the personal word and the spoken word (see also Joel 2:10, 11; 3:16; 2 Thess. 2:8; Ps. 2:5).

In *verse 3* Christ identifies Himself with His people Israel, for it is in close association with Him that the restored nation is to become His servant, and it is in Israel that the Lord will yet be glorified on the earth.

In this relationship, and in view of the bitter experiences which will have preceded that time of glory, *verse 4* strikes a note almost of despondency, though it is only of a momentary character, and in a certain way it may be referred to Christ in the time of His suffering and rejection by Israel: **"But [R.V.] I said, I** have labored in vain, I have spent My strength for nought and vanity [i.e., to no purpose]"; but this is not an utterance of unbelief or despair, for immediately the heart expresses the assurance of the truth, "yet surely My judgment is with the Lord, and My recompense with My God."

The service we seek to render often seems to produce little or no result. In addition to ineffectiveness there come circumstances of extreme difficulty and trial, which tend to weigh down the heart. And if Satan could accomplish his purpose, he would use all this to cast us down into despair and if possible cause us to cease from the work and turn back through perplexity and distress. Here then is a passage designed by the Spirit of God to give us to consider all such circumstances in the light of God's all-wise counsels, so that while in the midst of conflict we may be encouraged to share His vision and know that our judgment is with Him, and that with Him is the recompense for our seemingly fruitless work.

The language of *verse 5* and what follows is clearly that of the Messiah, who here bears testimony to the object for which He is the Servant of Jehovah, namely, "to bring Jacob again to Him, and that Israel be gathered unto Him" (R.V.). It is Christ alone who will do this, and a still wider purpose is in view in *verse 6*.

The parenthesis between (note the R.V. brackets) expresses the delight of the Lord Jesus in the Father's approval. His statement "I am honorable in the eyes of the Lord, and My God is become My strength" is introduced by the word "for," which expresses the fact that His work in the restoration of Israel is especially pleasing to the Father. It is clear, too, that His resurrection is in view. In the darkness of Calvary He said "My God, My God, why hast Thou forsaken Me?" He was "crucified through weakness." Now He declares that His God has become His strength. This is to be taken with chapter 52:13, which predicts that the Lord's Servant would be "exalted and extolled and be very high."

The "Yea" at the beginning of *verse 6* introduces an extension of the scope of Christ's work of salvation, as well as a confirmation of what has just been stated as to the salvation of Israel. The delighted heart of Jehovah looks on to the worldwide fullness of blessing: "It is too light a thing [or rather it is only a small thing] that Thou shouldest be My Servant to raise up the tribes of Jacob, and to restore the preserved of Israel: I will also give Thee [more expressive than "make Thee"] for a light to the Gentiles, that Thou mayest be My salvation unto the end of the earth."

This has a present application to the work of the Gospel in fulfillment of the command of the Lord Himself to go into all the world and preach the gospel, and to be His witnesses "unto the uttermost part of the earth." The complete fulfillment will take place in the Millennial age. Both are comprehended in Romans 11:12, where the present application is described as "the riches of the world" and "the riches of the Gentiles," and this is followed by the exclamatory prediction of what the restoration or "fullness" of Israel will mean for the world.

In *verse 7*, in the continuation of His utterance to His Servant (for it is still Christ who is primarily in view), we are reminded again of the time of His humiliation. That was a necessary basis for the carrying out of the work of saving grace. So He is called the One **"whom man despiseth"** [see 53:3 and cp. 50:6, 7], and **"whom the nation abhorreth,"** referring to His treatment by the Jews, and, thirdly, in a very suggestive phrase, **"a Servant of rulers."**

This provides an instance of the very real way in which the Lord Jesus identified Himself with the nation of Israel. That nation had become a servant of rulers. This was the result of its departure from God. At the same time there were men such as Daniel, Ezra, and Nehemiah who, while they were suffering with their people, served Gentile rulers in the fear of the Lord. So Christ, in the days of His flesh, made Himself subject to Roman rulers, handing Himself over to their will that He might fulfill the great purposes for which He had come. Included also are such beneficent deeds of mercy as that which He wrought for a centurion. In these many ways the verse points to His Self-humbling.

The outcome of it all will be seen in the coming day of glory, when **"Kings shall see and arise; princes, and they shall worship; because of the** LORD **that is faithful,** even **the Holy One of Israel, who hath chosen Thee"** (cp. 52:15, which foretells that kings shall shut their mouths because of Him, R.V. margin). How great the change of attitude from that of the present time! How startling will be the revelation of the Lord of glory in a world that has lain in darkness, superstition and alienation from God!

Verse 8 tells how Jehovah heard the prayer of His Servant when, in the lowly condition which He shared with His people, He "offered up prayers and supplications with strong crying and tears unto Him that was able to save Him from death" (Heb. 5:7). Here He says to Him: **"Thus saith the Lord, In an acceptable time** [in a time of favor] **have I answered Thee, and in a day of salvation have I helped Thee: and I will preserve Thee, and give Thee** [or set Thee] **for a covenant of the people, to raise up the land, to make them inherit the desolate heritages; saying to them that are bound, Go forth; to them that are in darkness Shew yourselves."** It was an acceptable time when God raised Him from the dead, and since Christ identifies Himself with Israel the words will become true of the nation in fellowship with Him in its restored condition.

That Christ Himself is made "a covenant of the people" indicates the Personal bond which will hereafter unite the nation to Him as the result of His having been heard and helped. The exiled prisoners will be freed and, being restored to their land, will manifest themselves as His people.

The verses which follow give one of the most glorious descriptions of the effects of Christ's Second Advent. The promises far exceed anything that took place in the return from captivity under Cyrus. The people are depicted as a flock returning home: **"They shall feed in the ways,"** that is to say, they will be able to have sufficient supplies of food on their journeys without going long distances to get food. **"On all bare heights shall be their pasture."**

They will know neither hunger nor thirst, nor will they suffer from the heat of the sun. And all this will be due to the fact that the Lord **"that hath mercy** on them" will lead them in Person; **"even by the springs of water shall He guide them"** (*v. 10*).

In their return from all parts of the world their journeys will be characterized by entire freedom from obstacles and difficulties. **"And,"** He says, **"I will make all my mountains a way, and My high ways shall be exalted** (*v. 11*). Comfortingly He speaks of "My mountains" and "My ways." They are His by creation and therefore He can order for their alteration so as to make everything favorable for the return of His people.

All this is applicable to our present experiences. The mountains of difficulty which face us in our pilgrim path can become highways of communion with God and of joyous fellowship with His people, if we trust in the Lord with all our heart and present to Him our whole being for the fulfillment of His will.

In the coming day Israel will be gathered to their appointed earthly center from all parts of the world: **"Lo, these shall come from far: and, lo, these from the north and from the west; and these from the land of Sinim"** (*v. 12*). The west seems to be a comprehensive term, and would include districts in Africa as well as Western Europe and the Americas. Some regard Sinim as referring to the Near East. The Sinite is mentioned in Genesis 10:17. But there can be little doubt that the geographical scope is far wider, and that, as several Orientalists have maintained, the reference is to the land of China. In very ancient times Tsin was the name of a feudal kingdom in Shen-si, the first king of which began to reign in 897 B.C., and it is not at all improbable that the existence of the Chinese was well-known in Palestine and Western Asia generally. Accordingly the prophecy has in view the gathering of Jews from the uttermost parts of the world (cp. *v. 6*).

Such a prospect calls forth the jubilant summons to the heavens, the earth and the mountains to rejoice and to break forth into singing, **"for the Lord hath comforted** [a prophetic perfect tense] **His people, and will have compassion upon His afflicted"** (*v. 13*). Verse 14 records the grievous lament of the nation in its long period of suffering. The tribulation has been judicial indeed, but unbelief, instead of repentance toward God, complains of being forsaken by Jehovah and forgotten by the Lord.

The complaint elicits an expostulation and an assurance, to the effect that His love not only is as inalienable as a mother's love but exceeds it. So far from forgetting Zion (which again stands for its inhabitants), He says **"I have graven thee upon the palms of My hands: thy walls are continually before Me"** (*v. 16*). Jews had a custom of marking on their hands, or elsewhere, a delineation of the city and the temple, as a sign of their devotion to, and perpetual remembrance of, them. The Lord graciously adopts the figure to confirm His assurance. However great the devastation wrought by Gentile powers might be, the walls are ever before Him in their restored and perfected condition in the future.

To be graven on the palms of His hands is suggestive of the closest identification with Himself, of His unchanging love, and of His constant mindfulness of us in all His emotions and activities. Often, in our unbelief, remissness and forgetfulness, we lose sight of our preciousness in His sight in Christ. What is here conveyed in figure finds its fullness of expression in the outflowing of the Lord's heart to the disciples in the upper room, "Even as the Father hath loved Me, I also have loved you: abide ye in My love" (John 15:9).

Verses 17 to 21 reaffirm the promise of the eventual gathering of the scattered outcasts of the nation back to their land. **"Thy children make haste"** (a variant reading is "thy builders"). The exiles enter: the destroyers and wasters go out. The children whom Zion thought she had lost come in crowds (*v. 18*). With a confirming oath Jehovah assures her that her people will be like the ornaments with which a woman decks herself and like the beautiful girdle which a bride fastens round her bridal attire (R.V.).

And the reason is (note the "For" of *v. 19*) that, notwithstanding the recovery and productiveness of the districts which had been desolated and rendered untenable and the removal of those that had swallowed her up, there will not be room for all her inhabitants. Her children will say in her hearing (i.e., will call to one another) that the place is too narrow, and room must be provided.

Her people had been exiles and wanderers and she had been left "solitary" (or "barren"). Now she finds herself surrounded by a multitude of her children. How, she wonders, had they been "borne" to her (R.V., margin—not "begotten")? Who had brought them up? **"Where were they?"** (R.V.). The answer is about to be given.

Sometimes the Lord refrains from manifesting His dealings and, in testing our faith, keeps us waiting till the appointed time for the disclosure of His actings and significance. Far greater the joy when the unfolding comes than if there had been no mystery, no darksome circumstances, and far greater the glory of His grace.

> "God moves in a mysterious way
> His wonders to perform
>
> Behind a frowning providence
> He hides a smiling face
>
> Blind unbelief is sure to err,
> And scan His work in vain;
> God is His own interpreter,
> And He will make it plain."

The close of the forth-ninth chapter, from *verse 22*, gives the Lord's answer to the surprised questions arising from Zion in verse 21. He shows how the multitude of scattered Israelites will be delivered from their exile and those who oppressed them, and be gathered to their own land. He will employ the Gentile nations to take their part in accomplishing this gathering. **"Behold,"** He says, **"I will lift up Mine hand to the nations, and set up My ensign to the peoples."** The lifting up of His hand suggests that some marked sign or indication will be given to all the nations as to what is to be done. The setting up of a standard is a frequent figure in Isaiah: see 5:26; 11:10, 12; 18:3; 62:10 (one of the many indications that there was only one author of this book). The military metaphor may point to some connection with the Lord's interposition in the warfare of Armageddon (see end of the chapter).

Other metaphors follow. The nations will bring Zion's sons **"in their bosom,"** and her daughters **"shall be carried upon their shoulders."** Just as foster fathers give diligence to care for those committed to them, and nurses give their best in caring for the children they nourish, so will kings and princesses devote themselves to the welfare of God's ancient people. They will pay homage to them to the utmost, and subject themselves to them, doing them the most lowly and menial service. The statement that they shall **"lick the dust of Thy feet"** points to the submission of those who before had taken part in oppressing them (see Ps. 72:9; Mic. 7:17).

By all this Zion will recognize Jehovah and His ways: **"thou shalt know that I am the Lord."** Then follows the comforting promise, **"and they that wait for Me shall not be ashamed."** In 40:31 the promise is that "they that wait upon the Lord shall renew their strength." In the present passage the promise is negative: they will not be put to shame. Here too the exercise of patience is in view, in the endurance of all that is difficult and adverse until the Lord's time for deliverance comes.

We wait *upon* Him in prayer. We wait *for* Him in the confident assurance that present conditions of trial and sorrow will have a future of joy and peace such as can come only by the direct and manifest intervention of the Lord Himself.

In the next verses the tyrants with all their power and malign intentions are in view. The rhetorical question in *verse 24* is divided into two distinct parts: **"Shall the prey be taken from the mighty"** (it certainly will, and not merely the Chaldeans are in view, but the Beasts of Rev. 13); "or the captive host of the righteous be delivered?" (margin). The captives are not lawful captives, as the text seems to indicate, though that would be true of those who had been taken into captivity by the Chaldeans under God's ordering; but the time in view is far beyond the return from captivity under Cyrus, and is yet future. Hence the marginal reading is to be preferred, which shows that the captives are the righteous ones whom the Lord will snatch from the hands of the Antichrist, whom Satan will instigate to endeavor to exterminate the Jews.

The assurance is given that the Lord Himself will contend with those that contend with His people. The passage again points to the time of Armageddon (Har-Magedon) and the Second Advent. With the statement **"I will feed them that oppress thee with their own flesh; and they shall be drunken with their own blood"** (cp. Rev. 14:20). All the world will discover and recognize that Jehovah is Israel's Savior and Redeemer, **"the mighty One of Jacob."**

All the efforts of the combined nations to establish "peace and safety" in the earth, however sincere the motive, however good the intention may be, are foredoomed to failure. The world's last great conflict, in which the Jewish question will be uppermost, will see the fulfillment of the Scriptures which make known that righteousness can be established in the earth only by the Personal Advent of Christ in judgment upon the foes of God and in the deliverance of His people.

ISAIAH 50

Two prophetic facts stand out prominently in this chapter: (1) the responsibility attaching to Israel for her state of rejection, and (2) the steadfastness and faithfulness of the Servant of Jehovah.

In *verse 1* the Lord asks two questions by way of protest, each repudiating the idea that the evils which had befallen the nation were the result of arbitrary dealings on His part. Nay, their state was due to their transgressions.

"Where," He says, "is the bill of your mother's divorcement, wherewith I have put her away?" (R.V.). This is a denial by the Lord that He had broken off the relation in which He stood to Zion (Israel's mother). He had betrothed Zion to Himself, and she had no bill of divorce to show, by means of which He had put her away, thus removing the possibility of receiving her back in case she should have married another (see Deut. 24:14, and especially v. 4). Her sad condition of being put away was not caused by any such proceedings.

Further, He asks "or which of My creditors is it to whom I have sold you?" That Israel was sold and exiled was true, but Jehovah had not been in the position of being indebted to creditors. In other words, His having given her into the hands of Gentile powers was not through His giving way to their constraint, as if He was discharging a debt by so doing. Nay, they were sold for their iniquities, and Zion, their mother, was put away for their transgression. The mother suffered through the perverseness of her children. Sinners often put down the evils that come upon them to any cause except their own transgressions.

But there are further questions, questions in a different manner of divine protestations, telling of Jehovah's power in the exercise of mercy, and all leading to a personal testimony by Messiah Himself.

"Wherefore, when I came, was there no man?" (*v. 2*). The past tense is prophetic. He "came," not merely by His prophets, nor would He come simply by deliverance from captivity. He would come in the Person of His Servant, the Messiah-Redeemer Himself. But how was it that there was no man, none willing to receive the message? (cp. 53:1). How was it that "when He called, there was none to answer"? His hand was not shortened (an emblem of weakness) that it could not redeem (cp. 59:1). He who could dry up the sea, make rivers a wilderness, clothe the heavens with blackness and make sackcloth their covering (telling especially of His retributive judgments upon Babylon), had power to deliver. And with this in view, He would send His Servant. Eventually He came, and declared at the outset of His ministry, that He had been sent "to proclaim release to the captives . . . to proclaim the acceptable year of the Lord"

(Luke 4:18). Instead of receiving Him and His message, they cast Him forth to destroy Him.

So now there follows, in *verse 4* in the words of Christ Himself, a description of His testimony as the Sent One, His obedience to Him who sent Him, His sufferings and His vindication.

God spake to prophets by special and periodic revelations, by visions and dreams. With the Servant of Jehovah it was different. Here He discloses the secret of His inner life in the days of His flesh, and the secret source of His ministry and ways: **"The Lord God hath given Me the tongue of them that are taught, that I should know how to sustain with words him that is weary: He wakeneth morning by morning, He wakeneth Mine ear to hear as they that are taught."** A joyous lowliness and condescension breathe through His illustration taken from discipleship. In the days of the fulfillment of this prophecy He says "My teaching is not Mine, but His that sent Me" (John 7:16); again, "as the Father hath taught Me, I speak these things" (8:28), and "I speak the things which I have seen with My Father" (8:38); and again, "the Father which sent Me, He hath given Me a commandment, what I should say, and what I should speak" (12:49; cp. 14:10, 24).

How He "sustained with words" the weary is told out in the Gospel narratives, both in His public ministry (e.g., Matt. 11:28) and in the comfort He gave to the widow, the diseased, the distressed and the tempest-tossed.

The Lord daily listened to His Heavenly Father's voice. In this He sets us an example. It was His joy to say "I do always the things that are pleasing to Him" (John 8:29), and it is only as we are attentive to His voice day by day that we can fulfill His will, enabling us to say with the apostle, "we make it our aim . . . to be well-pleasing unto Him."

He says **"The Lord God hath opened Mine ear, and I was not rebellious, neither turned away backward"** (*v. 5*). This was the very perfection of obedience. Compare Psalm 40:6, where, however, the word rendered "to open" signifies "to dig," which may either refer to the custom of boring a servant's ear, in token of perpetual service (Exod. 21:6), or be figurative simply of devotion to God's will. Here in Isaiah a different word is used, with the latter meaning. The Lord Jesus knew all the suffering that lay before Him, and with undeviating steadfastness He pursued His pathway to the Cross.

To that consummating act *verse 6* points: **"I gave My back to the smiters, and My cheeks to them that plucked off the hair: I hid not My face from shame and spitting."** With striking detail this prophecy predicts what the Lord actually endured as recorded in the Gospel. He set His face to His persecutors without faltering, knowing that the words that follow would be fulfilled, that the Lord God would help Him and that He would not be ashamed.

His example is an incentive to us, when called to suffer the pressure of fierce antagonism, so that with fixity of purpose we may fulfill that which the Lord has committed to us. We can never suffer as He did, but our life and testimony can be marked by the same characteristics as those which marked His. "We must through much tribulation enter the Kingdom," but to suffer for His sake makes it all a glory and joy.

He looked to the future with confidence, and so may we. He says, **"For the Lord God will help Me; therefore have I not been confounded** [He had not suffered Himself to be overcome by mockery and opposition]: **therefore have I set My face like a flint, and I know that I shall not be ashamed"** (*v. 7*, R.V.).

The design of our Father is to give us such confidence in Him and in the assurance of His help, that we may be free from every tendency to despair under the weight of trouble. If we are walking in the path of obedience we can ever be assured of His present help and of deliverance and victory in His own way and time.

The Lord knew that, in spite of every accusation both by man and by the spiritual foe, He would be triumphantly vindicated. He says **"He is near that justifieth Me; who will contend with Me? let us stand up together** [i.e., let the foe draw toward Me]: **who is Mine adversary? let him come near to Me"** (*v. 8*). He does not say "He will justify Me" but "He is near" that will do so, which declares His consciousness of the presence of His Father, as, for instance, when standing before Caiaphas and his associates and before Pilate and his men of war.

His justification took place in His resurrection. He was "declared to be the Son of God with power, according to the spirit of holiness (that is the sinlessness which marked Him as the Holy One of God), by the resurrection of the dead" (Rom. 1:4). This is further borne out by the clause in 1 Timothy 3:16, "justified in the spirit" (referring directly to His resurrection).

A second time He says **"Behold, the Lord God will help Me."** Such repeated expressions are characteristic of Isaiah's prophecies.

As for God's accusers and foes they shall all **"wax old,"** or rather, fall to pieces like a worn-out garment, a prey to the moth, an insect which, working slowly and imperceptibly, accomplishes thoroughly its deadly destruction (*v. 9*).

That finishes the testimony of Messiah Himself. Just as the chapter opened with the declaration of Jehovah, so it closes. Here it is addressed first to the believer who fears the Lord and obeys the voice of His servant, a title which looks back to what has been stated concerning Him in verses 4, 5 that is, to the one who follows in His steps (*v. 10*).

A believer may be walking in darkness circumstantially and have no light, and in such conditions may be tempted to despondency. Sometimes a situation seems hopeless. A variety of trials and adverse circumstances may crowd upon him. Here then is the message, uplifting and soul-stirring. **"Let him trust in the Name of the Lord, and stay upon His God."** True faith is tested faith, and proves its reality by standing the test. God is "a very present help in trouble." Faith not only accepts this as a fact, but learns to lean upon God Himself and to prove the power and love of His almighty arm. That turns our darkness into light. The heart is cheered and, more still, is empowered to rise victorious over all that opposes, rejoicing in the light of His countenance.

The next words (*v. 11*) are addressed to unbelievers and to their presumptuous self-confidence. They kindle a fire and gird themselves about with firebrands, and walk proudly in the flickering flame which they have kindled. Not only so, their fire is kindled against the Lord and against His Christ. For this the divine retribution is inevitable. They must suffer from the effects of the burnings which they have kindled. It comes from the hand of Jehovah Himself. Their activities, with all their malice and hard-heartedness are brought to a terrible end and they **"lie down in sorrow,"** a contrast to the joyous restfulness of the believer who stays himself upon His God!

ISAIAH 51

The subject of this chapter is the promise of salvation for Israel on a righteous basis and the removal of the cup of wrath.

The Lord now addresses those among His people who are faithful and, following after righteousness, long for salvation and the fulfillment of the promise to Abraham. They share his spirit of faith in refraining from making mere earthly things and pursuits the objects of their ambition. Abraham was himself the rock from which the stones, of which the house of Jacob was built, had been hewn, and Sarah was the hollow of the pit from which they had been digged. For the reference here is to the fact that, in the advanced and barren condition of the married life of Abraham and Sarah, the Lord wrought by His own supernatural power in response to Abraham's faith (*vv. 1, 2*).

In this connection the R.V. of Romans 4:19–21 should be noted. Its correct rendering brings out more forcibly than the A.V. the character of Abraham's faith: "And without being weakened in faith he considered his own body now as good as dead (he being about a hundred years old), and the deadness of Sarah's womb: yea, looking unto the promise of God, he wavered not through unbelief, but waxed strong through faith, giving glory to God and being fully assured that, what He had promised, He was able also to perform."

All this was the origin of the nation of Israel and the Lord calls them, in the figurative language of the rock and the pit, to remember this, and further reminds them that **"when he was but one I called him** [R.V.], **and I blessed him and made him many."** Hence the strengthening assurance of comfort for Zion and her waste places and the blossoming out of her wilderness **"like Eden, and her desert like the garden of the Lord; joy and gladness shall be found therein, thanksgiving and the voice of melody"** (*v. 3*). Just as joy came to Sarah after a long period of unfruitfulness, so Israel, after its long time of trouble and desolation, shall yet be made to rejoice.

The paragraph beginning at *verse 4* speaks of the times when the restoration of Israel will issue in blessing for all the world, and then later in the passing away of the whole of the old creation. The present message of the gospel is not here in view. The Lord makes the promise, **"a law shall go forth from Me, and I will make My judgment to rest for a light of the peoples** [i.e., the Gentiles]" (*v. 4*). The law is not that of Sinai but stands for instruction which God will give through the instrumentality of Israel. That He will make His judgment to rest is, more literally, "I will make a place for My right." Hence the Lord declares that His righteousness is near, that His salvation is gone forth, and that His arms will judge the nations, that is, they will come under the judgment which His arms will inflict.

But the result of the judgment is that the remaining nations who survive it, even the far distant isles, will rely upon His arm. For that which ministered judgment will subsequently act in mercy and salvation. Thus the might of God's power, represented by His arm, will be exercised in two great contrasting ways (*v. 5*).

Not only will sin exist during the Millennial age, the whole of the old creation has been defiled by it. The heavens are to vanish like smoke, the earth is to fall to pieces like a garment, and its inhabitants are to die out as if they were nothing (this seems to be the meaning of the phrase rendered **"in like manner"**), *verse 6* (cp. 2 Pet. 3:13).

Those who are saved (these are comprehended in the phrase "My salvation") will never perish, and God's righteousness will stand forever. And now, in a striking parallel between this passage and the one in 2 Peter, there follows an appeal to those who know God's righteousness and share it, **"the people in whose heart is My law"** (*v. 7*). In the Isaiah passage they are exhorted not to fear the reproach of mortals or to be alarmed at their revilings. The persecutors are to perish just as a garment is consumed by a moth and wool by a worm (*v. 8*). A Jewish proverb says that "the worm is brother to the moth." God uses little things to accomplish great ends, whether by way of judgment or for purposes of grace.

The order here is salvation and righteousness; in the preceding verse it was righteousness and salvation. The whole is in the chiasmic order; the order is reversed again in *verse 8*.

These promises must have aroused in the hearts of the faithful a longing for the promised salvation (*v. 9*). They knew that the arm of the Lord could bring it about. Was it not His arm that overthrew Pharaoh and his hosts? The mention of Rahab has reference to Egypt, and the dragon to Pharaoh himself, with an allusion doubtless to the power of Satan acting through him (*v. 10*). The Egyptians are vividly described as having been cut into pieces. Pharaoh himself was not drowned in the waters but was "pierced." The memory of past deliverance and the assurance of future deliverance call forth the vivid appeal, uttered three times, for the arm of the Lord to awake.

It is good for the soul to recall the mercies of God in days gone by, but it is needful not to be occupied merely with a retrospect, but to let the power of the hope do its purifying work. The double view strengthens the power of prayer, prayer not merely for deliverance but for what will accomplish the glory of God. This meets with a response on His part far exceeding the mere expectation of deliverance.

What follows is scarcely exceeded anywhere in Scripture in the beauty of its language and in the sweetness of the assurance given to God's people as to their future. It begins not with the word "Therefore," but with "And," connecting the promise with the appeal, not by way of conclusion but with the closer combination, expressing the assurance more directly and decisively: **"And the ransomed of the Lord shall return and come with singing unto Zion; and everlasting joy shall be upon their heads: they shall obtain gladness and joy, and sorrow and sighing shall flee away"** (*v. 11*). All this speaks gloriously of the Millennial blessedness to be enjoyed by Israel. The prospect is enhanced and strengthened by the retrospect of past trials and sufferings.

So it is with the still brighter prospect that we enjoy who are members of the Church. Our present experiences of sore trial and affliction are brightened by the hope, a hope that "sweetens every bitter cup."

Verses 12 to 15 continue in a different way the comfort ministered by the Lord. Many of His people were in fear because of the oppressor, and doubtless in the coming day, in the time of "Jacob's trouble," the oppression of the man of sin will tend to have a similar effect. To this time the present passage seems to point. The Lord speaks of Himself as their Comforter. This being so, what had they to fear? **"Who art thou,"** He says, **"that thou art afraid of man that shall die, and of the son of man which shall be made as grass** (lit., "made a blade of grass")?" The tyranny of the Antichrist will be short-lived. The Lord has ever had His own way and time for delivering His earthly people.

Fear is the offspring of forgetfulness of God. The realization of the presence and power of the Lord is the all-sufficient antidote. Again and again the Lord reminds Israel that He was their Maker and that His power had stretched forth the heavens and laid the foundations of the earth. Why then should they continually stand in dread of the fury of the oppressor even when he was preparing to destroy?

The *14th verse* is rightly put in the R.V. as a promise: **"The captive exile** [lit., he that is bowed down, i.e., bound in fetters in prison] **shall speedily be loosed; and he shall not die and go down into the pit, neither shall his bread fail."** While the conquest of Babylon by Cyrus is probably immediately in view here, the prophecy will ultimately have its fulfillment in the coming time when Jews, suffering privation in exile among the nations under the Antichrist, will be set at liberty to come back to their land in recognition of their Redeemer Messiah.

The Lord pledges His all-sufficiency for this, in that He terrifies the sea when its waves roar, by putting His restraint upon it. That is probably the true meaning in *verse 15*. The Hebrew verb is the same as that rendered "rest" in verse 4. The reference here does not seem to be to the dividing of the sea when Israel was delivered from Egypt, but to the roaring of the waves which by His word are frightened into stillness. That is what the Lord did on Lake Galilee. The waters of the sea are interpreted in Scripture as symbolizing the restlessness and tossings of the nations (see Ps. 65:7; 98:7 Isa. 17:12, 13; Ezek. 26:3; Luke 21:25, 26 and Rev. 17:15). The greatest turmoil among the nations will prevail during the latter part of the rule of the man of sin, and especially at the time of the warfare of Armageddon. But the Lord will still that tempest by His Personal intervention.

Verse 16 tells how the Jews will become His messengers. He will put His words in their mouth (the perfect tense is prophetic). He will cover them in the shadow of His hand, not only protecting them but equipping them for His purpose in view. This purpose is stated as follows: **"that I may plant the heavens and lay the foundations of the earth, and say unto Zion, Thou art My people."** The last clause refers to Millennial conditions and accordingly the planting of the heavens and the founding of the earth may point to changed conditions in the universe when the Kingdom of righteousness and peace is established. For the forces of nature both in the heavens and the earth will not be used any more for the exercise of divine judgments, as has often been the case and must again be so before the Lord comes in glory. There is doubtless also a reference to the new heavens and earth which are to be created hereafter.

The messenger of the gospel may apply to himself the comfort of the assurance "I have put My words in thy mouth." He is "the Lord's messenger in the Lord's message"; his testimony is effectual only as he adheres to the truth of Scripture. Again, as His messenger he is under His protecting care, covered by the shadow of His hand, indicating the pleasure the Lord has in one who rightly ministers His truth.

The last paragraph of this chapter, beginning at *verse 17*, describes in vivid language the effects of the judgments inflicted upon the nation as a result of its persistent rebellion against God. Jerusalem is depicted as a woman lying on the ground in a state of helpless stupefaction through having drained to the dregs the cup of staggering, the cup of the fury of the Lord. Not one among all her sons was able to guide her or, taking her by the hand, to lift her up. Devastation, ruin, famine and the sword had come upon her, and the prophet himself, like Jeremiah in his lamentations, could not find how to comfort her. Her sons, instead of assisting her, were lying helpless at the corners of all the streets, like an antelope taken in a hunter's net and exhausted by vain struggles to be free (*vv. 18–20*).

Deliverance could come only from God, and in His pity and mercy He promises to bring it (*vv. 21–23*). He remembers that they are His people, and describes Himself as the One who pleads, or, rather, conducts, their cause as their Advocate or Defender. And inasmuch as the nations whom He has used, and will yet use for the punishment of His people, overstep the limits of the power committed to them, and, acting as the agents of the evil one and priding themselves in their despotism, wreak their vengeance upon His people, God will take **"the cup of staggering, even the bowl of the cup of His fury,"** and will make their tormentors drink it. They thought they would trample upon the nation just as foes tread upon a street. God reverses the position and brings human pride down to utter degradation.

All this will yet be enacted in the coming time of "Jacob's trouble," when Satan's efforts to destroy Israel reach their height.

ISAIAH 52:1–12

In this beautiful section, we see a combination of prophecies regarding the nature of the Messiah's message of judgment, and the amazing promises and blessing that He will bestow on His people. While prophetic in nature, this is one of the more encouraging sections for the people of God.

Again the call of the Lord comes to Zion to awake and put on her strength and to Jerusalem to put on her beautiful garments. Here, as in the two preceding instances, the call is the result of what precedes. She has been in a state of utter prostration and covered with dust, powerless under the fury of her enemies and robbed of her royal and priestly robes, wearing instead the chains of captivity around her neck. From all those who had defiled and degraded her she would be delivered.

But she was not only to arise but was to take her seat in a position of restful dignity and authority. Strangers will not be allowed to pass through her any more (cp. Joel 3:17; see also Nah. 1:15, where the R.V. rightly translates "the wicked one," i.e., the Antichrist). Babylon has sat as a queen but would be brought down to the dust; Jerusalem would be raised from her dust and sit upon her throne of glory (*vv. 1, 2*).

The promises which follow in *verses 3 to 6* are set, with their comfort, in the background of past misery. The Lord's people are reminded that they **"were sold for nought"** (R.V.), they were handed over to Gentile powers; not that the Lord might gain any advantage from that; His sole purpose was to bring them to repentance under His chastening rod. No money would be paid for their redemption. That would be accomplished by His sovereign grace and almighty power. Their deliverance would emanate from Himself solely and absolutely.

So with redemption from the power of sin and Satan. Man can do nothing to effect it. It must be "according to the riches of His grace" (Eph. 1:7; Col. 1:14; 1 Pet. 1:18, 19).

As illustrations, the oppression of two Gentile powers is mentioned, Egypt and Assyria. For though the actual oppression is recorded only of the latter, it is evidently intimated in regard to the former, according to the principle of parallelism. Israel went down to Egypt "at the first" (R.V.) simply to sojourn there until the famine in Canaan was over. After their bondage, their deliverance was wrought by the outstretched arm of the Lord. They are reminded of this again and again throughout their history. On the other hand, the Assyrians invaded their territory and drove them into captivity as the instruments of God's disciplinary dealings. Let them remember each case, now that similar trouble had come upon them by Babylonian aggression.

The rhetorical question asked by the Lord Himself in *verse 5*, **"What do I here?"** has been interpreted in several ways. The right meaning seems to be "What advantage do I gain in the midst of My people?" as is indicated by the next clause, **"seeing that My people is taken away for nought."** And then as to the enemy themselves, **"they that rule over them do howl."** This is not the howling of misery (that idea seems to have led to the A.V. rendering "make them to howl"); here the verb is used of the blustering war cry of the oppressors and it was in that spirit that the Name of the Lord was blasphemed continually by them.

The shrieking and the blaspheming would be made to cease by the direct power of God. The Name so despised by the Gentiles will be made known to His people. His nature, character and power as represented by His Name will be revealed to them in the day of their redemption. His self-manifestation will cause them to know the voice of their Redeemer; see 63:1, where, in answer to the astonished question of His people as to who He is, He replies, "I that speak in righteousness, mighty to save." Here in *verse 6*, in view of that assured event, He says **"Behold, it is I,"** or, as in the margin, "Here I am." He will make known not only the character of His Person and attributes, but His very presence as their Deliverer.

This is how the Lord reveals Himself in our times of tribulation and difficulty. He uses such circumstances by way of increasing our knowledge of Himself, His character, His power and His grace. It is when we come to an end of ourselves that He makes Himself known to us. Wits' end corner provides the turning at which the Lord manifests to us not only our own helplessness but His almightiness. We may be like Peter, who, finding himself going down to a watery grave, cried out "Lord, save me." Christ planned the whole circumstance so that His ardent follower might know the strength of His arm and His power to do more than deliver. How often in the midst of the troubles of His disciples He said (that with which this passage in Isaiah ends) "It is I!"

Verses 7 to 10 consist of a triumphant exultation consequent upon the news of the great deliverance wrought for the Lord's people in the eyes of all nations. Wars will have been made to cease to the ends of the earth. Peace will prevail because God reigns and Jehovah is returning to Zion.

"How beautiful upon the mountains are the feet of him [or "them"—the pronoun is collective] **that bringeth good tidings, that publisheth peace!"** The feet of the messengers are lovely to behold (not the sound of the footsteps but the appearance of their feet), beautiful not only because of their buoyant rapidity, but because of the rapture of heart which lends character to their movement, and the very nature of their errand.

The mountains are those of the Land, and especially those north of Jerusalem. What are natural obstacles are made highways for God's heralds. He had declared "I will make all My mountains a way." The world will cry "peace and safety" (1 Thess. 5:3)—the old delusion, that man is his own savior! Destruction will come upon them, confounding their politics and chasing away their cherished dreams. God's Christ alone can bring deliverance, and at His Coming the messengers publish "peace and salvation." Not the "safety" of an imagined security, but the salvation wrought by the arm of the Savior Himself!

So it will be. But so it is now in respect of the messengers of the Gospel and its good news; and for this we have the confirmatory quotation in Romans 10:15, where "the mountains" is omitted, for the emblematic becomes the actual in the Gospel. The apostle exults in that in which he was himself such an assiduous messenger! And it is ours to share in the activity and the joy. The feet of one who goes forth with the evangel, at home or abroad, are lovely in the sight of Him who died to provide both the message and the messengers.

There are three blessings pronounced in the message, *peace, good*, and *salvation*; *peace* with God through the blood of Christ, instead of alienation; *good*, that which benefits and profits, instead of evil, the blighting effect of sin; *salvation*, which not only saves from death and judgment, but ministers continual preservation, with its eternal realization, instead of doom and eternal perdition.

The "watchmen" (or watchers) in *verse 8*, who **"lift up the voice together,"** rejoicing with singing, are the prophets (Isaiah himself being one), like those who look out into the distance as from a watch tower. They are distinct from the messengers just mentioned, who will bear the news of the Kingdom when Christ's Millennial reign is ushered in. Contrast the blind watchmen, the false prophets, in 56:10. These faithful watchers, who saw future events from afar, are described in 1 Peter 1:10–12 (cp. Isa. 21:8, 11 and Hab. 2:1–3).

The day is coming when they will **"see, eye to eye, when** [or, rather, "how"] **Jehovah returns to Zion,"** lit., "makes Zion to return" (the same construction as in Ps. 85:4). They will see the Lord restoring Zion, as vividly as one person is to another when he looks straight into his eyes (see Num. 14:14, R.V. margin). No wonder they will join in a chorus of praise. Those who foretold these things apart from one another during the course of many centuries will, in one great company and in bodily presence, utter their joy before Him who has been the great Subject of these prophecies.

In *verse 9* the ruins of Jerusalem are called upon to do the same. The language is vivid, it visualizes and depicts the glory of restoration after the long periods of desolation: **"Break forth into jubilation, join in singing, ye ruins of Jerusalem."** And the reason is twofold, God's word and work: the word of consolation, **"The Lord hath comforted His people"**; the work of delivering power, **"He hath redeemed Jerusalem."** His word has been carried out in act. "Jesus . . . was mighty in deed and word" (Luke 24:19). Moses "was mighty in his words and works" (Acts 7:22). Compare 2 Thessalonians 2:17.

Comfort and deliverance, these are the constant ministration of the Holy Spirit in our sorrows and distresses, our trials and dangers: comfort *amidst* them, deliverance *from* them! We may rejoice in the consolation, and be confident of the deliverance.

Verse 10 first looks back from future fulfillment. **"Jehovah hath made bare His holy arm in the eyes of all the nations."** The metaphor is that of a warrior, removing all coverings and accoutrements from his arm so as to exert his power to the utmost. The foolish misconceptions the nations have had about God will be mightily dispelled. Their refusal to acknowledge the Person, facts and claims of His Son will meet the force of His direct interposition. **"All the ends of the earth shall see the salvation of our God."**

Verses 11 and 12 deal with another side of the circumstances, and give a view of the setting free of the exiles. They are bidden to go out from the scene of their captivity. The language of the command bears reference to Babylon, but Babylon here stands for more than the city itself, it speaks of world conditions, as the preceding context shows. They are commanded to touch no unclean thing. They are not to take with them the Babylonish gods, as they did when they took of the spoils of Egypt. The vessels they are to carry home are **"the vessels of the Lord."** This points to the return under the decree of Cyrus, when the vessels taken by Nebuchadnezzar were to be restored (Ezra 1:7–11). Again, unlike the exodus from Egypt, they would not go out in haste nor by flight. Their attitude, instead of that of fugitives, was to be one of complete preparedness for the resumption of the worship of the Lord in His Temple. For this the requisite is absolute purity.

Yet they would need His guidance and protection, and of this they are assured: **"for Jehovah will go before you; and the God of Israel will be your rearward."**

All this has its direct messages for those who, themselves vessels, set apart to the Lord for His use (2 Tim. 2:21), have a holy responsibility to keep themselves unspotted from the world, and to cleanse themselves "from all defilement of flesh and spirit, perfecting holiness in the fear of the Lord." And as to the promises, all that is here assured and much more, is gathered up in the pledge, "I will be to you a Father, and ye shall be to Me sons and daughters, saith the Lord Almighty." The relationship divinely established at the new birth finds its practical expression on His part in our experiences and circumstances in a manner impossible if the condition is not fulfilled.

ISAIAH 52:13–53

This prophetic section describes the great theme of the suffering, rejected, atoning, and exalted Servant of Jehovah. Many incorrectly see the "Suffering Servant" as the nation of Israel. However, the reader will see contextually that this amazing portion of Scripture is buried in the middle of Isaiah's words regarding a Deliverer, the Savior, who would redeem and restore Israel.

The connection with what has just preceded is significant. Deliverance from captivity has just been in view, deliverance from Babylon, and deliverance yet future and final. Babylon itself was not actually mentioned and is not spoken of again in Isaiah.

Deliverance can be wrought alone by Jehovah's Servant, whether for Jew or Gentile. So the Lord calls attention to Him, first to His prosperous dealing, then to His exalted position itself (*v. 13*). There follows a brief mention of His humiliation as antecedent to the coming manifestation of His power and glory (*vv. 14, 15*). And all this, in its condensed form, is the very theme which, having been thus introduced, is expanded in the twelve following verses.

"**Behold, My Servant shall deal wisely.**" Two meanings are contained in this word, wisdom (one feature of which is prudence) and prosperity. These might be combined in a fuller rendering, "shall deal wisely, with consequent prosperity." Strikingly this describes His life on earth, in all that He said and did, with its prosperous effects, and in maintaining His testimony without surrendering His life till the appointed hour. No greater prosperity ever accrued from any act than from the giving up of that life in His voluntary and atoning sacrifice.

"**He shall be exalted and lifted up, and shall be very high.**" Three stages are in view, His Resurrection (the word rendered "exalted" signifies to rise up in exaltation), His Ascension (the thought is that of a glorious ascent), and His position at the right hand of God (see Acts 2:33, Phil. 2:9; Heb. 1:3 and 13).

"**Like as many were astonished at Thee** (with the change from a statement of fact concerning Him to an utterance addressed to Him; cp. chap. 49, vv. 7, 8) **. . . so shall He startle** (R.V. margin) **many nations.**" The similarity of the verbs in these corresponding statements is to be noted. In the degradation and disfigurement which man inflicted on Him many were astonished; in the coming manifestation of His glory He will astonish (cause to leap and tremble in astonishment) many nations; "startle" is the meaning here, not "sprinkle" (as the grammatical phraseology makes clear).

The fact that "**His visage was so marred more than any man, and His form more than the sons of men**" was the cause of the astonishment of those who beheld Him. The soldiers hit Him with a mock scepter one after another on His face and His thorn-crowned brow, till His features were unrecognizable. The form of scourging administered was that by means of which the flesh was cut away from breast as well as back. So Psalm 22:17 foretold: "I may tell all My bones; they look and stare upon Me."

In the coming Day the astonishment at His power and glory will be so great that kings will be overpowered into speechlessness, struck dumb at the sight of what they had never heard of. More still, they will be made to grasp the reality and significance of the stupendous manifestation: "**that which they had not heard shall they understand.**"

There follows immediately the reason why they had not heard. The cause lay with Israel. They (not the prophet) are the mourning and repentant speakers in the next verse. They acknowledge with lamentation their unbelief. As a nation they had refused to believe the message proclaimed to them. That is the meaning of the rhetorical question rendered in our Versions, "**Who hath believed our report?**" (*v. 1*). See the R.V. margin. The word rendered "report," means that which was heard, that which was declared, and the reference is to the Gospel preached at Pentecost and afterwards, which was persistently rejected by the nation. Witness Paul's protests and lament (Acts 13:46; 18:6; 28:28; Rom. 9:1; 11:7, 8; 1 Thess. 2:14–18).

So with the manifestation of God's power in Christ: **"to whom hath the arm of the Lord been revealed**?" is a prophetic question expressing the confession to be made in the coming day of repentance, that Israel had in its unbelief failed to recognize what God had wrought in raising Christ from the dead. All that follows is a full acknowledgment to be made of the great facts concerning Him when the nation is restored.

They did not realize that **"He grew up before Him** [Jehovah] **as a tender plant, and as a root** [a sprouting root] **out of a dry ground"** (v. 2).

The pleasantness of Christ in the eyes of Jehovah, in the days of His childhood and growth into manhood, as a tender twig and the verdant shoot, is set in contrast with the barren and enslaved condition of the nation.

They saw nothing in His appearance to make them feel naturally attracted to Him, nothing of comeliness or beauty to delight their natural senses. On the contrary, **"He was despised and rejected of men; a man of sorrows, and acquainted with grief"** (v. 3). The special meaning of the word rendered "grief" is sickness, or disease. The former clause marks His life as one characterized by the inward smart of experiencing the effects of the sins and sorrows of those around Him; the latter clause marks Him as One uniquely capable of complete acquaintance with various forms of illness.

The latter part of the verse expresses still more strongly the attitude of the people as a whole. It shows the character of their despisings: **"and as one from whom men hide their face He was despised, and we esteemed Him not."** Men hide the face from, or turn away from, that which is considered unbearable to behold. Their estimate of Him is put very strongly; they regarded Him as nothing. All this records the depths of remorse with which the nation hereafter will recall their attitude shown Him in the days of His flesh.

In *verses 4 to 6*, they enter into the subject more deeply, confessing that His sufferings were of quite a different nature from what they had supposed them to be. The sufferings of the Cross are now in view.

The change of their ideas is marked by the opening word **"Surely"** or **"Verily."** The statement **"He hath borne our griefs, and carried our sorrows,"** expresses more fully what was mentioned in the preceding verse as to His being a man of sorrows and acquainted with grief. It tells how the Lord bore in His own Person sufferings which were other than His own. Matthew quotes this in connection with His deeds of healing and deliverance (Matt. 8:16, 17). Yet that statement does not speak of His making a substitutionary atonement.

Verse 4 takes us directly to the Cross, for only to that could the statement apply, **"yet we did esteem Him stricken, smitten of God, and afflicted."** In their blindness they looked upon His sufferings as the punishment of His own sins, which they must have regarded as especially great.

But now, under the power of the revelation of the great facts, there comes an entire reversal of their opinions. This is marked in a special way by the series of emphatic personal pronouns in the plural in what follows. **"But He was wounded** for our transgressions, He was bruised for our iniquities: the chastisement of our peace was upon Him" (*v. 5*).

The words rendered "wounded" (or pierced) and "bruised" are the strongest terms to describe a violent and agonizing death. There is stress on the "our" in both statements. The chastisement which was administered to Him by God was that which makes for our peace (the word *shalom* is comprehensive and describes not simply a peaceful state, but well-being in general); **"and with His stripes we are healed"**—not the Roman scourging; the margin gives the literal rendering, "bruise" (so in the Septuagint, and see 1 Pet. 2:24, margin). The expression conveys in condensed form the stroke of Divine judgment inflicted upon Him. The healing, the spiritual soundness which we receive, is expressly set in direct contrast to the bruising or Divine stroke to which He submitted.

Now comes the climax of conscience-stricken admission on the part of the penitent nation: **"All we like sheep have gone astray, we have turned every one to his own way,"** and then the grateful realization and recognition of the tremendous fact, **"and Jehovah hath laid on Him the iniquity of us all"** (*v. 6*).

What the nation will hereafter acknowledge is true of the whole human race. Man has substituted his own will for God's will. Being granted the power of self-determination, a feature which, among others, marks him as made in the image of God, he has used that power to go "his own way" and make himself ego-centric instead of God-centric.

In this universal condition of guilt and misery the grace of God has interposed. Sending His own Son "in the likeness of sinful flesh and as an offering for sin" (Rom. 8:3, R.V.). He made to meet upon Him the whole weight of our iniquity and the righteous wrath due to it.

The third paragraph, *verses 7 to 9*, describes His sufferings, death and burial. **"He was oppressed** ["treated unsparingly"], **yet He humbled Himself** [i.e., He suffered voluntarily] **and opened not His mouth; as a lamb that is led to the slaughter, and as a sheep that before her shearers is dumb; yea, He opened not His mouth."** This all expresses His voluntary endurance and is apparently set in striking antithesis to the straying away, in the first part of verse 6.

The scene passes next to the unrighteous judicial verdict passed upon Him, and from thence direct to Calvary. **"By oppression and judgment** [a hendiadys, i.e., one sentiment conveyed by two expressions, here signifying "by an oppressive judicial sentence"] **He was taken away** [Matt. 26:66; 27:22–31, and see Acts 8:33, which translates the Septuagint], **and as for His generation, who** *among them* **considered that He was cut off out of the land of the living? for the transgression of my people was He stricken,"** or "was the stroke upon Him." This is preferable to the R.V. margin, "to whom the stroke was due." The stress of the passage is what Christ endured.

This section, which has described the character of His sufferings and the manner of His death, closes with a statement as to His burial: **"And they** [R.V.; i.e., "His generation"] **made His grave with the wicked** ["with sinners"], **and with the rich** ["a rich man"] **in His death."** The first part of this would seem to refer to the intention of the rulers, who would have had Him ignominiously buried with the two robbers. The Roman authorities, however, granted the body to Joseph of Arimathaea, the "rich man" (Matt. 27:57).

The Hebrew word rendered "death" is in the plural; this is expressive of the violent character, not to say the comprehensive nature, of His death.

In what follows, the A.V. rendering **"because He had done no violence, neither was any deceit in His mouth"** is probably correct, rather than the R.V., "although . . ." The clause is to be connected with what immediately precedes. The fact of His freedom from sin made it fitting that He should receive an honorable burial, instead of being cast into a criminal's grave, to which his enemies would have committed Him.

The last section of the chapter gives a threefold testimony concerning the experiences of His soul. We are taken into the inner sanctuary of His Being. Again, *verses 10 and 12* speak of the dealings of Jehovah with Him, judicially in respect of His death and compensatingly in respect of His reward. *Verse 11* speaks of the outcome of His Sacrifice and His own satisfaction therein and the justifying grace He ministers to others.

The statement **"Yet it pleased the Lord to bruise Him"** speaks of the determinate counsel of Jehovah in causing man's sin to be subservient to the actings of His grace, in the suffering inflicted upon His sinless Servant on the Cross. That He **"put Him to grief"** speaks of the extreme distress brought upon Him.

What follows is probably rightly rendered as in the margin: **"When His soul shall make an offering for sin,"** i.e., a trespass offering, a sacrifice offered to God with the effect of clearing the sinner from his guilt. The sin offering was presented by the priest from the point of view of the offerer, but the trespass offering had especially in view the demands of God's justice. That is what is indicated here. This is the first of the three statements as to His soul.

This voluntary act of surrendering His life (a life with which God was ineffably pleased) to meet God's righteous demands concerning man's guilt, is shown to have the following results (*in vv. 10–12*) relating to Christ Himself:

1. **"He shall see His seed."** An Israelite was regarded as conspicuously blessed if he had a numerous posterity, and especially if he lived to see them (Gen. 48:11; Ps. 128:6). Here then we have an intimation of the exceeding joy of Christ in seeing the results of His sacrifice in the countless multitude of His spiritual posterity from among Jew and Gentile.

2. **"He shall prolong His days,"** another blessing regarded as a high favor among Israelites (cp. Ps. 91:16; Prov. 3:2, 16). Here, however, the reference is to the unending resurrection life of the Lord, and to the joy that breathes through His words "I was dead, and behold I am alive forevermore" (Rev. 1:18).

3. **"The pleasure of the Lord shall prosper in His hand."** That is to say, the predeterminate counsels of God shall have their joyous realization. The phrase "in His hand" points to His Mediatorial and High Priestly work, as well as to the exercise of His authority and power in His Kingdom.

4. **"He shall see of the travail of His soul, and shall be satisfied."** This is the second mention of the soul of Christ in the passage. All the glory that follows and will follow will be viewed by Him as the outcome of His atoning sufferings, which will never cease to be present to His mind as the all-necessary and all-sufficient means by which His heart is satisfied in the redemption of those that have become His own possession. This is true both in the progressive work of saving grace and in its entire fulfillment when the Church is complete and Israel is saved.

5. **"By His knowledge shall My righteous Servant justify many."** There is stress upon the word "righteous." There could be no justification for others, no reckoning of righteousness, were it not for His flawless righteousness, by which alone He was competent to render Himself voluntarily as a propitiatory Sacrifice.

The phrase translated "by His knowledge" may be rendered in two ways, either "by knowledge of Him" or "by His own knowledge." Regarding the former, to know Him is life eternal (John 17:3; 1 John 5:20; cp. 2 Pet. 1:3); this is the objective sense. The other is the subjective. In chapter 11:2, one of the seven spirits which were foretold as resting upon Christ is "the spirit of knowledge." Again, one of the qualifications of a priest is that his lips keep knowledge (Mal. 2:7), so that people may seek the law at his mouth. Further, in Matthew 11:27 the Lord says that knowledge of the Father belongs only to Himself and "to whomsoever the Son willeth to reveal Him." In the whole passage both the priestly and the mediatorial work of Christ is unfolded as well as the prospect of His regal glory (see 52:15 and 53:12). Because of what He is in His own Person as well as in this threefold office, and because of His absolute knowledge as the Son of God, He would effect the justification of many. That is to say, He would make righteous all that come unto God by Him. But only on the ground of His vicarious sacrifice, and this is why the statement **"And He shall bear their iniquities"** immediately follows. By reason of this He is an eternal Priest, qualified to dispense all that accrues from His offering.

There yet remains another glorious effect of His sacrificial death. Jehovah will **"divide Him a portion with the great, and He shall divide the spoil with the strong."** The Septuagint renders it, "I will give Him the mighty for a portion." The thought is not that of dividing into portions, but of assigning. "The great" and "the strong" are general terms, and do not specify particular individuals; they do not refer to specially prominent persons or those who are mightier than others, but to all who by reason of faithful adherence to His will are to be made sharers in His regal authority when His Kingdom is established.

The Father and the Son cooperate, and the Son will "divide the spoil with the strong." The latter are mentioned in Psalm 110:3 as volunteers in the day of His power, partaking with Him of the spoils of His triumph. The Septuagint renders this second statement, "He shall divide the spoils of the mighty" suggesting His triumph over His foes, and this meaning is accepted by many.

Again we are directed to the foundation work of His atoning sacrifice. The very establishment of His sovereign power in the earth will rest upon that finished work. It is here finally set forth in four statements. All the future glory, all that will accrue by way of reward to the faithful is because (1) **"He poured out His soul unto death"**; (2) **"He was numbered with the transgressors"**; (3) **"He bare the sin of many"**; (4) **"He made intercession for the transgressors."** The last two of these are set in striking contrast to the fact that He was numbered with the transgressors, and this is accurately set forth by the R.V. "yet" instead of "and." The former points to the unrighteous opinion of those who pronounced sentence upon Him and handed Him over to execution. Little did they realize that in what He endured on the Cross He was Himself the sin-bearer, and the closing statement refers especially to His intercessory prayer while He was being nailed to the tree. Then it was that He made intercession for the transgressors.

For the third time mention is made of His soul, and now in connection with His own act in pouring out His soul unto death. Concerning this He Himself said "I lay down My life for the sheep" and "I lay down My life that I may take it again. No one taketh it away from Me, but I lay it down of Myself. I have power to lay it down, and I have power to take it again" (John 10:15, 17, 18).

The details of this prophecy in chapter fifty-three grow in vividness and reach a climax in these last three verses.

ISAIAH 54

This prophetic chapter bursts out in exultation and rejoicing. Yes, after the prophecies of the sufferings, sin-bearing, there is glory for the Servant of Jehovah for the ultimate deliverance that He will bring to His people.

Israel is called upon to rejoice with singing and shouting, as her state of barrenness would yield place to fruitfulness. The experiences of their ancestress Sarah had been a foreshadowing of this. The desolate condition of the people and their land was not to last indefinitely. Jehovah had not divorced her. The time will come when she will no more be termed "Forsaken" neither will the land be termed "Desolate," for **"as the bridegroom rejoiceth over the bride,"** so will God rejoice over her (62:4, 5) and her children will be more numerous than they were before she became desolate (*v. 1*).

She is therefore bidden to broaden out her tent and stretch out the curtains of her habitations, to lengthen her cords and strengthen her stakes, language metaphorically setting forth the extension of her territory so that there may be room for the increased population.

Accordingly the promise is given her, **"thou shalt spread abroad on the right hand and on the left; and thy seed shall possess the nations, and make the desolate cities to be inhabited"** (*v. 3*). The right hand and the left stands for both the south and the north, as in Genesis 15:18, Egypt and the Euphrates; also for the east and the west (see Gen. 28:14). There will be much more in the coming time than what was enjoyed in the reign of Solomon. They are to become the head of the nations, ruling over those who oppressed them (see Mic. 4:1–3). Cities desolated by war and pillage will become populous. Israel, repentant and converted, will then be the meek who shall inherit the earth.

Such are the Lord's ways. Enlargement follows curtailment when His chastening hand has done its work. When the disciplined soul learns to realize more fully what was accomplished at Calvary and bows in self-judgment before Him, spiritual enlargement is sure to result. Fruitfulness, which has suffered through impoverishment of soul, bursts forth in abundance, for the glory of the Lord and for the enrichment and blessing of others.

The passage that follows from *verse 4* onward is full of the tenderest promises and comfort, telling out the lovingkindness of the Lord, His covenant mercies, and the glorious future in store for the nation. Israel is no longer to fear, for she will not be put to shame. She is exhorted not to be confounded (or rather, as it may be rendered, "to bid defiance to reproach"). Her future will be so delightful that she will "forget the shame of her youth," the time when she was in bondage in Egypt. There she was like a virgin, but Jehovah who redeemed her betrothed her to Himself with a covenant of love (see Jer. 51:5), for her Husband was none other than her Maker (*v. 5*). He who had become her Husband was the One who brought her into existence, and He is **"the Lord of hosts,"** the One whose bidding the hosts above fulfill. In the Hebrew the words for Maker and Husband are plural, alike with *Elohim*, "God," the last divine title in the verse; they are thus expressive of the fullness of the relation and of His creatorial power.

Again, her Redeemer, the Holy One of Israel, is described as **"the God of the whole earth,"** indicating that the power to assist her belongs to Him and will be exercised because of the relation of love in which she stands to Him.

The relation had suffered a kind of disillusion, but Jehovah will yet call her back to Himself, **"as a wife forsaken and grieved in spirit, even a wife of youth, when she is cast off"** (*v. 6*). Wonderful is the restoring grace of God. He calls Israel back to Himself as a husband receives back the wife he loved in his youth. She has displeased Him, but she was not as one hated. On the contrary, the Lord regards the time in which He had forsaken her, the time of her captivity, as "a small moment" (*v. 7*).

The time of her captivity in the east had seemed long to the captives, and this is especially evinced in the intercessory prayer and supplications made by Daniel, who realized the terrible nature of God's disciplinary dealings in the time of the forsaking (see Dan. 9 and Jeremiah's Lamentations). Jeremiah says, "Wherefore dost Thou forget us forever, and forsake us so long time?" (Lam. 5:20). Viewing the still longer period from the unalterable character of His mercy, God speaks of it as a moment. He says **"with great mercies will I gather thee"** (*vv. 7, 8*).

At the beginning of *verse 8* the R.V. rightly renders the phrase **"In overflowing wrath,"** that is, in the gushing forth of indignation. It is with this that His **"everlasting kindness"** is set in contrast. The Lord then gives a pledge that He will never again be wroth with Israel or rebuke her. Similarly, He says, He pledged Himself to Noah and His descendants that He would never cut off all the flesh again by the waters of a flood. Just as the already existent rainbow was then set as a token of a covenant between Himself and the earth and every living creature, so now He speaks of His "covenant of peace" as that which will never be removed, and conveys the assurance that likewise, even when the mountains have departed and the hills have been removed, His kindness shall never depart from Israel. For He is **"the Lord that hath mercy on thee"** (v. 10).

Just as Noah and his family came forth into a new world after the deluge, so after "the great tribulation" will God's redeemed earthly people come forth to Millennial blessedness. "Weeping may tarry [or come in to lodge] for the night, but joy cometh in the morning" (Ps. 30:5, where God's anger is said to last "but for a moment," just as here in Isa. 54:7, 8; cp. 2 Cor. 4:17).

Thus does the Lord, while administering the necessary unjoyous chastening of His people, fix His heart and keep His eye upon the "peaceable fruit of righteousness." Never does He cease to have our highest and best interests in view.

From *verse 11* to the end of the chapter the future glory and happiness of God's earthly people is described in a beautiful variety of ways, which serve to set forth the coming deliverance and its issues in contrast to their present woes. This latter condition He describes in tender terms: **"O thou afflicted, tossed with tempest, and not comforted"** (v. 11). The tempest expresses the fury of Gentile powers in their Satanically inspired determination to crush Israel to the uttermost. Of Jerusalem, which at the height of the storm will become the center of the world's last great war, He says **"I will set thy stones in fair colors, and lay thy foundations with sapphires. And I will make thy pinnacles** [or minarets, not "windows," A.V.] **of rubies, and thy gates of carbuncles, and all thy border** [R.V.] **of pleasant stones."** All this represents the reflection of the glory of God Himself. The jewels which God has hidden in the earth, and which man has unearthed for purposes of his own avarice and self-glorification, have been designed for the purpose of setting forth the glory of Christ's attributes and character, and while they will be literally used to beautify the earthly Jerusalem, they will thereby be a continuous reminder and token to God's people of the glories and grace of Christ their Redeemer.

So the twelve precious stones, set in the breastplate of the high priest of old, set forth the glory and grace of Christ in His High Priestly ministry. And as from that breastplate the words of light and instruction were given for the impartation of the mind of the Lord to His people, so in the coming day the natural glory of Jerusalem, instead of ministering to human pride, will convey the mind and will of God as revealed in the Messiah.

This is what is immediately promised, for *verse 13* says: **"And all thy children shall be taught of the Lord; and great shall be the peace of thy children."** That is to say, they will all be disciples (see the R.V. margin). They will not need human instruction. This promise Christ Himself quoted when He said to the murmuring Jews: "Every one that hath heard from the Father, and hath learned, cometh unto Me," John 6:45. The two words in that verse in the original, "taught of God," are combined into one adjective in 1 Thessalonians 4:9, lit., "God-taught." Just as believers are taught of God to love one another, so in Israel, as those who will be "taught of the Lord," love will characterize them all. It naturally follows that peace will prevail. For where love is in exercise joy and peace inevitably exist (cp. Col. 3:14, 15).

All this is the outcome of the knowledge of the Lord. Israel will not need to teach every man his neighbor and every man his brother, saying, "know the Lord": for they will all know Him "from the least to the greatest" (Jer. 31:34). But all this happiness will be enjoyed on the basis of Divine righteousness: **"in righteousness shalt thou be established,"** *verse 14* (see chap. 11:5).

No longer will foes oppress them. They will be far from oppression. They are not to fear a repetition of their troubles. They are to be far from terror; it will not come near them again. Their enemies may gather together, but all who dare to do so will fall because of them. Jerusalem will be invincible (*v. 15*). God has created the smith who blows the coal fire and produces a weapon for his work (or "according to his trade"); He has also created the waster (or destroyer) to destroy (*v. 16*). The very creative power of Jehovah is to be used to defend His people. Accordingly no weapon formed against them shall prosper. And then, just as every hostile weapon fails, so Jerusalem, quickened into the knowledge of the Lord, and therefore conscious of its Divine right, will convict every accuser as guilty and therefore subject to punishment. **"Every tongue that shall rise against thee in judgment thou shalt condemn"** (*v. 17*).

The closing statement of the chapter sums up all the preceding promises, and describes them as **"the heritage of the servants of Jehovah."** What is the rightful reward of the great Servant of Jehovah in His exaltation, is differently described in respect of His servants, for their heritage is of grace. And whereas He is Himself "Jesus Christ the righteous," the righteousness granted to His people is likewise a matter of grace: **"their righteousness is of Me, saith Jehovah."** That is how Jerusalem is to be established. Israel will not be able to claim anything of this by their own merit, any more than we can who are "justified freely by His grace through the redemption that is in Christ Jesus."

ISAIAH 55–57

In these last three prophetic chapters in Isaiah, we see a major shift from judgment and impending deliverance from the Servant of Jehovah to an incredible invitation to the people to come and to partake of the spiritual provision given by Him. All that is required is to hear His voice, listen to His promise of forgiveness, and to repent. While this section isn't a prophecy per se, it is prophetic in the sense that even yet today, "while it is called today," if anyone would hear and respond to Jehovah's invitation, he will be saved.

The invitation is to **"every one that thirsteth,"** and the provision made consists not of the material benefits of water, wine and milk. These are metaphorically used of higher things than the natural products. The spiritual significance of water has been mentioned in 44:3, where the reference is to the Holy Spirit, as in John 7:38. Similarly in regard to wine (see 25:6, 7). So we must understand the mention of milk (see 1 Pet. 2:2, where the reference is to the Word of God). In Scripture the Spirit of God and the Word of God are often associated.

Moreover, the purchase is to be made **"without money and without price"** (v. 1). This is all of divine grace. The possession of the spiritual blessings is, from the point of view of the recipients, dependent solely upon a sense of need and a readiness to accept them.

With this invitation we may compare the words of the parable in Matthew 22:4, and the contrast, expressed in *verse 2* of this fifty-fifth chapter, reminds us of the contrast between grace and works in Romans 11:6. The paradox of buying without money is suggestive of spiritual bankruptcy. Israel was spending money and labor upon idols. Hence the solemn appeal of the opening word of the chapter; for the exclamation "Ho" is not simply a matter of invitation, it casts a reflection upon the state of those who are adopting their own devices instead of listening to the voice of the Lord.

The Lord follows His remonstrance with the gracious words **"hearken diligently unto Me, and eat ye that which is good, and let your soul delight itself in fatness"** (v. 2). Often in Scripture where two commands are given the second suggests the good result of obeying the first (cp. Gen. 42:18).

The satisfaction of the soul can be obtained only in the path of the obedience of faith. By diligently listening to the voice of God and fulfilling His will we can enjoy real spiritual delight. Moreover, what the Lord here holds out is something more than meeting our need. He designs to give us an overflowing satisfaction. This is indicated by the word "fatness" (see, for instance, Pss. 36:8 and 63:5). This is "the riches of His grace."

He now bids His people to incline their ear and come unto Him, to hear, that their soul may live (v. 3) or revive (cp. John 14:6). Much the same thing was said later to the church in Laodicea. In such conditions the Lord calls upon the individual to hear His voice (Rev. 3:20), and the provision He makes for the responsive heart is to find in Him the very life and sustenance of the soul.

There is much in these first three verses of the chapter that affords matter for a Gospel message, but the appeal is directly to the backslider, whose soul needs the reviving that can be effected only by returning to the Lord.

"And I will make," He says, **"an everlasting covenant with you, even the sure mercies of David."** In human affairs a covenant is made and ratified by each of the parties to it. Here the Lord undertakes the obligations Himself, and the covenant is virtually a promise. So in Galatians 3:17, 18, where "covenant" and "promise" are used interchangeably. Moreover, the Greek word there used, *diatheke*, does not in itself contain the idea of joint obligation, it denotes that which is undertaken by one alone. The sole condition for the recipient is that he shall incline his ear and come. He will not thereby be putting his signature to a covenant; his acceptance of the invitation ensures the fulfillment of the "covenant of promise."

The phrase "the sure mercies of David" receives its interpretation in Acts 13:34, which quotes from the Septuagint: "I will give you the holy and sure *blessings* [lit., things] of David." Paul uses this as the second of three quotations from the O.T. to prove that they were fulfilled in the Person of Christ, the first foretelling His birth (v. 33, see the R.V.; there the raising up of Jesus speaks of His being raised up in the nation, in His life on earth, cp. v. 23), the second foretelling His resurrection, the third His incorruptibility. What God promised to David (e.g., in 2 Sam. 7:16), and will yet be fulfilled to him in the future earthly Kingdom, can be established in that day only in and through the Person of Christ Himself, by reason of His resurrection and exaltation, and in the glory of His Millennial reign.

David was, and yet will be, God's appointed **"witness to the peoples"** (the nations), and their **"leader and commander"** (see Ezek. 34:24; 37:24). Israel, possessed of worldwide dominion, will "call a nation that they knew not" (referring to Gentile peoples in general), and the nation that knew not Israel will run to them (indicative of swift means of travel), "because of Jehovah their God," and **"for the Holy One of Israel."** Now there is no such reciprocal recognition; the opposite is the case. But in the day of Messiah's reign, Israel will be glorified by Him (*vv. 4, 5*). In *verse 6* there is a general appeal: **"Seek ye the Lord while He may be found, call ye upon Him while He is near."**

What follows is an appeal to the backslider; he is called upon to forsake his way and his thoughts, and to return unto the Lord. A return implies the retracing of one's steps to that which was formerly enjoyed. The unregenerate man can turn, but a return is for him who has gone back from that fellowship with God which he once experienced. He waits to have mercy upon him and to "pardon abundantly" (lit., "He will multiply to pardon"), *verse 7*.

The foregoing appeal to forsake their own way and thoughts, and, by returning to God, to yield themselves to Him, is urged by reason of the fact of the utter difference between the ways and thoughts of God and the self-willed and foolish ways and thoughts of men (*vv. 8, 9*; cp. 40:27; 9:14).

The waywardness of the backslider plunges him into unbelief and misery. He finds that his purposes are frustrated by a mightier power than his, and the thorny path that he has chosen brings him into spiritual gloom and uncertainty.

To all this God sets His actings and decrees in striking contrast. Just as He has absolute control over the rain and the snow and the produce of the earth, and man can do nothing to alter that which God has established by His creative power, **"so shall My word be,"** He says, **"that goeth forth out of My mouth: it shall not return unto Me void** [or, fruitless], **but it shall accomplish** [or, "till it has accomplished"] **that which I please, and it shall prosper in** [or, "has prosperously carried out"] **the thing whereto I sent it."** That is to say, it will not return without having achieved the purpose for which the Lord sent it (*vv. 10, 11*).

His Word is His messenger (see 9:8; Pss. 107:20; 147:15–19). His Word is here personified. It runs like a swift messenger, accomplishing God's will with its vital power both in nature and amidst humanity. A word is the expression of thought. It is part of the person himself. So Christ is called the Word of God. He had declared Him (told Him out), John 1:18. "Everything that proceedeth out of the mouth of the Lord" provides spiritual food by which man lives (Deut. 8:3). Just as what comes from the soil of the earth is produced by the rain and the snow, so with the soil of the human heart and the Word of God.

How great a responsibility therefore devolves upon one who is God's messenger! If the messenger's heart is in full communion with the One who sends him, his message will accomplish God's pleasure and prosper in the object for which it is sent.

In *verse 12* the Lord graciously applies the principles relating to His Word to the promise of unspeakable blessing for Israel in the coming day. **"For ye shall go out with joy,"** that is to say, life's activities will be carried on without the haste of fear (cp. 52:12), **"and be led forth with peace"**: they will never again have to fight their way through foes or flee from them: **"the mountains and the hills shall break forth before you into singing, and all the trees of the field shall clap their hands."** Nature will be brought into unison with God's purposes of grace toward His people (cp. Ps. 98:8, where the clapping of the hands is applied to streams and billows of water). There will be a sympathy, so to speak, between nature and the joyous hearts of God's redeemed. No longer will the natural creation be subjected to vanity. The creation itself "shall be delivered from the bondage of corruption into the liberty of the glory of the children of God" (Rom. 8:21, R.V.).

"Instead of the thorn shall come up the fir tree [or cypress], **and instead of the briar shall come up the myrtle tree,"** a humble, sweet-smelling, beautiful evergreen; from the Hebrew word for it comes the name Hadassah, the original name of Esther (Esth. 2:7): **"and it shall be to the Lord for a name, for an everlasting sign** (or memorial) **that shall not be cut off"** (*v. 13*). What God will bring about in the blessedness of the Millennial Kingdom will have a twofold effect: it will tell forth His glory and will be a constant reminder to His people of His attributes and actings of grace and power.

The opening words of this chapter [56], **"Keep ye judgment and do righteousness,"** recall the admonition in verses 6 and 7 of the preceding chapter. The thoughts and the ways of Israel were not those of the Lord (*v. 8*). The glorious promises which followed in that chapter were incentives to the wicked to forsake his way and the unrighteous man his thoughts; they were also preparatory to the present injunctions. Let them fulfill practical righteousness and they would thus become conformed to the righteousness of God's character and dealings. And the reason why they should do so is twofold: **"for My salvation,"** He says, **"is near to come** [the salvation expressed in the preceding promises], **and My righteousness to be revealed."** Righteous dealing has as its basis the relationship into which God brings His people. It was a covenanted relation with Israel, involving the fulfillment of righteousness on each side. God fulfilled His part and He was ready to manifest it if they turned from their unrighteous ways and fell into line with His. If they only realized how near His salvation and His righteous dealings were in their manifestation, this itself should have impelled them to respond to His promise and command.

A special blessing is held out to him who keeps God's command, and to the son of man **"that holdeth fast by it, that keepeth the sabbath from polluting it, and keepeth his hand from doing any evil"** (v. 2).

As to the sabbath, ours is a perpetual sabbath keeping; "there remaineth [i.e., continueth perpetually] a sabbath rest for the people of God" (Heb. 4:9). We ourselves can only enjoy this rest in Christ if we keep our hand from doing evil.

The stranger who had joined himself to the Lord (and there were not a few who, professing the religion of Jehovah, had joined His people) might be tempted to fear that after Israel was restored to their land the Lord would separate him from them, depriving him of the privileges he had enjoyed. The fear was ill-founded, for if they "held fast by His covenant," God would bring them to His Holy mountain, and make them joyful in His house of prayer; their burnt offerings and sacrifices would be accepted upon His altar: for His house "would be called a house of prayer for all peoples." And He who will gather the outcasts of Israel, will gather others to him beside "his own" that were gathered (vv. 6–8, R.V.).

There were others who might be tempted to despair, considering their condition and all that was taking place. There were the eunuchs, concerning whom a prohibition was given in Deuteronomy 23:1. But even to these a promise is given of a **"memorial** [A.V., place] **and a name better than of sons, and of daughters,"** an everlasting name that would not be cut off (vv. 4, 5), on condition that they refrained from profaning the sabbath and held fast by the Lord's covenant. The party wall would be pulled down, which separated the eunuchs from fellowship with the congregation of Israel. All humanly erected barriers to fellowship are destined to be removed in the coming day.

Verse 9, which the R.V. marks as the beginning of a paragraph, probably commences a new subject and forms the beginning of chapter 57. The watchman and the shepherds in Israel had given way to selfishness and debauchery. They had abandoned their responsibilities toward God's people and, instead of giving warning, they were blind to the impending danger. They were **"dumb dogs,"** unable to bark. Instead of watching they were **"dreaming, lying down, loving to slumber."** Accordingly the Lord gives an invitation to the beasts of the field and the forest, metaphorically representing Gentile powers, to come and devour (vv. 9–12).

All whom the Lord makes responsible to act as shepherds over His flock need to guard themselves against gradual decline from their duty and against either lording it over the charge allotted to them or becoming possessed of sordid aims to acquire filthy lucre (1 Pet. 5:2, 3).

In contrast to the evil watchmen and shepherds and rulers, who were simply engaged in debauchery and self-indulgence, there were the righteous, who stand out conspicuously by reason of the fact that they are taken away from the coming evil, that is to say, from the impending Divine judgments. Their removal is unheeded. They are characterized as "merciful" (or rather, godly, R.V. margin). They **"enter into peace; they rest in their beds, each one that walketh in his uprightness"** (or "straight before him," *[ch. 57] vv. 1, 2*). While the godly suffer by oppression, and by distress at what is going on around them, they do not lose their blessedness in the sight of God or their reward hereafter. They die in faith and go to enjoy the eternal peace of the spirits of the just made perfect (Heb. 12:23).

Far better it is to suffer death for righteousness' sake than to endeavor to enjoy ease and freedom from trouble by making compromises with the world.

A striking change in the prophet's utterances follows. There is first a warning to the evildoers to draw near to listen to the voice of God (*v. 3*). Frequently in Scripture a man's moral character is indicated by a reference to his father (2 Kin. 6:32), or his mother (1 Sam. 20:30), or both parents (Job 30:8). Accordingly those who were in captivity and continued the idolatry which had brought upon their fathers the judgment of their overthrow by the Chaldeans, are called **"sons of the sorceress, the seed of the adulterer and the whore."**

All that follows, in *verses 4 to 11*, is addressed to those who had gone into captivity. The reference to the oaks and the green trees (*v. 5*) points to those forms of tree worship by which different trees were regarded as the special abodes of different deities. Abominable orgies were associated therewith. The slaughter of the children "in the valleys and under the clefts of the rocks" was not that carried out in sacrifice to Moloch in the valley of Hinnom, but that connected with the worship of Baal (Jer. 19:5; Ezek. 16:21). In *verse 6* the reference is to stone worship, end the libations poured out thereon. In *verses 7 to 9* the idolatrous worship is further described in the metaphorical phraseology of adultery, in its faithlessness toward God.

All this wickedness involved much toil and weariness (*v. 10*); yet the people were so far gone in their alienation from the Lord, that instead of realizing the hopelessness of their condition they found **"a quickening of their strength"** (R.V.), and continued to make alliances with the heathen. The longsuffering of God did not produce repentance, but His silence by way of helping His faithful ones would not be indefinitely postponed.

There are dangers in forming associations with those who do not adhere to the Word of God, under the pretext of being regarded as charitable, and, on the other hand, as a result of urgent advice that we must all make common cause against powerful adverse forces. Faithfulness to the Lord demands our maintaining the honor of His Name at whatever cost. And as the Lord came to the help of His faithful ones in captivity, so He will in these times of laxity and apostasy.

The alliances the people were making were the outcome of fear. They took refuge in lies and did not remember God; nor did they lay it to their heart (*v. 11*).

Forgetfulness of God and a seared conscience go together. The fact that God does not intervene by way of judgment leads the hardened heart to be void of the fear of the Lord: **"Have not I held My peace even of long time, and thou fearest Me not?"** He says.

In *verse 12* the statement **"I will declare thy righteousness"** does not indicate that those with whom God was remonstrating were themselves righteous. The very opposite was the case. It was what Israel in its blind condition regarded as their own righteousness. It was a lying righteousness and its true character would be declared, i.e., exposed and judged by the Lord. This is confirmed by what follows: **"and as for thy works, they shall not profit thee. When thou criest, let them which thou hast gathered deliver thee; but the wind shall take them, a breath shall carry them all away"** (*v. 13*).

The Lord now addresses His faithful ones among His people in captivity, and gives the assurance, **"he that putteth his trust in Me shall possess the land, and shall inherit My holy mountain."** The way is to be made for the return of the captives, and the message to be given is, **"Cast ye up, Cast ye up, prepare the way, take up the stumbling block out of the way of My people."** This receives light from 62:10, which looks on to the final gathering of Israel from among the nations (cp. 40:3, 4). The stumbling block speaks of any and every obstruction standing in the way of the return (*v. 14*).

In the last paragraph of the chapter the Lord gives a message of combined glory and grace, concerning His twofold dwelling place, the high and holy place in Heaven and the contrite and humble spirit on earth. The latter will be the condition of His earthly people after the restoration.

If we humble ourselves under the mighty hand of God (1 Pet. 5:6). He will exalt us, or, as He says here in Isaiah, He will revive our spirit and our heart. Contrition and humility are as cause and effect. As one has said, "The selfish egotism which repentance breaks has its root in the heart; and the self-consciousness, from whose false elevation repentance brings down, has its seat in the spirit."

If the Lord were to contend continually and always be wroth, the spirit of the object of His righteous anger would fail before Him **"and the souls which He has made"** (*v. 16*). Here significantly the Lord gives a reminder that the very existence of the soul is due to His creative power, and this is His touching appeal for contrition and humility before Him. In spite of His creative mercy, it became a necessity for Him to destroy the whole human race, save for eight souls, at the time of the Flood. The spread of the physical corruption consequent upon the unlicensed moral depravity of the race, and their persistent lack of repentance, would have terminated in a more terrible way than even by the Flood. The present statement seems to have a connection with the promise made after judgment had been inflicted, that God would not utterly destroy the race again.

Perhaps in fulfilling that promise, and certainly by reason of His covenant with Abraham and his seed, the Lord now makes a promise to Israel that, having smitten him for his covetousness (or rather, selfishness) and for the turning away of his own heart (margin), He would heal him, and lead him, and restore comforts unto him, and particularly to those who mourned by reason of their wanderings (*vv. 17, 18*).

Verse 19 shows that the effects of God's dealings will divide the nation in twain. For those who became contrite and humble there would be "peace, peace," in all their scattered condition, those who were far offend those who were near. The doubling of the word conveys its perfection and perpetuity, i.e., "perfect peace," as in 26:3. This will produce worship and songs of praise; hence the Lord introduces the promise of peace by the statement, "**I create the fruit of the lips.**"

On the other hand there will be the impenitent, the wicked, for whom there is no peace, who **"are like the troubled sea; for it cannot rest, and its waters cast up mire and dirt"** (*vv. 20, 21*).

THE BAPTIST'S TESTIMONY

John the Baptist was the last prophet of Christ. When Jesus comes to him, John calls him "the Lamb of God," the one "who taketh away the sin of the world." John is not only prophetically linked to Isaiah and Elijah in his utterances and stern warnings to the people, but he is also a fulfillment of prophecy in that he would be that last forerunner of the Messiah.

Following the introduction, or prologue, comes the first main division of John's Gospel, from 1:19 to the end of chapter 12. This especially narrates the public testimony of Christ, by word and work. The narrative begins by resuming the witness of John the Baptist, now to priests and Levites sent by the Pharisees to Bethany beyond Jordan where John was baptizing.

John had by this time drawn the attention of the Sanhedrin. He had proclaimed the approach of a new era (Matt. 3:2). Hence the sending of the priests and Levites to inquire whether he himself was the Messiah. These came from the Pharisees; the Sadducees were not so interested, they were more submissive to the Roman power. For the Baptist it was a time of crisis. Hence his emphatic declaration, that he was neither the Messiah nor Elijah nor **"that prophet"** (Deut. 18:15) but **"the voice of one crying in the wilderness** [an intimation of the spiritual state of the nation], **Make straight the way of the Lord, as said Isaiah the prophet"** (v. 23).

Then came the question as to the reason for his baptizing. It had the appearance of treating Jews as if they were mere proselytes, and of implying that they were defiled and needed cleansing. The answer he gives reveals that to him the Lord Jesus is more than all His credentials. He has no time to argue about himself; his answer is to point them to Christ. **"I baptize with water; in the midst of you standeth One whom ye** (emphatic) **know not, even He that cometh after me, the latchet of whose shoe** [i.e., the thong of whose sandal] **I am not worthy to unloose"** (vv. 26, 27), one of the most menial acts of slaves.

THE LAMB OF GOD

Verse 29 begins the Baptist's testimony to the people, by reason of Christ's coming on the scene in person on the following day. And now He who has been described as the Word, the Creator, the Son of God, is pointed out as **"the Lamb of God,"** the one **"who taketh away the sin of the world."** The **"Behold"** is an interjection, not a command. His hearers would understand what the mention of a lamb signified, and might recall the language of Isaiah 53. But they must know that He is the Lamb of God, and that as such, that is by the atoning efficacy of His sacrifice, He takes away, not merely the sin of Israel ("my people," Isa. 53:8), but the sin of the world. Christ will restore the world's broken relation with God. In this matter it has been necessary for God to take the fact of sin into consideration, but Christ's sacrifice will be the eternal foundation of the renewed relation.

It was given to John the Baptist for the first time to designate Him as "the Lamb of God." The phrase is not found in the Old Testament, though typical intimations and foreshadowings abound therein. The nearest expression is in Genesis 22:8. The verb rendered "taketh away" denotes either to lift and bear or to take away, here both senses may be combined, for the word points to Christ's expiatory sacrifice and its effects. This is here said of "the sin of the world"; not the sins, but that which has existed from the time of the Fall, and in regard to which God has had judicial dealings with the world; hereafter the sin of the world will be replaced by everlasting righteousness.

John recalls his testimony of the previous day (v. 15) and the reason why he baptized with water (v. 31); it was that Christ was to be manifested to Israel. But there was more than this. That which would identify to the Baptist the person in a twofold way was the descent of the Holy Spirit upon Him.

3

END TIMES
PROPHECIES

WITNESSES TO THE SECOND ADVENT

We must go back to the very beginnings of human history for the initial announcement of the Second Advent. No sooner had sin come into the world than God pronounced the doom of the Tempter whose malignant craft had affected man's moral collapse. The Seed of the woman should bruise his head. That judicial sentence embodies the first prophecy of the Second Advent. Prophecies continued throughout the Old and New Testaments—Enoch, Job, Balaam, Moses, Hannah, David, Isaiah, Jesus, and His Apostles. This large section gives a wonderfully crafted overview of the Second Advent that will provide the reader with a clear biblical prophetic summation from Genesis to Revelation.

REVELATION 19:11–21 (R.V.)

"And I saw the heaven opened; and behold, a white horse, and He that sat thereon, called Faithful and True; and in righteousness He doth judge and make war. And His eyes are a flame of fire, and upon His head are many diadems; and He hath a name written, which no one knoweth but He Himself. And He is arrayed in a garment sprinkled with blood: and His name is called the Word of God. And the armies which are in heaven followed Him upon white horses, clothed in fine linen, white and pure. And out of His mouth proceedeth a sharp sword, that with it He should smite the nations: and He shall rule them with a rod of iron: And He treadeth the winepress of the fierceness of the wrath of Almighty God. And He hath on His garment and on His thigh a name written, KING OF KINGS AND LORD OF LORDS.

"And I saw an angel standing in the sun; and he cried with a loud voice, saying to all the birds that fly in midheaven, Come and be gathered together unto the great supper of God; that ye may eat the flesh of kings, and the flesh of captains, and the flesh of mighty men, and the flesh of horses, and of them that sit thereon, and the flesh of all men, both free and bond, and small and great.

"And I saw the beast, and the kings of the earth, and their armies, gathered together to make war against Him that sat upon the horse, and against His army. And the beast was taken, and with him the false prophet, that wrought the signs in his sight, wherewith he deceived them that had received the mark of the beast, and them that worshiped his image: they twain were cast alive into the lake of fire that burneth with brimstone: and the rest were killed with the sword which came forth out of his mouth: and all the birds were filled with their flesh."

REVELATION 11:15–18 (R.V.)

"And the seventh angel sounded; and there followed great voices in heaven, and they said, The Kingdom of the world is become the Kingdom of our Lord, and of His Christ: and He shall reign forever and ever. And the four and twenty elders, which sit before God on their thrones, fell upon their faces, and worshiped God, saying, We give Thee thanks, O Lord God, the Almighty, which art and which wast; because Thou hast taken Thy great power, and didst reign. And the nations were wroth, and thy wrath came, and the time of the dead to be judged, and the time to give their reward, to Thy servants the prophets, and to the saints, and to them that fear Thy name, the small and the great; and to destroy them that destroy the earth."

WITNESSES TO THE SECOND ADVENT

The Second Coming of Christ is shown in Scripture to consist of two distinct events, namely, (1) the rapture of the Church to meet the Lord in the air (1 Thess. 4:13–17), followed by a period of divine retribution upon the rebellious condition of humanity; (2) the appearing of the Lord Jesus in His glory with the Church and with His angels, at the consummation of this period, for the destruction of the Antichrist and those who are associated with him, for the deliverance of the Jewish nation from their oppressors, and for the establishment of the Kingdom of righteousness and peace (2 Thess. 2:7–10; Rev. 19:11–21). To these events there has been a long line of witnesses, and the number is not yet complete.

THE FIRST ANNOUNCEMENT

We must go back to the very beginnings of human history for the initial announcement of the Second Advent. No sooner had sin come into the world than God pronounced the doom of the Tempter whose malignant craft had effected man's moral collapse. The Seed of the woman should bruise his head. That judicial sentence embodies the first prophecy of the Second Advent. The crushing defeat which the Evil One sustained at Calvary by the Virgin-born Redeemer carried with it the inevitable doom by which that foe of God and man will, when Christ comes in glory, be bound by Him and cast into the abyss and shut up and sealed therein for a thousand years, thereafter to be cast into the Lake of Fire (Rev. 20:1–3, 10).

ENOCH'S PROPHECY

The next testimony, chronologically, is to be found in the epistle of Jude in a statement of fact not recorded in the Old Testament. Speaking of the ultimate doom of ungodly men, he says: "And to these also Enoch, the seventh from Adam, prophesied, saying, Behold, the Lord came with ten thousands of His holy ones, to execute judgment upon all, and to convict all the ungodly of all their works of ungodliness which they have ungodly wrought, and of all the hard things which ungodly sinners have spoken against Him" (Jude 14, 15). The word "came" is in the past tense, because by Hebrew usage the past tense was idiomatically employed in predicting the future, a testimony indeed to the certainty of the events foretold. Here, then, was a witness among the antediluvians to the fact that Christ would come to judge the world in righteousness.

JOB'S ASSURANCE

We now pass to the patriarchal age. The weight of evidence points to the likelihood that Job lived about the time of Abraham. We learn from the twenty-second chapter of Genesis that Uz was Abraham's nephew (v. 21, R.V.), and there is good reason for the supposition that this Uz gave his name to the land in which Job dwelt (Job 1:1). There is a remarkable passage in Job's sixth discourse in which his complaints give place for the moment to confident assurance of resurrection. Several of the great foundation truths of the gospel are packed into this brief utterance. He says, "I know that my Redeemer liveth, and that He shall stand up ["stand triumphantly" is the thought conveyed by the word] at the last over my dust (see R.V. marg.); and after my skin hath been destroyed, yet from my flesh shall I see God: Whom I shall see for myself, and mine eyes shall behold, and not another" (marg., not as a stranger) (Job 19:25–27).

The word "earth" here is the same as that rendered "dust" in Genesis 2:7; 3:19. It is true that Christ will stand on the Mount of Olives, when He comes to deliver Zion (Zech. 14:4), but Job is here speaking of the resurrection power of His Redeemer and how it will affect his mortal remains. He vividly describes the Lord as taking up a position as a mighty One over his dust, with the result that though his body has gone to disintegration yet in his flesh he will see God. Job's prediction then constitutes a striking testimony to the fact of the Second Advent.

JACOB'S PREDICTION

Almost two centuries later, Jacob, on his deathbed, in pronouncing prophetic blessings upon his sons, declares that "The scepter shall not depart from Judah, nor the ruler's staff from between his feet, until Shiloh come; and unto Him shall the obedience of the peoples be" (Gen. 49:10). Shiloh means the Peacemaker, and the context shows that not the place but the person, the Messiah, is in view. Abraham rejoiced to see His day (John 8:56), and the same anticipation is here expressed by his grandson. Whatever partial fulfillment of Jacob's prophecy there may have been in the past, the complete antitypical fulfillment cannot take place until Christ comes to reign. Then, and not till then, the willing obedience of the peoples will be offered to Him.

BALAAM'S PROPHECY

The next testimony to the Second Advent is Balaam's prophecy: it takes up and expands that of Jacob. That it relates to the time under consideration is made clear in Balaam's introductory words to Balak, "I will advertise thee what this people shall do to thy people in the latter days" (Num. 24:14). The time indicated is literally "the end of the days," a phrase which is found in other eschatological passages, e.g., Isaiah 2:7; Daniel 10:14; Micah 4:1. The phrase signifies the time when the promises of salvation made to Israel will have their fulfillment. It points, as has been well said, to the accomplishment of a prophetic announcement.

The prophecy is as follows: "I see Him, but not now: I behold Him, but not nigh: there shall come forth a star out of Jacob, and a scepter shall rise out of Israel, and shall smite through the corners of Moab, and break down all the sons of tumult. And Edom shall be a possession, Seir also shall be a possession, which were his enemies; while Israel doeth valiantly. And out of Jacob shall one have dominion, and shall destroy the remnant from the city" (Num. 24:17–19).

This prophecy cannot be rightly applied to the first advent. The details do not relate to the humiliation and sufferings of Christ, but to the glories which are yet to be. The mention of "the sons of tumult" has reference to the gathering of the nations at the end of this age in their effort to crush the Jews. The prophecy clearly relates to the time when Christ will come for their deliverance and establish the government of Israel in the earth.

THE SONG OF MOSES

We next come to the Song of Moses, a prophecy uttered just before his death. It is recorded in Deuteronomy 32, which gives a concise history of Israel from the time prior to their actual existence, when the divine providence was arranging the geographical distribution of the various nations in view of the future settlement of Israel in their land (v. 8), until the final overthrow of their adversaries at the Second Advent (vv. 40–43). The history thus covers the long period from the dispersion from Babel to the issue of the warfare of Armageddon.

The main part of the song is devoted to a record of the waywardness of Israel in spite of the mercies of God, and to a prediction of the inevitable judgments which must consequently come upon the nation. They must be delivered over to their adversaries, until the divine vengeance has done its necessary work. Yet final deliverance will come, "The Lord shall judge His people, and repent Himself for His servants, when He seeth that their power is gone." Their foes, at whose hands they have suffered the woes of the Great Tribulation, will themselves be visited with the wrath of God.

The close of the prophecy, as correctly rendered in the Revised Version, makes a striking allusion to the doom of Antichrist and to the kings of the nations allied under him, the passage thus being remarkably coincidental with Revelation 17:12–14, and other passages relating to Armageddon. The foe is overthrown by the Son of God Himself, and the nations of the world, delivered from the tyranny and misrule of their despots, are invited to rejoice with liberated Israel. God's people and their land shall be blessed with peace and rest. With this prediction of the glorious intervention of Messiah the song terminates. From verse 39 to verse 42 the speaker is Jehovah.

We will quote in full the closing utterances relating to the Second Advent: "If I whet My glittering sword (see Isa. 34:5–8 and 66:16; and Rev. 19:15, 21), and My hand take hold on judgment; I will render vengeance (see 2 Thess. 1:8, R.V.) to Mine adversaries, and will recompense them that hate Me. I will make Mine arrows drunk with blood (see Isa. 34:3, 7; 63:4; Ezek. 39:17–20; Hab. 3:11; Rev. 14:20), and My sword shall devour flesh; with the blood of the slain and the captives, from the head of the leaders of the enemy ('the head' is prophetic of Antichrist; 'the leaders' indicates the potentates gathered under him; see especially Ps. 110:6; Rev. 17:12–14, 17; 19:19–21; Dan. 7:24–27; and Hab. 3:13). Rejoice, O ye nations [Gentile peoples who are to be blessed in the Millennium] with His people [Israel]; for He will avenge the blood of His servants (see Rev. 6:10; 11:17; 13:7; 19:2), and will render vengeance to His adversaries, and will make expiation for His land, for His people" (see Isa. 34:8; 63:4; Ezek. 39:20–22; Joel 3:16; Hab. 3:16; and the Psalms, *passim*).

The Septuagint inserts, "and let all the angels of God worship Him" after "Rejoice, O ye nations, with His people," and this Septuagint version is quoted in Hebrews 1:6, which is a Second Advent prophecy, and should read, as in the Revised Version, "And when He again bringeth the Firstborn into the world, He saith, And let all the angels of God worship Him." The Father brought His Firstborn into the world at His Incarnation; He will do so again when He comes in glory.

HANNAH'S SONG

Passing now to the time of the birth of Samuel the prophet, whose ministry inaugurated the line of Israel's kings, we come to the prophetic Psalm prayed by his mother when she brought her child to Eli in the house of the Lord for his lifelong service therein. As with many other Spirit-controlled utterances, the theme passes from the immediate circumstances, in this case relating to the birth of the child, to events which have to do with the judgments of the Lord in the earth and the establishment of His Kingdom. The closing words of her song thus testify to the Second Advent: "They that strive with the Lord shall be broken in pieces; against them shall He thunder in Heaven. The Lord shall judge the ends of the earth; and He shall give strength unto His king, and exalt the horn of His Anointed" (1 Sam. 2:10).

The last two sentences are clearly prophetic of millennial blessing, and inasmuch as the Scripture teaches that the millennium will be preceded by the overthrow of the combined foes of Israel, the preceding clauses can only be rightly taken in their fullest meaning as applicable to that time. We may compare, for instance, the breaking in pieces of those who strive against God with Daniel 2:35, 44, and the prediction concerning God's thundering upon them with Revelation 16:18. Whatever may have been in Hannah's mind as to her own circumstances, she was speaking as a prophetess, and her words, inspired of God, were doubtless of wider significance than she herself realized.

This then is the list of the outstanding testimonies to the Second Advent from the time of Adam until Israel's entrance into the land of Canaan. It consists of God's declaration to Satan, and the prophecies of Enoch, Job, Jacob, Balaam, Moses and Hannah. There are other intimations, but those which have been mentioned are the definite utterances. The occasions are separated at comparatively lengthy intervals, the details, however, becoming increasingly distinct and the prophecy expanding as history proceeds.

THE TIME OF THE KINGS

We now come to a period when the witness is more constant; it begins with the establishment of the kingdom under David and extends throughout the time of the kings of Judah and Israel, on through the captivity and the restoration, until the close of prophetic testimony in the nation under the era of the Law.

It is not our purpose here to consider in detail the wonderful series of predictions in the Psalms and the prophets relating to the Lord's Return in glory. The Psalms contain a large number of references to it. It may indeed be said to form one of the main subjects of their prophecies.

THE PSALMS

In the second Psalm, for instance, which together with the first, forms an introduction to the whole book, the intervention of the Lord in Person in the affairs of the world is foretold. The gathering of the kings of the earth and the rulers together against Messiah, as mentioned in the opening words, had only a partial fulfillment at the time of the death of Christ. The statement that the Lord shall speak unto the nations in His wrath and vex them in His sore displeasure has not yet received accomplishment, but will be fulfilled immediately prior to the setting of God's king upon His "holy hill of Zion" at the beginning of the Millennium (vv. 5, 6).

The Psalms are largely occupied with the sufferings and prayers and preservation of the godly remnant of the Jews in the time of the Great Tribulation. The experiences of David form an historical basis for the prophetic and divinely inspired utterances which relate to the experiences of God-fearing Jews who will at the close of this age suffer at the hands of the Antichrist. These Psalms are not merely the history of past events. They are the utterances of the Spirit of Christ, Who, through the Psalmists beforehand, was sympathetically identifying Himself with His oppressed people, the Jews. "The testimony of Jesus is the spirit of prophecy." The facts that the Antichrist is to be Satan's human instrument in his final effort to crush the nation of Israel, and that Christ will Himself come to their deliverance and hurl the tyrant to his doom, accounts for the character of the language of what have been called the imprecatory Psalms. That God's vengeance would eventually be dealt out upon the adversaries of Israel had long been foretold, as we have seen.

SO-CALLED IMPRECATORY PSALMS

The Psalms which breathe the spirit of vengeance were penned, not for the use of the Church, but for the Jewish people, and in fellowship with God and His counsels. Complaints against these denunciatory psalms, on account of their vindictive character, are the outcome of a misunderstanding both of their spirit and purpose. They were not written for an age when the Church is bearing witness in the gospel and is taught to pray for her enemies and persecutors, nor in regard to Israel were they written in the spirit of mere human spite and vengeance. Israel's treatment of their enemies is not a matter of mere human revenge. It is always primarily a vindication of the claims of God. That the Antichrist and those associated with him in their rebellion against the Most High should be denounced and overthrown is only consistent with the divine counsels.

The Spirit of God, knowing beforehand the solemn events that will characterize the close of this age, and the intense suffering through which the Jews must pass at that time at the instigation of the devil, caused the Psalms to be written for the use of God-fearing Jews at this future period. The cry for vengeance is a cry which God has determined to answer at the Second Advent. Only as we grasp this divinely foretold situation can we understand the full meaning and scope of the book of the Psalms. If the Psalms denounce rebellious nations, they also contain long-suffering warnings as to the need of repentance, and if they frequently foretell the doom of the foes of God and His people, there are also predictions of final mercy and blessing for the world, and this bright theme, which likewise characterizes the whole, provides the grand subject of the final series of songs. The wrath of God upon the Antichrist and the gathered foes of God will be a necessary step preliminary to the establishment of peace on the earth, and this can be brought about only in the way indicated, at the hands of the Messiah Himself.

THE PSALMS AND ISAIAH

These themes which run through the Psalms likewise constitute a large part of the testimony of the prophets. Isaiah's testimony is largely parallel to that of the book of Psalms. Let the reader compare the words of the second Psalm, "Thou art My Son," and "Yet have I set My King upon My holy hill," and "I will give Thee the nations," with Isaiah 9:6, 7, "Unto us a Son is given; and the government shall be upon His shoulders . . . of the increase of His government and of peace there shall be no end, upon the throne of David, and upon His Kingdom, to establish it." Compare, as further examples, the sufferings and glories of Messiah in Psalm 22 and other Psalms with the similar themes in Isaiah 52:13–15 and 53; Psalm 137 and its denunciation of Babylon with Isaiah 47; Psalm 46:6, and similar passages foretelling the doom of rebellious nations, with Isaiah 63:1–6, etc.; the cries for deliverance in the so-called imprecatory Psalms, with such passages as Isaiah 64; the numerous Psalms of praise for deliverance, e.g., Psalms 46 and 47, with Isaiah 63:7, etc.; and, finally, the closing Psalms of millennial prosperity with the close of Isaiah's prophecies, 66:10 to end. Joel's prophecy predicts the circumstances of the warfare of Armageddon, and describes the intervention of Messiah as the treading of the winepress of God's wrath, amplifying the prophecy of Isaiah 53:3, and foreshadowing that at the close of Revelation 14.

THE WITNESS DURING THE CAPTIVITY

The prophets of the time of the Captivity, Ezekiel and Daniel, provide a testimony of a special character. The events connected with the Second Advent are foretold in these prophecies more precisely than in any that preceded. The general outline given in previous records is here largely filled in, many details, however, being reserved for the New Testament. In Ezekiel the subject bears more especially on Israel as a whole. In Daniel the range of prophecy is narrower; it has to do with the Jews in relation to the times of the Gentiles and the way in which the Second Advent will bring them to a close.

POST-CAPTIVITY TESTIMONY

The prophets of the time subsequent to the return from captivity continue the theme, Zechariah giving details not previously supplied, as to the effects of the war upon Jerusalem, and the way in which the Lord will appear for deliverance.

The witness of the Old Testament prophets closes with the testimony of Malachi, "The Lord, Whom ye seek, shall suddenly come to His Temple; and the Messenger of the covenant, Whom ye delight in, behold, He cometh, saith the Lord of Hosts. But who may abide the day of His coming? and who shall stand when He appeareth? for He is like fuller's soap; and He shall sit as a refiner and purifier of silver, and He shall purify the sons of Levi, and purge them as gold and silver; and they shall offer unto the Lord offerings in righteousness. Then shall the offering of Judah and Jerusalem be pleasant unto the Lord, as in the days of old, and as in ancient years" (Mal. 3:1–4). The prophecy closes with the promise that Elijah shall be sent to the nation before "the great and terrible Day of the Lord" come. Here the voice of prophecy ceases until the appearance of Christ in the days of His flesh.

THE WITNESS OF CHRIST

The witness to the Second Advent, resumed by the Lord, was continued by His apostles until the cycle of revelation was completed. This period is characterized by a greater continuity of testimony and a greater fullness of revelation than during the preceding ages. Our Lord begins His testimony at the very outset of His public ministry. Just after His baptism He makes known to His disciples that they will see "the Heaven opened, and the angels of God ascending and descending upon the Son of man," obviously a Second Advent scene (John 1:50). His teaching on the subject is given both publicly and privately.

Each of the four Gospel writers records it, the details being appropriate to the general scope and design of his Gospel. Matthew, Mark and Luke devote whole sections to the prediction of the events and the circumstances attending it. The Gospels of Matthew and Mark view it especially in relation to the Jewish nation (the fig tree, Matt. 24:32; Mark 13:28); Luke's Gospel views it as it will affect both the Jews and the Gentile nations (the fig tree and all the trees, Luke 21:28). The Gospel of John gives the Lord's predictions as to the resurrection. This has a special bearing on Christ's testimony to His deity (John 5:28, 29; see the whole passage from v. 17). In this Gospel, too, the Lord unlocks further secrets to His disciples respecting His return, which are not disclosed in the Synoptists.

APOSTOLIC TESTIMONY

The apostles were thus prepared for their post-pentecostal witness, the last item in their instruction being given immediately after the Ascension, in the words of the two men who stood by them in white apparel and confirmed the Lord's own promise, by declaring that He Who had just been received up into heaven would so come in like manner as they had beheld Him going (Acts 1:10, 11).

PAUL'S EPISTLES

As to the apostolic testimony, a perusal of the New Testament reveals the striking fact that only two of its writings, and these the brief and intimately personal epistle to Philemon and third epistle of John, do not contain a reference to the Lord's Second Coming. It has a prominent place in each of the four groups of Paul's epistles.

In the first group, consisting of Galatians and 1 and 2 Thessalonians, the subject finds an incidental mention in Galatians, in chapter 6:9, and perhaps also in chapter 1:4; in 1 Thessalonians the Lord's return is the prominent theme; in 2 Thessalonians the apostle shows that the Rapture of the Church, the Parousia of Christ and His coming in glory with the Church for the destruction of the Man of Sin, formed regular subjects of his oral instruction in the churches (see 2 Thess. 2:5).

Of the second group Romans abounds in references to the subject. 1 Corinthians makes frequent mention of it, from the first chapter onward, and devotes the greater part of a whole chapter to it. The second epistle does not contain as many references to it as the first, yet it receives prominence in the fifth chapter.

In the third group, the epistle to the Philippians and Colossians all give prominence to it. Paul did not lose the power of the hope, or become slack in his testimony concerning it, as his years advanced. His imprisonment in Rome certainly did not damp his ardor regarding it.

This is clear, too, in the pastoral epistles. He keeps the Lord's return before Timothy and Titus as the consummation of their service and testimony. Timothy is to keep the commandment "without spot, without reproach, until the appearing of our Lord Jesus Christ" (1 Tim. 6:14). To suffer here will be to reign with

Him hereafter; to deny Him will meet with His denial of a reward at His Judgment Seat (2 Tim. 2:12). Paul charges him "in the sight of God, and of Jesus Christ, who shall judge the quick and the dead, and by His appearing and His kingdom," to "preach the Word, be instant in season, out of season" (2 Tim. 4:1, 2). The Lord will in that day give the crown of righteousness to all them that have loved His appearing (4:8). Titus is reminded that the grace of God instructs us to be "looking for the blessed hope and appearing of the glory of our great God and Savior Jesus Christ" (2:13).

The subject is constantly before us in the epistle to the Hebrews, from the sixth verse of the first chapter onward (see remarks above in connection with Deut. 32). It is presented to us especially as the believer's hope (6:18, 20; 10:23, R.V.; 11:10); his desire (11:16); his expectation (9:28; 11:10); and his power for patience and faith in doing the will of God (10:36–38).

THE EPISTLE OF JAMES

James, in his epistle, exhorts us to be patient, and establish our hearts, since the coming of the Lord is at hand. If we are not to murmur one against another it is that we may not be judged, for the Judge standeth before the doors, that is to say, He is ready to enter the tribunal, a figurative way of expressing that the Second Coming is near at hand.

THE APOSTLE PETER

Peter points to the coming of Jesus Christ as that which will bring the recompense of the trial of our faith here (1:7). We are to set our hope perfectly on the grace that is then to be brought to us (1:13). He presents Christ as the One who is ready to punish the quick and the dead (4:5), and warns us that the end of all things is at hand (that is, the end of all present affairs). If we are to rejoice in suffering for Christ here, it is because ours will be exceeding joy at the revelation of His glory (4:13).

The Lord's Second Coming is still more prominent in his second epistle. It is viewed there as the time of our entrance into the eternal kingdom of the Lord (1:11). It is compared to the dawn of the day and the rising of the day star (1:19). In the last days mockers will scoff at the idea of the Lord's coming (3:4). Yet the Second Advent will introduce the Day of the Lord (3:10), which will be a day of judgment and the destruction of ungodly men. We are to be looking for and earnestly desiring this great event, and in view of it are to live in all holiness and godliness (3:11, 12), so that we may be found in peace without spot and blameless (3:14).

THE FIRST AND SECOND EPISTLES OF JOHN

The apostle John earnestly pleads with his spiritual children that they may so abide in Christ that neither he nor they may be ashamed before Him in His

Parousia (1 John 2:28). While it is not yet made manifest what we shall be, we shall certainly be like Him, and this hope is to be a purifying power within us (3:2, 3). God's love is made perfect with us, that we may have boldness in the Day of Judgment (4:17).

There are two references to the subject in his second epistle. Firstly, he says that "many deceivers have gone forth into the world, even they that confess not that Jesus Christ cometh in the flesh. This is the deceiver and the Antichrist" (v. 7). The original has the present participle here, "coming," so that the Authorized Version "has come" is wrong. That rendering seems to have been due to the idea that John was necessarily referring to the Incarnation.

The Antichrist will deny, not the well-established fact that a person known as Jesus Christ lived in the first century, but that He has been raised from the dead, and lives and is "coming in the flesh." How significant is the blasphemous teaching of the International Bible Students' Association, otherwise known as Millennial Dawnism, which declares that Christ is only a Spirit, and that His coming took place as a Spirit in 1914! This is a plain anti-Christian denial that "Christ cometh in the flesh."

The second reference is in the next verse, where the apostle desires that the converts may look to themselves that they may not lose the things which have been wrought on their behalf, but that they may receive a full reward (v. 8), that is to say, at the Judgment Seat of Christ, after He has come to receive the Church to Himself (see 1 Cor. 4:5).

THE EPISTLE OF JUDE

To Jude's quotation of Enoch's prophecy of the judgment which is to be executed on the ungodly at the Second Advent, we have made reference before. His closing doxology is uttered in view of the time when we shall be set before the presence of Christ's glory without blemish with exceeding joy.

THE APOCALYPSE

As to the Apocalypse, the Second Advent is practically its entire theme. In its three parts Christ is seen as the Judge, first in His own person (ch. 1), then of His saints (chh. 2, 3), then of the world (ch. 4:2); all culminating in the establishment of His kingdom upon earth.

In reviewing the testimony recorded in Scripture one cannot but be struck with the regular increase in the volume of witness given in the various periods. We have noticed this increase as we passed in our review from the Antediluvian, Patriarchal and Mosaic times to the period of the kings of Judah and Israel, and thence to the Captivity and the Restoration. Light on the subject shines with still greater intensity of brightness in the testimony of our Lord and His apostles, the climax being reached in the Apocalypse.

THE POST-APOSTOLIC WITNESS OF THE CHURCH

The New Testament shows what prominence was given in all apostolic testimony to the subject of the Lord's Second Coming. Nor could it be otherwise, for being the hope of the gospel it forms an essential element therein. Imagine gospel ministry being carried on year after year with the hope of the gospel ignored.

The post-apostolic writings of early Church history make clear that the subject continued to engage the hearts of Christians universally for a considerable time. The hope was kept bright amongst them by the persecutions they experienced. Subsequently when prosperity replaced tribulation, and the Church, succumbing to the patronage of the world and its rulers, attained to affluence and political prestige, the Lord's return was lost sight of. Departure from the teachings and principles inculcated by Christ and His apostles blighted the hope which they had inspired. The rise of popery quenched the testimony. The humanly-devised, flesh-gratifying scheme of establishing the Church as a political power over the nations was radically inconsistent with the expectation of the Rapture and the Second Advent.

THE TWO WITNESSES OF REVELATION 11

The Apocalypse shows that the world having been given over to delusion under the power of the Antichrist, with the apostate Jewish nation politically restored and in covenant treaty with Him, the Lord will send two witnesses to Jerusalem, the object of whose ministry will be to turn the hearts of the Jews to God and to expectation of the Advent of their Messiah. Their testimony will last for 1260 days, or three and a half years (Rev. 11:3).

Their names are not given. That Elijah will be one of them is likely. For this passage in Revelation 11 would seem to be connected with the prophecy in Malachi, "Behold, I will send you Elijah the prophet before the great and terrible day of the Lord come. And he shall turn the heart of the fathers to the children, and the heart of the children to their fathers" (Mal. 4:5, 6). Christ also, while showing that John the Baptist fulfilled the prophecy in a preliminary way, predicted that Elijah would eventually come and restore all things (Matt. 17:11).

The statement that the two witnesses are "the two olive trees and the two candlesticks [or rather, lampstands], standing before the Lord of the earth" is undoubtedly an allusion to Zechariah 4, the symbolism being appropriate to the giving of testimony. They will be sent to maintain the rights of God and to vindicate His sovereignty over the earth, in view of the satanic denial of those rights by the Antichrist. The ratification of their testimony will be the establishment of the Lordship of Christ over the earth at His appearing. That the two witnesses will be actual persons seems abundantly clear from the context.

THE JEWISH REMNANT

Whether through their instrumentality, or by other means, a large number of witnesses will be raised up to take part in bearing testimony to Christ and

His approaching Advent. A large proportion of these will consist of the godly company of Jews called in the Psalms and other Old Testament prophecies "the remnant." As in the case of the two witnesses, a considerable number of these will be slaughtered by the Beast and his agents (Rev. 6:9). Against them Satan will manifest his fiercest fury, but without permanent success, for "they overcame him because of the blood of the Lamb, and because of the Word of their testimony; and they loved not their lives even unto death" (12:11). Multitudes of the Jews are, however, to be preserved from death, and will form the nucleus of the nation in its regenerated condition after Christ has come to deliver it (12:14–16).

There is also to be the proclamation of

"THE EVERLASTING GOSPEL"

which will have a worldwide effect in turning men from allegiance to the Antichrist to await the Second Advent. The words of this gospel are told us: the message is, "Fear God, and give Him glory; for the hour of His judgment is come: and worship Him that made the heaven, and the earth, and sea, and fountains of waters" (14:6, 7). "Worship God" is an eternal gospel. It suits all periods. At the time when it will be proclaimed throughout the earth the world at large will be worshiping the Man of Sin. Hence the command to worship God.

Thus the world will be divided, not as it is now into three divisions, the Jews, the Gentiles, and the Church of God, but into those, on the one hand, who worship God and are waiting for the appearing of Christ in glory as the Son of man, and those, on the other hand, who worship the Beast, and who must suffer punishment in consequence. The Gentile nations will, it would seem, be greatly affected by the witness of the multitudes of godly Jews who will have been converted from the apostasy of the nation.

THE GREAT FULFILLMENT

Thus the long line of witnesses from the divine prediction in the Garden of Eden to the multitude who will stand for the truth at the end of this age, all bearing testimony to the great event which is to bring deliverance to the world from the antagonism and deception of Satan, will be completed.

The Lord Jesus Christ, who has in His own person already fulfilled so much of Scripture prophecy, will suddenly and completely ratify all its testimony as to His glorious and triumphant appearing. The wheels of divinely appointed destiny turn with unerring movement and with undeviating course. All the combined hostility of the powers of darkness, all the anti-God and anti-Christian amalgamations of humanity, can never frustrate the accomplishment of God's purposes.

He who has issued His irrevocable and unalterable decree on behalf of His Son, "I will give the nations for Thine inheritance, and the uttermost parts of the earth for Thy possession," will fulfill His Word and confirm the witness He has raised up, when "He sets His King upon His holy hill of Zion"; and in the grand inauguration of the kingdom, and the exercise of His sovereign power, His saints who have borne their testimony will have their part.

> For the flight of ancient specters,
>> That had shaded with their gloom
> Both the castle and the cottage,
>> Both the cradle and the tomb;
> For the hope of holy triumphs,
>> In the eras yet to be;
>
> For the pledge to captive millions,
>> Of release and jubilee—
>>> Blessed be God, our God, alone,
>>> Our God, the Everlasting One,
>>> Who spake the Word, and it was done!
>
> For the watchword of the prophets,
>> That "the just shall live by faith";
>
> For the Church's ancient symbol
>> Of the life that comes through death;
> For the standard of apostles,
>> Raised aloft and full unfurled,
> Glad deliverance proclaiming
>> To a crushed and trampled world—
>>> Blessed be God, our God, alone,
>>> Our God, the Everlasting One,
>>> Who spake the Word, and it was done!
>
> For the martyr's song of triumph,
>> On the wheel or scorching pyre;
> For his strength of meek endurance,
>> On the rack or torturing fire;
> For the noble witness-bearing
>> To the Christ the Lamb of God,
> To the One unchanging Priesthood,
>> To the One atoning blood—
>>> Blessed be God, our God, alone,
>>> Our God, the Everlasting One,
>>> Who spake the Word, and it was done!
>
> For the everlasting gospel,
>> Which in splendor has gone forth,

> Like a torch upon the mountains,
>   Of a reillumined earth;
> For the temple flung wide open,
>   At whose gates the goodly train
> Of the nations had been knocking,
>   But in vain, so long in vain—
>   Blessed be God, our God, alone,
>   Our God, the Everlasting One,
>   Who spake the Word, and it was done.
> —Dr. Horatius Bonar

THE LORD'S SECOND ADVENT

The Advent of the Lord is His coming into the world. At His first advent Jesus came as a baby, wrapped in swaddling clothes and humility. In contrast, at His second advent He will "glorify the House of His glory," and will "make the place of His feet glorious" (Isa. 60:7, 13). He will set up His Kingdom of righteousness and peace. The Second Coming of Christ is the hope of the Gospel. Indeed, Jesus is "the hope of glory," and those who are His will experience resurrection, rapture, and reunion. The second advent, then, can refer to the Day of the Lord, the Parousia, the Marriage Feast, the Judgment of nations, and the Millennium.

The Personal Return of the Lord is a doctrine essential to the Gospel. Preaching which eliminates it is defective in one of the main elements of the message of Life. To omit this subject is to leave out "the hope of the Gospel." That is how Scripture speaks of this part of the evangel. When exhorting the saints at Colossae to continue "in the faith grounded and steadfast," the apostle adds, "And be not moved away from the hope of the Gospel, which ye heard, . . . whereof I Paul was made a minister" (Col. 1:23). That he is referring to the Lord's Second Coming is clear from the contents of the epistle. He has already spoken of "the hope which is laid up for you in the heavens, whereof ye heard before in the word of the truth of the Gospel" (1:5). He subsequently speaks of Christ Himself as "the hope of glory" (v. 27), and specifically mentions the facts of the hope when he says, a little further on, "When Christ, who is our Life, shall be manifested, then shall ye also with Him be manifested in glory" (3:4).

THE HOPE

The hope, then, of which the apostle speaks, is not simply the prospect of experiencing the bliss of the heavenly state, nor is it the rapture of the saints when the Lord comes to the air. He will indeed fulfill His word of promise, "I come again and will receive you unto Myself," then the saints, both those who have fallen asleep and those "that are alive, that are left unto the coming of the Lord," will, as a united company, all with glorified bodies, be "caught up in the clouds, to meet the Lord in the air" (1 Thess. 4:15–17). But this great act of resurrection power will itself be anticipatory of the consummating event when the saints are manifested with Him in glory. That is what Scripture speaks of as "the hope."

The Gospel which proclaims that Christ became Incarnate, died for our sins, rose from the dead, and is seated at the right hand of God, "a Prince and a Savior," also proclaims His return. He who at His first Advent partook of flesh and blood (Heb. 2:4, R.V.), and in His resurrection-life is still "Himself man, Christ Jesus" (1 Tim. 2:5), is to have a Second Advent. The Father who testified of Him concerning His first Advent, "Thou art My Son, this day have I begotten Thee" (Heb. 1:5), will again bring "His Firstborn into the world" (v. 6).[1] He who was "despised and rejected of men," put to shame and crucified as a malefactor, is to be glorified where He was crucified; He is to be acknowledged and acclaimed as King in the place where that title was assigned to Him only in scorn. Where men bowed the knee to Him in mockery, there He is to be worshiped and adored. This is "the blessed hope." He is going to have His rights here in the place where He was rejected.

A DISTINCTION

The Coming of the Lord to receive us to Himself is not His Second Advent to the earth, it is preliminary to it. The former is indeed a hope, a bright expectation in the heart of the believer, a purifying power in his life; "every one that hath this hope set on Him, purifieth himself even as He is pure." But "the hope of the Gospel" carries us on to the ultimate event, to the day of "the revealing of the sons of God" (Rom. 8:19), the day when the kingdom of darkness shall yield place to the Kingdom of Light, when "the kingdom of the world" will have become "the Kingdom of our Lord, and of His Christ" (Rev. 11:15, R.V.).

The Advent of the Lord is His coming into the world. At His First Advent He came in lowly guise: "He emptied Himself, taking the form of a servant, being made (*margin*, 'becoming') in the likeness of men" (Phil. 2:7). "Born of a woman," He was wrapped in swaddling clothes and laid in a manger. He came not to a palace but to a laborer's cottage, not to a throne, but to a cross. At His Second Advent He "will suddenly come to His Temple." He will "glorify the House of His glory," and will "make the place of His feet glorious" (Isa. 60:7, 13). In the days of His flesh He made the place of His feet glorious by acts of lowly kindness and tender mercy. He made the place of His feet glorious when nailed to the Cross, in His consummating act of redeeming grace. He is yet again to do so at His Second

---

1 It is important to observe the position and force of the word "again" in this verse, as accurately rendered in the R.V.; here it is not used to introduce a quotation, as in verse 5. The position of the word in verse 6 puts it into immediate connection with "bringeth"—"And when He again bringeth in the Firstborn into the world." Whereas at His birth there was "a multitude of the heavenly host praising God," at the occasion of the Second Advent He saith, "And let all the angels of God worship Him." That verse 6 speaks of His Second Advent indicates that verse 5 refers to His Incarnation.

Advent when His enemies are made His footstool, when, as the Deliverer of His earthly people, He sets up His Kingdom of righteousness and peace.

Only then will the hope of the Gospel be consummated. That hope is in the heart of God Himself. For that day He waits. He will not rest until He has set "His king upon His holy hill of Zion" and has made Jerusalem "a praise in the earth."

CHRIST'S OWN EXPECTANCY

While the Scriptures set before us the Lord's return as the hope of believers, it is especially presented as the object of Christ's own expectancy. The hope is essentially His hope, and we can only rightly experience the power of its anticipation as we so view it. His eager anticipation breathes in His words to the disciples in the Upper Room: "If I go and prepare a place for you, I come again, and will receive you unto Myself; that where I am ye may be also," and further, in His prayer that follows: "Father I will that they also whom Thou hast given Me be with Me where I am." So again four times in the book of Revelation His message rings out, "I come quickly," first in the letter addressed to the church at Philadelphia (3:11), and then finally three times at the close of the book (ch. 22:7, 12, 20).

His coming to receive the Church to Himself is, however, only the first step in the accomplishment of that for which He waits. For the Rapture of the Church will be but preliminary to a series of events which will culminate in His overthrow of the foes of God, and the setting up of His kingdom on earth. His expectancy in this respect is frequently brought out in the Gospels, and in the statement in the epistle to the Hebrews, "He sat down on the right hand of God, from henceforth expecting till His enemies be made the footstool of His feet" (Heb. 10:13). He cannot be satisfied while the usurper holds sway over the world which He came to redeem. At His Second Advent He will banish this archenemy from the scene, take the reins of sovereignty, and, governing the world in righteousness, will at length abolish all rule and all authority and power, and hand over the kingdom to the Father (1 Cor. 15:24, 25). In longsuffering patience He waits till the purposes of God for the present age have been accomplished. Probably this was in the apostle's mind in his desire for the saints in Thessalonica, "The Lord direct your hearts into the love of God and into the patience of Christ" (2 Thess. 3:5, R.V.), which would thus mean "the Lord direct your hearts to love as God loves, and to be patient as Christ is patient."

THE DAY OF CHRIST

A clear distinction is made in the Word of God between the circumstances connected with the coming of the Lord to receive the Church to Himself and His coming with the Church and with all His angels, for the execution of divine retribution upon the foes of God, and for the establishment of His kingdom in the world. The Resurrection and Rapture of the saints will introduce "the Day of our Lord Jesus Christ" (1 Cor. 1:8). His coming to the earth in judgment will introduce "the Day of the Lord" (1 Thess. 5:2). The former is otherwise called "the Day of Christ" (Phil. 1:10; 2:16), "the Day of Jesus Christ" (Phil. 1:6), "the Day of the Lord Jesus" (1 Cor. 5:5; 2 Cor. 1:14). These terms are applied, as the context shows in each case, to the period beginning with the Rapture, when the saints will be with the Lord, and will stand before His Judgment Seat to receive the things done in the body. The apostle exhorts them, for instance, to be "sincere and void of offense unto the Day of Christ" (Phil. 1:10). God, who has begun a good work in them, will perform it "unto the Day of Jesus Christ" (1:6). He assures the saints at Corinth of the confirming work of God in them, so that they may be "unreproveable in the day of our Lord Jesus Christ" (1 Cor. 1:8). Looking forward to the same time he says, "We are your glorying even as ye also are ours in the day of our Lord Jesus" (2 Cor. 1:14). Believers are so to live now that they may be "sincere and void of offense unto the day of Christ" (Phil. 1:10).

THE PAROUSIA

A comparison with similar Scriptures shows that the term "Parousia" is applied to the same scene and circumstances. This term is sometimes rendered "coming," which, however, is not an adequate translation. It signifies literally "a being with," or "presence," and is so rendered, e.g., in Philippians 1:26; 2:12. We never read simply of a parousia to persons, but always of a parousia with them. That the Rapture introduces the Parousia of the Lord with His people and that in that period the Judgment Seat of Christ will be set, is clear from what follows. In writing to the Thessalonians Paul uses the term in a way which makes it impossible to view it as applicable merely to the moment of the Lord's descent into the air. He says, "For what is our hope, or joy, or crown of glorying? . . . Are not even ye, before our Lord Jesus at [or rather "in"] His Parousia" (1 Thess. 2:19)? The fruit of the apostle's service on their behalf will then be seen. Again, he desires that the Lord shall so work in them that they may be "unblameable in holiness, before our Lord and Father, at [lit., "in"] the Parousia of our Lord Jesus Christ with all His saints" (3:13). Obviously this does not refer to the coming of the Lord in glory with His saints and His holy angels to overthrow His foes, but to the period when the saints will be with Christ after the Rapture. Further, the apostle desires that God may sanctify them wholly in order that their "whole spirit and soul and body may be preserved entire, without blame, in the Parousia of our Lord Jesus Christ" (5:23).

The apostle John, anticipating the same time, says, "Now my little children, abide in Him; that, if He shall be manifested, we may have boldness, and not be ashamed before Him in His Parousia" (1 John 2:28). In other words he desires that both he himself, and they who have been the objects of his care, may have boldness and not be ashamed at the Judgment Seat of Christ. Similarly Paul desired that the saints at Philippi should be blameless and harmless, and should shine as lights in the world, that he might have "whereof to glory in the Day of Christ," that he had not run in vain, neither labored in vain (Phil. 2:16). For then the work of each shall be made manifest, "for the Day shall declare it," that is, the Day of Christ. That which abides will meet with a reward. "If any man's work shall be burned he shall suffer loss, and he himself shall be saved, yet so as through fire" (1 Cor. 3:13–15). John desires that his spiritual children shall not lose these things which he had wrought, but that they shall receive a full reward (2 John 8). Then, too, the rewards promised by the Lord Jesus in the second and third chapters of Revelation to those who overcome, will be assigned.

THE DAY OF THE LORD

The phrase "the Day of the Lord" is used in an entirely different connection. It never refers to the events which we have been considering, but relates to the Lord's judgment of the world at His personal intervention in its affairs, that is to say, to the time when "He shall come in flaming fire, rendering vengeance to them that know not God and to them that obey not the Gospel," and "to be glorified in His saints, and to be marveled at in all them that believed" (2 Thess. 1:7–10; cp. Col. 3:4). The apostle distinguishes the Day of the Lord from the Parousia, in 2 Thessalonians 2. He writes "touching [or rather, "in the interests of"] the Parousia of our Lord Jesus Christ, and our gathering together unto Him," i.e., at the Rapture. Some confusion had arisen in the minds of the converts between the Parousia and the Day of the Lord since he wrote the first Epistle.[1] Some were supposing that the latter period had already begun. He warns them, therefore, not to be deceived into thinking "that the day of the Lord is now present" (see the R.V., which gives the correct rendering). He had spoken of the Rapture and the Parousia in the first epistle (5:4, e.g.), and also of the Day of the Lord. The latter would come "as a thief in the night" and bring "sudden destruction" upon the world (5:2, 3). If, then, as they supposed the Day of the Lord had begun, they might well be in perturbation of mind. He now assures them that the Day of the Lord will not take place till two other events have transpired, namely, "the falling away" and the revelation of the Man of Sin. His career of anti-Christian rule will be suddenly terminated by the Lord Jesus Himself, who will slay him "with the breath of His mouth," and bring him to naught "by the manifestation of His coming," literally, "the outshining of His Parousia." That is one and the same event with His revelation from heaven "with the angels of His power in flaming fire" (1:7, 8). The apostle Paul, to whom especially, it should be remembered, was

---

1 That they are distinct periods, the following considerations go to show:

1, "whereas the Day of the Lord is a subject of Old Testament prophecy, the Parousia is not:

2, "the scene of the Day of the Lord is the earth; the scene of the Parousia is the air:

3, "the Day of the Lord, since it is a period of judgment and punishment, is to be anticipated with dread; the Parousia, since it is a period of rest and reward, is to be anticipated with joy:

4, "from the Day of the Lord believers are to be delivered, saved; in the Parousia they are to meet the Lord and be with Him:

5, "angels are prominent in connection with the Day of the Lord; they are not mentioned in connection with the Parousia."

(*Notes on the Epistle to the Thessalonians*, by Hogg and Vine.)

committed the truth of the mystery relating to the Rapture (1 Cor. 15:51), does not teach that certain events must transpire before that takes place.

THE MANIFESTATION OF THE PAROUSIA

The Epiphany, or shining forth, of the Parousia, which introduces the Day of the Lord, is what Christ spoke of when He said that "as the lightning cometh forth from the east, and is seen even unto the west, so shall be the Coming [or Parousia] of the Son of man" (Matt. 24:27). Christ and the saints in resurrection life and glory will then be revealed to the world, which He will come to judge in righteousness. This sudden manifestation of Christ as the Son of man will terminate the fierce persecution carried on by the Antichrist, a persecution chiefly directed against the Jews. The Lord says that "immediately after the tribulation of those days, the sun shall be darkened, and the moon shall not give her light, and the stars shall fall from heaven, and the powers of the heavens shall be shaken: and then shall appear the sign of the Son of man in heaven; and then shall all the tribes of the earth mourn, and they shall see the Son of man coming on the clouds of heaven with power and great glory" (Matt. 24:29, 30). The phrase "the sign of the Son of man" is subjective, that is to say, His appearance will be the sign itself.

Luke adds that before this there will be "distress of nations, men fainting for fear and for expectation of the things which are coming on the earth" (Luke 21:25, 26; compare Acts 2:20, quoted from Joel 2:30). These and other passages make clear that the coming of the Son of man in power and great glory will introduce the Day of the Lord. Perhaps the most vivid description of the details of this intervention are given in Revelation 19. The strife of Armageddon will be hushed to stillness. The Jewish nation will be delivered from its tyrant and his confederates, and from its long period of unbelief. They will look on Him whom they have pierced and mourn and repent. The beast and the false prophet will be cast alive into the Lake of Fire. Satan will be bound for a thousand years and cast into the abyss.

THE MARRIAGE AND THE MARRIAGE FEAST

It would seem that following upon this there will be an earthly celebration of the marriage of the Lamb, which has taken place in heaven. For before the events just mentioned the announcement is made in heaven that "the marriage of the Lamb has come,[1] and His wife has made herself ready. And it was given unto her that she should array herself in fine linen, bright and pure; for the fine linen is the righteous acts of the saints" (19:8). For these acts they will have been rewarded. That the celebration of this heavenly union takes place on the earth is indicated in several places in the Gospels, in each of which the Revised Version rightly gives "the marriage feast" instead of "the marriage" or "wedding." See the Revised Version of Matthew 22:2, 3, 4, 9. Thus it is from an earthly scene that the man

---

1 The tense is the aorist, or past, and signifies that the marriage has taken place.

without the wedding garment is cast into the outer darkness. See also Matthew 25:10 and Luke 12:36.

THE JUDGMENT OF THE NATIONS

Again, it is when the Son of man comes in His glory and all the holy angels with Him, that He will sit on the throne of His glory, and the nations of the world will be gathered together to be judged before Him (Matt. 25:32–46). The kingdom of the world will have become "the Kingdom of our Lord and Savior Jesus Christ, and He shall reign forever and ever," (Rev. 11:15). Sin, however, will not be eradicated from the earth during the Millennial period. Even the personal presence of Christ, and the establishment of His kingdom will not accomplish the regeneration of the human heart. That alone can be effected on the ground of His death.

THE MILLENNIUM

At the end of the first century of the Millennium a generation will have arisen which will know only Millennial experience, and will therefore be familiar only with the circumstances of the world's peace, and of the absolutely righteous and firm government of the King of kings. At the close of this period, therefore, there will be a large number who will yield ready allegiance to the Evil One, when he is permitted to make his final attempt against God. Then, and not till then, will every enemy be subdued. Christ must reign "till He has put all His enemies under His feet. Then He will deliver up the kingdom to God, even the Father; when He shall have abolished all rule and all authority and all power. And when all things have been subjected unto Him, then shall the Son also Himself be subjected to Him that did subject all things unto Him, that God may be all and in all" (1 Cor. 15:24–28).

THE COMING PRIEST-KING

In Scripture, Jesus' kingship and priesthood are intertwined. Christ is presented as the Priest-King, first in Genesis, then in the Psalms, the Prophets, and the epistle to the Hebrews, and finally in the Apocalypse itself. Here, the writer presents a biblical overview of the royal priesthood of Christ, from Genesis to Revelation.

The book of Genesis is the book of beginnings; the Apocalypse is the book of issues. In the latter we find matters that have been dealt with in preceding parts of Scripture brought to their consummation. It is our purpose now to consider the way in which Christ is presented as the King-Priest, first in Genesis, then in the Psalms, the Prophets, and the epistle to the Hebrews, and finally in the Apocalypse itself. The subject stands out in the Word of God conspicuously in various parts of the whole volume. The association of kingship and priesthood in

Christ is set forth figuratively and prophetically in the Old Testament, antitypically in Hebrews, and by intimation in the book of Revelation.

MELCHIZEDEK

The first mention in Scripture of the combination of the kingly and priestly functions in the person of Christ is in the Genesis record concerning Melchizedek, that unique character described as "King of Salem . . . priest of God Most High" (Gen. 14:18). The biography of this king-priest is remarkable. It is intentionally abbreviated, as the epistle to the Hebrews makes clear. There we learn that Melchizedek "was made like unto the Son of God" (Heb. 7:3). That is to say, the history was so framed that, both by what is omitted and what is narrated, the details might prefigure the Son of God. The divine inspiration of the narrative is seen, not only in the narrative itself, but also in the withholding of everything save that which would serve the purpose intended.

That Melchizedek was made like unto the Son of God is sufficient to show that he was not, as some have supposed, the Son of God Himself. In the biography in Genesis he is "without father, without mother, without genealogy." Nothing is mentioned as to the length of his life, nor are we told of his death. The termination of the biography is as striking in its suddenness as the introduction. In this way the history of the man represents the everlasting existence of the Son of God.

RIGHTEOUSNESS AND PEACE

But there is more than this. Melchizedek was, firstly, King of Salem. His name denotes "King of righteousness." Salem signifies "peace." Both the personal name and that of the locality were divinely arranged, in order that as king of righteousness and peace he might prefigure the future glories of the Lord Jesus Christ in the day when His sovereign power will be displayed in the earth, and God's King will be set upon His holy hill of Zion. In that day "Israel shall be saved and Judah shall dwell in safety," for God "will raise unto David a righteous Branch, and He shall reign as King and deal wisely, and shall execute judgment and justice . . . and this is His Name whereby He shall be called, Jehovah Tsidkenu," i.e., "the Lord is our righteousness" (Jer. 23:5, 6). "Righteousness and peace will kiss each other," "Righteousness will go before Him" and will set the nation of Israel "in the way of His steps" (Ps. 85:10, 13, R.V., margin). Then throughout the earth "the work of righteousness shall be peace; and the effect of righteousness quietness and confidence forever" (Isa. 32:17).

A ROYAL PRIEST

But Melchizedek was not only king of Salem, he was also "priest of God Most High," and both in this office, and in what he performed on behalf of Abraham, he prefigured the person and priestly work of Christ and the royal character of

His priesthood. This is interpreted for us again in the seventh chapter of Hebrews, the object of which is to show that the priesthood of Christ was not after the inferior Levitical order, but after the kingly order of Melchizedek. The points in that chapter in this respect, after the first three introductory verses, are as follows:

Firstly, Abraham paid tithes to Melchizedek, but Abraham was the forefather of Levi and his sons, and so the Levites representatively paid tithes to the king-priest Melchizedek in the person of their ancestor Abraham (Heb. 7:4–6).

Secondly, Melchizedek blessed Abraham. Now "the less is blessed of the better." If Abraham, whom God had brought into covenant relationship with Him and was thus so highly privileged, was blessed of Melchizedek, how great must have been the position of the latter, and accordingly how much superior is the position of Christ whom he prefigured! (v. 7).

Thirdly, here men that died received tithes, but in the Genesis record "one of whom it is witnessed that he liveth." The omission of the record of Melchizedek's death placed him in a superior position in this respect (vv. 8, 9).

Fourthly, Christ sprang out of the royal tribe of Judah, a tribe of which nothing was spoken concerning priests. This was, therefore, a token that His priesthood would be of a royal character (vv. 13, 14).

Fifthly, the Levitical priesthood was based upon the "law of a carnal commandment." That of Melchizedek was "after the power of an endless life" (literally, an indissoluble life) (vv. 15–17).

Sixthly, the Levitical priests were so constituted without any oath, but Christ with an oath; as the Psalmist says prophetically of Christ in the 110th Psalm, "The Lord hath sworn . . . Thou art a priest forever after the order of Melchizedek" (Ps. 110:4). The priesthood of Christ was established upon an oath uttered by Jehovah Himself (vv. 20, 21).

Seventhly, the Levitical priests were many in number; death hindered them from continuing. Christ, as intimated in the record of Melchizedek, abideth forever and therefore "hath His priesthood unchangeable" (vv. 23, 24).

THE PRIESTLY PROVISION

Again, the priestly act of Melchizedek, in bringing forth bread and wine for Abraham, was prefigurative of the service of Christ as the High Priest of His people in ministering to them of Himself in resurrection life and power as the outcome of His atoning death. The blessing Melchizedek pronounced was an immediate preparation for Abraham's victory in resisting the tempting offer made to him by the king of Sodom. So now, the Lord's people depend upon Him for strength to resist the overtures of the world and every form of temptation.

But the narrative in Genesis points further than to the present age. The blessing bestowed by the king-priest upon Abraham was anticipative of what Christ will be to Abraham's descendants, the restored nation of Israel, in the Millennium. Then, as we shall see more fully from other Scriptures, Christ will be a priest upon His throne, acting mediatorially for the redeemed nation.

To this time

THE TITLE GOD MOST HIGH

in the narrative of Genesis 14 points. It is a Millennial title. It is brought out in its Millennial connection in Psalm 91, e.g., which consists, prophetically, of a dialogue between the Lord and the godly remnant of His faithful ones of the Jewish people in the time of "Jacob's trouble" at the close of this present age. They will be under His protecting care during their time of tribulation. They, who have made the Most High their habitation, will be delivered by the immediate power of the Lord and will be set on high after the destruction of their foes. The closing promise of the psalm, "I will be with him in trouble: I will deliver him and honor him, with long life will I satisfy him and shew him My salvation," will then be made good to them in Millennial blessing. Having dwelt, during the terrors of the reign of Antichrist "in the secret place of the Most High," and lodging (such is the meaning of the word rendered "abide") for the night of the nation's tribulation "under the shadow of the Almighty," they will see their enemies destroyed and will possess the inheritance promised to them in the covenant made by God to Abraham.

God made Himself known through Melchizedek to Abraham as the possessor of heaven and earth, and as such Christ will be revealed and acknowledged in the Millennial age. How strengthening this blessing must have been to the patriarch, living his simple tent life, occupying only the ground where his encampment was pitched, albeit assured by Jehovah of his eventual possession of the whole land! The word of the living God through the king priest was a nourishment to his soul, and with that same word he met the tempter, refusing to be enriched in the slightest degree by the worldly monarch, and resting solely on the promise and power of God. Melchizedek's message, telling of God as "the possessor of heaven and earth," was an echo of the Lord's own words to Abraham as recorded in the preceding chapter, when God made promise to him saying, "All the land which thou seest, to thee will I give it and to thy seed, forever."

The priestly monarch's appointment as king of Salem was divine, for this very Salem will be the seat of God's government of the earth when He sets His King upon His holy hill of Zion. With what pleasure must Jehovah have looked down upon Melchizedek, amidst the darkness and degradation of the Canaanitish nations, foreshadowing as he did, both in his person and his position, what the Son of God is yet to be in the day of His manifested glory!

PSALM 110

We shall see how this is brought to its issue in the book of Revelation. We must here, however, consider other passages which associate the Lord's royalty and priesthood. The two are strikingly combined in the messianic Psalm 110. The psalm, written by David concerning his Lord, "great David's greater Son," begins with Christ's ascension, reveals him as a priest "after the order of Melchizedek," and foretells of the day of God's wrath as exercised through Him, and His subsequent government over the earth. The theme of the psalm is Jehovah's Priest-King. The opening stanza speaks of His exaltation to the throne. "Jehovah saith unto My Lord, Sit thou at My right hand, till I make Thine enemies Thy footstool," words quoted by Christ Himself to the Pharisees when He inquired of them, "What think ye of Christ? Whose Son is He?" clearly indicating the prophetic character of the psalm, and illustrating the way in which the Lord declared Himself to be the embodiment of Old Testament prophecy.

THE PATIENCE OF CHRIST

The first verse covers the whole of the present age. It is a time in which, while the Lord is acting as the High Priest of His people, and is exercising longsuffering toward the rebellious world, He is also patiently anticipating the day of the exercise of His sovereign authority in casting out God's foes from His rightful domain, and establishing His kingdom where now the usurper holds sway. Having offered one sacrifice for sins He forever[1] sat down on the right hand of God, "from henceforth expecting till His enemies be made the footstool of His feet" (Heb. 10:12, 13). It is this patience of Christ of which the apostle Paul speaks when He says, "The Lord direct your hearts into the love of God, and into the patience of Christ" (2 Thess. 3:5).

THE ROD OF HIS STRENGTH

The psalm next speaks of the time when he will personally intervene for the overthrow of His enemies and the establishment of His kingdom: "The Lord shall send forth the rod of Thy strength out of Zion: rule thou in the midst of Thine enemies" (v. 2). The sending forth of the rod is here suggestive of the subjugation of enemies (see R.V., margin, and cp. Exod. 7:19; 8:5, 16, 17; 14:16). It symbolizes the exercise of the almighty strength of God in putting down His adversaries in the earth. In the day of the Lord's great controversy with the nations, the day when He will "sit to judge the nations around about" (Joel 3:12), "the Lord shall roar from Zion, and utter His voice from Jerusalem; and the heavens and the earth shall shake; but the Lord will be a refuge unto His people, and a stronghold to the children of Israel" (v. 16; cp. Amos 1:2). "The Lord of Hosts shall come down to fight upon Mount Zion and the hill thereof" (Isa. 31:4). So at the close of Psalm 110, "The Lord at Thy right hand shall strike through kings in the day of His wrath. He shall judge among the nations, He shall fill the places with dead bodies; He shall strike through the head over [see margin] many countries."

---

1 The word "forever" should be taken with what follows rather than with what precedes. When Christ comes to receive the Church to Himself, and again when He comes in revealed glory, He will still occupy His position at the right hand of God. That is His inalienable dignity. No king is always actually sitting on his throne. Wherever he may be he is still said to be "on the throne." "The right hand of the throne," where Christ has "sat down with His Father" (Rev. 3:21) will ever be His place of honor. Position, not posture, is what is in view.

THE PSALM AND THE ANTICHRIST

The individual indicated in this last clause is doubtless the Beast spoken of in Revelation, chapters thirteen and seventeen, with whom the ten confederate kings are to receive authority for a brief time (Rev. 17:12). He it is whom the Lord Jesus "shall slay with the breath of His mouth, and bring to nought by the manifestation of His Parousia" (2 Thess. 2:8). The same potentate is the subject of the prediction uttered by Moses in his song in Deuteronomy 32, where the Lord says, "If I whet My glittering sword and Mine hand take hold on judgment, I will render vengeance to Mine adversaries, and will recompense them that hate Me. I will make Mine arrows drunk with blood, and My sword shall devour flesh; with the blood of the slain and the captives, from the head of the leaders of the enemy" (vv. 41, 42). The time referred to is obviously the close of the present age, for the next verse tells of the deliverance of the Jews and the liberation of their land. The Gentiles are thereupon invited to rejoice with God's people. "Rejoice, O ye nations, with His people: for He will avenge the blood of His servants, and will render vengeance to His adversaries, and will make expiation for His land, for His people" (v. 43). After the clause, "Rejoice ye nations with His people," the Septuagint Version has, "and let all the angels of God worship Him." This is quoted in Hebrews 1:6, and refers, not to the first Advent of Christ, but to His second Advent. It reads, "And when He again bringeth in the Firstborn into the world, He saith, And let all the angels of God worship Him." The word "again" has been misplaced in the Authorized Version. It goes with the word "bringeth in." God brought His Son into the world the first time at His Incarnation. He will bring Him in again when He comes in glory to reign over the earth. Then will His enemies be made His footstool. Of that time the passage in Deuteronomy 32 speaks. "The head of the leaders of the enemy" is the Antichrist.[1]

HIS SAINTS AS VOLUNTEERS

The third verse of Psalm 110 speaks of the saints who will come with Christ in glory at this time, and of the faithful ones who have been preserved during the time of Jacob's trouble: "Thy people shall offer themselves willingly in the day of Thy power" (literally, "Thy people are freewill offerings"). That is, they consecrate themselves as freewill offerings to the Lord, enjoying the fullness of communion with Him, and rejoicing in the consummation of the glory of their Redeemer, and the manifestation of His power in the deliverance of the Jews from their tyrants and the earth from its groanings. They present themselves to Him for the service to which He will appoint them.

There is a striking coincidence between this verse and 1 Chronicles 29. Upon the completion of David's conquests he prepared for the establishment of the kingdom under Solomon. Having assembled the people and related to them

---

1 With these passages the following Scriptures should be especially associated: Isaiah 24:21–23; 26:20, 21; 34:1–9; 63:1–6; Daniel 2:34, 35; 7:26, 27; Joel 2:10, 11; 3:9–20; Zechariah 14:1–9; Revelation 14:20; 19:12–51. See also Psalm 2 and others.

his preparations for the house of God, he asked, "Who then offereth willingly to consecrate himself this day unto the Lord?" "Therefore the princes of the fathers' houses, and the princes of the tribes of Israel, and the captains of thousands and of hundreds, with the rulers over the king's work, offered willingly . . . with a perfect heart they offered willingly to the Lord" (1 Chron. 29:5–9). All this was a foreshadowing of the time predicted in the psalm we are considering. In the day of the Lord's humiliation His followers all forsook Him and fled. How different the vast assemblage of His shining hosts and faithful ones in the coming day! "In the beauties of holiness, from the womb of the morning" He will have the dew of His youth.

"THE DEW OF THY YOUTH"

The phrase "in the beauties of holiness," corresponds, in regard to character, to the arraying of the priests in holy garments. The saints who will be attendant upon Christ in the day of His manifested glory as the Priest-King, will themselves constitute a royal priesthood. They are also, as the psalm puts it figuratively, the dew of the Lord's youthful ones, strong and active to render Him service. Addressing His people Israel, the Lord said, "Ye shall be unto me a kingdom of priests and a holy nation" (Exod. 19:6), and of the Church the apostle Peter says, "Ye are an elect race, a royal priesthood, a holy nation" (1 Pet. 2:9). So the apostle John, in the opening doxology of the Apocalypse, says, "Unto Him that loveth us, and loosed us from our sins by His blood, and He made us to be a kingdom, to be priests unto His God and Father; to Him be the glory and the dominion forever and ever, Amen" (Rev. 1:5, 6). So, again, in chapter 5:10, "Thou madest them to be unto our God a kingdom and priests, and they reign upon the earth." And again at the close of the book, "Blessed and holy is he that hath part in the first resurrection: over these the second death hath no power; but they shall be priests of God and of Christ, and shall reign with Him a thousand years" (20:6). In the list of David's officials mentioned in 2 Samuel 8, on the occasion of the establishment of his kingdom, his sons are described as priests (v. 18, R.V.). The margin has "chief ministers." The word seems to foreshadow the combination of royalty and priesthood to which the other Scriptures just mentioned refer.

THE WOMB OF THE MORNING

"The womb of the morning" does not refer merely to the physical light of day. The expression is figurative of the fact that those who will be with Christ at His Second Advent have been born of God. In the first chapter of John Christ is described as the Light which, coming into the world, lighteth every man. Though the world knew Him not, and they that were His own received Him not, "as many as received Him, to them gave He the right to become children of God, even to them that believe on His Name, which were born . . . of God." Here then He who is spoken of as the Light is at the same time the One by whose grace and power men are born of God and become the followers of Christ.

When the light of the millenial day shines upon the world and the Sun of Righteousness arises with healing in His wings, the children of God, His redeemed saints, will come with Him. They are all "sons of light and sons of the day" (1 Thess. 5:5), God's infinite, eternal day. The marginal reading is, "Thy youth are to Thee as the dew." The dewdrops sparkling in the early morning sunlight each reflect the full-circled image of the heavenly orb. So each saint will shine resplendent in the complete likeness of the Son of God.

Note also the significance of the "Thou hast." His youthful ones are not only a kingdom of priests, arrayed in the beauties of holiness, they are "a people for His own possession" (Titus 2:14; 1 Pet. 2:9). They are each one the gift of the Father to Him (John 17:2, 6, 9, 11). They will then be seen by all creation to be one with Him, even as He is one with the Father (John 17:11, 21, 22), and thus the world will know that the Father has loved Him (v. 23).

The scene thus referred to in the psalm is described in more detail in Revelation 19, where the Lord is pictured coming forth with His hosts. "The armies which are in Heaven followed Him upon white horses, clothed in fine linen, white and pure" (v. 14). "The fine linen is the righteous acts of the saints" (v. 8). These garments of glory and beauty are symbolic of the rewards bestowed for faithfulness in service here, and not only so, but in this glorious array they will show forth the character of the Lord Himself, as they did in their life on earth by their acts of righteousness.

DIVINE RETRIBUTION

The filling of the places with dead bodies (Ps. 110:6) is a divine retribution upon those who in their cruelty will seek to exterminate God's earthly people. In this respect the language of the seventy-ninth Psalm is deeply significant. There the psalmist tells, in language which, though written in the past tense, is prophetic of the persecution to be inflicted by Antichrist in the future, how the nations have come into God's inheritance, have defiled His holy temple, and "have laid Jerusalem on heaps." "The dead bodies of Thy servants," he says, "have they given unto the beasts of the earth. Their blood have they shed like water round about Jerusalem" (vv. 1–3). Now in Psalm 110, the fact that Messiah is to "fill the places with the dead bodies" of Israel's foes, is distinctly retributive. We should connect with this Ezekiel 39:17–21, and Revelation 19:17–21, which describe the birds of prey as being gathered to feed on the carcasses of the slain. The prayer, at the close of the seventy-ninth Psalm, for vengeance upon the enemy, and similar impreca-tory passages in the Psalms, contain language which will, at the time referred to, be entirely appropriate. For the godly in the nation will be in fellowship with the Lord in His necessary judgments upon Antichrist and those who have associ-ated themselves with him in rebellion against the Almighty. Such language does not breathe mere human vindictiveness and spite. It is language inspired by the Holy Spirit with a view to the time when God in righteousness must judge the world. "Wherever this kind of sentiment is expressed by the writers of Scripture, the underlying motive is not vindictiveness against personal enemies, but antagonism against the enemies of God, enemies upon whom a divine sentence of wrath has been passed."[1]

THE ROYAL PRIESTHOOD

All this first part of the psalm is introductory to the declaration in verse 4, "The Lord hast sworn, and will not repent, Thou art a Priest forever after the order of Melchizedek." We shall see presently the significance of this union of kingship with priesthood, and its application to the government of the world. Here in the psalm Christ is seen acting both as the Mediatorial Priest of His people Israel, and as their king coming forth for their deliverance to establish His throne in their midst and to associate the nation with Himself in the affairs of His earthly kingdom. He first sits as king over the water-flood, when the nation passes through its great tribulation, and then as king in their midst, giving strength to His people and blessing them with peace (Ps. 29:10, 11).

The closing verse of the psalm, "He shall drink of the brook in the way; therefore shall He lift up the head," firstly represents the Messiah as a conqueror refreshing himself after his decisive victory over the foe. The land and its people, then delivered from the oppressor, will minister spiritual refreshment to Him in the accomplishment of His glorious intervention on their behalf. In a special way He will then "see of the travail of His soul and be satisfied." The lifting up of the head speaks of His triumph when, the kingdom of Antichrist having been destroyed, "the kingdom and dominion and the greatness of the kingdoms under the whole Heaven shall be given to the people of the saints of the Most High . . . and all dominions shall serve and obey Him" (Dan. 7:27).

Appropriately the poet sings of "great David's greater Son." David was great in that he was the king of God's own choice and appointment, in contrast to Saul. As king of Salem he was the direct successor to Melchizedek. No king had ruled in Jerusalem by direct divine appointment from Melchizedek's time till David was established in his throne. Saul's kingship was the outcome of the self-will of the people. But Melchizedek himself was superior to David in authority, because he combined priesthood with kingship. David could not occupy such a position. Messiah, David's lord, though "of the seed of David according to the flesh," is "a Priest forever after the order of Melchizedek."

ZECHARIAH'S PROPHECIES

There was a period of about a thousand years between the witness to the royal priesthood of Christ given by Melchizedek, and that given by David. Some five hundred years later the prophet Zechariah received a message from the Lord to the effect that Messiah would rule over Israel as Priest-King. Ezekiel had prophesied that both "miter and crown" would be removed. "This shall be no more,"

---

1 "The Divine Inspiration of the Bible" (by the Author).

said he—that is to say, the priesthood acting for and under the king—"until He come Whose right it is" (Ezek. 21:25–27). The words of the prophet had become true. The earthly monarchy had by this time ceased in the nation. Consequent upon the long continued apostasy and disobedience on the part of both kings and people, in spite of all the Lord's remonstrances and warnings through His prophets, the Chaldeans under Nebuchadnezzar, acting as God's instruments of chastisement, had overthrown Jerusalem and carried away both king and people into captivity. At the time of Zechariah's prophecy the divinely predicted period of the seventy years of the captivity of Judah was drawing to its close. It was in the year 520 B.C., the second year of Darius (the year that is, before the history of the book of Esther opens), that the Lord said to Zechariah through His angel, "I am returned to Jerusalem with mercies; My House shall be built in it, saith the Lord of Hosts" (Zech. 1:16).

The prophecy concerning Christ as the coming Priest-King is recorded in the sixth chapter. That marks a division of the whole book of Zechariah into two parts. It is the climax of a series of visions given to the prophet. After the close of the sixth chapter, where the prediction is recorded that the Lord will raise up One who shall be a Priest upon His throne, no more visions are related. The rest of the book is devoted to direct prophecy.

The Four Horses, Four Horns, and Four Smiths

The first vision, that of the four horses (1:8), indicates the providential dealings of God in regard to His people Israel.

The second vision, that of the four horns and four smiths (1:18–21), presents a view of the great gentile powers, permitted by God to control His people and their land, and the necessary retributive judgments of God upon these powers as a result of their tyranny and misrule. The subject of His dealings with these various nations, and their treatment of the Jewish people, does not lie within the scope of this pamphlet. The four powers are the same as those referred to in the book of Daniel.

The Man with the Measuring Line

The third vision is that of the man with the measuring line about to measure Jerusalem. This indicates the preciousness of Jerusalem to God. In spite of all the aggression and cruelty of gentile powers the Lord declares that He will be to Jerusalem "a wall of fire round about, and Himself the glory in the midst of her" (2:5). Israel would be delivered from the nations that had held her captive. They would suffer divine judgment for their treatment of His people. "For thus saith the Lord of Hosts, After glory [i.e., with a view to glory] hath He sent Me unto the nations which spoiled you; for he that toucheth you toucheth the apple of His eye. For, behold, I will shake My hand over them, and they shall be a spoil to those that served them: and ye shall know that the Lord of Hosts hath sent Me." The next words show that the scene is millennial, and does not refer merely to the return from the captivity in Chaldea: "Sing and rejoice, O daughter of Zion: for, lo, I come, and I will dwell in the midst of thee, saith the Lord. And many nations shall join themselves to the Lord in that day, and shall be My people: and I will dwell in the midst of thee, and thou shalt know that the Lord of Hosts hath sent Me unto thee. And the Lord shall inherit Judah as His portion in the holy land, and shall yet choose Jerusalem. Be silent, all flesh, before the Lord: for He is waked up out of His holy habitation" (2:10–13).

Joshua the High Priest

The fourth vision is given in chapter 3. This is a vision of Joshua the high priest standing before the angel of the Lord, and Satan standing at his right hand to be his adversary. We are now shown the power of the evil one, put forth to endeavor to hinder the fulfillment of God's purposes regarding Jerusalem. The filthy garments with which the high priest was clothed betoken the defiled condition of the nation. Satan is rebuked, the defilement is cleansed, the priest is clothed with royal apparel, and has a fair turban set upon his head. This is an intimation of what is to come in chapter six, and is anticipative of the kingly priesthood of Christ there predicted. Here, too, as in the sixth chapter, Messiah is spoken of as a Branch. The branch is symbolic both of increase and fruitfulness, and the promise is accordingly given that under Messiah's benign rule every man "will call his neighbor under the vine and under the fig tree." There will be abundance for all, and unity and liberality will characterize the people.

The Lampstand and Olive Trees

The fifth vision, recorded in chapter four, is that of the golden lampstand and the two olive trees by it. These are symbolic of the means by which God will yet give light in the world to His earthly people. It has been suggested that they represent the royalty and priesthood of Christ, the Spirit's power maintaining the light of testimony concerning Him and His government over, and care for, the nation. If so, we have in these symbols another anticipation of the union of kingship and priesthood in the person of Christ.

From the two trees two branches are seen immediately adjacent to the two spouts "that empty the golden oil out of themselves." The branches are interpreted as "the two sons of oil who stand by the Lord of the whole earth" (v. 14). They are referred to again in Revelation 11:4, and are there seen to be two witnesses who will be sent unto the nation during the reign of Antichrist, to bear witness concerning the approaching Advent of the true Messiah. The actual kingship and priesthood of Christ Himself so shortly about to be exercised in His manifested glory will doubtless form the subject of their witness as against the devilish dual control by Antichrist.

The restoration under Zerubbabel (vv. 7–10) and the laying of the foundation of the house as foretold in the vision, were anticipative of the fuller restoration in a day to come. The seven eyes on the stone (v. 9) indicate the searching gaze of the Lord of hosts, under which the iniquity of the people, having been marked and dealt with, will be removed. And not only so, His eyes watch over the course of events which under His providence are to issue in this.

The Flying Roll and the Ephah

The sixth vision, chapter five, is that of the flying roll, followed by that of the ephah with the talent of lead within it. The previous vision presented the establishment of God's sovereign power and worship in the midst of the nation; this one sets forth His judgment upon the wicked in Israel in the last days. The roll contains a curse for those who sin against God and against their neighbor. The talent of lead is interpreted as a woman that sits in the midst of the ephah and is described as "wickedness." It finds its source in Babylon. Apparently it will be reestablished and exposed in its evil character in the land of Shinar in the nation's dark hour of apostasy and association with Antichrist.

The Four Chariots

The seventh vision, chapter six, is that of the four chariots with their different colored horses. They are interpreted as being the four winds of heaven "which go forth from standing before the Lord of all the earth." They are no doubt indicative of the divine disposal of the affairs of the world. During the times of the Gentiles God largely allows man a free scope for his energies. As a result of this man endeavors to assert his own rights, despite the fact of the Fall and its effects. The god of this world, ever disputing the claims of the Lord to govern the earth, leads men and nations, under the guidance of their sin-blighted reason, to seek to establish themselves in the world according to the dictates of their self-will. The aim of Satan is to bring about universal combination of the peoples of the world against the Lord and against His Christ. Yet God remains sovereign, and is determined in due time to assert His claims and vindicate the rights of His Son, who will come upon the scene with His almighty power, to give the deathblow to human authority. This, which is so vividly depicted in the vision given to King Nebuchadnezzar, of the stone that fell upon the feet of the image, crushing the whole structure (Dan. 2), forms one of the leading subjects of the visions and prophecies of Zechariah.

JOSHUA, THE HIGH PRIEST

The visions being finished, the way is open for the glorious prediction concerning Christ and the combined power which He is to exercise. The word of the Lord came to Zechariah commanding him to take some of the returned exiles, and, going with them into the house of Josiah, to fashion a crown of silver and gold (the plural, "crowns," denotes here the various circlets forming one crown), and set it upon the head of Joshua, the son of Jehozadak, the high priest. The prophet was thereupon to say, "Thus speaketh the Lord of Hosts, saying, Behold the Man whose name is the Branch; and He shall grow up out of His place, and He shall build the temple of the Lord; and He shall bear the glory, and shall sit and rule upon His throne; and He shall be a Priest upon His throne: and the counsel of peace shall be between them both" (Zech. 6:9–13). The crown was to be to the returned exiles a memorial in the temple. There was doubtless an intimation in all this of the then impending restoration of the temple and its worship, after the return from captivity; but what took place then cannot possibly exhaust the meaning of the passage, which is clearly messianic in its character, and foretells the time, as we have seen in other Scriptures, when Christ will perfectly unite in Himself the offices of king and priest over God's people.

THE BRANCH

We should note that the humanity of Christ is first set forth. The introductory words, "Behold the Man," stand in striking contrast to the similar utterance by Pilate in the day of our Lord's humiliation. Christ is here symbolically described as the Branch, as He was in the third chapter; only there He was spoken of as "My Servant the Branch." Here He is "The Man." All this corresponds to the prophecies of Isaiah from chapter 42:1 onwards, where Christ is called Jehovah's Servant. The passage beginning with the 13th verse of the fifty-second chapter, which is really introductory to the fifty-third, opens with the call, "Behold My Servant." Then follows the prophecy of His humiliation and grief, as the Man of Sorrows, wounded for our transgressions and bruised for our iniquities. There, too, He is seen to be the "tender plant," the "root out of a dry ground." So now in Zechariah He is "the Man whose Name is the Branch," who will "grow up out of His place." While this may refer to the place of His earthly humiliation, which is yet to become the scene of His earthly glory, yet the language of the original (literally, He shall grow up from Himself) suggests that His increase would be by His own power. The Septuagint has "from beneath Himself." Similarly Isaiah had said, "In that day shall the Branch of the Lord be beautiful, and the fruit of the land [margin, "earth"] shall be excellent [or rather, majestic] and comely for them that are escaped of Israel" (Isa. 4:2).

In Jeremiah his fruitfulness as the Branch is associated with His kingship: "Behold, the days come, saith the Lord, that I will raise unto David a righteous Branch, and He shall reign as king and deal wisely, and shall execute judgment and justice in the land. In His days Judah shall be saved and Israel shall dwell safely: and this is His Name whereby He shall be called, the Lord is our righteousness" (Jer. 23:5, 6). We may note here the association with the name Melchizedek, "King of righteousness." God's king is Himself "the righteous Branch," and is also "Jehovah Tzidkenu" (v. 16). A different word rendered "Branch" is used in Isaiah 11:1 and Psalm 80:15, though the thought is the same.

The various titles of Christ in these passages correspond to the distinctive characteristics of the Lord in the four Gospels: in Matthew, His Kingship (cp. Jer. 23:3); in Mark, His Servant character (cp. Zech. 3:8); His Manhood in Luke (cp. Zech. 6:12); His Godhead in John (cp. Jer. 23:6).

KINGSHIP AND PRIESTHOOD

The prophecy next foretells the union of the two chief offices in Messiah's person: "He shall build the Temple of the Lord: and He shall bear the glory, and shall sit and rule upon His throne; and He shall be a Priest upon His throne: and the counsel of peace shall be between them both."

Nimrod

Many have been the attempts, on the part of aspirants to absolute monarchy, to obtain the joint control of the political and religious life of the communities under them. Temporal power is doubly strong if it combines spiritual power with it. Control the conscience and you control the man. Nimrod was the first. From the narrative in Genesis he seems to have originated the scheme of establishing a kingdom among men. "The beginning of his kingdom was Babel" (see Gen. 10:10, R.V.). From thence he invaded Assyria and built Nineveh and other towns. There is historic evidence to show that he and his queen Semiramis likewise instituted a religious system of nature worship, characterized by elaborate rites and ceremonies under an order of priesthood, of which he was the head. He thus acquired both political and religious leadership.

Julius Caesar

By means of the same combination Julius Caesar also reached the zenith of his power. After becoming dictator of the Roman republic he received from the people the office of Pontifex Maximus, that is, the chief pontiff of the Roman pagan religion. He had transferred from Pergamos to Rome the entire order of the Chaldean priesthood, which had been established there ever since the expulsion of the priests from Babylon by Darius, in 539 B.C. Driven from the eastern city, they had settled down at Pergamos under the patronage of the Lydian king, Attalus. The gorgeous ritual of the Babylonish religion added splendor and influence to the double domination of Caesar. From that time onward the union was maintained, first by the emperors and then by the popes, until the papacy lost temporal power.

Constantine the Great

A further instance is the case of Constantine the Great. In the fourth century A.D. his aspirations after supremacy in the Roman Empire, and the desire to unite its disintegrating elements, led him to adopt what was obviously the wisest policy for the attainment of his end. The churches by that time had become politically influential; forsaking the path appointed for them by Christ, they had attained to worldly greatness, and were now an organization to be reckoned with by any aspirant after world power. What could suit Constantine's aim better than to make Christianity, such as it had become, the state religion? This political and religious combination materialized in A.D. 325.

Antichrist

A yet future illustration, and indeed the last human effort to achieve the union, is foretold in Scripture in regard to the final world ruler of this age, who is described in Revelation 13 as "the Beast." That chapter predicts his domination in each respect. Proclaiming himself to be God, and supported by the false prophet, the "Second Beast," he will demand and receive the worship of the world (Rev. 13:8). With the assistance of his colleague he will likewise establish his supremacy in matters relating to commerce (vv. 16, 17).

In none of the cases in the past, however, has the association proved efficacious or durable, nor will the Antichrist achieve lasting success. The history of civil and international conflicts has been very largely a history of the antagonism between politics and religion, of strife between church and state. Again and again the ecclesiastical power has attempted to dominate the political. Many a war can be traced to this cause. Where success has attended the association, it has not been characterized by peaceful conditions for any great length of time. Disintegration marks all human efforts to establish such a union. The disruptive element lies within man himself. The Antichrist, with all his consummate powers, energized by Satan himself, will witness the collapse of his universal organization, and will be "brought to nought" by Christ at His Second Advent (2 Thess. 2:8). "The stone cut out of the mountain without hands" will irretrievably crush his worldwide domination (Dan. 2:45).

The passage in Ezekiel to which reference has already been made, undoubtedly speaks, as to its ultimate fulfillment, of the overthrow of the combined religious and political denomination of the Antichrist, and of their permanent establishment in the person of Christ Himself. The Revised Version gives the correct rendering: "And thou, O deadly wounded wicked one, the prince of Israel, whose day is come, in the time of the iniquity of the end; thus saith the Lord God: Remove the miter and take off the crown: this shall be no more the same: exalt that which is low, and abase that which is high. I will overturn, overturn, overturn it: this also shall be no more, until He come whose right it is; and I will give it Him" (Ezek. 21:25–27). Though the prophecy had no doubt immediate reference to Zedekiah, yet the Spirit of God directed the words so that they might prophetically apply to the Antichrist. That this is so is indicated by the time mentioned, namely, "the time of the iniquity of the end." The removal of the miter indicates the destruction of his religious leadership, the removal of the crown, the overthrow of his sovereignty. With the way in which he is addressed as the "deadly wounded wicked one" we may compare the similar statement concerning the Beast in Revelation 13:3.

One alone is destined successfully to combine kingly and priestly power. The Lord Jesus Christ shall be a priest upon His throne. Never under Him will the spiritual power be at strife with the civil. "The counsel of peace shall be between them both."

THE APOCALYPSE

While the kingship of Christ stands out clearly in the book of Revelation, His priesthood is not specifically stated. Yet it is there by intimation in several passages. As to His sovereignty, at the very outset of the book He is declared to be "the Ruler of the kings of the earth." His is "the glory and dominion forever and ever" (1:5, 6).

In the opening vision He reveals Himself in the combined character of priest and judge. He is "clothed with a garment down to the foot, and girt about at the breast with a golden girdle" (1:13). There can be little doubt that the garment is suggestive of the apparel of the high priest. Concerning this, Dr. Edersheim says, "The priest's coat was woven of one piece. Like the seamless robe of the Savior, its object must have been symbolical. In point of fact, it may be regarded as the most distinctive priestly vestment, since it was put on only during actual ministration, and put off immediately afterwards. Accordingly, when in Revelation 1:13, the Savior is seen in the midst of the lampstands girt about the breasts with a golden girdle, we are to understand by it that our heavenly high priest is there engaged in actual ministry for us. Similarly, the girdle is described as about the 'breasts,' as both the girdle of the ordinary priest, and that on the ephod which the high priest wore, were girded there, and not round the loins. Lastly, the expression, 'golden girdle,' may bear reference to the circumstance that the dress peculiar of the high priest was called his 'golden vestments,' in contradistinction to the 'linen vestments' which he wore on the Day of Atonement."[1]

His high priestly office is perhaps further symbolized by the fact that He holds the seven stars in His right hand, suggesting His maintenance of the service and testimony of the churches. At the same time He is a priest upon the throne, for He says to the church at Laodicea, "He that overcometh, I will give to him to sit down with Me in My throne, as I also overcame, and sat down with My Father in His throne" (3:21). Accordingly, the combined authority which He is yet to exercise in manifold glory on behalf of Israel He already possesses in regard to the church.

THE SHEPHERD-PRIEST

The seventh chapter speaks of the ministry of Christ to those who will pass through the great tribulation into the Millennial Kingdom. "The Lamb which is in the midst of the throne shall be their Shepherd, and shall guide them unto fountains of water of life" (Rev. 7:17). A priest and his ministry are sometimes represented in Scripture under the figure of a shepherd and his work. Jeremiah speaks of the priests as shepherds. (See Jer. 23:1–11, and compare Ezek. 37:1–4). The writer of the epistle to the Hebrews, in setting forth the glories of Christ as the High Priest of His people, speaks of Him also as "The Great Shepherd of the sheep." He who as the Lamb of God laid down His life for them has thereby

---

1 Edersheim. "The Temple: Its Ministry and Services," p. 98.

become their shepherd. While He will ever be "the Lamb which is in the midst of the throne," thus occupying His kingly position and authority, He will also be the Shepherd-Priest to those who are brought through the great tribulation. His sovereign power, priestly ministry, and pastoral care, will all be engaged on their behalf.

THE PRAYERS OF THE SAINTS

The eighth chapter presents Him again as a priest. The angel who stands at the altar, with "the golden censer and much incense," can scarcely be any other than Christ Himself. Only Christ could present the prayers of the saints (v. 4). No creature-ministry can render prayers effective. The symbolism represents mediatorial work between God and man, which is wrought by Christ alone (1 Tim. 2:5). "The smoke of the incense, with the prayers of the saints, went up before God out of the angel's hand."

Again, this ministry is seen to be exercised in connection with the throne. The golden altar from whence the prayers ascended was before the throne. Since it is occupied by Christ Himself, His priestly ministry is here associated again with the exercise of His sovereignty. The coexistence of the two positions is not only possible in His case, but is in accordance with the Scriptures we have already considered. His is both sovereign authority and priestly ministry toward God for His people.

It is in response to these prayers—not, be it noted, the present prayers of the church, but the prayers of the godly midst the Jewish nation in the coming time of "Jacob's trouble," that the angel takes the censer, fills it with fire from the altar and casts it into the earth. The signs which immediately follow introduce the sounding of the seven trumpets, and when the seventh angel sounds there follow great voices in heaven, saying, "The kingdom of the world is become the kingdom of our Lord and of His Christ: and He shall reign forever and ever" (11:15). The church is not called to pray for vengeance upon adversaries. Under the tyranny of Antichrist the faithful remnant of God-fearing Jews will rightly take up the language of the so-called imprecatory psalms, and their prayers will be entirely consistent with the retributive judgments of God then to be executed upon the world. That will be a day, not of gospel grace, but of divine wrath. That is why the prayers of the saints, ascending from the golden altar, are answered by fire therefrom upon the foes of God.

The meting out of divine vengeance upon iniquity is not incompatible with the discharge of the priestly function where the circumstance demands it. Phinehas, for instance, who was of the priestly line in Israel, executed the retributive vengeance of God when he put to death Zimri and Cozbi, who by their iniquity had brought trouble upon the people. For this his priesthood was permanently established. "Phinehas, the son of Eleazar, the son of Aaron the priest," said the Lord, "hath turned My wrath away from the children of Israel, in that he was jealous with My jealousy among them, so that I consumed not the children of Israel in My jealousy. Wherefore say, Behold, I give unto him My covenant of peace; and it shall be unto him, and to his seed after him, the covenant of an everlasting priesthood; because he was jealous for his God and made atonement for the children of Israel" (Num. 25:7, 13). In such a capacity Christ is presented in those chapters in the Apocalypse which describe His intervention in the affairs of the world in the coming day of wrath.

THE SECOND ADVENT

In chapter nineteen, where the Lord is seen coming in His glory and power to execute vengeance upon the world in the consummation of its rebellion, the description given of Christ answers to that in the first chapter. "His eyes are as a flame of fire, and upon His head are many diadems." "He is arrayed in a garment sprinkled with blood." All this is symbolic of His sovereign power and His righteous judgments. The blood which stains His garment is not that of the Cross, but of the foes of His earthly people. He comes to undertake their cause and to deliver them from the merciless oppression of Antichrist and his fellows who are then threatening them with extinction.

"The armies which are in heaven followed Him upon white horses, clothed in fine linen, white and pure. And out of his mouth proceedeth a sharp sword, that with it He should smite the nations: and He shall rule them with a rod of iron: and He treadeth the winepress of the fierceness of the wrath of almighty God. And He hath on His garment and on His thigh a name written, King of kings and Lord of lords" (19:14–16). The Beast and the False Prophet are taken and consigned to their doom, and the kings of the earth and the armies that were gathered together under them are destroyed. This is followed by the binding of Satan, who is to be cast into the abyss for the thousand years. It is in this manner that the Second Advent of Christ, in manifested glory, with His angels and with His saints, is to take place. These acts of righteous judgment, exercised after so long a period of the patient forbearance and longsuffering of God, will be the necessary preliminaries to the inauguration of the millennial kingdom. Those who had been slaughtered by the Beast and who had refused to worship him and his image and to receive his mark, will live and reign with Christ a thousand years (20:4). Those who are then raised, and all who have part in the first resurrection, are to be "priests of God and of Christ and are to reign with Him a thousand years" (v. 5).

This priestly sovereignty will be exercised by all who have received rewards at the Judgment Seat of Christ. They form part of the armies in heaven which follow Him "upon white horses, clothed in fine linen, white and pure" (19:14). "The fine linen is the righteous acts of the saints." The service which we render to Him in this short life of probation is determining day by day the character of the rewards we are to receive hereafter, and the place we are to occupy in His eternal kingdom. Let us therefore seek grace to serve Him faithfully and loyally while opportunity is given to us, that we may be able to say with the apostle when our life's work is finished, "I have fought the good fight, I have finished the course, I have kept the faith; henceforth there is laid up for me the crown of righteousness which the Lord, the righteous Judge, shall give to me at that day" (2 Tim. 4:7, 8). It is to be given "to all them that have loved His appearing."

THE TESTIMONY OF JOB

Job speaks of Christ as His Kinsman-Redeemer with reference to the resurrection of his body hereafter, when he says, "I know that my Redeemer (Heb. *goel*, Kinsman-Redeemer-Avenger) liveth, and that He shall stand up (i.e., stand victoriously) over the dust (i.e., the dust of his body—not the earth—see *margin*), and after my skin hath been thus destroyed, yet from my flesh shall I see God" (Job 19:25, 26).

In one other passage *apolutrōsis* is used to include the deliverance to be granted to God's earthly people at the coming of the Son of man (Luke 21:28).

The ransom price (*lutron*) paid by the Lord Jesus in giving up His life for the redemption of man (Matt. 20:28; Mark 10:45), was spoken of in our last chapter.

The Old Testament, alike with the New, makes clear the distinction between the ransom and the redemption. "No man can by any means redeem (Heb. *padah*, to release, to liberate) his brother, nor give to God a ransom (Heb. *kopher*, a cover, a redemption-price paid down) for him: for the redemption (Heb. *pidyom*, a redeeming deliverance) of their soul is precious (costly), and must be let alone forever" (Ps. 49:7, 8).

THE TIMES DETERMINED

God doesn't change and neither do His plans; his divine will is prophetic in nature. With Him, the future is as assured as the past. Jesus arrived in the world when the time was right, and His death came in the fullness of time as well. We live in times that have been appointed for the spreading of the Good News. The work of the gospel depends, not upon our own efforts, but upon the power of the Spirit of God and our willing obedience in presenting ourselves to Him who worketh in us "both to will and to work for His good pleasure."

The steps taken by God in the carrying out of His plans have been eternally predetermined both as to time and mode of accomplishment. Nothing can change them, nothing can thwart them. His acts are the expressions of His character. His immutability shines out in the actings of His providence. God's designs are as unalterable as His nature; His modes of procedure vary, His plans never change.

Variation in His methods does not indicate inconsistency in His designs. If He is said to repent, that does not argue the nonachievement of His purposes, it simply signifies a necessary alteration of His attitude consequent upon a change in the attitude of His creatures toward Him. Any such alteration on His part is but consistent with, and is an exhibition of, the immutability of His attributes.

With Him the future is as assured as the past. He dwells in an eternal present. Hence, what is yet future is often spoken of in the past tense. This is strikingly illustrated, for instance, in the second Psalm. Nations may rage, peoples imagine a vain thing, kings may set themselves, and rulers take counsel together against the Lord and against His anointed. All is foredoomed to failure. The purposes of Jehovah are sure. He does not even say: "Yet *will* I set My King upon My holy hill of Zion." The predetermined act is as good as accomplished. In the climax of the predictions the language changes from the future tense to the past. He says, "Yet *have* I set My King."

What is thus true of all God's works receives a special testimony in Scripture concerning His redemptive acts, such as the incarnation of His Son as a preliminary step to the atoning sacrifice of the Cross, and again the sending forth of the gospel on its worldwide mission, and eventually the revelation of Christ in glory for the deliverance of Creation from its bondage.

The time of the Incarnation is indicated in various ways, and is signalized as "the fullness of the time," "the consummation of the ages," and "the end of the times." "When the fullness of the time came, God sent forth His Son, born of a woman, born under the Law, that He might redeem them which were under the Law, that we might receive the adoption of sons" (Gal. 4:4, 5). The phrase, "The fullness of the time," suggests that everything which the divine counsels had appointed in the course of the preceding ages had been fulfilled. Step after step had been taken according to God's predetermination, and exactly at the appointed time. The nation into which "the Seed of the woman" should be born, had been formed, developed, trained and preserved. We may trace in the book of Genesis the measures taken by God for the formation of Israel prior to its existence, and from the book of Exodus onward the whole design of the training and preservation of the nation works out in the Old Testament with a continuity of development which impresses the reader with the manifold wisdom of God and the inspiration of His Word. For the Jews the Law had done the work designed for it in shutting up all under sin. The affairs of the gentile world just prior to the birth of Christ give evidence that everything was ripe for that event.

The next phrase, "The consummation of the ages," presents the same fact in another aspect. That is the phrase used by the writer of the epistle to the Hebrews, and mistranslated in the Authorized Version by "the end of the world." "Now once at the consummation of the ages hath He been manifested to put away sin by the sacrifice of Himself" (Heb. 9:26). Here again the birth of Christ is in view, and the great object for which He came to earth. The Cross, for the suffering of which a body was prepared for Him (Heb. 10:5), was the climax of God's dealings with man. All preceding ages had led up to these crowning acts of divine grace. All succeeding ages will look back to them.

Again, "Christ . . . was manifested at the end of the times" (1 Pet. 1:20), i.e. at the close of those ages which had led up to this climax. Cp. Hebrews 1:2, R.V.

The time of the atoning sacrifice itself is similarly spoken of. With the Cross immediately in view the Lord said, "The hour is come, that the Son of man should be glorified" (John 12:23). It was the Father's glory that He had in view when He said, "Now is My soul troubled; and what shall I say? Father, save Me from this hour. But for this cause came I unto this hour." For what cause? Surely that by His death He might glorify the Father. His next words suggest it: "Father, glorify thy Name." At once the Father's answer comes, "I have both glorified it, and will glorify it again" (vv. 27, 28). The beginning of the next chapter speaks of the time as "His hour"; "before the feast of the Passover, Jesus, knowing that His hour was come that He should depart unto the Father, . . . riseth from supper" (13:1–4). Again, on the night of the betrayal, He begins His prayer with the statement, "Father, the hour is come." That was the hour for which He had come into the world, the hour of the consummating act of His obedience to the Father, the hour of the completion of the work the Father had given Him to do.

As with the incarnation and the atonement, so with the work of the gospel. The special time appointed for it is alluded to by Paul in his first epistle to Timothy: "Christ Jesus . . . gave Himself a ransom for all; the testimony to be borne in its own times" (1 Tim. 2:6, R.V.). As the statements concerning the incarnation pointed on to the cross as being the object in view, so this statement of the times appointed for the gospel points back to the cross as the basis of the testimony to be given.

The word rendered "times" might be more suitably translated "seasons." A season suggests that a particular feature characterizes the period indicated. The work of the gospel is that which signalizes the present era. The divine plan of this testimony was succinctly stated by James at the gathering of the apostles and elders in Jerusalem as recorded in Acts 15. God is visiting the Gentiles "to take out of them a people for His Name" (v. 14)—a people, that is, who should own His authority and represent His character.

"A people for His Name" is a description of the Church. The Church is eternally to exhibit, in union with Christ and under His headship, all that the name of the Lord signifies. The gospel, while provisionally universal in its scope, is not universal in its effects, nor is it destined to be so. It is the instrument of God's grace toward men, proclaiming salvation through the death of His Son, but its purpose is the formation of the Church, which will in itself eternally be the exhibition of "the exceeding riches of His grace" (Eph. 2:7). During the present era the Church is being taken out from among the nations, each individual who believes being given "out of the world" to the Son by the Father (John 17:6). At the second coming of Christ the Church will be taken physically out of the world in resurrection life, to its destined heavenly home and sphere, the dead in Christ being raised and the living transfigured (1 Thess. 4:15–17; Phil. 3:20, 21).

This design and scope of the gospel was embodied in the teaching of the Lord prior to His ascension. We behold Him amidst His disciples, His redeeming work accomplished, His heart's affection engaged on behalf of mankind for whom He had given up Himself. "Jesus came to them and spake unto them, saying, All authority hath been given unto Me in heaven and on earth. Go ye therefore, and make disciples of all the nations, baptizing them into the name of the Father and of the Son and of the Holy Ghost: teaching them to observe all things whatsoever I commanded you: and lo, I am with you alway, even unto the end of the age" (Matt. 28:18–20).

But this was not all. They could not go until the appointed time, a time to be marked by God by an act which would usher in the new era of the gospel. The evangel had been provided through the death and resurrection of His Son, the work itself must be carried on by the presence and power of the Spirit. Nothing could be done until He was sent. Before leading the disciples out to the place of the Ascension, the Lord, having opened their mind, that they might understand the Scriptures, said unto them, "Thus it is written, that the Christ should suffer, and rise again from the dead the third day; and that repentance and remission of sins should be preached in His Name unto all the nations, beginning from Jerusalem. Ye are witnesses of these things. And behold I send forth the promise of My Father upon you: but tarry ye in the city, until ye be clothed with power from on high."

The place and character of this mission of the Holy Spirit in the divine plan call for further consideration. Suffice it here to say that the discharge of our responsibilities in the work of the gospel depends, not upon our own efforts, but upon the power of the Spirit of God and our willing obedience in presenting ourselves to Him Who worketh in us "both to will and to work for His good pleasure" (R.V.).

THE EXPECTANCY OF CHRIST

Believers are waiting for the return of their Lord; patient expectancy is a hallmark of Christian hope. Jesus' attitude towards the future is also de scribed as one of expectancy. The objective He has in view is His triumph over everything that opposes the will of God by the establishment of the Kingdom of God upon the earth.

> *"God loves to be longed for, He longs to be sought,*
> *For He sought us Himself with such longing and love:*
> *He died for desire of us, marvelous thought!*
> *And He yearns for us now to be with Him above."*

When men permit themselves to contemplate the future, when they project their thoughts beyond the grave, the natural tendency of the mind is to become overcast by fear. Fear draws its strength from the unknown, and is accentuated by the consciousness of failure and the sense of accountability. Fear demoralizes men, robs them of courage and of hope, and drives them to new depths of evil. Fear, anticipating the adverse verdict of the Day of Judgment, causes suffering even here and now; "fear hath punishment." There is but one way of dealing with fear, this natural tenant of the human mind; fear must be cast out. But how? Love alone is equal to the task. "There is no fear in love; but perfect love casteth out fear." "Perfect love," that is the love manifested in the death of the Lord Jesus Christ. It is only in the knowledge of the purpose of His death that the believer is able to think without fear of the Day of Judgment, for "as He is, even so are we in this world" (1 John 4:17, 18).

The tenses must be closely followed here. The apostle does not say as He is so we shall be, nor that as He was so we are, but quite plainly, and by the addition of the unmistakable phrase "in this world," as He is now at the right hand of the Majesty on High, so are we here and at this present time. What, then, is His place or condition there to which our present state here corresponds? Surely this, that He, after He had borne our sins in His body on the tree, experiencing there that separation from God which is the consequence of sin, was raised from among the dead and exalted to the throne of God. He is thus on the other side of the Judgment, so to speak; having suffered in the flesh for sin He has now passed out of any relation with sin, i.e., He is no longer a sin-bearer (1 Pet. 4:1).

And as He is, so are all they that have put their trust in Him. The Christian is not a man who contemplates the Day of Judgment with mingled feelings, hoping that it will see him exculpated on the ground of the death of Christ, and yet fearing lest it should not. Rather he is one who shall not come into the Judgment of that Day at all ("shall never stand in the dock," John 5:24), since he knows himself to be already justified by Christ and accepted in Christ, seated with and in Him in the heavenlies (Eph. 2:6). This the perfect love of God has accomplished for him, and the assurance of this has set him free from fear.

THE PROMISE TO THE SON

John's statement is a particular instance of a general principle; the principle itself is capable of wide application. Thus if it is asked why the Scriptures insist so much on the waiting attitude of the believer, that he is ever to be on his watch for the coming of the Lord, the answer assuredly is that that is the attitude of the Lord Himself toward the future, and that as He is in this respect, so also are we. Or, to express the same thing in another way, God has called us "into the fellowship of His Son Jesus Christ our Lord" (1 Cor. 1:9). But fellowship at the least means this, that those in fellowship with one another share each other's hopes, they have a common outlook, their hearts are set on the same ends. If it is true, as John declares, that "our fellowship is with the Father and with His Son Jesus Christ," then this fellowship must extend to the purpose of the Father for the Son and to the expectation of the Son Himself (1 John 1:3). It is not conceivable that the hope of the believer could be of any potency, that it could have any actuality, that it could even exist, were it not primarily the hope of the Lord Himself.

Now this plain deduction from the known facts is fully confirmed by the testimony of Scripture. The Father's purpose for the Son is declared in such words as those of Psalm 110:1, 2:

> "The Lord saith unto my Lord,
> Sit Thou at My right hand,
> Until I make Thine enemies thy footstool.
> The Lord shall send forth the rod of Thy strength out of Zion:
> Rule Thou in the midst of thine enemies."

In the second Psalm the Father addresses the Son:

> "Ask of Me and I will give Thee the nations for Thine inheritance,
> And the uttermost parts of the earth for Thy possession."

In complete correspondence with these words the writer of the epistle to the Hebrews says concerning Christ, that "He, when He had offered one sacrifice for sins forever, sat down on the right hand of God; from henceforth expecting till His enemies be made the footstool of His feet" (Heb. 10:12, 13). (H-J, p. 156).

To have the mind set upon that consummation, to refuse the world's plans for permanent government in favor of God's plan for the universal and eternal Kingdom of Christ, is to be to that extent in fellowship "with the Father and with His Son Jesus Christ." To ignore the declared purpose of God is to put oneself outside that fellowship, insofar as this purpose is concerned, and, as an inevitable consequence, to fail to appreciate the ways of God with men alike in the past, the present, and the future.

THE CONSTITUENTS OF HOPE

The attitude of Christ toward the future is here described as one of expectancy, and the objective before His mind is His triumph over everything that opposes the will of God by the establishment of the Kingdom of God upon the earth. And he who among men is in fellowship with Christ will have his heart set upon that consummation also.

Toward the end of his letter, written to the believers at Thessalonica to correct some misconceptions concerning his teaching about the coming of the Lord, the apostle prayed for them, "The Lord direct your hearts into the love of God, and into the patience of Christ" (2 Thess. 3:5). That is, that lifted above the level of merely natural love, the love of affinity of aim and taste, they should learn to love each other, and all men, after the pattern and measure of the love of God. Similarly, that they might learn to be patient in their hope, even as Christ is patient until the fullness of the time for His return comes in. That it is the patience of the risen Lord in His present session in the heavens of which the apostle is thinking seems clear. For one reason, because the language suggests a present condition of mind rather than a past experience, and for another because the title "Christ" is appropriate to Him in His exaltation to the throne of God, whereas the name "Jesus" brings to mind the years preceding the Cross, as in Hebrews 12:2, "Looking unto Jesus . . . Who . . . endured." "This Jesus" has, in His resurrection, been made "Christ" (Acts 2:36).

THE WORD OF MY PATIENCE

The apostle John speaks of the share that he and those to whom he wrote had "in the tribulation and kingdom and patience which are in Jesus" (Rev. 1:9). This arresting sentence suggests how deeply "the disciple whom Jesus loved" had been impressed by the patience of his Master in the days when his own slowness to believe, and that of his companions, and their consequent slowness to understand, made constant and heavy demand upon it. But the Lord's patience was not a virtue that had served its end and passed with the occasions that life among fallen men provided. It is in exercise still as He beholds the afflictions of His people in the world, and the reign of iniquity that can be brought to an end only when His Kingdom is established in the earth.

His sympathy with His own, whose sorrows touch Him with a poignancy beyond our experience, and His compassion for the masses of men, "distressed and scattered as sheep not having a shepherd" (Matt. 9:36), are still what they ever were, burdens upon His heart. And if He charges us to "let patience have its perfect work" that is because patience is working perfectly in Him. If we are to await the hour of our deliverance that is because He, too, is awaiting "the fullness of the time" that will bring Him from heaven again to be our Savior and the Deliverer of the whole Creation (Phil. 3:20; Rom. 8:21).

The Lord is quick to mark the response of the soul to His message. "Because thou didst keep the word of My patience, I also will keep thee from the hour of trial, that hour which is to come upon the whole inhabited earth, to try them that dwell upon the earth" (Rev. 3:10). "My patience," says the Lord, for His is the source of ours, and ours can only be because it is His first, and we share it by the ministry of the Spirit. "For of His fullness we all received, and grace for grace."[1] The grace of our patience is evoked by, and answers to, the grace of His.

> "On the earth the broken arcs;
> In the Heaven, a perfect round."

The two words translated "wait" in 1 Thessalonians 1:10 and Hebrews 9:28 are carefully chosen to meet the spiritual condition of the readers in each case.

---

1 So far as the utterances of the Lord Jesus are recorded He did not Himself use the word "hope" save in Luke 6:34, "If ye lend to them of whom ye hope to receive," and John 5:45, "Moses, on whom ye have set your hope." Neither of these passages is concerned with the Christian hope. Nor do any of the New Testament writers speak of the Lord's "hope," what He expects to happen, but of His purpose, what He "shall" or "will" do.

In the first passage the word used suggests the thought of abiding quietly, for the Thessalonians needed sobering and to be reminded that so they had been taught from the outset.[1] The ebbing faith, the waning hope of the Hebrews, on the other hand, are stimulated by the word which suggests the tiptoe, the out-stretched neck, of intent expectancy.[2] The ideas are combined at Romans 8:25, "if we hope . . . then do we with patience [expectantly] wait.[3]

THE SAFEGUARDS OF HOPE

Patient expectancy is thus the characteristic element in the Christian hope. The suggestion of uncertainty, inseparable from the word in its ordinary use of human affairs, is eliminated from it in those New Testament passages which speak of the coming of the Lord. In this hope there is no faintest trace of the possibility of an unforeseen contingency, or of an insuperable obstacle, or of a changed plan, such as disturb the calculations of the most farsighted among men. We may say, indeed, that the Lord Himself shares this hope, or rather that His purpose is our hope; and as the first is guaranteed by His power to bring the universe into subjection to Himself, so the second "putteth not to shame" those who cherish it in fellowship with Him (Phil. 3:20; Rom. 5:5).

Hope is liable to abuse; with eagerness there is a tendency to relaxation of discipline and to neglect of duty, as at Thessalonica, for this condition is reflected in both the epistles to the church there, and particularly in the second. Or patience may degenerate into lethargy and indifference, as seems to have been the case with those to whom the apostle Peter addressed his second epistle. The Christian hope is the happy mien; it is an expectant patience, a patient expectancy. The Christian lifts up his head to look for his approaching salvation. He looks toward heaven "as with outstretched neck" for his Lord's return. But not less does he "trade" diligently with that Lord's "pound" until He be pleased to return (Luke 19:13; 21:28). This is the paradox of the Christian life; working he waits, and waiting he works.

"In the night in which He was betrayed" the Lord Jesus spoke, for the first time so far as the records show, of His purpose to return in person for "His own that are in the world." Of their resurrection in response to His voice they had already heard from Him, and of His coming in the glories of heaven to put His enemies to confusion they had heard Him speak publicly again and again (John 6:39; Matt. 16:27; 24:30). But now, in the holy privacy of the Upper Room, and on the eve of His departure from them, with the cold shadow of the Cross already fallen into His heart, He addresses Himself to the comfort of men who must soon know the desolating sorrow of a bereavement the possibility of which had not heretofore entered their minds. But the separation from those who had

---

1 *anti* = "answering to," John 1:16.

2 *anamenō.*

3 *apekdechomai.*

"continued with Him in His trials," and whose sympathy in them was to Him unpriced, meant something to His own heart also.

THE SECRET OF THE LORD

For His sympathy with men is the complement of His desire for their sympathy with Him. God created man with social instincts; he was not made for solitude; companionship is the law of his life. Therefore in this as in all things "it behoved Him . . . to be made like unto His brethren," and for this reason, that, first of all, they were made like unto Him (Heb. 2:17; Gen. 1:26, 27). Hence it is that the desire of the redeemed to be with the Redeemer is the reflection, and the fruit, of His desire for their presence with Him.

Now this personal feeling seems audible in the words He spoke for their comfort, as though He found in them a comfort of His own. "I go to prepare a place for you," He said, "and if I go and prepare a place for you, I come again, and will receive you unto Myself; that where I am, there ye may be also" (John 14:2, 3). Never before had He used the first personal pronoun when He spoke of His return—in the wider circle of His public ministry and to His opponents he usually spoke of the coming of the Son of man. In this speech there is an arresting directness, the sense of intimacy and immediate personal concern. It is "the secret of the Lord," and it is for "them that fear Him." It was His secret, now it is theirs also, for He shares it with them, because He loves them "unto the uttermost." How shall the world that knows neither Him nor them know their secret? (1 John 3:1). And, again, how shall their joy in that secret exceed His own? If it is to make their hearts glad, that can only be because it has first gladdened His.

The language of the apostle Paul suggests the same desire of the Lord for the presence with Him of His redeemed. "Christ . . . loved the Church and gave Himself up for it . . . that He might present the Church to Himself a glorious Church, not having spot or wrinkle or any such thing; but that it should be holy and without blemish before Him." It is to this end, and because of His own interest in its completion and perfection, that He is said to "nourish and cherish it." At the appointed time He is to have the joy of receiving the Church to His Father's house, of causing it to stand with Himself, partaker of His holiness and meet companion in, and instrument of, His universal reign (Eph. 5:25–29). (F, p. 156).

The comfort and glory of the Church in that day is not the primary thought in the passage, however, but rather what that day will bring to Him in the accomplishment of a purpose which involved such costly sacrifice, and in the attainment of which His love sustained Him to the end of His toil.

THE LORD'S MEMORY

In the last of the series of five impressions of the glory and the sufferings of Christ—in this order—which occupy Isaiah 52:13—53:12, the prophet declares of the Messiah that "He shall see of the travail of His soul, and shall be satisfied" (v. 11). The perfection of the manhood of the Lord Jesus consists in the perfection of all the elements essential to manhood, and among these memory has its place as well as sympathy. Memory is the power of the mind to reproduce the past in its original form and color, to recall into the present the experiences of the past without loss of reality. With men memory fails; impressions can never be renewed to their full value; the heights of an old joy can never be attained again; into the depths of an old sorrow we can never again be plunged. Thus the defects of memory mean loss indeed, but not loss without compensation. Were our griefs to be continued, or could they be renewed in their first acuteness, the heart of man would fail, life become intolerable. Time by weakening memory assuages grief under the merciful hand of God.

But we may not conceive it to be so with the Lord. To Him the past can have lost nothing. No pang endured is forgotten. The price paid has not lost its value because it is so long since it was paid.

> " . . . Mine affliction and My outcast state, the wormwood and the gall,
> My soul hath them still in remembrance . . ." (Lam. 3:19, 20).

And on that day when He shall say "Behold, I and the children which God hath given Me," there will be no regret. Looking back over the past, realizing to the full all our redemption cost, He yet declares it to have been worthwhile!

COMPENSATION

When certain Hebrew Christians showed signs of relaxing confidence under the attacks of their multiplying adversaries, attacks now fierce, now subtle, they were reminded of the hidden power that had sustained the heroes of their race under the sorest afflictions and that had impelled them to fine achievements. They had endured as seeing the unseen God; they had put their trust in Him that in His own time He would recompense them in the city for which He had taught them to look, and of which He is both architect and builder. And yet, brilliant examples of the power of faith though these were, even their greatest had failed, and failed in that very thing of which they, in the general tenor of their lives, and at so many critical junctures in their lives, were shining examples. Always men fail at their strong points; there is something at work that forbids perfection to the children of Adam. These witnesses to the faithfulness of God are to be remembered, indeed, but beyond all things else must the Christian run his race "looking unto Jesus, the author and perfecter of faith."[1] They were leaders of the faithful; He is leader-in-chief. They were illustrations of the way and power of faith; He is its consummator. He trusted God from His birth; He lived in the fear of God; He died with the words of faith upon His lips (Ps. 22:9; Isa. 11:3; Luke 23:46).

---

1 There is neither article nor pronoun in the original. The reference is not to "the faith once for all delivered to the saints," nor yet to any operation within the believer whereby faith is begotten and strengthened, but, as the content demands, to the life of realized dependence and uninterrupted faith of the Lord in the days of His flesh.

And throughout His sustaining thought is of "the joy that was set before Him"; because of that "He endured the Cross, despising shame" (Heb. 12:1, 2).

Thus the prophetic vision is reproduced historically; but the point of view is necessarily different. Here the price has still to be paid; the rough and thorny way is as yet untrodden; the agony of the Cross is still in the future; the cup awaits Him. And the joy that is to be the issue sustains Him "to the uttermost." Whereas in Isaiah's vision the journey is already accomplished; the goal has been reached; the shame and the agony are exhausted; the cup has been drained. The retrospect confirms the prospect: the joy realized does not fall short of the joy anticipated. The prize in possession is no less than it seemed in prospect. The compensation for the sorrow of the lonely death is the gladness of the fellowship in resurrection.

This joy, moreover, is not merely the joy of the Son; no less is it the joy of the Father also, and of the Holy Spirit. The joy of the shepherd over the found sheep, of the woman over the recovered coin, is boldly declared to be the reflection of the joy in heaven over a sinner restored to God. It is noteworthy that this joy in heaven is not said to be the joy of the angels, but "joy in the presence of the angels." The words seem to be chosen to suggest the joy of God. For just as the angels are in His presence so is He in the presence of the angels. And this joy over the repentant soul even here and now, becomes an "exceeding joy" in that day when the Son presents the hosts of the redeemed to His Father, saying, "Behold, I and the children which God hath given me" (Luke 15:7, 10, 22–24; Heb. 2:13).

AT THE GATE OF NAIN

An incident in the life of the Lord Jesus, recorded in Luke 7, provides a picture in which may be discerned the joys of that day. As He approached the gate of Nain there met Him a funeral procession, a widow's only son carried out to burial. Moved with compassion for the sorrowing woman He bade her dry her tears. But more than words is needed to stay the flood of grief. The astounded crowd heard Him address the figure upon the bier: "Young man, I say unto thee, Arise." The writ of the Prince of Life runs in the realm of the dead! The lad sat up and began to speak. But the Lord does not only snatch the prey from the mighty. He binds up broken hearts and wipes tears away from all faces. So "He delivered him to his mother," and made effective His command "Weep not." Her son is not only brought back from the gates of the tomb, he is restored to her as a gift from the Lord.

So, that eventide, was sorrow turned into joy. They who witnessed the scene rejoiced that God had visited His people. The lad was glad to see the light of the sun again and to be with his widowed mother. The mother was glad—how much more glad!—to receive her son alive from the dead. And surely gladdest of all was the Lord Himself thus to taste beforehand the victory of the Cross.

There are degrees of gladness, heart differs from heart in power to enjoy. It is experience of sorrow that gives capacity for joy. The spectators were not involved in the tragedy; however its unexpected issue may have touched them, it was not to them a vital thing. The lad, whatever sorrows he had known, was young, and grief does not strike its roots deeply in the heart of youth. Small, therefore, was his capacity for joy in comparison with those whose span had been longer upon the earth, but such as it was the Lord met and satisfied it. But the mother—the years had brought to her more of bitter than of sweet. In sorrow and anguish she had travailed for her son (John 16:21) and now she had closed his eyes in death. Husband, family, all were gone; what an experience of sorrow hers had been; what capacity for joy it had given to her heart! This, too, the Lord satisfied to the full. And what of the Lord Himself? "A Man of sorrows and acquainted with grief," what experiences of sorrow, actual and in anticipation, were His! Outside the gate of Nain that day we may be sure that the gladdest heart was His own.

So shall it be in that other day within the gates of heaven. The little graves shall be opened and they that sleep therein shall be made glad to the measure of their capacity for joy. And those who lived longer and sorrowed more will be made glad also, each after his measure. But the "exceeding joy" is the joy of God. It is the joy of the Father Who gave His Son to death that that day might be brought about. It is the joy of the Son Who "Himself took our infirmities and bare our diseases," "Who His own self bare our sins in His body upon the tree" that He might have with Him forever those for whom He died, and to Whom it is said,

> "Thy God hath anointed Thee
> With the oil of gladness above Thy fellows."
> —Hebrews 1:9

It is the joy of the Holy Spirit Who led Him to the Cross and through Whom He "offered Himself without blemish unto God" (Heb. 9:14) and Whose present ministry enables the Christian to "rejoice in hope of the glory of God."

THE RESURRECTION AND THE RAPTURE

In the midst of His teaching, Jesus referred to the resurrection of the dead, particularly that of those who believe in Him. Here, the Lord's words on this subject are taken in order and expounded upon, from His response to the Pharisees and Sadducees to His disciples carrying on His words to the church. The reader will get a birds-eye prophetic vantage point of some key themes such as Christ's death, resurrection, the rapture, a new body, and the believer's eternal home.

THE TEACHING OF THE LORD

When the Lord Jesus appeared among the Jews as a public teacher they had long been divided into two main religious parties, Sadducees and Pharisees. The former though smaller in numbers were the more wealthy, and socially and politically the more powerful, the latter were the more popular party. The doctrinal difference between them is thus defined by Luke—"The Sadducees say that there is no resurrection, neither angel nor spirit: but the Pharisees confess both" (Acts 23:8). To the Sadducees the resurrection was an irrational fancy; to the Pharisees it was a hope. The Sadducees did not reject the Old Testament Scriptures, but they did not discover there the hope of resurrection as the Pharisees did.

Whether or no the dead would be raised was thus an open question among the Jews. It is true there is little in the Old Testament concerning resurrection or a future life, still the doctrine is present. Hence the Lord in His reply to a Sadducean interlocutor declared that the error of his school arose out of ignorance of the Scriptures and of the power of God, thus justifying the Pharisees in their hope (Luke 20:27–40).

REASONING FROM THE SCRIPTURES

On this occasion the Lord deduced from the words of Moses in Exodus 3:15, "the God of Abraham, the God of Isaac, and the God of Jacob," that inasmuch as God was still their God though they had died, they were in fact living persons still; for if to die means to cease to exist, then He would be the God of the nonexistent, plainly an absurd conclusion. Therefore the dead, i.e., those whose bodies have seen corruption, continue to live, for their spirits still hold fellowship with God. And to this the inevitable corollary is that they will one day be raised.

The other recorded references of the Lord to the resurrection, and particularly to the resurrection of those who believe on Him, are the subject of this chapter. His utterances will be taken in the order in which they were spoken, so far as that can be ascertained. We shall endeavor to learn His mind as He Himself unfolded it to those who, while they believed that the dead would ultimately be raised, had no certain knowledge of the extent of the resurrection, whether all men, Jews and Gentiles, were to partake in it, or Jews only; or how, or when, that resurrection would take place. We are to forget, for the moment, all that was subsequently revealed on the subject, and, as far as may be possible, to put ourselves in the place of those to whom the Lord originally spoke.

Subsequent communications of the Holy Spirit, made through the apostles, to supplement the words of the Lord and to complete the revelation, will form the subject of other chapters.

THE INNER SANCTUARY—HIS BODY

The first passage with which we are here concerned is John 2:19–22, where He referred, under a figure, to His own resurrection. "Destroy this temple," He said, "and after three days I will raise it up." It was to His own body He alluded, though at the time no one of His hearers perceived His meaning. Hence the words provided His enemies with one of the accusations upon which they ultimately secured His death, and John records that the disciples themselves understood their significance only after His resurrection from among the dead (Matt. 26:61).

After John the Baptist had been thrown into prison, and the Lord Jesus had begun to attract general attention, the disciples of the former came to inquire about the purposes and claims of the latter. The Lord drew their attention to the works in which He was engaged, in which power was at the service of beneficence, and in His recapitulation of these works He included the raising of the dead. The two evangelists who recorded the words do not set the incident in the same relation to the events of the Lord's ministry. Luke inserts the visit of these disciples in his narrative between the raising of the widow's son at Nain and the raising of Jairus's daughter. Matthew, who does not include the incident at Nain, places it after the raising of the girl. (See Luke 7:11–17, 22; 8:49–56 and Matt. 9:23–26; 11:5.) It seems probable, that, here at least, Matthew's is the chronological order. Certainly the words "the dead are raised" seem to suggest that more than one person had, at that time, been restored to life.

All this was intended to familiarize the minds of the disciples, and of His hearers generally, with the idea of resurrection, and to show them the possibility of the return of dead persons to life. It is the way of God to lead the believing mind into the light by easy stages, and to furnish it with aids to an understanding faith. These were first steps toward that larger thought which He was about to begin to unfold to them.

The next passage that calls for notice is the paragraph on hospitality, Luke 14:12–14, with its concluding words, "thou shalt be recompensed in the resurrection of the just."[1] The reference to resurrection here is incidental only; the Lord is not expounding the doctrine, nor is He adding anything by way of new revelation. He alludes to it as something His hearers would understand without further explanation. (See Acts 24:15.) Two things are clear from this statement; that there is to be a resurrection of a class of people described as "the just," and that they are thereafter to be rewarded for kindness shown in this life to the needy.

The rest of the Lord's teaching on this subject is found in the Gospel of John, which simplifies matters from the chronological point of view. We have now only to take the words He spoke in their order as there recorded, and of these the earliest is found in chapter 5, verses 28 and 29.[2]

---

1 It is not possible in every case to settle the order of occurrence of the Gospel incidents, or to fix with precision the time at which certain words were spoken. It is impossible to say that Luke 14:14 is actually the first reference to the resurrection in the teaching of the Lord. Whether it is placed before or after the discourse of John 5 is, however, not material in this connection.

2 See Appendix, Note A.

THE SON, CREATOR AND QUICKENER

The Lord had healed a long-standing case of physical weakness; to the scandal of the Jews He had done this on the Sabbath day. To their expostulations He replied in words that involved a claim to equality with God. This deepened their hatred, and strengthened their determination to put Him to death. Not only did He not repudiate the construction they had put upon His words, He confirmed it, and enlarged it into an assertion of a unique relation with God, Whom He called not "our" but "My Father." And that this might be made unmistakable, the Father, He declared, had committed to Him the dispensation of all judgment, so that to refuse to the Son the honor due to the Father, whether as Savior or as judge, is to dishonor God.

Moreover, as the Father is the source of life, so also is the Son; the honor due to God the Creator is His also. Hence it is that all who believe on Him themselves become partakers of life, here and now. And not only so, those who will to hear His voice now are quickened, the rest remain untouched, they continue in their natural state of "alienation from the life of God" (Eph. 4:16). But "the hour cometh in which all that are in the tombs shall hear His voice and shall come forth; they that have done good unto the resurrection of life; they that have practiced [so marg.] ill, unto the resurrection of judgment." So absolute is the jurisdiction of the Son over the destinies of all men, in life and in death, in time and in eternity, so immediate is His control, so imperative His word.

This declaration of the Lord enlarges the scope of the resurrection, and confirms the Pharisees in their reading of the Scriptures (Acts 24:15); for whereas Luke 14:14 speaks only of "the resurrection of the just," this present passage speaks of the resurrection of all men. The class there described as to their character, "the just," are here described as to their conduct, they "have done good." There the dead are said to be raised to reward, for their works are in question. Here they are said to be raised to life, for the purpose of the Lord is to declare that His claim to deity will ultimately be vindicated in this act of quickening.

The next utterance of the Lord which deals with this subject is found in John 6, where those who are to be raised are further described. That the same persons are intended is to be presumed, each separate description presenting a characteristic common to all who are to share in "the resurrection of life." It may be convenient to tabulate these descriptions here. They are:

The Just	Luke 14:14
Those who have done good	John 5:29
Those who are given by the Father to the Son	John 6:39
Those who behold the Son and believe on Him	John 6:40
Those who are drawn by the Father to the Son	John 6:44
Those who eat the Flesh and drink the Blood of the Son of man	John 6:54

"These are they that are accounted worthy to attain to that age, and the resurrection from [lit., out of] the dead . . . and are sons of God, being sons of the resurrection" (Luke 20:35, 36).

The time of the resurrection is now declared. It is to take place "at the Last Day," a phrase which occurs but once again in the recorded teaching of the Lord.[1]

DEATH AND RESURRECTION AT BETHANY

Lazarus had been dead four days at Bethany, and the Lord had made no sign. He had not come to him in response to the message that His friend was sick, nor had any message from Him reached the sisters to relieve their anxiety; or if one had come, it could have been only: "This sickness is not unto death, but for the glory of God, that the Son of God may be glorified thereby" (John 11:4). And these words could only mean to them that Lazarus would not die of the sickness that had brought him low. Yet he had succumbed to it. Thus was their faith most sorely tried.

The sisters had hoped for help; now they longed for comfort. "If He had been here, Lazarus had not died," was the regretful refrain as they reviewed their sorrow while the silence of the Lord remained unbroken. At least this was the thought uppermost in the mind of each when they saw the Lord. To Martha, who met Him first, He replied: "Thy brother shall rise again." Martha, busy woman though she was, and somewhat burdened with the care of the home and its guests (Luke 10:40), is nevertheless in touch with the teacher; she has fresh in her mind the last thing He had said about resurrection. She could, moreover, identify her brother as one of those whom the Lord described when He spoke of His purpose to raise certain from the dead. Accordingly she replies in the true disciple spirit: "I know that he shall rise again in the resurrection at the last day." But the Lord had not said anything about the last day when He spoke of the raising of Lazarus. There was an immediate boon for the home at Bethany. Nevertheless the new and nearer promise did not abrogate the older and more remote. It remains true that Lazarus will be raised again at the last day. This is a significant illustration of the Lord's ways. Ultimate and final blessings are often promised first; subsequent promises may have previous fulfillment but they do not cancel those given earlier. Neither do earlier assurances of ultimate blessing prevent the Lord from revealing His purposes to do yet other things while these still wait.

THE FAITH OF MARTHA

To return to Martha; it was to this busy woman of domestic affairs He chose to carry the revelation of His purpose a long step in advance. He said to her, "I am the resurrection and the life: he that believeth on Me, though he die yet shall he live: and whosoever liveth and believeth on Me shall never die. Believest thou

---

1 John 12:48. See Appendix, Note B.

this?" The words are apparently inconsistent; the second clause seems to be an absolute statement admitting of no exception, whereas the first clause provides for an exception. Martha did not understand them, and she was too honest to pretend she did. But not only was hers an intelligent apprehension of the teaching of the Lord; to spiritual knowledge she added spiritual understanding. "The word of the Lord tried" her, as it tried Joseph when he lay forgotten in the prison (Ps. 105:19), and as it tries every faithful soul that submits itself to be exercised under it. Faith triumphs. Martha appeals from the word, the meaning of which she did not perceive, to the Lord Who spoke it and Whom she had learned to trust. "Yea, Lord," she answered, "I have believed that Thou art the Christ, the Son of God." No remonstrance falls from His lips. Why should it? He speaks as we are able to bear His word, and this saying had to lie unexplained for many years, twenty at least, until the time came for the discovery of its hidden meaning.

It is necessary now to notice one feature common to all the passages so far quoted in this chapter. In no one of them is the presence of the Lord indispensable to the accomplishment of His purpose. It is not necessary that the Lord should return to this earth in order to raise the dead. All that He has undertaken to do He could do from heaven. The power of the voice of the Son of God is not diminished by distance. He Who at Cana could heal the son of the nobleman at Capernaum, twenty miles of hill and vale notwithstanding, could if He chose to do so, empty the graves of earth without leaving His Father's throne, (John 4:46–54).

Soon after the raising of Lazarus came the Lord's last meal with His disciples. During the conversation that followed He said to them, "I come again, and will receive you unto Myself," and in these words intimated for the first time His purpose to come in person for His own. But these words do not themselves suggest whether His promise to receive His people is to be redeemed before that glorious appearing of which He had spoken in public (Matt. 24:30, e.g.), or simultaneously with it, or subsequently to it. All this He left for a later day.

THE TEACHING OF THE APOSTLES (I)

The Lord's own teaching concerning resurrection . . . may be summarized thus. Those who refuse to acknowledge His claims to paramount authority over the lives and destinies of all men, and particularly over their own, who neglect His teaching concerning the way of life and the way of living, who pursue mean and worthless ends,[1] who refuse their rights to God and to men, these are to be raised to the judgment of the Great White Throne[2] (John 12:48; 5:29; Rev. 20:11–15).

Those who, being the gift of the Father, and having been drawn by the Father to the Son, live because they commit themselves to Him and depend upon Him,

---

1 *Phaulos*, "ill"; the same word is used in John 3:20.

2 Judgment is not equivalent to trial here; this is the ratification of the condemnation under which men lived while upon earth and from which they refused to escape when God provided a way through the Cross. See John 3:18.

who seek to render what is due to God and to men, who do the things that are good, these are to be raised to life and reward (John 6:39, 40, 44, 54; Luke 14:14; John 5:29).

It is to be observed that in neither case are these descriptions of different classes of men. The characteristics mentioned are complementary one of the other, and mark all who belong to that particular class. For those who are drawn to Christ and believe on Him, learn of Him what the Christian life is, and receive from Him power to live it. Whereas those who refuse Christ refuse with Him His counsel and His strength, and thus, by their own choice, are left to their own resources. The Christian man is so one with Christ that the Son of God has become to him at once a living Savior and a living hope.

Moreover, the Lord is Himself to come to gather His redeemed to Himself when the hour for the accomplishment of His purpose arrives. All this is to be learned from the Lord's own words, but so far as the records go, He Himself carried the revelation no further, not even after His resurrection, though His presence among the disciples under such conditions must have illuminated the word for them, as, indeed, it does for us.

The words to Martha are not included in this summary. They seem to have been left by the Lord in designed obscurity until the time became ripe to display the counsel of God that lay hidden in them.

ACTS AND THE EPISTLE OF JAMES

After the ascension of the Lord and the descent of the Holy Spirit, the apostles and the disciples carried the gospel far and wide. A selective record of their activities is provided in the "Acts of the apostles," but such references to resurrection as are found therein are either apostolic testimonies to the resurrection of Christ (4:33) addressed to the Jews (13:34) or to the Gentiles (17:31), or are restatements of the beliefs of the Pharisees (23:6), beliefs in which, as we have seen, the Lord confirmed them. But neither by Luke himself, nor by any one of the speakers whose words he reports, is the doctrine carried forward a step beyond the point at which it had been left by the Lord Jesus.

The epistle of James calls for notice next, as it may very well be the earliest of the New Testament writings. It need not detain us, however, for it does not contain any specific reference to resurrection at all, and only one to the coming of the Lord (5:7, 8) where the reader is exhorted to be patient in view of the imminence of the Parousia of the Lord, which is said to be "at hand." But neither does James supplement what had already been revealed.

THE EPISTLES OF PAUL

Next in order of time are the epistles of Paul, and of these the earliest is either that to the Galatians or those to the Thessalonians. In the former, however, there are but two references to the coming of the Lord, or perhaps three (1:4; 5:5, 21), and these are rather allusions to matters of knowledge common to the writer and to his readers, than statements of doctrine. Hence neither do they contribute anything to the end now in view.

Paul's Teaching at Thessalonica

The epistles to the Thessalonians offer a mine of wealth to the student of prophecy, and, as we shall find, carry the revelation of the manner of the fulfillment of the purpose of the Lord a considerable stage further than any utterance that preceded them. From the opening part of the first epistle we learn that during his brief stay at Thessalonica the apostle had taught the converts, "to wait for His [God's] Son from Heaven, Whom He raised from the dead, even Jesus, which delivereth us from the wrath to come" (1:10).

"'The wrath to come' is to be understood of the calamities wherewith God will visit men upon the earth when the present period of grace is closed."[1] (H-J, p. 156). The wording of the A.V., "which delivered," seems to make the reference to be to the deliverance of the believer from condemnation which Christ accomplished at the Cross. The tense is present, however, indeed the word is a title, "our Deliverer"; but the deliverance contemplated is not past but future; and it is a deliverance which can be accomplished only by one who has been raised from among the dead.

How this deliverance is to be effected the apostle does not seem to have declared, indeed there is no evidence that he himself had up to this time received any revelation on the subject. His stay among these new converts had been but brief, and in the interval between his sudden departure from their city and the writing of this letter, he had heard that some of their number had died. Not only had these losses plunged them into sorrow; they were perplexed by them, uncertain as to the consequences to their fulfillment of the promise of the Lord to come to deliver them from the threatened calamity. And this perplexity would be the greater if, as is possible, the deaths were the result of persecution. Might not that mean that they had been the victims of the very catastrophe—the Day of the Lord—from which they had been promised deliverance?

Paul's Letter to Thessalonica

Hence this letter, and particularly that section of it which begins at chapter 4, verse 13. The apostle first declares that "them also that are fallen asleep through [marg.] Jesus will God bring with Him." That is, when God "again bringeth the Firstborn into the world" (Heb. 1:6), He will also, and by the instrumentality of the person who died for them, bring with Him those who had fallen asleep. The reference is to the event to which the Lord Himself first referred at Caesarea Philippi, "the Son of God shall come in the glory of His Father with His angels" (Matt. 16:27), and of which He spoke many times thereafter. For up to the time

---

1 From a note on the passage in *The Epistles to the Thessalonians, With Notes Exegetical and Espository.* By the same Writers.

of the writing of the epistle nothing earlier than this appearing of the Lord had been revealed. (H-J, p. 156).

But how? They were dead; their bodies given over to corruption. How then can they come with the Lord when He appears in His glory? Verse 15 meets this difficulty. There is a word from the Lord to reassure them. Now this "word" is plainly not a quotation from the Old Testament; nothing like it is to be found there. Neither is it an utterance of the Lord Jesus during His ministry upon earth. Nothing resembling these words is on record in the Gospels. What the apostle is about to write to them is a freshly given revelation. The Spirit of God through him is fulfilling the promise of the Lord Jesus to His disciples, "when He, the Spirit of truth, is come, . . . He shall declare unto you the things that are to come" (John 16:13). The things that the Lord Himself refrained from saying, because the time was not ripe, nor were hearts prepared, the Holy Spirit would reveal. And in particular the words of the Lord to Martha (John 11:25, 26) that had so long waited explanation, are now made plain. When the Lord comes as described in these words, those who have believed upon Him will be divided into two classes, "we that are alive," and, "the dead in Christ." There is no statement elsewhere in Scripture that any are to be removed from the earth prior to this time. And of these two classes all are accounted for in the words "shall rise" and "shall . . . be caught away." There is no room in such an inclusive statement for another class, living or dead, to be left behind when these are taken.[1] (G-F, p. 156).

The words of the Lord correspond to those of the apostle, and the meaning of the earlier utterance is made clear by the latter. "He that believeth on Me, though he die [lit., even if he were to die] yet shall he live," stand over against "the dead in Christ shall rise first." "Whosoever liveth and believeth on Me shall never die," is explained by, "We that are alive that are left unto the Presence [marg.] of the Lord." The two classes had their typical representatives at Bethany. Lazarus, who had died, and Martha and Mary, who waited for the Lord in life. So it has been always, so must it be unto the end. And inasmuch as the time of the Lord's descent is unknown, because unrevealed, living believers describe themselves as "we that are alive, that are left."[2] Not that they are thereby guilty of the folly of asserting that the Lord will assuredly return in the lifetime of any particular believer, but because the proper attitude of Christian people is enjoined upon them by the word of the Lord: "What I say unto you I say unto all, Watch" (Mark 13:37).

THE RAPTURE

The second epistle to the Thessalonians does not advance the doctrine we are now considering. But before we leave these epistles we may notice two things. That which in the Old Testament and in the Gospels is the hope of resurrection,

---

1 See Appendix, Note C.

2 See Appendix, Note D.

becomes, from the writing of the letter to the church of the Thessalonians, the hope of resurrection and rapture. This later word, which is defined as "the act of conveying a person from one place to another," is the translation of a Greek word which is rendered "snatch" in John 10:12, 28, 29, and "caught away" in Acts 8:39. Thus the rapture of the saints, or "of the church," is an entirely Scriptural expression, and describes vividly the instantaneous removal of those who are in Christ, whether living or dead, at the word of the Returning Lord.[1]

The other matter that calls for notice is that, so far as the revelation has been carried up to this point, there is nothing to indicate that any change will pass on the bodies whether of the dead in Christ or of living believers.

THE TEACHING OF THE APOSTLES (II)

Next in chronological order is the first epistle to the Corinthians, in which the doctrine of the indwelling of the Holy Spirit in the body of the believer is enunciated for the first time in the words: "Know ye not that your body is a temple of the Holy Spirit which is in you, which ye have from God?" (6:19). This indwelling has a very important bearing on the rapture of those in whom He has taken up His abode, as we shall see a little later on.

In chapter fifteen the apostle deals with the resurrection at some length. Now whereas it is quite true that the words "resurrection of the body" do not occur in Scripture, it is also true that in Scripture the word resurrection is used exclusively of the body, never of the soul or spirit.[2]

Hence when the apostle speaks of "the resurrection of the dead," verse 42, he has in mind the bodies of the dead, for this is the subject with which he is dealing, and of course only the body dies.[3] The "it" which follows can, therefore, refer only to the body. But there is to be a change, and this is suggested in a general way in the series of contrasts that follow. This change is to be accomplished by the quickening power of "the last Adam," and its effect will be to transform the body of the believer from conformity with an earthly into conformity with a heavenly type; that is, his new, or resurrection, body will be congruous with, and fitted for, the heavenly environment to which he is destined.

Change there must be, however, for, the apostle affirms, "flesh and blood," that is, "we that are alive, that are left unto the presence of the Lord," while in that condition, "cannot inherit the Kingdom of God." And as for the dead in Christ, "neither doth corruption inherit incorruption" (v. 51). Now this is the first intimation of the necessity for such a change; no earlier word, spoken or written, suggests it. The revelation concerning the rapture and the resurrection

---

1 See Appendix, Note E.

2 Philippians 3:11 is not really an exception to this rule. An exceptional form of the word there is used, *exanastasis*, and the intention of the apostle seems to be to assert his desire to walk "in newness of life" (Rom. 6:4). *Anastasis* has also another range of meaning in the New Testament; the statement of the text refers, of course, only to those passages in which resurrection is in view.

3 See Appendix, Note F.

had exercised the minds of Christians who felt the difficulty of forming a mental picture corresponding to the apostle's words. This difficulty found expression in the question of verse 35, "How are the dead raised? With what manner of body do they come?" Nature, indeed, pointed the way to a solution of their perplexity; as far as nature could take them, therefore, they must go with nature. But nature unaided is not enough. When nature fails, God speaks.

"Behold," proceeds the apostle, "I tell you a mystery," that is, a secret, something that could not be discovered, or otherwise learned, save as God Himself is pleased to reveal it. And this mystery is, not that "we shall not all sleep," for that had already been made known in the letter to the Thessalonians, but that "we shall all be changed, in a moment, in the twinkling of an eye, at the last trump;[1] for the trumpet shall sound, and the dead shall be raised incorruptible, and we shall be changed. For this corruptible must put on incorruption, and this mortal must put on immortality.[2] But when this corruptible shall have put on incorruption, and this mortal shall have put on immortality, then shall come to pass the saying that is written, Death is swallowed up in victory," (G-F, p. 156).

"Then," but not until then, when the Lord comes, for this victory complete and final, is "through our Lord Jesus Christ," the "Life-giving Spirit," "the Son," Who "quickeneth whom He will" (v. 45; John 5:21).

THE CHRISTIAN AND DEATH

In this second letter to the Corinthians the apostle, laboring under a sense of physical weakness and of the hardships he had endured for the gospel's sake, contemplates the possibility that his bodily frame might prove unequal to the strain. That the "earthly house of this tabernacle," a temporary dwelling in any case, "should be dissolved" does not dismay one the assurance of resurrection; "knowing that he who raised up the Lord Jesus shall raise up us also with Jesus, and shall present us with you" (2 Cor. 4:14; 5:1).

In contrast with 1 Thessalonians 4:15, where he associates himself with those who are to be alive and upon the earth when the Lord descends to meet them in the air, he here associates himself with those who will have already fallen asleep, and who will, therefore, be no longer among the mortal but among the corruptible, before that event takes place. That he is not in either place forecasting what he believes to be in store for himself or for his contemporaries seems sufficiently clear. Nowhere in his writings does the apostle commit himself to the belief that the Lord would return in his lifetime.[3] He does not foreclose the possibility however; rather he is ready for it, and hails it with joy, and would have all Christians rejoice with him. He who a few sentences earlier had spoken of his confident hope of resurrection, here declares that in this body "we groan, long-

---

1 See Appendix, Note G.

2 See Appendix, Note H.

3 See Appendix, Note D.

ing to be clothed upon with our habitation which is from heaven . . . that what is mortal may be swallowed up of life" (5:2–4). That is, as he had already expressed it, that "this mortal" might "put on immortality" (1 Cor. 15:53).

However deeply he may have been impressed by the possibility of death bringing his service to an end, his ardent desire was that the Lord might come to call him to the meeting in the air. Not that he feared death; should that be the will of God for him, he can look death steadily in the face, for he had learned to say "O death, where is thy victory? O death, where is thy sting?" So now he declares that he is "always of good courage" in view of the possibility of the separation of the spirit from the body; and reiterates it with emphasis; "we" (it is normal Christian privilege and should be normal Christian experience) "we are of good courage, I say, and are willing rather to be absent from the body, and to be at home with the Lord." For death itself, enemy as it most surely is, but ushers the Christian into the presence of his Lord.

THE RESURRECTION AND THE ETERNAL HOUSE

The fifteenth chapter of the first epistle to the Corinthians, and the earlier part of the fifth chapter of the second, are not contradictory but complementary the one of the other. The first establishes the continuity of the spiritual with the natural body, "it is sown . . . it is raised." The second establishes the suitability of the changed body to the new conditions for which it is destined, "a building from God, a house not made with hands, eternal, in the heavens." The words change and resurrection imply this continuity, indeed, but that does not mean that the body which is to be is identical, as to the particles of matter of which it composed, with the body that is now. "That which thou sowest, thou sowest not the body that shall be . . . so also is the resurrection of the dead" (1 Cor. 15:37, 42).

And yet when wheat is sown so also is that which is reaped wheat; but not that particular grain of wheat which was dropped into the earth. In this characteristic of nature the apostle finds an analogy with the body in death and resurrection. The illustration must not be pressed too far. From one grain of wheat an abundance is raised. That is the glory of the grain; it died and, because it dies, does not abide alone. The glory of the resurrection body is different; sown in corruption, dishonor, and weakness, it is raised in incorruption, glory, and power.

"WHAT MANNER OF BODY?"

It is easy to go beyond what is written here. The apostle John warns us that it is not yet made manifest what we shall be (1 John 3:2), and the language of Paul implies as much. Where Scripture is reticent we may not attempt to be explicit. The identity of the body does not depend at all on the identity of the particles that compose it, for these come and go from moment to moment. So long as the body lives it is in a state of flux, receiving new supplies of material from food and air to replace what has become effete and waste. The body of the man is the body of the child developed; throughout life it is looked upon as the same body, and is called without qualification "my body." Nevertheless there is no particle of matter that has remained in that body during its growth from childhood to manhood.

The scar remains in the body through all the years of a man's life, though the actual particles of matter that sustained the injury have long since passed away from it. So with the resurrection of the dead. "With what manner of body do they come?" Each in his own, given him by God, though no particle therein should have had a place in that which clothed the spirit here. The body is not less the same on that account, any more than the body of the man is a different body from that of the child because of the exchange of matter particles in the process of nutrition, growth and repair.

THE INDWELLING SPIRIT

It has been noticed already that the earliest mention of the indwelling of the body of the believer by the Holy Spirit is found in the epistle that deals at length with the resurrection of that body. In 2 Corinthians there are two references to this indwelling, one in chapter 1, verse 22 ". . . God; Who also sealed us, and gave us the earnest of the Spirit in our hearts," the other in chapter 5, verse 5, "Now He that wrought us for this very thing [the change from mortality to immortality] is God, Who gave unto us the earnest of the Spirit." This it is, the apostle proceeds, that gives the believer courage in the face of death, for the indwelling of the Spirit is also God's pledge, or earnest, that they who die and whose bodies see corruption shall be raised from death in bodies incorruptible.

At the close of the argument of the seventh chapter of the epistle to the Romans, which follows 2 Corinthians in order of time, the apostle described the present habitation of the spirit of the believer as "the body of this death," words which by themselves might be taken to countenance the pagan doctrine of the inherent evil of matter, verse 24. Against this misconception, however, he shortly provides. In chapter 8, verse 11, he calls it, as in the letter to the Corinthians, the mortal body or body capable of, and liable to, death. And in harmony with the teaching of his earlier letters he declares that this mortal body is to be quickened,[1] it is to be "swallowed up of life." The quickener is God, "Him that raised up Jesus from the dead," and the ground on which it is to be quickened is that here and now it is already the dwelling place of the Holy Spirit, "because of His Spirit that dwelleth in you," according to the well supported reading of the margin.[2]

In 1 Corinthians chapter 6, verse 19, the mention of the indwelling of the Holy Spirit has an immediately practical end in view. The body in which He has taken up His abode must itself be kept holy. But has the body that is thus honored no other future than to be discarded as an irreclaimably evil thing? This wrong

---

1 See Appendix, Note J.

2 The Holy Spirit is not said to have raised the Lord Jesus. Neither is He elsewhere said to raise the believer. It is unlikely that this passage is an exception to the rule.

deduction is promptly repudiated; since it is a temple of the Spirit of God it also has a glorious future, "body of death" though it be.

REDEMPTION, PAST AND FUTURE

The argument is repeated in verse 23. "We which have the firstfruits of the Spirit, even we ourselves groan within ourselves, waiting for our adoption, to wit, the redemption of our body." Redemption has a double use in the New Testament. In one series of passages it refers to the Cross, where the price was paid, as in Ephesians chapter 1, verse 7; in the other it refers to the coming of the Lord when He will take possession of that which He purchased. (E-G, p. 156). "This body of death" has been redeemed from its bondage, and when He comes it will be delivered into the glorious liberty, which is the inheritance secured for it by the offering of the body of Jesus Christ once for all, and which is assured to us by the grace of the Spirit in taking up His abode therein (Heb. 10:10).

In one of his later letters the apostle again brings the two things into the same relationship. "Having . . . believed, ye were sealed with the Holy Spirit of promise, which is an earnest of our inheritance, unto the redemption of God's own possession" (Eph. 1:14; see also 4:30). When the man turned to God in Christ, then He was sealed for God (the mark of finality and security) to be His forever, and the Spirit came to make His abode in the body of the man, to be an earnest of the purpose of God that that body, being the peculiar property of God in virtue of the redemptive act of the Cross, should, at the coming of the Lord, be to the praise of the glory of God, exhibiting His power to redeem what is mortal and corruptible from the power of death and the grave. Thus the body in which the power of sin, both in life and in death, is now so abundantly manifested, that it is even called "this body of death," becomes "God's own possession." In it the salvation of God is made evident, both in life and in death, whereof the Holy Spirit who dwells therein is the power and the pledge.

CONFORMITY TO THE TYPE, CHRIST

Reverting to Romans 8, in a verse intermediate between those on which we have already dwelt, verses 11 and 23, namely, verse 19, a hint is given of the climax of the revelation concerning the resurrection and rapture of the Christian. "The earnest expectation of the creation waiteth for the revealing of the sons of God." The reference to "the sons of God," where "the Son of God" might have been expected, is somewhat surprising. Later the apostle explains, "whom He foreknew, He also foreordained to be conformed to the image of His Son, that He might be the Firstborn among many brethren," verse 29. In 1 Corinthians chapter fifteen, verses 47–49, there is a similar hint, but, as might be anticipated from the analogy of the progressive method of the revelation, a slighter hint. And in what was probably his last communication to any church, so far as these have been preserved, the purpose of God in this regard is categorically stated. "Our citizenship is in heaven; from whence also we wait for a Savior, the Lord Jesus

Christ; Who shall fashion anew the body of our humiliation, that it may be conformed to the body of His glory" (Phil. 3:20, 21). Thus the inevitable question is answered. To be changed—but into what likeness? Into the likeness of our Lord, and this not morally only; the body spiritual which is to replace the body natural, is to bear the image of that in which He showed Himself in the Mount of Transfiguration, and in which He appeared to John in Patmos, and in which He will yet appear when He comes to establish the rule of God upon the earth.

And by whom and by what power is this to be accomplished? The words of the Lord were "I will raise him up at the Last Day"; "all that are in the tombs shall hear His voice [the voice of the Son of God] and shall come forth"; and "I come again and will receive you unto Myself." It is both "by means of Jesus" and "with Him" that God will bring the dead in Christ, when He comes to reign. Christ Himself it is, then, Who is to "fashion anew" this body of sin and of pain "according to the working whereby He is able to subject all things unto Himself."[1]

THE LIMITS OF REVELATION

So far Scripture carries us. Not every question is answered. There remain many things impossible to say or to hear now. Impossible for God to say, for earth has no language wherein to describe these heavenly things. Impossible for us to hear, for as yet we have had no experience to enable us to bridge the gulf, to pierce the veil, that separates the material from the spiritual world. And this the apostle John asserts when he writes that "it is not yet made manifest what we shall be." But if, in the meantime, satisfaction is denied to the intellect, there remains at least comfort for the heart, for, "we know that, if He shall be manifested, we shall be like Him" (1 John 3:2). It is enough for the disciple that he be as his teacher, for the servant that he be as his Lord. Than this he cherishes no higher ambition. And this ambition will be realized to the full "when we shall see Him even as He is."

THE PAROUSIA OF THE LORD

His words were unequivocal; their directness and simplicity forbid their being explained away by a spiritualizing interpretation. He was going from them in bodily presence; in bodily presence He would return and receive them to Himself. Jesus explained many times to the disciples regarding His departure and "soon return"; here these events are highlighted, along with the distinctions between the rapture and the Day of the Lord.

"The midnight is past, the bright Star of the Morn
    Soon shall appear;
Soon the last briar, soon the last thorn,
    Soon the last tear.

---

1 Such power is essentially diving. No higher power is conceivable. Nor is it conceivable that He Who wields this power should Himself be other than God.

Heavenly Lover, come quickly! O come!
No longer Thy blood-bought this desert would roam;
The soul-stirring shout that shall gather them home
They are waiting to hear."
From *The Story of the Glory*—Boyd

Our Lord's discourse to His disciples on the night of His betrayal was calculated not only to comfort them in the sorrows they would experience after His departure, and to strengthen them to endure trial and opposition, but also, while conforming their faith in Himself during His absence from them, to direct their hearts to the prospect of His return. Spiritually present with all His followers throughout the age then about to commence, He would eventually return, but not merely in the spiritual sense. "I go," He said, "to prepare a place for you. And If I go and prepare a place for you, I come again, and will receive you unto Myself; that where I am, there ye may be also"; and further, "A little while and ye behold Me no more, and again a little while, and ye shall see me" (John 14:2, 3; 16:16). Such language could not indicate a spiritual coming. His words were unequivocal; their directness and simplicity forbid their being explained away by a spiritualizing interpretation. He was going from them in bodily presence; in bodily presence He would return and receive them to Himself. In His resurrection body "He showed Himself alive after His passion . . . appearing unto them . . . and assembling with them." No phantom form rose from their midst at His ascension. With that same tangible body "He was taken up," and thereupon His promise was renewed by the assurance given by the heavenly messengers, "This Jesus, which was received up from you into heaven, shall so come in like manner as ye beheld Him going into heaven" (Acts 1:3, 11). (H-J, p. 156).

AN EVENT YET FUTURE

Albeit nineteen centuries have elapsed, His promised advent has not yet taken place. The end of the age throughout which He assured His followers of His spiritual presence with them has not yet come. The descent of the Holy Spirit at pentecost was not the "Second Advent," nor has the promise of His return been fulfilled either in the spiritual experiences of believers or at their departure to be with Him at their decease. All such ideas are precluded at once by the words of the apostle Paul, that "the Lord Himself shall descend from heaven with a shout, with the voice of the archangel, and with the trump of God: and the dead in Christ shall rise first: then we that are alive, that are left, shall together with them be caught up in the clouds, to meet the Lord in the air: and so shall we ever be with the Lord" (1 Thess. 4:16, 17). Clearly no spiritual advent is signified here. Nor has this prediction had its fulfillment on any occasion in past history. For the object of the descent herein stated is nothing less than the instantaneous removal of the completed Church by the Lord in person. Christians still fall asleep and await resurrection, and thousands await the day of rapture. (E-G, p. 156).

Equally clear is the statement of the apostle in his first epistle to the Corinthians: "We shall not all sleep, but we shall all be changed, in a moment, in the twinkling of an eye, at the last trump: for the trumpet shall sound, and the dead shall be raised incorruptible, and we shall be changed. For this corruptible must put on incorruption, and this mortal must put on immortality" (1 Cor. 15:51–53). The same event is described as in 1 Thessalonians 4, the effect of the resurrection being, however, chiefly in view here, while there the action of the Lord is prominent.

THE MEANING OF "PAROUSIA"

The resurrection and rapture of the saints foretold in these passages constitute the initial event of what the New Testament calls "the Parousia of the Lord." Paul uses the word in the passage in 1 Thessalonians just referred to. "For if," he says, "we believe that Jesus died and rose again, even so them also that are fallen asleep in [marg. through] Jesus will God bring with Him. For this we say unto you by the word of the Lord, that we that are alive, that are left unto the coming [the parousia] of the Lord, shall in no wise precede them that are fallen asleep" (1 Thess. 4:14, 15). (F-H, p. 156).

Now the word "parousia" is a transliteration of the Greek word which is frequently rendered "coming," a rendering which, however, is quite inadequate. "Coming" is, indeed, misleading, and responsible for considerable misunderstanding and variety of judgment. There is indeed no single English term which exactly fits the meaning. Hence the value of the addition to our vocabulary of the transliterated word. "Parousia" literally signifies "a being with," "a presence." Not infrequently it is so rendered. It thus denotes a state, not an action. We never read of a parousia *to*, always of a parousia *with*. Paul tells the Philippian converts of his confidence that he will be with them "for their progress and joy in the faith, that their glorying may abound in Christ Jesus in him through his presence, his parousia, with them again." Further, he exhorts them as they have been obedient during his presence, his parousia, so much more in his absence, his apousia, to work out their own salvation with fear and trembling (Phil. 1:26; 2:12). In a Greek document of almost the same period as that in which the New Testament was written, a person states that attention to her property necessitates her parousia in a certain city. These examples suffice to show that, while of course the initial act of arrival is essential to a parousia, the word signifies the more or less prolonged period following the arrival.[1]

---

1 Cremer, *Biblico-Theological Lexicon of New Testament Greek*, p. 238, says, "It is only . . . without giving the word its full force, that we can apply the name of *parousia* to the second advent. It is not easy to explain how the term came to be used in this sense." The difficulty is removed when it is recognized that *parousia* is always in Scripture used in its primary sense ("a being present, presence," Liddell & Scott), and that it is never an alternative name for what ordinarily is called the Second Advent, that is, "the Appearing of the Glory of our great God and Savior Jesus Christ." In each case of its occurrence with reference to the Lord the margin of the Revised Version has "Gk., presence." This is not an alternative rendering to that given in the text, but the

We take a further example from the New Testament to show that several passages where the word is rendered "coming" receive their true explanation only when the extended period just pointed out has its due consideration. Thus when Peter says, "We made known unto you the power and coming [parousia] of the Lord Jesus Christ . . . we were eyewitnesses of His Majesty" (2 Pet. 1:16), he is referring, not to a sudden and momentary manifestation of the Lord, nor to His future advent, but to the period of His transfiguration before the disciples. "For," says the apostle, "He received from God the Father honor and glory, when there came such a voice to Him from the excellent glory, This is My beloved Son, in whom I am well pleased; and this voice we ourselves heard come out of heaven, when we were with Him in the holy mount" (vv. 17, 18). The power and glory of the Lord's Parousia in the Mount of Transfiguration were no doubt anticipative of His future Parousia with His saints, but the passage refers directly to the past, not to the future. The importance of the word in this passage, however, lies not only in the illustration it gives of the meaning "presence" rather than "coming," but in its indication of a set period of time marked by well defined limits. This has a special bearing upon an aspect of the Lord's Second Coming, which calls for subsequent consideration.

THE TEACHING OF 1 THESSALONIANS

In writing to the Thessalonians Paul makes constant use of the term in a way which makes it impossible to view it as applicable merely to the moment of the Lord's descent into the air. Speaking regretfully of his enforced absence from them, and looking forward joyfully to the certainty of reunion, when Satan's hindrances will be things of the past, and the Lord shall have gathered His people to Himself, he says, "For what is our hope, or joy, or crown of glorying? Are not even ye, before our Lord Jesus at [lit., in] His parousia? For ye are our glory and our joy" (1 Thess. 2:19, 20). Obviously the apostle is thinking of the time and circumstances immediately following upon the rapture of the saints rather than the moment of the rapture itself. The fruit of his service on behalf of the converts would then be seen, both in their presence before the Lord and in the praise and reward they would receive from Him at His Judgment Seat. That would provide abundant compensation for all the trials and afflictions experienced in his labors in the gospel. The converts themselves constituted his hope, which would attain its realization at the time of review; they were also his joy, a present joy, to be consummated at that time; they were his crown of glorying, ample reward to him

---

literal meaning of the word. It is to be regretted that "presence" does not appear in the text in its twenty-four occurrences.

Cremer quotes some suggestive words from Ewald to the effect that the Parousia of Christ corresponds perfectly with the Shekinah of God in the Old Testament. For him also the doctrine of the Coming of Christ is obscured because the word should regulate the theology, and not the theology prescribe the meaning of the word. Yet the neglect of the simple law of exegesis is responsible for some at least of the confusion into which the Hope of the Gospel has been thrown in the minds of many Christians.

for the fulfillment of the work committed to him, apart from the crown he would himself receive at the hands of the prize-giver. (F-H, p. 156).

Referring again to the same period, he says, "The Lord make you to increase and abound in love one toward another, and toward all men, even as we also do toward you; to the end He may stablish your hearts unblameable in holiness before our God and Father, at [lit., in] the coming [the parousia] of our Lord Jesus with all His Saints" (3:13). The word "coming" is clearly unsuitable here. It makes the verse appear to indicate the Advent of the Lord with His saints. That will take place at the close of the Parousia; at its commencement He will come for them, and it is to the circumstances of that intervening period itself that the apostle directs our thought in this passage.

His desire for the converts was that their Christian character might be so developed and perfected in this life that at the Judgment Seat in the Lord's Parousia they might stand clear of every possible charge against them. The substitution of "Parousia" for "coming" sets the passage in its true light, and is appropriate to the words which follow. We may observe here that the Parousia is to be with "all the saints"; no saint will be absent, none will have been left behind at the Rapture.

The Parousia period is again in view at the end of this first epistle, where the apostle, as a climax to a series of closing exhortations, expresses wishes for the converts similar to that which we have just been considering, and desires "that the God of peace Himself may sanctify them wholly, and that their whole spirit and soul and body may be preserved entire without blame at [lit., in] the Parousia of our Lord Jesus Christ" (v. 23). They were saints, or sanctified ones, by virtue of their calling. To this he desired that their daily life might correspond, so that, practically devoted to God and kept by His power in every part of their being, they might be found free of blame in the presence of the Lord when their works would be reviewed by Him.

THE TEACHING OF THE APOSTLE JOHN

In anticipation of that time, the apostle John manifests the same jealous care of the spiritual well-being of the subjects of his past labors. "And now, my little children," he says, "abide in Him; that, if He shall be manifested, we may have boldness, and not be ashamed before Him at [or rather in] His parousia" (1 John 2:28). Again the issues of the present life are in view as they will be seen at the Judgment Seat of Christ. That in the words "if He shall be manifested" the apostle is referring to the Lord's coming for His Church is obvious from the succeeding context, where, using the same phrase, he says, "We know that if He shall be manifested, we shall be like Him; for we shall see Him even as He is." The hypothesis is no expression of doubt as to whether the Lord will be manifested; it conveys a warning to the saints to keep in prospect the possibility of the event at any time. The manifestation of the Lord to His saints, and their rapture by Him will be simultaneous. (E-G, p. 156).

The aspirations expressed in the close of the verse go beyond that initial event of the Parousia to the circumstances of the Judgment Seat of Christ. He desires that at that time both he who has cared for the converts to whom he was writing, and they who have been the objects of his care, may have boldness and not be ashamed before the Lord. That would depend upon their present spiritual condition. Would they abide in Christ, and "let that abide in them which they had heard from the beginning"? Or would they backslide and give heed to those who were seeking to lead them astray? By this would be determined their gain or loss of reward in the Parousia. Nor would the issue affect them alone; John who himself had shepherded them was interested in the consequences. The fruit of pastoral care seen in the steadfastness of the believers would lead to joy and boldness in that solemn scene; on their part in the reward bestowed upon them, on the apostle's part in the realization that his labor had not been in vain. On the other hand, faithlessness would lead to shame, through their failure to obtain a reward.

Thus the apostle is not cautioning them against a possibility that when the Lord comes they will shrink back from Him in shame on account of failure, and be left to remain on earth while others who have been faithful are taken away. The scene is heavenly, and the circumstances are those of the Judgment Seat of Christ. The teaching of John is in entire harmony with that of Paul in the passages considered above.

The apostle Peter also, in exhorting elders to a faithful discharge of their pastoral responsibilities toward the flock of God, similarly refers to the manifestation of Christ as the terminus of such service, and points them to the immediately succeeding time of reward for it. "Tend," he says, "the flock of God which is among you, exercising the oversight, not of constraint, but willingly, according unto God; nor yet for filthy lucre, but of a ready mind; neither as lording it over the charge allotted to you, but making yourselves ensamples to the flock. And when the Chief Shepherd shall be manifested, ye shall receive the crown of glory that fadeth not away" (1 Pet. 5:2–4). The manifestation of Christ for the removal of His saints from the earth is thus, in this passage also, shown to be the preliminary to His review of their earthly service when they stand before his Judgment Seat.

OTHER DESCRIPTIONS OF THE SAME PERIOD

The Parousia, then, is not a momentary event, but a period during which Christ will be present with His saints after coming into the air to receive them to Himself, and will test their works as His servants with a view to rewarding them. The period is otherwise described by the following expressions, "the day of Christ" (Phil. 1:10; 2:16), "the day of Jesus Christ" (Phil. 1:6), "the day of the Lord Jesus" (1 Cor. 5:5; 2 Cor. 1:14), and "the day of our Lord Jesus Christ" (1 Cor. 1:8). It will be observed that in each of these designations one or both of the titles "Jesus" and "Christ" is used, and an examination of the passages will show that the reference is in each case to the time of the Parousia, and that this group of expressions is to be distinguished from "the day of the Lord," which latter refers to a period of an entirely different character. We will take the passages in the epistle to the Philippians first.

In recording his joy in the constant fellowship of the Philippian converts in the furtherance of the gospel, Paul asserts his confidence that "God who began a good work in them would perfect it until the day of Jesus Christ" (Phil. 1:6). That is to say, that through the power of God their steadfastness would continue throughout the time of their earthly service so that all would be estimated at its true value by Christ in the day when they would appear before Him at His Judgment Seat. Again, as he had prayed for the Thessalonian converts in view of the Parousia, that they might walk in love and be found blameless at that time, so now he prays for those at Philippi, "that their love may abound yet more and more in knowledge and all discernment; so that they may approve the things that are excellent; and be sincere and void of offense, until the day of Christ" (1:9, 10), a clear identification of that period with the Parousia. Similarly, as he regarded the Thessalonians as his hope and joy and crown of glorying before the Lord in His Parousia, seeing that their faithfulness and steadfastness were the fruit of his labor, so now he exhorts the Philippians "that they may be blameless and harmless and shine as lights in the world, holding forth the Word of life; that he may have whereof to glory in the day of Christ, that he did not run in vain, nor labor in vain" (2:15, 16). Thus, once more, the thought and language concerning that day are identical with those concerning the Parousia.

So at the outset of his epistle to the church at Corinth he expresses the assurance that the Lord will confirm them unto the end, that is, the end of their course on earth, so that they may be "unreproveable in the day of our Lord Jesus Christ," and reminds them of the faithfulness of God to undertake this confirmation, since He had called them into the fellowship of His Son (1 Cor. 1:8, 9). Parallel, again, with the sentiments in the other epistles above referred to is the expression, in the second epistle to the Corinthians, of his joy in the converts in prospect of that day. "We are your glorying," he says, "even as ye also are ours, in the day of our Lord Jesus" (2 Cor. 1:14).

The addition of the first clause of this verse is an appeal against the efforts and influence of the enemies who were seeking to depreciate the apostle's character and service in the eyes of the Corinthian church, and thus to undermine his work. Had he not brought the gospel to them? Were not the blessings they had received due to his ministry? Not only would they be his joy in the coming day as the fruit of his toil, but they would then rejoice in seeing him rewarded for his faithful service and testimony on their behalf.

Again, in giving instruction as to the discipline of one who was guilty of moral obliquity the apostle views the circumstances in the light of the same period of judgment. Discipline was necessary not only for the present welfare of the church, but for the ultimate benefit of the erring individual. He was "to be delivered unto Satan for the destruction of the flesh, that the spirit might be saved in the day of the Lord Jesus" (1 Cor. 5:5). The word "day" is constantly associated with judgment, inasmuch as the day, in contrast with the night, reveals things in their true character. Thus Paul says concerning his own service, "With me it is a very small thing that I should be judged of you, or of man's judgment [lit., man's day]: yea, I judge not mine own self. For I know nothing against myself; yet I am not hereby justified: but he that judgeth me is the Lord. Wherefore judge nothing before, until the Lord come, who will both bring to light the hidden things of darkness, and make manifest the counsels of the hearts; and then shall each man have his praise from God" (1 Cor. 4:3–5).

Man's day is the time when man passes judgment on things. The day of our Lord Jesus Christ will be the time when He will pass judgment on the service of His saints. "Each man's work shall be made manifest; for, the day shall declare it [i.e., the day in which Christ judges the work will manifest its real character] because it is revealed in fire; and the fire itself shall prove each man's work of what sort it is. If any man's work shall abide which he built thereon, he shall receive a reward. If any man's work shall be burned, he shall suffer loss; but he himself shall be saved; yet so as through fire" (3:13–15).

THE DAY OF THE LORD—A DISTINCTION

Clearly, all these passages refer to the time and circumstances of the Parousia of Christ with His saints. On the other hand, "the Day of the Lord" is never used in reference to these events; it relates always to the Lord's judgment on the world and His personal intervention in its affairs, a subject which calls for more detailed consideration in another chapter.

In this connection, however, it is important to observe the correct reading of 2 Thessalonians 2:2, where the Revised Version rightly gives "the Day of the Lord" instead of "the Day of Christ" as in the Authorized Version. As the passage is connected with the Parousia we must consider it somewhat closely.

In the first chapter Paul had spoken of the future revelation of the Lord Jesus from heaven, "with the angels of His power in flaming fire, rendering vengeance to them that know not God, and to them that obey not the gospel of our Lord Jesus." At that time His saints, having been with Him in His Parousia, will accompany Him in manifested glory; "He shall come to be glorified in His saints, and to be marveled at in all them that believed" (2 Thess. 1:7–10). "When Christ . . . shall be manifested, then shall ye also with Him be manifested in glory" (Col. 3:4). The divine vengeance then rendered will usher in the Day of the Lord, and the apostle speaks of it in order to prepare for correcting a wrong impression entertained by the Thessalonian converts concerning that day. They were being told that the Day of the Lord had begun already, and their minds were consequently disturbed in relation to the Rapture and the Parousia. Paul had himself written to them that Christ would come and gather to Himself in resurrection power both their departed who had fallen asleep and the living together with them, and that certain events were destined to take place in the world prior to the beginning of the Day of the Lord. If, then, the latter had already set in, they might well be perplexed and troubled concerning His promised coming to receive them unto Himself.

Accordingly he must write again to correct their ideas concerning both events, and show the distinction between the Parousia and the Day of the Lord. In reminding them of the conditions which were inevitably to exist in the world ere that day begins, he would at the same time be regulating their view regarding the Parousia. This he does at the commencement of chapter two, as follows:

"Now we beseech you, brethren, touching [the Greek preposition, *huper*, is, lit., on behalf of, i.e., with a view to correcting your thoughts about] the coming [the parousia] of our Lord Jesus Christ, and our gathering together unto Him [i.e., at the rapture of the saints, as mentioned in 1 Thess. 4:17]; to the end that ye be not quickly shaken from your mind [i.e., become unsettled in your convictions and the steadfast purposes consequent upon them], nor yet be troubled, either by spirit, or by word, or by epistle as from us [i.e., a letter purporting to be from Paul], as that the Day of the Lord is now present [i.e., has already commenced]: let no man beguile you in any wise: for it will not be [i.e., the Day of the Lord will not set in] except the falling away [the apostasy from God and His truth] come first, and the man of sin be revealed."

Thus an understanding of the conditions which must necessarily precede the Day of the Lord would set their mind at rest concerning the Parousia. The apostle shows them that the man of sin is to be overthrown by the Lord "at the manifestation of His coming" (v. 8). Literally the phrase is "at the epiphany of His Parousia" or "the shining forth of His Presence." This event coincides with "the revelation of the Lord Jesus" mentioned in 1:7, and marks the close of the Parousia. (H-J, p. 156).

THE PAROUSIA REVIEWED

Briefly summing up, the Parousia is a period which will commence with the coming of Christ into the air to raise the dead saints, change the living, and receive all together to Himself. They will render an account of their stewardship at His Judgment Seat, receiving rewards or suffering loss according to the measure of their faithfulness. The time of the duration of the Parousia is not definitely intimated in Scripture. Heavenly in its character it stands in contrast to circumstances in the world, which, after the removal of the church, will come under the judgments of God. At the conclusion of the Parousia the Lord will come with His angels and with His saints in manifested glory for the overthrow of His foes, an event which is described as "the manifestation of His Parousia."[1]

---

1 The beginning of the Parousia of Christ is prominent in 1 Corinthians 15:23; 1 Thessalonians 4:15; 5:23; 2 Thessalonians 2:1; James 5:7, 8; and 2 Peter 3:4; its course in 1 Thessalonians 2:19; 3:13; Matthew 24:3, 37, 39; and 1 John 2:28; its conclusion in Matthew 24:27; and 2 Thessalonians 2:8. From the Writer's *Notes on the Thessalonians*.

THE JUDGMENT SEAT OF CHRIST

*The Judgment Seat of Christ is for believers. Everyone who stands before it
is there because they had become the children of God through faith in Christ
Jesus, because they had been redeemed through His blood, and had received
the forgiveness of their sins. The purpose of this judgment is to reward each
one's conduct. This takes the fear and misunderstanding out of this needed
task of God.*

The period . . . described in the New Testament as the Parousia, and the day of
Christ, are of peculiar interest to the Christian, for in it his course of life is to be
reviewed in order that he may be rewarded for all that he has done and suffered
during the time of his responsibility in the world. Now this judgment is to be
distinguished sharply from the judgment of the nations described in Matthew
25:31–46, for that is to take place after the appearing of the Lord in glory, and its
venue is the earth, whereas the judgment of which we now speak takes place "in
the air" and between the Rapture and the Second Advent. At the former some are
pronounced accursed and dismissed to eternal punishment, whereas at the latter
no such condemnation is possible, as the conditions under which it is to be held
plainly show. On the other hand, it is to be distinguished with equal clearness
from the judgment of the Great White Throne, which takes place after the final
catastrophe has overtaken Satan and his hosts at the close of the Millennium
(Rev. 20:11–15). The terms in which these three judgments are described preclude any possibility of confusing them. It is essential, however, that the different
writers must be allowed to know what they meant to say, and to have said what
they meant. It is too readily assumed that meaning one thing they said another,
or that, however differently they describe it, yet they all, and always, refer to the
same general judgment. The Scriptures certainly cannot be made to mean that
the world is rushing on to a final conflagration, to be followed by a universal
assize. The words in which the Holy Spirit has spoken are not responsible for the
widespread confusion of mind on the subject. Rather is that the result of careless
reading, or of failure to credit the writers of Scripture with ordinary intelligence
and honesty.

There are several passages in which the Judgment Seat of Christ is described;
the principle of these now fall to be considered.

The word, translated, Judgment Seat is *bēma* whereas the word used in each
of the other cases (Matt. 25:31; Rev. 20:11) is *thronos*, the English word throne.
This latter word is reserved in the New Testament for the symbol of authority in
the heavenlies, whether good or evil, including that of God Himself. The only
exception to this rule is the throne of David (Luke 1:32), which is referred to,
significantly enough, only in a prophecy concerning the rule over Israel of "great
David's greater Son." Even the throne of Imperial Caesar is called a *bēma*, as is
that before which the Lord Jesus was condemned to death by Pilate (Acts 18:12;
John 19:13). It will be seen, therefore, that the word lacks nothing in dignity

as a symbol of competent authority. Its associations are of the most impressive character. Solemn, indeed, must be the issues involved for all who stand before a tribunal so entitled.

The time of the Judgment Seat of Christ is to be learned from the language of the Lord, recorded in Luke 14:14, "thou shalt be recompensed in the resurrection of the just."

This Judgment Seat is twice named, once as "of God," and once as "of Christ" (Rom. 14:10; 2 Cor. 5:10). These are not two but one, however, for "neither doth the Father judge any man, but He hath given all judgment unto the Son; that all may honor the Son even as they honor the Father.... And He gave Him authority to execute judgment because He is [the] Son of Man" (John 5:22, 23, 27). That there is but one judge is also plain from 1 Corinthians 4:5, "judge nothing before the time, until the Lord come, Who will both bring to light the hidden things of darkness, and make manifest the counsels of the hearts; and then shall each man have his praise from God." The reference to His coming makes it evident that by Lord the apostle here means the Lord Jesus, while the praise is said to come from God. The words of the apostle are thus in harmony with those of the Lord Himself.

CHRISTIANS ALONE TO STAND THEREAT

As to the persons who are to come before this Judgment Seat many Scriptures testify. The passage in the first epistle to the Corinthians (3:10–4:5) contemplates the Christians at Corinth: "ye are Christ's," says the apostle, "ye are a temple of God." They had been built upon, and were themselves builders upon, the foundation, the Lord Jesus Christ. The passage in Romans 14:1–12 is equally explicit. A man might be weak in faith, indeed, but that is a description which can be true only of one who is in Christ. God has received him; he is the servant of God. These are brethren sinning against brethren, but still they "are the Lord's." The other leading Scripture (2 Cor. 5:1–10), also contemplates Christians, and like the others, Christians alone. "The Church of God ... with all the saints" is addressed (1:1). Sometimes the apostle speaks to them directly, "you," "your," as in 4:14, 15, for example; sometimes he associates them with himself, as in each of the verses from 1 to 9 of chapter 5. The conclusion is hardly to be resisted that in verse 10 also, "we" refers to Christians, and to Christians alone. There is no hint that the writer enlarges the scope of his address as he passes from one statement to another. The "we" who walk by faith, not by sight, who make it their ambition to be well-pleasing to God, who have received God's Spirit, who hope for the coming of the Lord, and who are yet of good courage in the face of death, are the "we" who "must all be made manifest before the Judgment Seat of Christ."

This follows also from the fact that this judgment takes place during the Parousia, and there is nothing said concerning others than Christians in connection with that. None save those who belong to Christ, living or dead, share in the Rapture that will usher us into the presence of the Lord when He descends into the air.

One other thing . . . must here be remembered. When Christians are taken away to be with the Lord Jesus they will be changed, "the body of our humiliation" will be "conformed to the body of His glory" (Phil. 3:20). It is clear, then, that the judgment with which we are now dealing is not concerned with the innocence or guilt of those who appear thereat. The matter of sin and salvation was, for them, settled long ago. At the Judgment Seat of Christ no question is raised of their right to share in the salvation which brings them into the Parousia. They are there because they had become the children of God through faith in Christ Jesus; because they had been redeemed through His blood, and had received the forgiveness of their sins. The purpose of this judgment is in another direction altogether. What that purpose is we may learn from a brief consideration of the Scriptures already mentioned.

SALVATION AND JUDGMENT

The broad principle underlying all God's dealings with men is, that salvation is always by grace, that judgment is always according to works. To this rule there is no exception. No one ever was saved, no one ever will be saved, because he deserves salvation. No one ever will be condemned save because the character of his ways demanded that he should be punished. No one will ever be rewarded save as in his ways and acts the reward has been earned. These are the right ways of God; their justice is beyond dispute.[1]

The apostle had heard tidings from Corinth that called for firm yet affectionate dealing with those whom he rightly regarded as his children in the gospel. He had laid the foundation of the church there and that foundation was Christ. Now they were building upon that foundation. What manner of building would it be? He does not seem to be addressing any particular class in the church. All are builders, each in his measure is adding something to the structure; it might be "gold, silver, costly stones," but then it might be "wood, hay, stubble." One or the other they must be building into it. No person can be a member of a church without modifying its character, in a good way or in a bad; without adding to its fabric either noble and worthy things or things mean and worthless. Let each person (not the men only, for no noun is expressed) "take heed how he buildeth." Why? Because "each man's [person's] work shall be made manifest: for the day shall declare it." That is, the day of Christ, as we have already seen. For worthy work there is a reward, for He has said, "Behold, I come quickly; and My reward is with Me, to render to each man [person] according as his work is" (Rev. 22:12). If, on the other hand, the building has been of a mean, unworthy character, then that person shall "suffer loss," though "he himself shall be saved [shall be caught away at the Rapture] yet so as through fire." The possibility is thus presented to

---

1 *Misthos*, usually renered reward, is rendered "wages" in Romans 6:23, and "hire" in 1 Timothy 5:18. That is, it refers to something earned, not merely bestowed.

the Christian that at that judgment he may be without the word of praise and the crown which it is the joy of God to give to every faithful soul.

THE CHRISTIAN AND THE CHURCH

It is in immediate connection with the life of the church that the apostle is speaking. The church in view here, however, is not "the Church which is His [Christ's body]," but the gathering in any place of those who name the Name of Christ, and in whose midst He is. The whole passage is intended to raise our conception of the responsibility of membership in such a church, and to teach us that each is expected by the Lord of the church to contribute his share to its corporate life, in view of the day when each must give account to Him. The thoughts of God concerning such churches are readily learned from the language he uses concerning this at Corinth: "Know ye not that ye are a sanctuary [marg.] of God, and that the Spirit of God dwelleth in [among] you?" What follows, then, if God dwells not in a house made with hands, but in the midst of His redeemed people? This, that what a man does to the church, that will God do to Him. "If any man destroyeth the sanctuary of God, him shall God destroy." And, conversely, if any man builds up, cheers, encourages, strengthens, by word or by example, the sanctuary of God, him will God assuredly reward (1 Cor. 3:10–17).

In the second epistle the apostle approaches the subject along a different line. Here the church is not directly before his mind, but the Christian in the whole round of his life. Of course the result is the same, for men do not live their lives in watertight compartments, and what a man is in his daily walk and conversation affects the church of which he is a member. He will be the same man, not a different one, on Sundays as on each of the other days of the week. The apostle is thinking of the certainty, and indeed of the near approach, of the end of opportunity for service. But whether it be by way of death, or by way of the immediate clothing upon with the new and heavenly body, this at least was assured, they would, one and all, "be made manifest before the Judgment Seat of Christ" (2 Cor. 5:10). The word "make manifest" suggests an open display. It is the summation of those other words in 1 Corinthians 4:5, "the Lord . . . will both bring to light the hidden things of darkness, and make manifest the counsels of the hearts."

The purpose of the words is plain. It is that we should neither do nor allow now that of which we know we would be ashamed then. The thought of the Judgment Seat of Christ is a deterrent from word and act inconsistent with the Name of the Lord, and a stimulus to the ambition to manifest every grace He manifested in His ways when He dwelt among men. It is true that our consciousness of sinfulness ("conscience of sins," Heb. 10:2), makes us shrink from the revelations of that day. But we need to correct our thoughts by at least two considerations. Then, with sin eliminated, we shall hate sin as sin, and as we ought to hate it now. We shall rejoice in the completeness of the Lord's victory over sin in us. Love of what is true will become so real that we shall have no desire to appear other than we are, as men have endeavored to appear ever since the day in which Adam and Eve attempted to hide themselves in the thicket from the eye of God.

We should not dread anything that to the Lord seems wise and right; otherwise the question might well be asked, Where is your faith? Moreover, do not our delinquencies and failures, in a word, our sins, bring the Name of the Lord into disrepute, causing it to be blasphemed? At that day His name will be cleared. What belongs to Him in us, the fruit of His Spirit, will remain to His praise and glory and honor (1 Pet. 1:7). The rest will pass; that will be to our loss, indeed, but would we have it otherwise? The loss will not be of the worthless material built into life, the "burning" of that will be deliverance, and insofar gain, not loss. The loss will be of the glory to God and of the reward to us that might have been ours had we lived in accordance with His Word.

"Knowing, therefore, the fear of the Lord," the apostle proceeds. Not "terror," as in the Authorized Version, as though he had the judgment of God upon the ungodly before his mind, warning them to flee from wrath to come. Rather he is thinking of the character of the Lord, His holiness and righteousness; of what is due to Him and what He requires of, and inspires in, us. He is thinking also of his responsibility to answer from his own life and service, and urging upon the Christians at Corinth, and upon us in our day also, to hold our walk and conversation, and to fulfill our appointed service, as those who must give account thereof to such a Lord.

SOWING AND REAPING

It is "the Lord, the righteous Judge" (2 Tim. 4:8), before Whom we are to be made manifest. And the principle on which He judges is declared, "whatsoever a man soweth, that shall he also reap" (Gal. 6:7). Hence the repetition of the word "destroy" in 1 Corinthians 3:17, to which attention has already been drawn. Hence, too, the words of 2 Corinthians 5:10, "that each one may receive the things done by means of [marg.] the body, according to what he hath done [lit., practiced], whether it be good or bad." The present body is the implement by which the will of the man is carried out; in the resurrection body the reward of his conduct will be received; if good, in some happy recognition as the wisdom of the Lord shall prescribe; if ill, in the loss of that which it would have rejoiced the Lord to give.

The words of Colossians 3:23–25 are in harmony with this principle also. "Whatsoever ye do, work from the soul, as unto the Lord, and not unto men; knowing that from the Lord ye shall receive the recompense of the inheritance: ye serve the Lord Christ. For he that doeth wrong shall receive again the wrong that he hath done [marg.]: and there is no respect of persons." The significance of the words is heightened by their context; they occur in the midst of a series of exhortations addressed to wives, husbands, children, servants and masters. Thus, and not otherwise, is life to be lived by all those, of whatever station in life, who hold the Name and the Word of the Lord in reverence.

"Shall receive again the wrong done." It may be difficult for us to conceive how God will fulfill this word to those who are already in bodies of glory, partakers of the joy of the redeemed in salvation consummated in spirit, soul and body. Yet may we be assured that the operation of this law is not to be suspended even in their case. He that "knoweth how to deliver the godly out of temptation, and to keep the unrighteous under punishment unto the day of judgment" (2 Pet. 2:9), knows also how to direct and to use the working of His law of sowing and reaping in the case of His children also. The attempt to alleviate the text of some of its weight by suggesting that the law operates only in this life, fails, for there is nothing in the text or context to lead the reader to think other than that while the sowing is here, the reaping is hereafter. It is clear that if it were not for this supposed difficulty of referring the words to the Christian in the condition in which, as we know from other Scriptures, he will appear at the Judgment Seat of Christ, the question whether that time and place were intended would not be raised.

The parallel passage in Ephesians 6:8 is varied in a direction that carries comfort, and gives courage to the Christian to be "zealous of good works." It runs thus, "knowing that whatsoever good thing each one doeth, the same shall he receive again from the Lord."

CONCERNING CROWNS

The reward is assured, equally so the loss; nevertheless it is also written concerning the crownless at that day that they themselves shall be saved, yet so as through the fire (1 Cor. 3:15). For the crowns of which the Scripture speaks are rewards that must be earned; they are not the common heritage of the saints, falling to them by the operation of grace and without regard to works. A crown is not the equivalent of salvation; it is an inducement offered to those who have trusted the Lord to manifest their faith in obedience. It is the reward of the race and the fight for them that strive, and that strive lawfully, that they may attain. In his words to the Corinthian believers the apostle is not concerned about his salvation, whether or no he will be taken away with all those "that are Christ's" at His Parousia. For him that is a matter settled when he was delivered out of the power of darkness into the Kingdom of the Son of His [God's] love, for from that moment he was reckoned among the redeemed, among those who had obtained the forgiveness of their sins "through the Blood of His [Christ's] Cross" (Col. 1:13). What did concern him was lest having urged others to run with purpose he himself should, through relaxed vigilance and effort, fail to win the Amaranthine Crown.[1]

---

1 Crowns, in the New Testament, are promised to the Christian as rewards for patient endurance or for faithful service. Cp.:

"An incorruptible crown," a general description applicable to all rewards promised to those who stand approved before the Judgment Seat of Christ (1 Cor. 9:25).

"The crown of righteousness," describing the character of the reward corresponding to the character of the giver (2 Tim. 4:8).

Years afterward, when the end of his service seemed very near indeed, the apostle wrote to the Philippians that he had but one ambition, that he might "gain Christ," that he might "know Him, and the power of His Resurrection, and the fellowship of His sufferings," that so he might become "conformed unto His Death." "If by any means," he continues, "I may attain unto the resurrection from the dead" (3:8–13). The word *exanastasis* is not elsewhere used in the New Testament. Is he now uncertain whether he will have any part in the resurrection and rapture of those that belong to Christ, the assurance of which it had pleased God to give to him many years before (1 Thess. 4:17) and to so many others through his voice and pen? Once more he is not concerned here about his salvation, for of that he had long been assured, and in it he had long rejoiced; whereas of this which now occupies him he declares that he is not yet in possession. Obviously not, if he is thinking of the resurrection of which he wrote in 1 Corinthians 15. Why should he pause to assert twice what was so evident? Moreover, a few sentences further on he declares himself to be among those who are waiting for the Lord from heaven (v. 20).

Is it possible that he has in mind an earlier resurrection than that of which he had previously written? To this solution there are at least two objections. He does not elsewhere refer to any such event. Moreover, the desire for resurrection would include the desire for death, and the apostle never elsewhere expressed himself in this sense. Of death, as we have seen in an earlier chapter, he has no fear; but he does not desire it. He looks, even longs for, the coming of the Lord. And if, earlier in this letter to the Philippians (1:23) he speaks of the prospect of death as a happy one, that is only in comparison with his toils and sufferings here, and in the assurance that to depart is to be with Christ, "to have died is gain."[1]

The "out-resurrection from among the dead," toward which the apostle aspires so warmly here, is that which he describes in Romans 6:4 as the "walk in newness of life." He had urged others to reckon themselves "to be dead unto sin, but alive unto God in Christ Jesus" (v. 11), and these words to the Philippians reveal the same ambition in his own soul. Having preached to others he did not wish himself to fail of the prize that awaits those who live as baptized persons should. The difference in the form of expression is accounted for by the

---

"The crown of life," describing the permanent nature of the reward, in contrast to the transient experience of trial in which it is won, and corresponding to the nature of the Living God Who gives it (James 1:12; Rev. 2:10).

"The crown of unfading glory," describing the reward of those who give themselves without ostentation, and without hope of gain, to the care of the flock in the absence of the Chief Shepherd (1 Pet. 5:4).

—From *Notes on the Thessalonians.*

1 Philippians 1:21. "The tense denotes not the act of dying but the consequence of dying, the state after death," *Lightfoot.* And so what the apostle contemplates after the spirit leaves the body is not quiescence, sleep, oblivion, but a nearer sense of the presence of Christ and a more intimate communion with Him than is possible now. See Appendix, Note F.

different purpose and method of the two epistles. In Romans, a more or less formal treatise, written to a church with which he had had no direct personal relationship, he is expounding and enforcing a doctrine. In Philippians, a letter breathing in every sentence the warmth of personal interest and feeling, because it is written to people whom he knew and loved as his children in the faith, he reveals the ambition of his own heart. In the one he is the teacher, propounding with authority the doctrines of the gospel. In the other he is the living example of the things he teaches. The "prize of the high calling of God in Christ Jesus" (Phil. 3:14) is the "incorruptible crown," "the crown of righteousness," of 1 Corinthians 9:25 and 2 Timothy 4:8.[1] It is probable that these rewards should be conceived of as suggested in the parable of the talents, "His Lord said unto him, Well done, good and faithful servant: thou hast been faithful over a few things, I will set thee over many things" (Matt. 25:21). For heaven is not a place of happy inactivity, of "ease with dignity," as though eternal youth could be happy, or even content, in idleness! Nor yet will that state be one in which energy is expended selfishly or aimlessly. For it is written that "His servants shall do Him service" there (Rev. 22:3).

THE EPIPHANY OF THE PAROUSIA

Many believe that the human race is capable of rising above all forms of misery, creating a golden age of world peace. The redemption of humanity from the evils which divide it must come about by the direct intervention of the Son of God, Who has already laid its foundation in His atoning sacrifice at Calvary. He Himself will introduce millennial blessing into the world, not by coming into a realm made ready for Him by human effort, but by the sudden overthrow of the mighty forces of evil, human and superhuman, which will continue their opposition unabated till the end of the present age.

> *"The vision is nearing,*
> *The Judge and the Throne!*
> *The voice of the Angel*
> *Proclaims "It is done."*
> *On the whirl of the tempest*
> *Its Ruler shall come*
> *And the blaze of His glory*
> *Flash out from its gloom."*

---

1 *Ano*, here rendered "above" appears again in Colossians 3:1, 2. This seems to fix the meaning of the word here. The apostle who urges the Colossians to "seek the things that are above, where Christ is, seated on the right hand of God," and to set their minds "on the things that are above, not on things that are upon the earth," declares that this also is his own aim. "The prize of the high calling" and "the things that are above" seem to be alternative expressions of the same idea.

We are to be occupied in this chapter with what Scripture states concerning the closing scenes of the present dispensation. The testimony of the sacred page at once discourages any hope that the deliverance of mankind in general from its miseries and sorrows is to be achieved by human effort, or by some evolutionary process of amelioration, or even by the preaching of the gospel. Not that the Word of God holds out no hope of the future deliverance of the human race. The belief that the golden age, sung by poets and depicted by idealists, will one day dawn, is confirmed in all parts of the book. For the introduction of this millennial era God has His own plans. Concerning these the writers of Scripture are in complete agreement. The agencies of civilization find no place in the divine scheme for the redemption of the world. The wisest and most powerful enterprises on the part of man cannot banish the cause of the evil which stands in the way of deliverance.

Let it be clearly understood that we are not disparaging humanitarian efforts for the alleviation of suffering and misery. It would ill become those who profess to be followers of Christ to do so. He Himself ever had a heart of compassion for the afflicted and woebegone, and expects those who acknowledge Him as Master and Lord to share His sympathies and to be ready to every good work. Did He not send His disciples out, not only to preach the gospel, but to heal the sick? We seek to show in another chapter that the expectation of the Lord's return, so far from being incompatible with such practical Christianity, is calculated to stimulate Christians to engage in it. Failure to do so, on the part of any who profess to look for His appearing, is only to their shame. We each have our part to do in seeking to diminish the sum of human wretchedness. Let not a word be uttered to underestimate or discourage schemes of improvement, philanthropic, social, economic, political! Yet we must not fail to point out that the root of social and national evils lies too deep for these agencies to eradicate.

Sin does not come merely by ignorance; therefore it cannot be removed by knowledge. Sin does not come merely by environment; therefore it cannot be expelled by improved circumstances. Sin does not come merely by poverty; therefore it cannot be annihilated by economic changes. The redemption of the race from the cause of the evils which divide it, and work mischief and misery in it, must come about by the direct intervention of the Son of God, Who has already laid the basis of this redemption in His atoning sacrifice at Calvary. He Himself will introduce millennial blessing into the world, not by coming into a realm made ready for Him by human instrumentality, but by the sudden overthrow of the mighty forces of evil, human and superhuman, which will continue their opposition unabated till the end of this dispensation.

THE END OF THE AGE

The Word of God gives a dark picture of the condition of the world at the close of the present age. The apostle Paul says, "In the last days grievous times shall come. For men shall be lovers of self, lovers of money, boastful, haughty, railers, disobedient to parents, unthankful, unholy, without natural affection, implacable, slanderers, without self-control, fierce, no lovers of good, traitors, headstrong, puffed up, lovers of pleasure rather than lovers of God; holding a form of godliness, but having denied the power thereof" (2 Tim. 3:1–5). There is certainly nothing to indicate in present-day conditions that the apostle's predictions will be stultified, nor yet his further forecast, that "evil men and impostors shall wax worse and worse, deceiving and being deceived" (v. 13).

Again, the Lord paralleled the state of humanity at the close of this era with that prevailing in the days of Noah immediately prior to the Flood, and, further, with that of the cities of the plain in the time of Lot. He says, "And as it came to pass in the days of Noah, even so shall it be in the days of the Son of man. They ate, they drank, they married, they were given in marriage, until the day that Noah entered into the ark, and the flood came, and destroyed them all. Likewise even as it came to pass in the days of Lot; they ate, they drank, they bought, they sold, they planted, they builded; but in the day that Lot went out from Sodom it rained fire and brimstone from heaven, and destroyed them all; after the same manner shall it be in the day that the Son of man is revealed" (Luke 17:26–30). Not that these pursuits were in either case evil in themselves. The sin lay in excluding God from their thoughts, the while they engaged in lawful occupations. This condition the Lord signalizes as characteristic of mankind at the end of the present era. The moral result of "refusing to have God in knowledge" is recorded in the Old Testament history of the times of Noah and Lot, and in the first chapter of Paul's epistle to the Romans.

A LEAGUE OF NATIONS

Again, men hope for universal peace and safety by the eventual abolition of militarism as the weapon of lust for conquest and supremacy, and by the establishment of international and democratic unity. Christ, Who has proved accurate in His prediction that during this dispensation "nation would rise against nation, and kingdom against kingdom, and that there would be great earthquakes, and in divers places famines and pestilences," also stated at the same time that, instead of the prevalence of rest and security at the end of the age, "there shall be signs in the sun and moon and stars; and upon the earth distress of nations in perplexity for the roaring of the sea and billows; men fainting for fear, and for expectation of the things which are coming on the world: for the powers of the heavens shall be shaken" (Luke 21:10, 11, 25, 26). In proof that the time of the end is here in view He immediately after said, "And then shall they see the Son of man coming in a cloud with power and great glory," an event which will introduce the next age. It must be clear therefore that human statescraft cannot achieve universal success.

Such a League of Nations, for instance, as is proposed today as a panacea for national wrongs, not only has been foretold in Scripture as the last resource of international politics, but its failure has likewise been predicted. The various Gentile empires which were to hold dominions of a more or less worldwide character were made known to the prophet Daniel. These were symbolized as beasts. The fourth and last beast, i.e., the final form of Gentile rule, was seen to have ten horns. The interpretation of the vision is as follows: "The fourth beast shall be diverse from all the kingdoms . . . and as for the ten horns, out of this kingdom shall ten kings arise" (Dan. 7:23, 24). In the preceding part of the chapter the beast is personified (v. 17) and the symbol stands both for the imperial head and for his dominion. A corresponding vision was given to the apostle John. He also saw a beast with ten horns, and the symbolism is again explained, but in greater detail: "The ten horns that thou sawest are ten kings, which have received no kingdom as yet; but they receive authority as kings, with the beast, for one hour [i.e., for a brief time]. These have one mind, and they give their power and authority unto the beast" (Rev. 17:12, 13). Obviously these ten kingdoms are contemporaneous. The potentates ruling over them agree to a certain policy in handing over their authority to a superior ruler. No such league has existed in human history as yet.

It is manifest, too, from this Scripture that the existence of the league will provide the opportunity for a man sufficiently strong to dominate the situation. Of this man, and of the way in which he and his confederacy and power will come to their end by the revelation of the Son of God in judgment upon them, more presently. Their overthrow is sufficiently clear from the words which follow: "These [i.e., the beast and his confederate kings] shall make war against the Lamb, and the Lamb shall overcome them; and they also shall overcome that are with Him, called and chosen and faithful" (v. 14).

This personal intervention of Christ in the affairs of the world marks the close of His Parousia with His saints in the air, which formed the subject of a preceding chapter. It thereby also constitutes, as we shall see, the introductory event of the Day of the Lord, Paul describes it as "the manifestation [lit., the epiphany, i.e., the shining forth] of His parousia" (2 Thess. 2:8); and the Lord Himself spoke of it as follows: "For as the lightning cometh forth from the east, and is seen even unto the west; so shall be the Parousia of the Son of man" (Matt. 24:27). The Parousia of the Son of man is the Parousia viewed from the earthly standpoint. His Parousia with His saints in the heavenlies will be made known to men only when it is revealed. From its purely heavenly standpoint, as synchronizing with "the Day of Christ," or the period of His Judgment Seat for the review of the service of His saints, the Parousia then terminates. He then will come forth with them in manifested glory, and the Day of the Lord will begin.

THINGS THAT DIFFER

Certain events, such as the Great Tribulation, signs and judgments from heaven, and great distress in the earth, are destined to precede the Day of the Lord, and thus are to be distinguished from it. This is clear from a comparison of the prophecy of Joel, quoted by the apostle Peter, with the words of the Lord concerning the time of the Great Tribulation. Joel's prophecy is, "And I will show wonders in the heavens and in the earth, blood, and fire, and pillars of smoke. The sun shall be turned into darkness, and the moon into blood, before the great and terrible day of the Lord come" (Joel 2:30, 31). Peter speaks of it as "the day of the Lord . . . that great and notable day" (Acts 2:20).

The Lord Himself, speaking of the Tribulation, says, "Immediately after the tribulation of those days, the sun shall be darkened, and the moon shall not give her light, and the stars shall fall from heaven, and the powers of the heavens shall be shaken: and then shall appear the sign of the Son of man in heaven: and then shall all the tribes of the earth mourn, and they shall see the Son of man coming on the clouds of heaven with power and great glory" (Matt. 24:29, 30).

The Great Tribulation is "the time of Jacob's trouble," i.e., the fierce persecution of the Jews by the Antichrist. (G-J, p. 156). The Day of the Lord is the time of the personal exercise of Christ's authority in the world, and will be ushered in by His appearing in glory. (J-B). The Day of the Lord is never spoken of in Scripture as referring to the Great Tribulation. The latter is also to be distinguished from the divine judgments to be manifested immediately before the Day of the Lord, the signs in the heavens and earth mentioned in the passage just quoted from Joel.

We have, then, a fixed order foretold. First, the Great Tribulation; second, signs in the sun, moon, and stars (Luke adds "distress of nations, men fainting for fear and for expectation of the things which are coming on the world, and the shaking of the powers of the heavens," Luke 21:25, 26); and, third, the revelation of the Son of man. Joel and Peter show that the signs in the heavens immediately precede the Day of the Lord; Christ showed that they immediately succeed the Great Tribulation, and immediately precede His manifestation as the Son of man. Accordingly His revelation in power and great glory, will be coincidental with the inception of the Day of the Lord. (H-J, p. 156).

That the Jewish people are to be the sufferers in the Great Tribulation is clear from the following Scriptures. Jeremiah prophesied that no period of tribulation will equal that of "Jacob's trouble," i.e., of the Jewish nation (Jer. 30:7). To Daniel it was foretold concerning his people, the Jews, that there would be a time of trouble "such as never was since there was a nation even to that time" (Dan. 12:1). The Lord said of the Great Tribulation that it will be "such as hath not been from the beginning of the world until now, no nor ever shall be" (Matt. 24:21). Wherever there are Jews at that time they will suffer in this worldwide pogrom. For, while prior to this they are to be nationally reinstated in Palestine, they will not all be resident there; considerable numbers will still be living in other countries. Accordingly, those who have been put to death in the Tribulation and are seen in the apocalyptic vision standing "before the Throne and before the Lamb," are said to have come "out of every nation, and of all tribes and peoples and tongues" (Rev. 7:9 and 14).

"The sign of the Son of man," is probably to be understood subjectively. There are to be preceding signs in the heavens, immediately after the Great Tribulation, but the sign of the Son of man is not to be classed with those. He will be His own sign. That is to say, the words may be understood as equivalent to "the sign which is the Son of man," and not as indicating a sign heralding His appearance. This is confirmed, perhaps, by the order of events given in Revelation 6, which correspond to that in Matthew 24. First there are preliminary judgments, war and famine and pestilence (vv. 1–8), then the signs in heaven (vv. 12, 13), and finally the appearance of the Lord in person, at the "shining out of His Parousia." That is the sign of the Son of man. The effect of this is that "the kings of the earth, and the princes, and the chief captains, and the rich, and the strong, and every bondman, and freeman, hide themselves in the caves, and in the rocks of the mountains: and they say to the mountains and to the rocks, Fall on us and hide us from the face of Him that sitteth on the Throne, and from the wrath of the Lamb: for the great day of their wrath is come; and who is able to stand?" (vv. 15–17).

THE MAN OF SIN

The Scriptures not only speak in a general way, as in the passages already quoted, of the conditions which will characterize the world at the close of the age; specific details are also given. Some of these now call for consideration, as leading up to the Day of the Lord.

We have seen, in the chapter on the Parousia, that in the second epistle to the Thessalonians Paul was correcting the notion that the Day of the Lord had already set in. In contradistinction to his teaching concerning the coming of the Lord for His saints, as ever the next thing to be expected, he now showed that certain events must precede the Day of the Lord. "That Day will not be," he says, "except the falling away [lit., the apostasy] come first, and the Man of Sin be revealed, the Son of Perdition, he that opposeth and exalteth himself against all that is called God, or that is worshiped; so that he sitteth in the temple of God, setting himself forth as God" (2 Thess. 2:3–5). Two clearly defined events are here foretold as destined to precede the Day of the Lord (1) the apostasy, the turning away from, and repudiation of, divine truth formerly adhered to, and (2) the revelation of the Man of Sin, called in verse 8 "the Lawless One."

Again, this latter revelation is to be preceded by another event. Lawlessness, the apostle says, was already at work in the first century, as a mystery, i.e., as something not recognized in its true character by the world at large, but made known by revelation. A certain principle was, however, at work, hindering the manifestation of the Lawless One until the time appointed for him. This principle is described as "that which restraineth" (v. 6). It found concrete expression in a person representatively described as "one that restraineth" (v. 7). This restraint against lawlessness will be exercised until the restrainer is "taken out of the way."[1] When this takes place the man himself, the embodiment of lawlessness, will be revealed.

But what as to the power and policy of this world-ruler? These are detailed in other Scriptures. In 2 Thessalonians Paul, who is pointing on to the Day of

---

1 A more literal, and not improbable, rendering is, "when it, i.e., lawlessness, becomes out of the midst," i.e., becomes fully and manifestly developed. See *Notes on Thessalonians*.

the Lord, passes over the interval of the government of the Man of Sin, save for a brief mention of his satanic power and deceitful influence, and speaks at once of his doom, declaring that "the Lord Jesus shall slay him with the breath of His mouth, and bring him to nought by the manifestation of His Parousia" (v. 8). The word rendered "manifestation" is literally "epiphany," i.e., a shining forth. This epiphany marks the close of the Parousia, the saints having been with the Lord hidden from the world since the Rapture. (F-H, p. 156).

The world itself will by this time have reached its climax of iniquity, men having only hardened their hearts against God by reason of the judgments premonitory of impending doom. "The rest of mankind, which were not killed with these plagues, repented not of the works of their hands . . . and they repented not of their murders, nor of their sorceries, nor of their fornication, nor of their thefts" (Rev. 9:20, 21). "They blasphemed the Name of the God which hath the power over these plagues; and they repented not to give Him glory . . . and they blasphemed the God of heaven because of their pains and their sores; and they repented not of their works" (16:9, 11). What a picture of the antagonism of the natural heart against God! What a witness to the helplessness of man to eradicate evil, to remove the curse from the earth! The testimony of Scripture is plain enough as to the darkness and evil which are to prevail at the close of this dispensation of "man's day." Nor can it be otherwise, since we are shown that mankind at large will still refuse to view sin according to the divine estimate, and to accept God's proffered pardon and grace through the sacrifice of His Son.

At length, human rebellion having reached its consummation under the Man of Sin, the Son of man appears in person to execute wrath upon him and upon all who own allegiance to him. He is "revealed from heaven with the angels of His power in flaming fire, rendering vengeance to them that know not God, and to them that obey not the gospel of our Lord Jesus" (2 Thess. 1:7, 8). One of the most ancient prophecies recorded in the Word of God foretold this solemn event, the past tense being used with prophetic significance, as is frequent in Scripture: "Enoch, the seventh from Adam, prophesied, saying, Behold, the Lord came with His holy myriads, to execute judgment upon all, and to convict all the ungodly of all their works of ungodliness which they have ungodly wrought, and of all the hard things which ungodly sinners have spoken against Him" (Jude 14, 15). Man's day will be over, the Day of the Lord will begin. (J-B, p. 156).

CLOSING EVENTS

We may now briefly enumerate some of the events in the world which will lead up to this divine intervention.[1] The Word of God foretells that the Man of Sin will obtain world dominion as the result of a confederacy of nations, the rulers of which will, with one consent, commit their power and authority to him (Rev. 17:13 with 13:8); that, having first supported, and then overthrown the combined religious systems of the world with the aid of these potentates

---

1 For a more detailed account, see "The Roman Empire in the Light of Prophecy," by W. E. Vine, M. A.

(Rev. 17:7, 16), he will "exalt himself against all that is called God or that is worshiped," and thus claiming deity, will demand, and receive, universal worship (2 Thess. 2:4 with Rev. 13:8); that he will be supported in this by another potentate described firstly as "another beast," and secondly as "the false prophet" (Rev. 13:11–15 with 19:20); and that they will establish a worldwide commercial system, prohibiting buying and selling save on the part of those who use the special mark officially appointed (13:16, 17). With the Jews, who will have been reestablished nationally in Palestine, he will at first enter into a covenant, but will subsequently break it, turning upon the nation with a view to its annihilation (Dan. 9:27). Thus will begin "the time of Jacob's trouble." "But he shall be saved out of it" (Jer. 30:7). Temporarily successful in his other enterprises, the Man of Sin will fail in this anti-Semitic campaign—fail through the intervention of the Lord Jesus, by Whom he will be destroyed. (H-J, p. 156).

The prophetic Scriptures to which reference has been made serve, perhaps, to throw light upon some of the world movements which are taking place at the present time. Certainly the trend of current events is not in a direction contrary to what the Scriptures have predicted.

HAR-MAGEDON

We must dwell more fully upon the manner in which the Jews will be delivered, since their deliverance coincides with the manifestation of the Parousia and with the commencement of the Day of the Lord. (H-J, p. 156).

The attempt to destroy the Jewish nation will form the climax of the aggression of the Antichrist against God, and will constitute a war waged against the Son of God, the Messiah of the Jews. The armies of the Gentile powers, placed at the disposal of their great leader, will be gathered together "against the Lord, and against His Anointed." Having by mutual consent given their power and authority unto "the beast," these kings of the earth, with their supreme warlord, "will war against the Lamb" (Rev. 17:13, 14). "I saw," says the inspired seer, "the beast, and the kings of the earth, and their armies, gathered together to make war against His army" (Rev. 19:19). It had been permitted to the arch-oppressor to prevail against the Jews in the Great Tribulation of which he was the instrument; he will not prevail against the Son of God; his success is only "until the Ancient of days came" (Dan. 7:21, 22).

The issues at stake will differentiate this war from all that have preceded; they have been waged for dynastic or territorial or commercial supremacy, this contest will be fought to decide whether world dominion is to rest in the hands of Satan or of Christ. This is the battle of Har-Magedon, "the war of the great day of God, the Almighty," which will introduce the Day of the Lord. Satan it is whose utmost power will energize his human instruments to force a decision: "And I saw coming out of the mouth of the Dragon, and out of the mouth of the beast, and out of the mouth of the false prophet [a trinity of evil], three unclean spirits, as it were frogs: for they are the spirits of demons, working signs; which go forth unto the kings of the whole world, to gather them together unto the war of the great day of God, the Almighty . . . and they gathered them together into the place which is called in the Hebrew, Har-Magedon" (Rev. 16:13–16).

THE FORCES OF THE VICTOR

This, then, on the one hand, is the description of the massed forces of evil, of humanity in alienation from God, combined in impious rebellion against the Most High, and satanically deceived by the "power and signs and lying wonders" of the Man of Sin; deceived "because they received not the love of the truth, that they might be saved," duped into believing the lie, because "they believed not the truth, but had pleasure in unrighteousness" (2 Thess. 2:9–12).

Now as to the forces of righteousness, the armies of the King of kings, Who comes to establish peace by the overthrow of militarism, Who

> "Comes to break oppression
> To set the captive free;
> To take away transgression,
> And rule in equity."

Terrible in its grandeur is the apostle's vivid description of the Lord and His hosts: "And I saw the heaven opened: and behold, a white horse, and He that sat thereon, called Faithful and True; and in righteousness he doth judge and make war. And His eyes are a flame of fire, and upon His head are many diadems: and He hath a name written, which no one knoweth, but he Himself. And He is arrayed in a garment sprinkled with blood: and His name is called The Word of God. And the armies which are in heaven followed Him upon white horses, clothed in fine linen, white and pure. And out of His mouth proceedeth a sharp sword, that with it he should smite the nations: and He shall rule them with a rod of iron; and He treadeth the winepress of the fierceness of the wrath of Almighty God. And He hath on His garment and on His thigh a name written, King of Kings, and Lord of Lords. And I saw an angel standing in the sun; and he cried with a loud voice, saying to all the birds that fly in mid heaven, Come and be gathered together unto the great supper of God; that ye may eat the flesh of kings, and the flesh of captains and the flesh of mighty men, and the flesh of horses and of them that sit thereon, and the flesh of all men, both free and bond, and small and great. . . . And the beast was taken, and with him the false prophet, that wrought the signs in his sight, wherewith he deceived them that had received the mark of the beast, and them that worshiped his image: they twain were cast alive into the lake of fire that burneth with brimstone: and the rest were killed with the sword of Him that sat upon the horse, even the sword which came forth out of His mouth: and all the birds were filled with their flesh."

Thus it is that the Man of Sin is to be brought to naught by the manifestation of the Parousia of the Lord Jesus. Thus will the Son of man, coming on the clouds of heaven with power and great glory, usher in the Day of the Lord, a day terrible in its inception, blessed in its continuance, when to the outpouring of righteous wrath shall succeed a righteous peace, under the sovereignty of the King of kings. We may compare the prophecy of Joel: "The Lord uttereth His voice before His army [a striking association with Paul's words, "the breath of His mouth," 2 Thessalonians 2:8, and with John's vision of the sword proceeding from the mouth of the Lord]; for His camp is very great; for He is strong that executeth His word; for the Day of the Lord is very terrible; and who can abide it?" (Joel 2:10, 11).

Comparing the two passages above mentioned, viz., Revelation 19:19–21 and 2 Thessalonians 2:8, which each refer in different ways to the overthrow of the Man of Sin and his forces, the Thessalonians passage gives the effect, and the Revelation passage the process; the process is short and sharp, as the effect is decisive. Further light is thrown on the two by the prophecy of Zechariah: "Then shall the Lord go forth, and fight against those nations, as when He fought in the day of battle. And His feet shall stand in that day upon the Mount of Olives. . . . And the Lord my God shall come and all the holy angels with thee" (Zech. 14:3–5).

The Day of the Lord, which will reveal the Church in the heavenlies, glorious with the glory of Christ, will at the same time bring deliverance to His earthly people the Jews. The scene is predicted in the last chapter of Joel as follows: "Proclaim ye this among the nations; prepare war; stir up the mighty men; let all the men of war draw near, let them come up. Beat your plowshares into swords, and your pruninghooks into spears; let the weak say, I am strong. Haste ye, and come, all ye nations round about, and gather yourselves together; thither cause thy mighty ones come down, O Lord. Let the nations bestir themselves, and come up to the valley of Jehoshaphat; for there will I sit to judge all the nations round about. Put ye in the sickle for the harvest is ripe; come, tread ye; for the winepress is full, the fats overflow; for their wickedness is great. Multitudes, multitudes in the valley of decision! for the day of the Lord is near in the valley of decision. The sun and the moon are darkened, and the stars withdraw their shining. And the Lord shall roar from Zion, and utter His voice from Jerusalem; and the heavens and the earth shall shake; but the Lord will be a refuge unto His people, and a stronghold to the children of Israel. So shall ye know that I am the Lord your God dwelling in Zion my holy mountain; then shall Jerusalem be holy, and there shall no strangers pass through her any more."

The manifestation of the Parousia and the introduction of the Day of the Lord thus constitute the closing stage of the Lord's Second Coming. (H-J, p. 156).

THE FINAL GENTILE WORLD-RULER AND HIS DOMINION

The apostle Paul speaks of him as "the Man of Sin, the Son of Perdition," and "the Lawless One" (2 Thess. 2:3, 8). His is to be the final attempt to monopolize world power, and his dominion is to be different in character from all that preceded it. This prophetically will be the rise of the Antichrist.

The influence of "the Prince that shall come" (Dan. 9:26) upon the destiny of the human race is of such a determining character that more is demanded than the brief reference to his power and his policy included in the last chapter. His is to be the final attempt to monopolize world power, and his dominion is to be different in character from all that preceded it. Happily the Word of God provides us with a sufficiently clear revelation concerning the closing drama of Gentile power to enable us both to form a broad view of the trend and destiny of national affairs, and to understand the manner in which His Kingdom of righteousness will be universally established in the earth.

In order to ascertain the character of the final Gentile world dominion and its Imperial head, we must first refer to those Scriptures which indicate the course of Gentile government over the land of Palestine. It is necessary to remember that the prophetic Scriptures relating to national governments bear directly and always on the land of the Jews. Palestine is the center of divine dealings with nations, the pivot upon which those dealings turn. "When the Most High gave to the nations their inheritance, when He separated the children of men, He set the bounds of the peoples according to the number of the children of Israel" (Deut. 32:8). With that statement all Scripture history regarding Gentile power is entirely consistent. The land was foreordained of God as the eventual seat of Messiah's kingdom.

THE VISION OF THE IMAGE

The second chapter of Daniel describes a vision of a great image seen by Nebuchadnezzar, the Chaldean monarch, the first Gentile potentate to hold dominion over the whole of Palestine after that country had been given to Israel to possess. His subjugation of the land began the long period afterwards called by the Lord "the times of the Gentiles" (Luke 21:24), that is, the period during which Gentile nations govern the country. Almost immediately after Nebuchadnezzar had annexed the land and carried the people into captivity, a divine revelation was given of the program of Gentile government over them and of the character of the various forms of that government. The vision just referred to was the means of this revelation in the first instance.

The image was divided into four parts which were interpreted as symbolical of four kingdoms. Nebuchadnezzar's was immediately identified as the first.

"Thou, O King," said the prophet, "art king of kings, unto whom the God of heaven hath given the kingdom . . . thou art the head of gold" (vv. 37, 38). The second and third, corresponding respectively to the breast and arms, of silver, and the belly and thighs, of brass, are subsequently shown to be the Medo-Persian and the Grecian, or Macedonian, kingdoms. Thus the prophet's prediction to Nebuchadnezzar, "after thee shall arise another kingdom" (v. 39), finds fulfillment in the historic record, "In that night Belshazzar the Chaldean king was slain, and Darius the Mede received the kingdom" (vv. 30, 31). The interpretation of a later vision, seen by Daniel, of a conflict between a ram and an he-goat, identifies the third kingdom with that of Greece: "The ram which thou sawest that had the two horns, they are the kings of Media and Persia. And the rough he-goat [which was seen to destroy the ram, v. 8] is the King of Greece" (8:20, 21; cp. 10:20).

THE FOURTH KINGDOM

The fourth kingdom was symbolized by the legs of iron and the feet partly of iron and partly of clay, or, rather, earthenware (2:33). That kingdom would be strong as iron, but inasmuch as the feet and toes of the image were part of iron and part of earthenware, the kingdom would exist in a divided condition. Further, while it would always contain the strength of iron, yet the admixture of the earthenware would eventually render the kingdom partly strong and partly brittle (vv. 40–42) (not "broken," but liable to break). This characteristic is especially mentioned of the period corresponding to the toes (v. 42). Thus the form of government of the fourth kingdom would pass through certain stages.

This fourth kingdom is not specifically mentioned in the book of Daniel, but its identification is not difficult. The history of the overthrow of the Grecian Empire by the Romans is well-known. The Roman power is, moreover, indicated in the ninth chapter of Daniel where, following the prophecy that the Messiah would be cut off, is the prediction that "the people of the prince that shall come" would destroy the city and the sanctuary" (v. 26). This the Romans carried out in A.D. 70.

THE VISION OF THE FOUR BEASTS

A further revelation of the course of Gentile government over the Jews, given to Daniel himself, is recorded in the seventh chapter. Four powers were represented in that vision as wild beasts, symbols appropriate for a revelation to a Jew, in contrast to those of the Gentile monarch's vision, and indicative of the treatment Daniel's people would receive from Gentile rulers.

The similarity of the description of the fourth beast to that of the fourth part of the image makes clear that the same power is in view in each case. "The fourth beast would be a fourth kingdom, differing from all others; it would devour the earth, tread it down and break it in pieces" (7:23)—an accurate representation of the Roman power.

It is to be noticed that in each interpretation the fourth kingdom is predicted as the last Gentile power, and that it receives its overthrow at the hand of God, Who will thereupon establish an everlasting Kingdom. "In the days of those kings [i.e., of the potentates represented by the toes of the image] shall the God of heaven set up a kingdom, which shall never be destroyed, nor shall the sovereignty thereof be left to another people; but it shall break in pieces and consume all these kingdoms, and it shall stand forever" (2:44). So of the final head of the empire, represented by the fourth beast, it is said, "The judgment shall sit, and they shall take away his dominion, to consume and to destroy it unto the end, and the kingdom and the dominion, and the greatness of the kingdoms under the whole heaven, shall be given to the people of the saints of the Most High: His kingdom is an everlasting kingdom, and all dominions shall serve and obey Him" (7:26, 27). Clearly, then, no worldwide imperial power is to rule between the Roman kingdom, in its final stage, and the Kingdom of Christ. (H-J, p. 156).

IS THE LAST THE ROMAN?

The inquiry may be raised as to how the Roman power can be the last of the Gentile empires which rule over the Jews as a nation, considering that the Roman Empire was overthrown in the fifth and succeeding centuries of the present era. Moreover, what of the Turkish dominion?

The book of the Revelation gives us light as to the first question. Here we are carried much farther in detail, just as the eighth chapter of Daniel gives fuller information than the second. This is in accordance with the progressive character of prophecy. We are shown, in the seventeenth chapter of the Apocalypse, that the power symbolized by the beast would, after a temporary lapse, be resuscitated. The apostle John received a vision of a beast with seven heads and ten horns, and carrying a woman. The identification of this beast with the fourth of Daniel's vision is established by the facts that each had ten horns, and that each becomes the object of divine judgment at the manifestation of the Son of God for the setting up of His Kingdom. (H-J, p. 156). The three periods relating to the power of the beast are thus indicated: "The beast that thou sawest was, and is not; and is about to come up out of the abyss"; and again, "he was, and is not, and shall come" (Rev. 17:8). This does not mean that it existed prior to John's time and was then nonexistent. The language is prophetic rather than historic, and simply implies (1) an existence, (2) a discontinuance, (3) a reappearance.

A TWOFOLD APPLICATION

We must notice that the symbol of a beast represents both the kingdom and its final ruler. This is the case in both the 7th of Daniel and the 17th of Revelation. In the former chapter the interpretation is as follows: "These great beasts which are four are four *kings*. . . . The fourth beast shall be a fourth *kingdom*" (Dan. 7:17, 23). In the Revelation the beast is seen with seven heads and ten horns (v. 3). Here the whole animal is termed a beast. In verses 9–11, however, the beast is symbolically identified, not with the whole animal, but with one of the heads. Moreover, the seven heads are described first topographically and then personally. "The seven heads are seven mountains . . . and they are seven kings; . . . and the beast . . . is himself also an eighth, and is of the seven." Clearly the beast again represents two distinct yet closely associated things. In the first eight verses of the chapter the language is indicative of dominion. Then the scope of the symbol is narrowed and the individual ruler comes into view. Thus the entire animal represents, not merely the ruler, but his kingdom, as in Daniel 7:23.

The fourth, or Roman, Empire, as a matter of history, existed in the closing part of the past dispensation and in the first few centuries of the present one, that is, before and after the point C in the diagram. For many centuries it has not existed as an empire, that is to say, it is now in the "is not" stage.

THE TURKS

The Turks, who overthrew the eastern part of the Empire in the fifteenth century, occupied Palestine until 1917, but never ruled over the Jews as a nation, i.e., as the nationally recognized possessor of Palestine. Their relationship with the Jewish people differs fundamentally from that of the Chaldeans, Medo-Persians, Greeks, and Romans. The Jews had been scattered from their land before the Turks took possession. Turkish domination is therefore not noticed in the Scriptures we have considered.

THE FINAL FORM

Intimation is given in Scripture as to the form in which the fourth kingdom will be resuscitated, possibly during the period represented by G-J on the diagram. Of the ten horns on the fourth beast in Daniel's vision it was said, "As for the ten horns, out of this kingdom shall ten kings arise" (Dan. 7:24). And of the ten horns of the beast of Revelation, "The ten horns . . . are ten kings, which have received no kingdom as yet" (Rev. 17:12). That they will be contemporaneous and confederate is obvious, from the statement that they have one mind and agree to hand their kingdom over to a federal head (vv. 13, 17). Moreover, the countries over which they rule are spoken of not as kingdoms, but as a kingdom, indicating community of interest as well as territorial unity.

Clearly, therefore, a league of nations is in view, and this is apparently to be the new form of the old empire. Its reformed condition will render it "diverse from all the kingdoms," i.e., from the three preceding empires (Dan. 7:23).

TERRITORIAL CONSIDERATIONS

As to the territories of this reconstructed fourth empire, we have no definite intimation in Scripture, though there are indications that they will embrace at least the area occupied by all the four powers, the Chaldean, Medo-Persian, Grecian, and Roman. When in the vision the stone smote the image on its feet the whole image was broken in pieces (Dan. 2:34, 35). (H-J, p. 156). When the fourth beast was destroyed the dominion of the rest of the beasts was taken away (7:12). Probably there will be an expansion of territory beyond the ancient limits. Certainly the whole world will acknowledge the authority of the final head of the empire (Rev. 13:7).

Several territorial changes which have taken place during recent centuries—i.e., in the "is not" period—and especially of late, have shown a remarkable return toward the configuration of the ancient Roman dominions. All the territory of North Africa which was within the ancient empire, but which was subdued later by Turkey, has gradually come under the government of countries which belonged to the Roman kingdom. Spain governs Morocco; France governs Algeria and Tunis; Italy, Tripoli; and Britain, Egypt. Again, Alsace and Lorraine and other territory west of the Rhine, formerly in the Roman province of Gallia, are now reverting to France. The Trentino, which formerly belonged to Italy, has been regained by it. Austrian territory, which in the Roman Empire was confined to the district west and south of the Danube, is again reduced to that limit. Syria, Palestine, and Mesopotamia have been recovered from the Turk and are now under the influence of nations which belonged to the Roman world.[1] Moreover, those countries which have been freed from Turkish control have resumed the Western civil institutions and organizations, which have all along been Roman in character. Other territorial changes in Europe seem probable, which will render the approximation to the ancient delineations the closer.

We are not justified, however, in concluding that the territories of the League of Nations, indicated by the passages relating to the ten horns of the beast, will necessarily be confined to the area which has just been under consideration. Whatever the arrangement may be, the fact of the League will prepare the way for the government of the final and all-controlling despot.

This is foretold in Scripture as follows: "Out of this kingdom shall ten kings arise: and another shall arise after them; and he shall be diverse from the former" (Dan. 7:24). "[The] ten kings . . . receive authority as kings with the beast, for one hour [i.e., for a brief period]. These have one mind, and they give their power and authority unto the beast" (Rev. 17:12, 13, 17).

THE IRON AND CLAY

Now the character of the power of the ten kings is indicated by the constitution of the toes of the image seen in the vision by Nebuchadnezzar. These were formed of a mixture of iron and earthenware (Dan. 2:42). As the different metals of the image obviously represent the character of the respective governments, the iron most appropriately symbolizes militarism. The earthenware is brittle—the fourth kingdom, in this form, was predicted to be "partly strong and partly brittle" (see marg.). This suggests an unstable form of government. That democracy is in view is extremely improbable. Many a republic has evidenced striking

---

1 See the writer's *The Roman Empire in Prophecy*, written in 1915.

stability. On the other hand, such revolutionary forces as those of Communism, Anarchy, Bolshevism, etc., have always been liable to speedy disintegration. Moreover, revolutions instigated by such forces have almost always given rise to despotism, as in the case of the French Revolution.

Again, militarism is essentially so different in character from the associations referred to that, as the prophecy says, they could not cleave together, any more than iron and earthenware do. That they might mingle for a time is possible, especially if the will of the people lay behind the combination. This is perhaps indicated in the words "they shall mingle themselves by [marg.—i.e., by means of] the seed of men" (v. 43). We can conceive, therefore, of the outbreak of such widespread revolution in the confederate kingdom of the ten potentates,[1] coupled with a condition of impoverishment consequent upon war, that they would willingly commit their power into the hands of a man of consummate ability who might be ready for the occasion.[2]

THE FINAL EMPEROR

Concerning this final Gentile emperor Scripture has much to say, more than we can refer to in the present volume.[3]

The apostle Paul speaks of him as "the Man of Sin, the Son of Perdition," and "the Lawless One" (2 Thess. 2:3, 8). He is to have a parousia (v. 9), a period commencing with his manifestation, and during which his power will be in exercise over the whole world. His parousia, apparently an imitation of the Parousia of Christ, will be "according to the working of Satan with all power and signs and lying wonders, and with all deceit of unrighteousness." In the language of the Apocalypse, "the Dragon gave him his power, and his throne, and great authority" (Rev. 13:2). Hence the rapidity of his rise to power and of the universal acknowledgment of his rule. "His stupendous power and brilliant abilities, the evidence of his superhuman origin, his phenomenal capacity for organization, and the consolidation of the empire under his absolute control, will cause the whole world to marvel at him."[4]

His Overthrow

Exalting himself in impious pride and blasphemy against all that is called God, and claiming and receiving universal worship, he and his supporters will make war against the Son of God. "These shall war against the Lamb, and the Lamb shall overcome them" (Rev. 17:14). That victory, synchronizing with the

---

1 The word rendered "king" does not necessarily denote a constitutional monarch; rather it represents the head of any state, of whatever type.

2 See *The Roman Empire in Prophecy*.

3 For a brief outline of his career, see *The Roman Empire in Prophecy*. See also *The Mystery of Iniquity*, by C. F. Hogg.

4 *The Roman Empire in Prophecy*.

Second Advent, the ushering in of the Day of the Lord (H-J, p. 156), is variously described in the Word of God. The overthrow of the Beast is the falling of the stone upon the feet of the image of Nebuchadnezzar's vision, the annihilation of all Gentile government. He who in the days of His flesh refused to accept the kingdoms of the world at the hands of Satan, and to evade the sufferings of Calvary, will then by virtue of those sufferings, and of His victory over His arch-adversary, come to deliver the earth from its oppressors and from unrighteous government in all its forms.

The two contrasting circumstances of the Cross and the Glory are vividly depicted by Isaiah: "Like as many were astonied at Thee (His visage was so marred more than any man, and His form more than the sons of men), so shall He startle [marg., which seems accurate] many nations; kings shall shut their mouths at Him; for that which had not been told them shall they see; and that which they had not heard shall they understand" (Isa. 52:14, 15). The astonishment of men who gazed upon His sufferings will have its counterpart in the astonishment with which His Second Advent will overturn the existing order of things and introduce the glory of His Kingdom.

THE KINGDOM OF THE KING OF KINGS

Then will be fulfilled the saying that is written, "The kingdom of the world is become the kingdom of our Lord, and of His Christ; and He shall reign forever and ever." Then will ascend the song of praise in heaven. "We give Thee thanks, O Lord God, the Almighty, which art and which wast; because Thou hast taken Thy great power, and didst reign. And the nations were wroth, and Thy wrath came, and the time of the dead to be judged, and the time to give their reward to Thy servants the prophets, and to the saints, and to them that fear Thy Name, the small and the great; and to destroy them that destroy the earth" (Rev. 11:15–18).

"The stone that smote the image became a great mountain, and filled the whole earth." The interpretation of this is to be found, not in the imagined universality of the success of the gospel in the present dispensation, but in such prophecies as those of Isaiah when he says that "out of Zion shall go forth the law and the word of the Lord from Jerusalem. And He shall judge between the nations and shall reprove many peoples: and they shall beat their swords into plowshares and their spears into pruninghooks; nation shall not lift up sword against nation, neither shall they learn war any more. . . . The loftiness of man shall be bowed down, and the haughtiness of men shall be brought low; and the Lord alone shall be exalted in that day" (Isa. 2:3, 4, 17). Jehovah's Servant, Israel's Messiah, "shall bring forth judgment to the Gentiles. . . . He shall not fail nor be discouraged, till He have set judgment in the earth; and the isles shall wait for His law" (62:1, 4). "The earth shall be full of the knowledge of the Lord as the waters cover the sea" (11:9).

"All the kingdoms shall become
His whose imperial brow with crown of thorn
The men of war in mockery did adorn.
Peace shall prevail, and every land shall own
His rightful sway, and low before His throne
Shall bow and worship; angels there shall kneel.
The soul of the vast universe shall feel
The quickening touch of its life-giving Head,
And shall break forth in song. The heavens shall shed
Into the lap of earth immortal joys,
And every living thing, with thankful voice,
Shall sweetly raise the universal psalm
Of glory unto God and to the Lamb."
　　　—Boyd

THE EFFECT OF THE HOPE

The apostle Peter speaks of the Second Advent as "a salvation ready to be revealed in the last time," and then describes the joy-inspiring power of the prospect for the believer in the midst of trial. Believers throughout the ages have found courage amidst persecution, comfort in sorrow, and a reason for diligence in the fact that Jesus offered a "better resurrection." A reward proportionate to their faithfulness awaits those who persevere. The realization of what is to take place in His Parousia is an incentive to purity of heart and life.

> *"O keep us, Jesus, Lord, until that day,*
> *Walking with girded loins, apart from all*
> *That savors of this world that Thee refused,*
> *Until Thou come with shout and trump, and we*
> *Behold Thee as Thou art and like Thee be."*
> 　　From *The Story of The Glory*—Boyd

The Christian's hope of the Lord's return is a certain hope, "an anchor of the soul, both sure and steadfast," a hope "laid up in the heavens": "He that cometh shall come, and shall not tarry." But more than this, it is a practical hope, influencing every part of the life, energizing and purifying it. It forms, indeed, an essential part of that new life imparted by the Spirit of God to the believer. One who is born of the Spirit is by Him directed to the constant expectation of the return of the Christ Who died for him and rose again. With other believers he "waits for a Savior from heaven, the Lord Jesus Christ" (Phil. 3:20). It is as much a spiritual instinct for the regenerate being to lay hold on the hope set before him as it is a natural instinct for the infant to cling to something material. No one is living up to his privileges, no one is living in the full light and power of gospel truth, whose heart is not enjoying the prospect of the Lord's Second Coming. Nor can a preacher of the gospel be faithful to his ministry if he omits therefrom that which constitutes the hope of the gospel. It will perhaps be helpful if we consider some of the effects of this hope upon the Christian life.

AN INCENTIVE TO DILIGENCE IN SERVICE

Anticipation of the Second Coming of the Lord is not indulgence in a mere spiritual luxury, nor does expectation of His return tend to make Christians unpractical. The expectation may be perverted into unscriptural theorizing and speculation; but the perversion of what is good neither disproves its essential goodness, nor provides an argument against its proper use. One of the most aggressively evangelical communities of the first century was the church of the Thessalonians. "From you," says the apostle, "hath sounded forth the Word of the Lord, not only in Macedonia and Achaia, but in every place your faith to God-ward is gone forth" (1 Thess. 1:8). Yet it is of these Christians that he also writes that they had turned to God from idols, not only to serve Him, but "to wait for His Son from heaven" (vv. 9, 10). They evidently did not find waiting for the Lord incompatible with service to God. Their expectancy neither damped their ardor nor repressed their zeal in the spread of the gospel and in other forms of practical Christianity. They were not stargazers. Paul speaks of their "work of faith and labor of love"; and these were only stimulated by their "patience of hope" (v. 3). The church at Corinth, likewise, both "came behind in no gift," and at the same time "waited for the revelation of our Lord Jesus Christ" (1 Cor. 1:7).

Paul himself, who certainly could never be accused of effortless Christianity, testified to the constantly practical effect the prospect had upon his life. In his defense before the governor Felix he boldly declared his hope toward God that there shall be a resurrection, and stated that "therein he exercised himself to have a conscience void of offense toward God and men alway" (Acts 24:16). It has been imputed to him that toward the end of his life his expectation of the Lord's Second Advent diminished. Yet in his letter to Titus, the last but one of those under his name in the New Testament, and written shortly before his death, he speaks of "looking for the blessed hope and appearing of the glory of our great God and Savior Jesus Christ," and regards the hope as part and parcel of a sober, righteous and godly life (Titus 2:12, 13).

How could the knowledge that Christ is coming hinder the work of the church, or paralyze its effort? Those who, like the Thessalonians of old, wait for God's Son from heaven, find the expectation of the event an incentive to greater devotion to the service of their Master. The nobleman in the Lord's parable, who entrusted his servants with his money, commanded them, "Trade ye herewith, till I come" (Luke 19:12, 13). He who spake the parable thus set His coming again as the goal toward which the energies of His servants were to be directed.

The churches were certainly not more aggressive in Christian activity during those centuries of the present era in which the hope of the Lord's return was well-nigh lost, than they have been since the hope was resuscitated as it has been now for over a century. Simultaneous with the revival of interest in His Second Advent, and with an increased intelligent apprehension of the testimony of Scripture concerning it, has been the revival of zealous effort for the spread of the gospel, and for the evangelization of nations lying in heathen darkness.

A STRENGTH FOR ENDURANCE

The apostle Peter speaks of the Second Advent as "a salvation ready to be revealed in the last time," and then describes the joy-inspiring power of the prospect for the believer in the midst of trial. In this salvation, he says, "ye greatly rejoice, though now for a little while, if need be, ye have been put to grief in manifold trials, that the proof of your faith, being more precious than gold that perisheth though it is proved by fire, might be found unto praise and glory and honor at the revelation of Jesus Christ" (1 Pet. 1:5–8). Two points may be observed here.

Firstly, the trials are for "a little while." The phrase is suggestive of expectancy of the Lord's return. It was frequently on the lips of Christ Himself: "A little while, and ye behold Me no more; and again a little while, and ye shall see Me" (John 16:16, 17, 19; see also 7:33; 12:35; 13:33; 14:19). The words remained with Peter, and find an echo in his epistle, both in the passage above quoted, and later on when he says, "And the God of all grace, who called you unto His eternal glory in Christ, after that ye have suffered a little while, shall Himself perfect, stablish, strengthen you" (v. 10). Nineteen centuries have rolled away and the Lord has not yet returned. Albeit the prospect is ever near to the Christian. It is still "a little while." The writer to the Hebrews views the time even more briefly: "yet a very little while (lit., yet a little while, how little! how little!), He that cometh shall come, and shall not tarry" (Heb. 10:37). Paul's way of putting it in the second epistle to the Corinthians, "Our light affliction, which is for the moment," is briefest of all (2 Cor. 5:17).

Secondly, there is a "needs be." Why exactly it should be so may remain a mystery here. But the faith, which itself is undergoing the testing, can rest in the assurance of a loving heart and an unerring wisdom which planned the trial, and in the prospect of the day of Christ, when the Lord will make fully known the value He sets upon the patient endurance of trial, and show how all has redounded to His "praise, honor and glory."

Suffering for Christ's sake is lustered by the glory beyond. "We are," says Paul, "Joint heirs with Christ; if so be that we suffer with Him, that we may be also glorified with Him. For I reckon that the sufferings of this present time are not worthy to be compared with the glory which shall be revealed to usward" (Rom. 8:17,18). The apostle is here looking on to the manifestation of the Parousia, when the Lord "shall come to be glorified in His saints" (2 Thess. 1:10). The glory is not merely that which will be revealed to them: "to usward" conveys the more comprehensive idea of the revelation of His glory first to, and then in and through, them. Of this he speaks as "the liberty of the glory of the children of God" (Rom. 8:21).

Of the effects of the prospect upon sufferings resulting from Christian testimony Peter has more to say. Those on whose behalf he was writing were the objects of fierce persecution; "a fiery trial," he calls it. They were not, however, to count that kind of thing strange. Three incentives were given them to rejoice therein, past, future and present. As to the past, they were to rejoice because they were partakers of Christ's sufferings: that looked back to Calvary. As to the future, there lay before them "the revelation of His glory"; then they would rejoice "with exceeding joy." As to the present, "if ye are reproached," he says, "for the name of Christ, blessed are ye; because the Spirit of glory and the Spirit of God resteth upon you" (1 Pet. 4:12–14). The power to endure reproach for Christ's sake comes from the Holy Spirit. He is "the Spirit of glory" because He is Himself the pledge of coming glory. The present blessedness of reproach for the name of Christ is an earnest of the reward to be bestowed hereafter for such suffering. "If we endure, we shall also reign with Him."

This patient endurance in view of resurrection glory was what characterized the faithful of the former age. They saw the promises and greeted them from afar, and, confessing that they were strangers and pilgrims on the earth, they sought after a heavenly country. Some "were tortured, not accepting their deliverance; that they might obtain a better resurrection"—not a different kind of actual resurrection from that of other saints, but a resurrection which would bring with it a reward proportionate to their faithfulness in enduring hardship and suffering instead of seeking to escape it by compromise of the truth and dalliance with evil (Heb. 11:13, 35). They anticipated the inspired estimate given in a later age by one like-minded with themselves, counting light their affliction which was for a moment, reckoning that it was working for them more and more exceedingly an eternal weight of glory, and looking, not at the things which are seen, the temporal things, but at the things which are not seen, the eternal.

Accordingly the writer to the Hebrews, turning from these faithful ones to the author and perfecter of faith, and reminding them how for the joy set before Him He endured the Cross, and, further, how and why He "suffered without the gate," exhorts them to go forth unto Him, bearing His reproach (Heb. 12:2 and 13:12, 13). And the inducement? The Lord Himself. "Unto Him!" He must ever be the great attraction. Nothing signifies apart from Him. But with Him there is a further inducement, namely, the future glories, of which He will be the center. With those in view the apostle speaks of the heavenly Jerusalem. "For we have not here an abiding city, but we seek after the city which is to come." The glory of that city takes its light from the Cross, and reflects it, in all its spirit-strengthening radiance, upon the sufferings of this little while.

"The Cross is all thy splendor,
　　The Crucified thy praise;
His laud and benediction
　　Thy ransomed people raise.
Upon the Rock of Ages
　　They raise thy holy tower;
Thine is the victor's laurel,
　　And shine the golden dower."

AN ENCOURAGEMENT IN CONFLICT

When Paul exhorts Timothy to "endure hardship as a good soldier of Christ Jesus," warning him against entangling himself in the affairs of this life, he points him to the reward hereafter, adding the metaphor of the crown received by the victor in the games. To be crowned he must contend lawfully. The reference to the second coming of Christ is indirect, yet real, for it is only when the Lord comes that the crowning day will come. The illustration of abiding by the laws of a game imparts the lessons of faithfulness and obedience to Christ in view of the reward, despite the efforts of spiritual foes to oppose and to defeat, and despite every inducement to desist from the struggle with sin within and with the hosts of spiritual wickedness without. Anticipation of the crown begets strength for the conflict.

And Paul not only exhorts, he presents the example of his own life. "I have fought the good fight, I have finished the course, I have kept the faith: henceforth there is laid up for me the crown of righteousness, which the Lord, the righteous judge, shall give to me at that day; and not only to me, but also to all them that have loved His appearing" (2 Tim. 4:7, 8).

True, the apostle realized that he might be near the end of his earthly course: "The time of my departure is come," he says. But that did not lessen for him the power of the hope. Clearly, too, he implies that, looking back through his Christian life, he has joy in being of the number of those who love the Lord's appearing. This love is more than a longing for the great event to take place. Paul evidently implies that it involves fighting the good fight, finishing the course, and keeping the faith. This had all been done in his case with the Lord's coming and the crown of righteousness in view. The love of His appearing imparted courage in the conflict, steadfastness in the race, and faithfulness in adherence to the truth. His own example, then, was calculated to be an encouragement to every believer similarly to set the heart's affection on the Lord's appearing. No more striking evidence could be given of the power of the hope to affect the Christian life. The perfect tense looks back from the Judgment Seat of Christ where the past conduct of each believer will be reviewed. According as each will there be seen to have lived his life and finished his course under the stimulating influence of the Lord's return, so will be his reward.

That the Lord watches constantly, and with a view to their reward, the spiritual conflict in which His servants are engaged is evidenced in a special manner in the letters to the seven churches in Asia, in each of which He addresses the overcomer, reminding him of the time when faithfulness will receive its recompense at His hands. The present opposition is subtle, unremitting, and varied, but the promises are sure: "To him that overcometh will I give. . . ." What seems to be the greatest reward is for the overcomer in the church in Laodicea, the low spiritual condition of which calls forth His most solemn rebuke; the church that was lukewarm, rich in this world, but wretched and miserable and poor and blind and naked spiritually. In this church "He that overcometh," says the Lord, "I will give to him to sit down with Me in My throne, as I also overcame, and sat down with My Father in His Throne" (Rev. 3:21). This is a special identification with Himself as the Great Overcomer, and the reward is that of highest authority in the future glories of His kingdom.

But what is it to be an overcomer? The term implies the existence of obstacles to the exercise of faith and difficulties in the path of faithfulness. In each letter the obstacles and difficulties are clearly indicated in the mention of the various evils in the churches, and the trials to which some are subjected. The overcomer is he who in loyalty to His Lord and reliance upon His power surmounts the difficulty, triumphs over the obstacle, and remains steadfast amidst declension.

The prospect of the Lord's speedy return is definitely given to the church in Philadelphia: "I come quickly: hold fast that which thou hast, that no one take thy crown." But what to the overcomer? Here, again, we are directed to the glory of the city that is to be. "He that overcometh, I will make him a pillar in the temple of My God, and He shall go out thence no more: and I will write upon him the name of My God, and the name of the city of My God, the New Jerusalem, which cometh down out of heaven from My God, and Mine own new Name" (3:12).

> "There is the Throne of David
>   And there, from care released,
> The song of them that triumph,
>   The shout of them that feast;
> And they who with their leader
>   Have conquered in the fight,
> Forever and forever
>   Are clad in robes of white."

A COMFORT IN SORROW

This is distinctly laid down by Paul both at the beginning and at the close of the passage relating to the subject in the fourth chapter of 1 Thessalonians. He prefaces his divinely given assurance of the fact that those who have fallen asleep will have part in the resurrection and rapture at the Lord's return, by stating that his object is to prevent needless sorrow. "We would not have you ignorant, brethren, concerning them that fall asleep; that ye sorrow not, even as the rest, which have no hope." Then, having shown how all are to be together again when the promised event takes place, and how all will be caught up to meet the Lord, he says, "Wherefore comfort one another with these words."

This hope is given us, then, not to preclude sorrow, but to mitigate it.

"Grief for the loss of friends is common to all, and is not inconsistent with acceptance of the will of God, neither does it deny the hope of the Christian. The Lord Jesus Himself wept in sympathy with the mourners at the grave of Lazarus (John 11:33–35). Paul, too, was apprehensive of the sorrow into which he would have been plunged had the sickness of Epaphroditus resulted in death (Phil. 2:27). The converts at Thessalonica grieved not merely for their own loss, they grieved also for the loss sustained, as the survivors supposed, by those of their number who had fallen asleep. It was to save them from grief on this account that the apostle wrote showing them that their fears were groundless. . . . Since, for the believer, to live is Christ, to die not loss but gain (Phil. 1:21), sorrow on behalf of departed saints is precluded entirely. For our loss we mourn, for their gain we rejoice."[1]

The knowledge that our loved ones who have fallen asleep are "at home with the Lord" should be sufficient to satisfy us completely as to their present felicity. To be at home with Him who loved us and gave Himself for us, is to be in the enjoyment of happiness which can be exceeded only by that of reunion in the resurrection and rapture with all the redeemed, and participation in the glories that are to follow. For those who mourn the loss of loved ones, the Lord both lusters the dews of sorrow by His love, and wills that the glory of His promised return should shed its comforting light into the darkness of our bereavements, and that the joy of that day should temper the sorrows of separation.

> "Haste, thou glorious morning! welcome shadeless day,
> Chasing with thy sunlight all our tears away;
> Haste, O wondrous moment, when 'midst radiant skies
> Sleeping saints and living at His word arise."

A Means of Molding Character

Men become like the objects of their worship. The character of the idolater receives an impress from the nature of his idol. "They that make them are like unto them." "If you think of Buddha and pray to Buddha," says the Eastern proverb, "you will become like Buddha." He whose heart's affection is set on Christ, inevitably becomes conformed to His character. "We all, with unveiled face, beholding as in a mirror the glory of the Lord, are [being] transformed into the same image from glory to glory, even as from the Lord the Spirit" (2 Cor. 3:18, marg.). There is first the unobscured vision, indicating heart occupation with Christ; then the transformation into His likeness. The more we learn of the Lord

---

1 From *Notes on the Epistles to the Thessalonians*.

by means of the mirror of the Scriptures, the more we let the vision of His glory operate within us, the more conformed to His likeness we become.

But such devotion to the Lord is in Scripture associated with the prospect of His return, and this is definitely stated to be a means of conformity to His character. "Beloved, now are we children of God, and it is not yet made manifest what we shall be. We know that, if He shall be manifested, we shall be like Him; for we shall see Him even as He is." There will be no defect in the image when the resurrection shout has accomplished its work. Meanwhile the transformation of character is gradual: "Every one that hath this hope set on Him purifieth himself, even as He is pure" (1 John 3:2, 3). The Authorized Version "in him" is ambiguous and lends itself readily to the idea that the hope is within the believer. This of course is true, but it is not in the verse. Christ is the attraction. The hope is not merely that the event will take place, it is a hope set on Him. The immediate outgoing of the heart to Him is coupled with the joyful anticipation of what we shall find ourselves to be when we see Him even as He is, and share in His resurrection glory. "We shall be satisfied, when we awake, with His likeness" (Ps. 17:8).

The realization of what is to take place in His Parousia is an incentive to purity of heart and life. When we remember that according as we have purified ourselves, abstaining from, or discarding, all that displeases Him, so will be our capacity to serve Him in the ages to come. We have enough to inspire us to eschew every form of evil and to devote our lives and energies to Him in loyal obedience. And the standard of purity is His own unsullied character—"even as He is pure." The more effectively the power of the hope works within us, the more like our Lord we become.

Peter likewise gives testimony to the power of the hope to mold character. "Gird up," he says, "the loins of your mind, be sober and set your hope perfectly on the grace that is to be brought unto you at the revelation of Jesus Christ" (1 Pet. 1:13). The tense he employs is the vivid present—"is being brought unto you"—as if to make the future event immediately real. Then, presenting the same standard of holiness as John does, he continues, "as children of obedience"—suggesting the likeness of child to parent—"not fashioning yourselves according to your former lusts in the time of your ignorance, but like as He who called you is holy, be ye yourselves also holy in all manner of living; because it is written, Ye shall be holy, for I am holy." To set one's hope perfectly on the Lord's Second Coming thus produces conformity to His holiness in a life of obedience, with the consequent shaping of a character which is the reflection of His own.

In the second epistle, too, he points to the Day of the Lord and the passing away therein of the heavens, the dissolution of the elements, the destruction of the earth and its works by fire, and exhorts us, in view of that day, to live in all holiness and godliness, and to look for and earnestly desire "the Parousia of the Day of God." With this prospect before us we are to "give diligence that we may be found in peace, without spot, and blameless in His sight" (2 Pet. 3:10–14).

In writing to Titus Paul speaks of two appearings, one past, the appearing of grace, which has brought salvation to all men, the other future, the appearing of glory, "the glory of our great God and Savior Jesus Christ." Grace instructs us to deny ungodliness and worldly desires, and to live soberly and righteously and godly in this present world, but ever with our eye upon the glory that is to be revealed at the Lord's Second Advent. That hope is, then, to influence us in all the conditions and relationships of life, producing sobriety in our individual experience, righteousness toward our fellows, and godliness toward God (Titus 2:11–13).

And when the Lord Himself, in the closing declaration of Holy Writ, predicts His speedy return, He gives solemn admonition as to the effects of His Advent upon character, and points to the recompense which He will administer in person: "He that is unrighteous, let him do unrighteousness still: and he that is filthy, let him be made filthy still: and he that is righteous, let him do righteousness still: and he that is holy, let him be made holy still: Behold, I come quickly; and My reward is with Me, to render to each man according as his work is. I am the Alpha and the Omega, the first and the last, the beginning and the end. Blessed are they that wash their robes, that they may have the right to come to the tree of life, and may enter by the gates into the city" (Rev. 22:11–14).

A SYNOPSIS OF THE BIBLE DOCTRINE OF THE SECOND ADVENT

This is a simple, systematic description of the events that are prophesied with regards to the Second Coming of Jesus Christ, beginning with His present role in heaven and ending with judgment before the Great White Throne.

A – B = The World, the human race in time and upon the earth.
C – D = The Ascension of the Lord Jesus Christ.
D – E = The Session of the Lord on His Father's Throne.
C – G = The concurrent period upon the earth.
E – F = The Descent of the Lord into the air.
G – F = The Rapture of the Redeemed.
F – H = The Parousia of the Lord with His Redeemed.
H – J = The Manifestation of the Parousia to the World, the Second Advent.

The diagram is intended to present to the mind, through the eye, the way of the Lord Jesus from His ascension until His feet stand again upon the Mount of Olives, as foretold through Zechariah, see chapter 14, verse 4.

The base line A-B represents the World, or Time, or the History of the Human Race on the one and in the other. The first event marked thereon, C, is the Ascension of the Lord, which is described in the New Testament in such terms as these: "He was taken up; and a cloud received Him out of their sight"; he "was carried up into Heaven"; He "passed through the Heavens"; He "ascended far above all the Heavens"; He "entered . . . into Heaven itself," where He is seated "far above all rule and authority and power and dominion, and every name that is named, not only in this age, but also in that which is to come"; "With His Father in His Throne"; "On the right Hand of the Throne of the Majesty in the Heavens" (Acts 1:9; Luke 24:51; Heb. 4:14; Eph. 4:10; Heb. 9:24; Eph. 1:21; Rev. 3:21; Heb. 8:1).

It is significant, however, that when the apostle has occasion to speak of the ascension of Christ, without previous reference to His heavenly origin, he is careful to add that before He ascended He descended; that is, he takes pains to guard against a wrong deduction from his words, as that the Lord had His beginning here. He was, indeed, born in Bethlehem of Judaea, but "His goings forth are from of old, from everlasting"; He "came forth from God" (Mic. 5:2; John 17:8).

CHRIST IN HEAVEN

The occupation of Christ during His present session in heaven, D-E, is variously described. "Whither as a forerunner Jesus entered for us"; "to appear before the face of God for us"; "to prepare a place for us" (Heb. 6:20; 9:24; John 14:2). He is "Great Priest over the House of God," "Whose House are we, if we hold fast our boldness and the glorying of our hope firm unto the end"; he "maketh intercession for us"; and "if any man sin," He is our "Advocate with the Father," and, as already noticed in an earlier chapter, He is also "expecting till His enemies be made the footstool of His feet" (Heb. 10:21; 3:6; Rom. 8:34; 1 John 2:1; Heb. 10:13).

The end of this session of the Lord on His Father's throne is described thus by the apostle Paul: "the Lord Himself shall descend from heaven, with a shout, with the voice of the archangel, and with the trump of God" (1 Thess. 4:16) (E-F). But the duration of the period, D-E, has not been revealed; hence in the diagram the line has been interrupted in the middle, to suggest the limitation of our knowledge in this respect.

Coterminous with the Lord's session in heaven is this age of Gospel preaching, of "the ministration of the Spirit" (2 Cor. 2:8). It began with the outpouring of the Holy Spirit, the gift of the Father and the Son (Acts 2:33). It is the age during which "the Church which is His [Christ's] Body" is being formed (Eph. 1:22, 23). The manner of its ending has been revealed in these words of the apostle: "the Lord Himself shall descend from heaven . . . and the dead in Christ shall rise first: then we that are alive, that are left, shall together with them be caught up in the clouds, to meet the Lord in the air" (1 Thess. 4:17) (G-F).

But concerning the duration of the age of the Church, C-G, nothing has been revealed, hence this line also has been interrupted.

The Fixing of Dates Forbidden

Attempts have again and again been made to supply this lack of revelation by calculations based upon biblical and other data, astronomical phenomena and what not, or by deductions drawn from analogies assumed to be discernible therein. That such attempts are vain is abundantly evident from the failure that has invariably attended them. The only fruit they have had has been to discredit prophecy and to bring its study into disrepute. These attempts, moreover, are not merely vain; they are wrong, inasmuch as they are forbidden in the Scriptures which themselves provide the material on which such calculations are supposed to be based.

The principle underlying all communications of the divine will was thus enunciated by Moses, "The secret things belong unto the Lord our God: but the things that are revealed belong unto us and to our children" (Deut. 29:29). The Lord Jesus said to His disciples, "Of that day and hour knoweth no one, not even the angels of heaven, neither the Son, but the Father only" (Matt. 24:36). The words "day" and "hour" here seem to be equivalent to "time" in its wider, as well as in its narrower, sense. That is, the time was unknown, whether the year or the month, the day or the hour. Nor was it ever afterward revealed. Indeed the words used by the Lord after His Resurrection and recorded in Acts 1:7, "It is not for you to know times or seasons, which the Father hath set within His own authority," seem to be intended to declare that the withholding from His children of this knowledge is designed and for a purpose, and is intended to remain in force until the event takes place. The prohibition is plain enough; to attempt that which He has thus forbidden is disobedience, neither less nor more, however speciously it may be disguised or excused.

The Condition of Watchfulness

The words of 1 Thessalonians, chapter 5, verses 1 and 2: "But concerning the times and the seasons, brethren, ye have no need that aught be written unto you. For yourselves know perfectly that the Day of the Lord so cometh as a thief in the night," may be paraphrased thus, "you well know that nothing more can be known about the date of the Advent than that it will come when least expected." True the apostle went on to say, "When they [i.e., the ungodly] are saying, Peace and safety, then sudden destruction cometh upon them. . . . But ye, brethren, are not in darkness that that day should overtake you as a thief." The difference between the Christian and the ungodly, however, is not that the former knows the time of the Advent, for he does not, but that he is watchful for it at all times. It is with him as with the master of the house in the parable, who, had he known the hour of the night at which the thief was coming, would have been on the alert about that hour. But the Christian being assured that his Lord is coming, and knowing not the time of His coming, is to be on the alert all the while the night lasts. In every age His ever appropriate word to all His people is, "Be ye also ready; for in an hour that ye think not He will come" (Luke 12:37–40).

Two reasons may be suggested for this silence as to the date of the Advent. In the first place it is left unrevealed in order to induce in the Christian an ever-watchful spirit. Were the day of his Lord's appearing known this incentive to instant readiness would be lost. True it is the Christian ought to need no such aid to loyalty, but that is not to the point here. God has been pleased, in His wisdom, to provide the incentive, and what He gives we need. "Take ye heed, watch and pray; for ye know not when the time is. . . . Watch therefore: for ye know not when . . . and what I say unto you I say unto all, Watch" (Mark 13:33–37). All such language, and there is much of it in the New Testament, presupposes our ignorance of the time of the Lord's return. That known the sanctifying power of the hope would disappear. Moreover, had that time been revealed subsequently to the use of these words and others of a similar tenor, then the force of the oft-repeated exhortation to watch would have been dissipated.

It was not, then, a temporary expedient that this hour should be unknown for a season; neither was it left hidden in such a way that the diligent, or the ingenious, might discover it. From our point of view it has been left unrevealed that we might be "like unto men that wait for their Lord" (Luke 12:36). And yet there may be a deeper reason still.

THE SOVEREIGNTY OF THE LIVING GOD

We must beware of the entirely unwarranted assumption underlying much of what is said upon this point, that the acts of God are fixed upon human almanacs, that His purposes are measurable by human calendars. Not the striking of a clock but the maturity of the conditions moves the hand of God. We must resist the tendency to think of Him as though He were limited to a merely mechanical activity; as if, like the Medo-Persian monarchs, He were the slave of His own laws. The state of the crops prescribes the time of the harvest. He waited for the iniquity of the Amorites to be filled to the full (Gen. 15:10). Nineveh repented, so the fortieth day did not see the destruction of the city albeit that was proclaimed by Jonah at His command. For the elect's sake the days of calamity are shortened, whereas the longsuffering of God lengthens the day of salvation. Yet these days are not two but one (Matt. 24:22; 2 Pet. 3:9). The same patience of God that wrings from the saint the cry, "O Lord, how long," puts the new songs of praise for salvation into the mouth of many a sinner.

It is difficult, rather it is impossible, for us to conceive of the full yet harmonious exercise of all the attributes of God. There seems to us some necessary antagonism between omniscience, which must know the end from the beginning, as well as all the steps of the way thither, and the dependence of any action of God upon the course and conduct of men. So also we ask how it is possible for God to be resisted if He is omnipotent? We must remember the inevitable limitations of our power to apprehend what it is to be God. God is omniscient and omnipotent; we cannot conceive of Him as anything less. But God is also a living and free person, and it is the prerogative of all living and free persons to adapt themselves to the changing conditions with which they have to deal. Are we to deny that to Him which we claim for ourselves? It is vain for us to reason that God cannot be this if He is that, cannot be the one if He is the other, when the very conditions of our being make it inevitable that we must ascribe that to God which, because of realized inconsistency or antagonism, would be inconceivable in ourselves. Moreover, the coming of the Lord is a proper subject for prayer. The Lord taught His disciples to say "Thy Kingdom come."[1] To John He said, "Yea, I come quickly"; and to Him John responded, "Amen: come, Lord Jesus." "The Spirit and the bride say, Come. And he that heareth, let him say, Come" (Matt. 6:10; Rev. 22:17, 20). Thus the Spirit prompts the Christian, and even utters Himself, the very petition the Lord Jesus taught His disciples to present to God. And if the coming of the Lord is a proper subject for prayer, it is not possible for us to conceive of its hour as already fixed. It is noticeable, too, that when the Lord declared that that hour did not lie within His knowledge, He said, not that though it had been fixed by the Father it had not been revealed by Him, but that the Father had reserved the matter within His own authority. Does not this suggest, at least, that the fixing of the hour is for the Father when, in His wisdom, He sees that the time is ripe?

Our apprehension of the perfection of deity is feeble as yet. Our knowledge of God is but partial, and being partial may present insoluble problems to our minds. We must be content to await the larger capacity and the increased knowledge that are to be made ours when the Lord comes.

THE MEETING IN THE AIR

To return: at a time unrevealed and hence undiscoverable, "they that are Christ's" are to be caught away "to meet the Lord in the air"; or as the words run literally "to a meeting with" (F). The word used is *apantēsis*, which occurs elsewhere only in Matthew 25:1, 6; Acts 28:15. The brethren who met the apostle at the Three Taverns returned with him to Rome; in the parable the virgins returned with the bridegroom to the place whence they set out. After this analogy those who are caught up to this meeting with the Lord in the air, are to return with Him to the earth, for we know that the earth is the appointed terminus toward which He is journeying when that meeting takes place.

---

1 This word "come" is sometimes taken to mean "grow," "increase," "spread," as though the kingdom were to be established by the preaching of the gospel. The kingdom of God comes when its king comes; not before and not otherwise. The stone in Nebuchadnezzar's dream only began to grow after it had destroyed the image (Dan. 2:35). Rightly understood the prayer is most appropriate to the time now present and to the heart and lip of the Christian. To pray "Thy kingdom come," is to pray "Amen: come, Lord Jesus." To pray for the coming of the king is to pray for the coming of the kingdom.

There is nothing in the Word, neither is there anything in the context, to indicate that the return to the earth must follow immediately upon the meeting in the air. Or, to express the same thing from another point of view, the Lord's descent from heaven to earth is not of necessity continuous. Indeed there are cogent reasons for the conclusion that that descent will be interrupted for a measurable interval at the point of meeting with His redeemed people.

THE PAROUSIA

When the Lord Jesus descends from heaven with the quickening word which is to work in the bodies of all His own, the living and the dead, the change to the new and heavenly condition, they are to be carried together to meet Him at His parousia (F). It is unfortunate that the English Versions should have adopted, or retained, "coming" as a translation of the Greek word *parousia*; it would have been clear gain had they done with it as with the Greek word *baptisma*, that is had they transliterated instead of translating it. "Coming" does not at all convey the meaning of the original word. The difference is that whereas "coming" is the name of an act and is equivalent to "arrival," "advent," *parousia* is the name of a state and is equivalent to "presence," which is, indeed, its literal meaning, as the margin of the Revised Version indicates. "Coming" is properly represented by a perpendicular line thus |; *parousia* by a horizontal line thus—. "Coming" is the act of arriving and hence does not denote duration, as *parousia* invariably does. It will be easy to test these statements by reference to the New Testament occurrences of the word. The effect of this confusion is evident in 1 Thessalonians 3:12, 13, for example, "the Lord . . . stablish your hearts unblamable in holiness before our God and Father, at the coming [*parousia*] of our Lord Jesus with all His saints." This seems to refer to the Second Advent, "the appearing of the glory of our great God and Savior Jesus Christ," "with ten thousands of His holy ones" (Titus 2:11; Jude 14) And so the classic commentators understand it, see Alford, Ellicott, Lightfoot, among others. But this conclusion is only possible, as Cremer somewhat artlessly remarks, when *parousia* is made to mean what, in fact, it does not mean. It is essential to an apprehension of the mind of the Spirit, and of the apostle, that the characteristic meaning of the word be preserved. To come with, and to be present with, are obviously different ideas, and would never be confounded in the pages of any secular writer. Why should it be supposed that they are synonymous in the Scriptures?

THE JUDGMENT SEAT OF CHRIST

The word used in this connection, then, demands that we conceive of an interruption in the descent of the Lord Jesus to the earth for an appreciable period of time, during which His redeemed people will be with Him at the place of meeting. How long the Parousia will occupy has not been revealed, hence the line F-H, which represents this session of the Lord with His redeemed at their place of meeting, has also been interrupted. Apparently it is during this session that the Judgment Seat of God—or of Christ, both terms are used—takes place (Rom. 14:10; 2 Cor. 5:10). This seems the inevitable deduction from a number of passages. The resurrection of the just is the time of reward for faithful service (Luke 14:14). And this resurrection of the just takes place at the opening of the Parousia (1 Cor. 15:23, etc.). At (en, in) the Parousia of the Lord Jesus the apostle hoped to meet his converts who would then be his glory. And those converts would themselves be presented there, for the appraisement of life and service (1 Thess. 2:19; 3:13).

The apostle John also expected to meet at the Parousia those to whom he wrote, and his language suggests that that would be a time of the reviewing of life alike for himself and for them (1 John 2:28).[1]

THE END OF GENTILE TIMES

Concurrent with the Parousia of the Lord with His redeemed in the air is the period represented by the line G-J on the diagram. It also is of an unrevealed duration, and hence has been interrupted. This period sees the rise and development of the final form of Gentile government as described in Revelation 13 and other passages. It includes the Great Tribulation, "the time of Jacob's trouble," under the persecuting power of the Antichristian monarch, whether he be called king or president, or whether another title be evolved for him more in keeping with the tendencies of the age.

The "times of the Gentiles" end only when a Jew assumes the sovereign power in Jerusalem. That is to say, when the Lord Jesus Himself appears to overthrow the world monarch and his empire. This catastrophe will be the effect of the manifestation of the Parousia; the veil that hides the host in the air is suddenly withdrawn, the presence of the Lord with His redeemed is manifested, "the kingdom of the world," becomes that of "our Lord and of His Christ, and He shall reign forever and ever" (Rev. 11:15).[2] This is represented by H-J.

During the period G-J, as in every preceding age, there will be a testimony for God in the world, a gospel preached whereby men may be saved, albeit the "Church which is His [Christ's] Body" having already been completed and caught away to meet Him, the salvation of those who then respond to the gospel does not carry with it membership in that body. (See Rev. 7; 11; 14:15; 15:1, 2; 20:4.) The gospel then, as now, will have for its center the once slain, now living, Lamb, and it will be made effective by the Holy Spirit, among both Jews and Gentiles.[3]

---

1 This passage and 1 Thessalonians 2:19 intimate plainly enough that the apostles expected to recognize those with whom they had been in contact in this life, and to be recognized by them.

2 The overthrow of the Turk in Palestine has not relieved the land from Gentile domination. The British also are Gentiles. Doubtless the change from the iron yoke of the Turk to the milder rule of the British is altogether for the better. But that does not alter the fact as stated.

3 There does not appear to be adequate ground for identifying "the restrainer" of 2 Thessalonians 2:7, with the Holy Spirit, or for the statement that He is to leave the earth with the completed Church. It

How this testimony for God may be carried over into the new circumstances when all who belong to Christ have been caught away, is not difficult to conceive. Sufficient to mention the multitudes to whom the gospel facts at least will be known, and the Bible and Christian literature generally, to suggest the possibilities of the situation. That persons are to be saved, and in large numbers, during the period between the rapture of the Church and the Day of the Lord, G-J, is clear from the passages in the Apocalypse referred to above. Moreover, in Joel's foreview of the time when "the great and notable Day of the Lord" is imminent, he concludes with these words, "And it shall come to pass that whosoever shall call upon the Name of the Lord shall be delivered." It is worthy of note that "whosoever" is the characteristic word which describes the scope of the gospel of the grace of God in this present age. It will be no less so in that which is to follow. The line of demarcation between the day of grace and the Day of Judgment is clearly drawn. When the Lord Jesus is revealed in fire, "rendering vengeance [just retribution is the meaning of the word] to them that know not God, and to them that obey not the gospel of our Lord Jesus," then it is that "the Master of the House has risen up, and shut to the door" (2 Thess. 1:8; Luke 13:25). Until that hour (H-J) grace reigns, and "whosoever shall call upon the Name of the Lord shall be saved."

The conditions during the period G-J, however, will not be more but less favorable for naming the Name of the Lord than in this. The spirit of satisfaction with the progress of humanity and hope for its acceleration will increase. There will be no toleration for the godly, while for those who refuse the truth there will be a strong delusion, and a consequent ready belief in the lie that the antichristian ruler, the first beast of Revelation 13, is the man of destiny, his dominion the universal empire, the guarantee of settled peace and uninterrupted prosperity. (See 2 Thess. 2:8–12.)

AFTER THE ADVENT

With events after the Second Advent (H-J) of the Lord Jesus the diagram is not concerned. The judgment of the nations then existent upon the earth will not long be delayed, for the scene is introduced in a way that fixes its relation in time with the Advent. "When the Son of man shall come in His glory, and all the angels with Him, then shall He sit on the throne of His glory: and before Him shall be gathered all the nations" (Matt. 25:31 ff.). This takes place, apparently, at the opening of the millennial reign. The characteristic of that reign may be learned from the symbol "a rod of iron" used to describe it (Rev. 12:5). That is to say the rule of the Prince of Peace and King of righteousness will be guaranteed by adequate force, for no other rule over unregenerate men is possible in any age.

---

is in these "last days," indeed, that God is to pour forth His Spirit upon all flesh (Joel 2:28-30). See *Notes on Thessalonians*.

This is to be man's final probation. As in all previous ages, so also in this. Immune from temptation from without, for during this period Satan is confined in the abyss, men will submit to force, now happily at the disposal of righteousness; but when the archenemy is free again to practice his deceits, they will readily respond to his approaches and once more assert themselves against God and the Anointed of God. The event is the final defeat of Satan and his doom.

Thereupon follows the resurrection of "the rest of the dead" and their judgment at the Great White Throne, where the Judge is the rejected Savior (Rev. 20:11 ff.; John 5:22 and 27). "From [His] Face the earth and the heaven fled away; and there was found no place for them." They make way for "new heavens and a new earth, wherein dwelleth righteousness" (2 Pet. 3:13).

THE CHURCH AND THE TRIBULATION

In order to gain a proper understanding of the Church and the Tribulation, time is taken to set forth a careful explanation of the term "Church" and how to apply it correctly to an explanation of future events. The Great Tribulation will take place when the "abomination of desolation spoken of by Daniel the prophet" would be seen standing "in the holy place." This event sets off the series of events that eventually lead to the Second Coming of Christ.

PART 1: THE SIGNIFICANCE OF THE WORD "CHURCH"

The question is frequently asked: "Will the Church go through the Great Tribulation?" This at once raises the prior question as to the use and significance of the word Church in Scripture. A widely held idea of the word is that it stands for the whole company of believers living on the earth at any given time. Such an interpretation is, however, nowhere endorsed in the New Testament.

TWOFOLD APPLICATION OF THE TERM

Apart from an application to the community of Israel, Acts 7:38 and Hebrews 2:12, the term *ekklesia* (church) is used in two respects. One denotes the complete corporate company of saints spoken of as the "Body" of Christ, comprising all the redeemed from among Jew and Gentile during the present era or age. Of that Body Christ is the Head, Ephesians 1:22, 23; 4:15; 5:23, 25; Colossians 1:18, 24. That is the company of which the Lord spoke in Matthew 16:18: "I will build My Church." It consists both of those who have fallen asleep in Christ, 1 Corinthians 15:18, and of saints who are living in the world, and of those who may yet be added through the gospel before the Rapture. What is said of this company in the epistles to the Ephesians and Colossians is comprehensive of all. The saints in heaven are still of "the body of Christ" and of "the household of God." They are not dismembered, because they are for the time being in the spirit state. When the Body is complete, the Lord will "descend from heaven with a shout, with the voice of the archangel, and with the trump of God; and the dead in Christ shall rise first; then we that are alive, that are left, shall together with them be caught up in the clouds, to meet the Lord in the air" (1 Thess. 4:16, 17, R.V.). Such figurative expressions as nourishing, cherishing and building up, as used in Ephesians, take in their scope the complete company which the Lord will ultimately present to Himself.

The view that the term "the Church" is also used to comprise all the saints in the world at any given time is not borne out by the teaching of Christ and His apostles. Such believers could not be spoken of as either "a body" or "the body" of Christ. At the inception of the present period only a small fraction of the Church, the Body of Christ, was actually in existence; since then those who have fallen asleep do not cease to form part of the complete corporate company. The use of the phrase "the Church on earth" is a contravention of the teaching of Scripture on this subject.

A CHURCH OF GOD

The other respect in which *ekklesia* is used is that of a local church; that is, a company of believers acting together in local capacity and responsibility. Of such a community the Lord spoke in Matthew 18:17. Each company is described as a church of God, or as the church of God in a given place, e.g., 1 Corinthians 1:2. In the plural such companies are similarly termed "churches of God," 1 Corinthians 11:16; 1 Thessalonians 2:14; 2 Thessalonians 1:4.

The passages which are regarded by some as supporting the view that the term "church" can be interpreted to consist of believers living in all parts of the world really teach the contrary when considered in the light of the immediate context or of the teaching of the epistle in which the word occurs. For instance, the passages in which the apostle Paul speaks of his persecuting the church, viz., 1 Corinthians 15:9; Galatians 1:13; Philippians 3:6, do not refer to all the believers in Palestine and elsewhere at the time, but to the local church in Jerusalem. That was the assembly of which it is said in Acts 8:3, "but Saul laid waste the church, entering into every house, and hailing men and women, committed them to prison." The next verse shows that many from that assembly were scattered abroad and went about preaching the Word. For some time their work would consist of testifying, and there is no evidence of the immediate formation of other churches, though that took place ere long. Some of those who were scattered had gone as far as Damascus, and Saul in his zeal went there, with the determination to bring them to Jerusalem for imprisonment. It is significant, by the way, that instead of the mention of an assembly at Damascus, Saul stayed with "certain disciples." That the persecuted belonged to Jerusalem is confirmed

165

by the question asked in Acts 9:29: "Is not this he that destroyed them which called on this name in Jerusalem?"

It is true that in the passages referred to the apostle does not mention the city of Jerusalem, but that is no indication that he was using the term in any but the local sense. There was no need for him to mention the locality. In 1 Corinthians 15:9, he had just been speaking of Jerusalem, and the Lord's appearances there after He was risen. In Galatians 1:13 it would be evident to his readers that he was referring to the church in Jerusalem; moreover, it is significant that in verse 22, with reference to those who were not known to him by face, he speaks of "the churches [not "the church"] of Judaea." In Philippians 3:6 the description he gives of the circumstances of his preconversion days centers in Jerusalem.

In Acts 9:31, R.V., where the singular is used, the context indicates that the word still bears the local sense. The saints had been scattered from Jerusalem throughout Judaea and Samaria and Galilee. It was they who had comprised the church at Jerusalem, from the time of pentecost until the persecution arose. The formation of other churches does not up to that time receive mention.

THE CHURCH ON EARTH—AN UNSCRIPTURAL PHRASE

Moreover, neither here nor in the other passages could they have been said to constitute "the Church on earth." These persecuted and scattered saints were not the only believers alive at the time, as is clear from the mention of some in Damascus.

It is true that when Saul was making havoc of the church the Lord in His divine interposition said: "Why persecutest thou Me?" But this affords no ground for the inference that there was such an entity as "the Church on earth." This identification of Himself with His persecuted saints could apply to any company of believers at any time who were suffering in this way, or to any single Christian; it does not betoken what is conceived of as "the Church on earth."

Neither can such an idea be derived from any use of the term "church" in the first epistle to the Corinthians. In 1 Corinthians 12:28 the context shows that the reference is to the local church at Corinth and not to a wider application of the term. In the preceding verse the apostle speaks of it as "a body of Christ" (there is no definite article in the original), a corporate company the members of which are to have the same care one for another (v. 25). This could not be said of believers constituting an assembly inclusive of those living in another land. What is here inculcated is the realization on the part of each member of a local church of the need of seeking the welfare of the fellow members of that church. How could that apply to those in a distant region?

The spiritual gifts mentioned in verse 28 all existed in the church at Corinth (the word "apostles" is used in its wider sense, as in 1 Thess. 2:6; Rom. 16:7; 2 Cor. 8:23). Yet whatever view is taken of the meaning of this verse, it could not apply to what is called "the Church on earth," a phrase unscriptural in its use and subversive in its import; for the position, establishment and destiny of the Church are heavenly. It constitutes "the Church of the firstborn who are enrolled in heaven" (Heb. 12:23, R.V.).

In 1 Timothy 3:16 it is the local church at Ephesus that is spoken of as "the house of God, which is the church of the living God, the pillar and ground of the truth," and not all the churches in the world as an amalgamated entity. The distinctly local application is evident throughout the epistle, the object of which is to give instruction "how men ought to behave themselves [the A.V. gives a wrong rendering here] in the house of God." The local application is again clear, for instance, in verse 16. Each assembly is "a house of God, a church of the living God." There is no definite article in the phrases in the original. The passage has no reference to such a company as "the Church on earth."

AN IMPOSSIBLE EVENT

To speak, then, of the Church as destined to go through the Great Tribulation, is to use phraseology which receives no support from Scripture, and betokens a misunderstanding of the significance of the term. Some might say that their use of the word in this respect is simply a convenient mode of expression to comprehend all true believers who will be living during the time of the Great Tribulation, and that to regard one who uses the term in this way as holding an erroneous view, is simply making a person an offender for a word.

Yet to speak of the Church's going through the Great Tribulation involves the impossibility that those who are already with the Lord (who still form part of the Church) would come down from heaven to suffer with their fellow saints on earth the Great Tribulation woes.

If those who hold the view referred to, adopted Scripture phraseology and taught that individual believers or believers gathered as local churches or assemblies, would experience the sufferings of the period so described, we could understand their meaning. Even so there is this to be considered, that individual Christians and local companies could not endure more horrible afflictions than have from time to time been meted out to fellow Christians in times of persecution in the past, and that not even the woes of the Great Tribulation will exceed the tortures and privations, with their vast variety, which have been the lot of believers during past centuries. The question remains whether living members of the Church are destined to share with the Jewish people their unprecedented tribulation.

THE GREAT TRIBULATION AND THE WRATH OF GOD

Let us see, then, what Scripture has to say with regard to the circumstances of that time. In the Lord's discourse to His disciples recorded in Matthew 24, He foretold that there would be "great tribulation, such as hath not been from the beginning of the world until now, no nor ever shall be" (v. 21). He indicated both the time of its occurrence and that of its termination.

TIME INDICATIONS AS TO THE TRIBULATION

It would take place when the "abomination of desolation spoken of by Daniel the prophet" would be seen standing "in the holy place" (v. 15). Immediately after the Tribulation "The sun shall be darkened, and the moon shall not give her light, and the stars shall fall from heaven, and the powers of heaven shall be shaken; and then shall appear the sign of the Son of man in heaven: and then shall all the tribes of the earth mourn, and they shall see the Son of man coming in the clouds of heaven with power and great glory" (vv. 29, 30). Obviously these events have not yet taken place.

THE PROPHECIES IN DANIEL AND MATTHEW

The same period and circumstances are foretold in Daniel 12:1, 2: "And at that time shall Michael stand up, the great prince which standeth for the children of thy people: and there shall be a time of trouble, such as never was since there was a nation even to that same time: and at that time thy people shall be delivered, every one that shall be found written in the book. And many of them that sleep in the dust of the earth shall awake, some to everlasting life, and some to shame and everlasting contempt" (Dan. 12:1, 2). The phrase "at that time," refers to what has just been related in the eleventh chapter, which predicts a war as destined to take place in Palestine. The unprecedented tribulation cannot therefore be regarded as extending through the present era since A.D. 70.

In Matthew 24 fuller details are given: "When therefore ye see the abomination of desolation, which was spoken of by Daniel the prophet, standing in the holy place (let him that readeth understand), then let them that are in Judaea flee into the mountains: let him that is in the housetop not go down to take out the things that are in his house; and let him that is in the field not return back to take his cloak. But woe unto them that are with child and to them that give suck in those days! And pray ye that your flight be not in the winter, neither on a Sabbath: for then shall be great tribulation, such as hath not been from the beginning of the world until now, no, nor ever shall be. And except those days had been shortened, no flesh would have been saved: but for the elect's sake those days shall be shortened" (vv. 15–22).

Three passages in the book of Daniel speak of this "abomination of desolation," the context making clear that the time referred to is yet future and will immediately precede the personal intervention of Christ for the overthrow of the desolator and the setting up of the millennial kingdom, "to bring in everlasting righteousness." The first passage indicates that the Antichrist will make a covenant with the Jews for a period spoken of as "one week" (or *hebdomad*), that in the middle of this period, he will break the covenant and mark the reversal of his attitude toward the Jewish people by the installation of the abomination that maketh desolate: "he shall make a firm covenant with many for one week: and for the half of the week he shall cause the sacrifice and the oblation to cease; and upon the wing [or pinnacle] of abominations shall come one that maketh desolate; and even unto the consummation, and that determined, shall wrath be poured out upon the desolator" (9:27).

The R.V. word "desolator" (correcting the A.V., "desolate") should be noted, for it is upon him and his associates that the divine wrath is to be executed. The Jews themselves, that is, the godly remnant, the objects of the fury of the Antichrist are, as a nation, to be the subjects of divine deliverance (Jer. 30:7); those of the nation who remain apostate and worship the image of the Beast will be subject to the wrath of God alike with all others who do so (Rev. 14:9).

The second passage similarly predicts the breach of the treaty by the Antichrist: "he shall . . . have indignation against the holy covenant, and shall do his pleasure: he shall even return, and have regard unto them that forsake the holy covenant. And arms shall stand on his part, and they shall profane the sanctuary, even the fortress, and shall take away the continual burnt offering, and they shall set up the abomination that maketh desolate" (11:30, 31). The last passage is 12:11, which states the length of the period of tribulation as a thousand two hundred and ninety days, from the time that the burnt offering is taken away and the abomination that maketh desolate set up.

"THE TIME OF JACOB'S TROUBLE"

Jeremiah 30:7 defines the character of the period as relating to the nation: "It is even the time of Jacob's trouble." Then follows the assurance that the nation, as a nation (that is obviously the significance of the name Jacob, the name being put by metonymy for his descendants) will be "saved out of it." The subsequent context shows that the deliverance will introduce the millennial period of peace and rest. Strangers will no more serve themselves of the people, and judgment will be meted out to the nations who have oppressed them (v. 11). This very passage states that while the Lord will save His own earthly people, He will "make a full end of all the nations whither they have been scattered."

The efforts of the combined Gentile powers under the Man of Sin to destroy the Jews from being a nation, to cut off their very existence from the earth (for this is to be the object of their fierce hostility in the period of desolation consequent upon the breaking of the covenant previously agreed upon by the Man of Sin), will be immediately met by a series of retributive judgments, not merely punitive or remedial, but retributive, by which the wrath of God will be poured out upon the foe, and upon all those (including persistently apostate Jews) who own allegiance to the Man of Sin.

This divine wrath, in its manifold judgments, which will be God's answer to the utter rejection of His claims and the denial of His very existence, His answer to men's allegiance to, and worship of, the Beast (Rev. 13:3–8), and to their unprecedented maltreatment of His earthly people, will affect the world, that is, "them that dwell on the earth" (Rev. 8:13; 12:12; 13:8, 14, e.g.).

THE DIVINE WRATH EXTENDING THROUGH A PERIOD

That the wrath of God will extend over a period instead of being confined to one final judgment at the revelation of Christ with the angels of His power, is made clear in Revelation, chapters 6 to 19. In chapter 15:1, concerning the seven last plagues, it is said that "in them is finished the wrath of God" (R.V.) The verb in the original signifies to bring to an end, to complete, to finish, not to fill up (as in the A.V.). The same word is used, for instance, in 10:7 ("finished") and in 11:7. It corresponds to the noun *telos*, an end. The word "finished" makes clear that the judgments poured out in connection with the seven vials or bowls do not constitute the whole of the divine wrath to be exercised. The successive events which form the consummating acts of this divine wrath, are given in detail in chapter 16, and these are all preliminary to the personal advent of Christ in judgment as described in 19:11 to 21. Moreover, that these seven judgments themselves cover a certain period, is clear from what is said, for instance, of the sixth, in which the kings of the whole world are instigated by the powers of darkness to gather together "unto the war of the Great Day of God, the Almighty" (16:14).

As the events which take place in the execution of the wrath of God under the pouring out of the seven last plagues out of what are figuratively described as "seven bowls," constitute the finishing of His wrath, it follows that the preceding similar events described in the earlier chapters are likewise to be recognized as belonging to this same period.

AN IMPORTANT DISTINCTION

This series of judgments in connection with the wrath of God, the immediate retribution by God upon the nations, is not to be identified with "Jacob's trouble," though the events will be concurrent. The judgment upon the Jewish nation as such, for their rejection of their Messiah and their persistent refusal to accept His claims, has consisted and will consist of bitter persecution at the hands of Gentile powers, reaching its culmination in the satanically instigated onslaught inflicted by the Beast (Rev. 12:13). At the time when the apostle wrote to the church of the Thessalonians the wrath had already begun to come upon the Jews and would proceed "to the uttermost" (1 Thess. 2:16). They were already a scattered people. Their land was under tyrants, their temple and city were about to be destroyed; heavier sorrows would come upon them, and, as the Lord Himself foretold, will do so, before final deliverance comes, Matthew 24:15–28. But God's wrath upon His earthly people, reaching its climax in the acts of the Man of Sin in "the time of Jacob's trouble" is one thing; the wrath of God to be poured out simultaneously upon that despot and his kingdom and all who associate with him, Jew or Gentile, is another. The two circumstances coincide but are to be distinguished.

TWO CONTEMPORANEOUS EVENTS

This is made clear in the Apocalypse, as well as in other Scriptures. The time of "Jacob's trouble" and the judgments of the wrath of God begin when "the abomination that maketh desolate" is set up. The judgments meted out to the worshipers of the Beast are not withheld until the Great Tribulation is over. God no longer will maintain His attitude of long-suffering, waiting for men to come to repentance. The retributive hardness of heart which will characterize the adherents of the Man of Sin, will determine their irretrievable doom. The "coming" of that "lawless one" (his *parousia*, obviously his presence in the world and not his mere arising to prominence) will be "according to the working of Satan with all power and signs and lying wonders, and with all deceit of unrighteousness for them that are perishing; because they received not the love of the truth, that they might be saved. And for this cause God sendeth them a working of error, that they should believe a lie that they all might be judged who believed not the truth, but had pleasure in unrighteousness" (2 Thess. 2:9–12).

One great distinction between "Jacob's trouble" and the wrath of God upon the Beast and his kingdom, lies in this, that there is to be no deliverance for the Beast and all who acknowledge him; the wrath of God upon them will issue in their entire removal from the earth to their appointed doom (Rev. 14:9–11). Deliverance, on the contrary, is assured to the God-fearing Jews as a nation, for the tribulation which they experience at the hands of man will not see their extermination, but the preservation of this converted and faithful "remnant," the nucleus of the leading nation of the earth in the Millennium. "Two parts . . . shall be cut off and die; but the third shall be left therein. And I will bring the third part through the fire, and will refine them as silver is refined, and try them as gold is tried: they shall call on my name, and I will hear them: I will say, 'It is my people'; and they shall say, 'The Lord is my God.' Behold, a day of the Lord cometh, when thy spoil shall be divided in the midst of thee. For I will gather all nations against Jerusalem to battle; and the city shall be taken, and the houses rifled, and the women ravished; and half of the city shall go forth into captivity, and the residue of the people shall not be cut off from the city. Then shall the Lord go forth, and fight against those nations, as when He fought in the day of battle. And His feet shall stand in that day upon the Mount of Olives, which is before Jerusalem on the east, and the Mount of Olives shall cleave in the midst thereof toward the east and toward the west, and there shall be a very great valley; and half of the mountain shall remove toward the north, and half of it toward the south. And ye shall flee by the valley of my mountains; for the valley of the mountains shall reach unto Azel: yea, ye shall flee, like as ye fled from before the earthquake in the days of Uzziah king of Judah: and the Lord my God shall come and all the holy ones with Thee. And it shall come to pass in that day, that the light shall not be with the brightness and with gloom: but it shall be one day which is known unto the Lord; not day, and not night: but it shall come to pass, that at evening time there shall be light. And it shall come to pass in that day, that living waters shall go out from Jerusalem; half of them toward the eastern sea, and half of them toward the western sea: in summer and in winter shall it be. And the Lord shall be King over all the earth: in that day shall the Lord be one, and His Name one" (Zech. 13:8–9). Man breaks and will break his covenants, but God's covenant with Abraham will ever abide.

REVELATION, CHAPTERS 6 TO 19

Before we return to this point of the subject, it is necessary to continue the consideration of the divine operations of judgment in the coming period, which constitute it as a time of the wrath of God upon the world, as well as a time of Israel's woe. For there is one fundamental truth connected with this, which has a direct bearing upon the question as to whether any of the saints who belong to the church, the body of Christ, are destined to pass through this period.

Previously to the pouring out of the seven vials or bowls there is a series of judgments to be executed under the sounding of seven trumpets. The events which are described as taking place in connection with these are obviously such as constitute measures of divine wrath upon "them that dwell on the earth" (see chapter 8, verse 7, to chapter 11, end). Nature itself is visited with disaster, as well as the circumstances and doings of men. After the sounding of the fourth trumpet a voice is heard pronouncing a threefold woe, "for them that dwell on the earth, by reason of the other voices of the trumpet of the three angels who are yet to sound" (8:13). Chapter 9 is descriptive of these further divine visitations, which, while they rise to a climax of retribution, meet with a refusal on the part of men to repent of their evil doings. After the sounding of the seventh trumpet, there is first an anticipative declaration in heaven as to the setting up of the kingdom of Christ upon the earth, and a retrospective statement looking back upon what has taken place as to the fury of the nations and the visitation of divine wrath upon them: "the nations were wroth, and Thy wrath came" (11:18, R.V.).

Tracing the events backward further, as characterized by wrath, we observe that previously to the sounding of the seven trumpets there are judgments carried out under the opening of the seals. These are described in chapter 6, and have the same features of divine retribution as those foretold in the subsequent chapters with reference to the sounding of the trumpets and the pouring of the contents of the seven bowls. The whole period covered by chapters 6 to 19 is thus seen to be one of the wrath of God upon the confederate nations and all associated with them, for their rejection of God and His Christ and their antagonism to His earthly people.

An Essential Difference

Without now considering, what to many seems obvious, that this closing period will on this very account be essentially contrary in character to that of the present time of the long-suffering of God and the preaching of the gospel of His grace, and that the latter will not continue into the period of wrath, yet the very fact that the wrath of God is to be poured out in the manner so clearly indicated in these chapters, must be regarded in the light of specific statements concerning the previous deliverance of believers who form part of the Church, the body of Christ (not, we say again, the Church on earth).

In 1 Thessalonians 5:9, the Scripture declares that "God appointed us not unto wrath, but unto the obtaining of salvation through our Lord Jesus Christ." The preceding verse makes clear that the salvation referred to is not deliverance from the perdition of hell (quite a different subject of salvation), but that which is to be brought unto us at the Lord's return to receive us unto Himself. With that event the passage from 4:13 to 5:11 deals. The wrath, then, from which we are to be delivered is that which is to descend upon "them that dwell on the earth," under the misrule of the Man of Sin.

This assurance in 5:9 throws light upon the statement in the 10th verse of the first chapter of this epistle, where the Lord Jesus is described, firstly, as the object of the expectancy of the saints, and, secondly, as "our Deliverer from the coming wrath." This is the plain meaning of the original. The R.V. has rightly used the present tense of the verb ("delivereth"). The A.V., "which delivered," is a mistranslation and is misleading; it has been responsible for giving a wrong impression as to the deliverance referred to. The construction is that of the definite article with the present participle of the verb, literally, "the delivering [One]," a construction commonly used as a title; for example, in Romans 11:26 the same phrase is actually translated "the Deliverer."

Ek and Apo

It has been urged that, since the preposition translated "from," *ek*, frequently means "out of" or "from the midst of," therefore this deliverance is destined to come while the wrath is being exercised, and that believers are to be delivered from the midst of its judgments. It is further argued that if the deliverance was destined to take place before the wrath descended, the preposition *apo*, away from, would have been used. As against such a view, in the first place, the preposition *ek* has a wider range of meaning than that which has just been represented. It is not always used in the way indicated. In 2 Corinthians 1:10 it is used in the statement, "who delivered us out of so great a death, and will deliver us." Here *ek* is plainly equivalent to *apo*, from, for death was not actually experienced, but was impending. In Matthew 17:9 it is used of descending *from* a mountain, not out of the midst of the mountain, for, as A. T. Robertson says, "we are not to suppose that they had been in a cave"; moreover, in the parallel passage in Luke 9:37, the equivalent preposition is *apo*. *Ek* is similarly used in Acts 12:7, "his chains fell off from his hands." Cp. *ek* in Acts 28:4, of the serpent hanging from his hand. Illustrations of the elastic use of this preposition in regard to circumstances of place, condition, or state, can be obtained from any comprehensive dictionary.

When, therefore, it is necessary to decide whether this preposition, in its use in 1 Thessalonians 1:10, signifies "out of the midst of," or "from that which is impending," the question is to be determined by a Scripture statement upon the subject concerning which no ambiguity is possible, and, as we have pointed out, such a statement is provided in the 9th verse of the 5th chapter, that "God hath appointed us not unto wrath, but to obtain salvation." This being so, believers who belong to the Church cannot be here to endure it, for the negative is followed by a positive assurance of salvation, the mode of which the context explains.

Appeal is made to Revelation 3:11, "I also will keep thee from the hour of trial, that hour which is to come upon the whole world, to try them that dwell upon the earth." Here, again, it is precarious to insist that *ek* means *out of* ("the hour"); moreover, the verb used in the promise is that of *keeping from*, not rescuing or even delivering, but guarding from it. It is not a promise of being kept through it, but of exemption from it. Even if the inference that this message, given to the assembly in Philadelphia, is of future and general fulfillment, no ground is afforded for the supposition that any members of the Church are doomed to pass through it.

A Specific Declaration as to Deliverance

The statement in 1 Thessalonians 5:9 is so definitely set in connection with the Lord's return to receive us to Himself, as a deliverance from the impending calamities to be suffered by the world under the righteous wrath of God at the close of the age, that we should regard this assurance as a fundamental part of the doctrines of the gospel relative to the return of Christ. To obtain salvation from this wrath and yet to endure it are clearly incompatible. And as the "wrath" and the "tribulation" are contemporaneous, to be exempt from the wrath of God carries with it exemption from "Jacob's trouble."

A Recapitulation

Recapitulating the subject as thus far treated, we have endeavored to show, firstly, that to speak of the Church as going through the Tribulation is to use unscriptural terminology and to convey the idea of what is actually an impossibility; secondly, that the time of the Great Tribulation is plainly indicated as immediately preceding the Second Advent, i.e., the manifestation of the Lord for the overthrow of His foes, the deliverance of Israel, and the setting up of His kingdom; thirdly, that the special characteristics of that Tribulation will be the unprecedented sufferings endured by the Jewish people at the hands of confederate nations under the human despots spoken of as the Beast and the False Prophet, following upon the setting up of "the abomination of desolation"; fourthly, that while the sufferings of the Jews at the hands of man will be the culmination of divine wrath upon His earthly people in punishment for their rejection of Christ, such wrath having come upon them "to the uttermost," this remedial punishment is to be distinguished from the retributive wrath of God poured upon Gentile nations, and upon Jews who remain in apostasy, a divine retribution because of their worship of the Beast, and their acceptance of his claims.

It is important to make this distinction quite clear even at the expense of a certain amount of repetition. The divine displeasure against the nation will be punitive and purgative; that against the Gentile powers will be purely retributive. The wrath of God upon His earthly people, exercised through the instrumentality of the Gentiles, under the Man of Sin, will thereby be mediate; the wrath poured out upon the Gentile powers and apostate Jews will be immediate.

Scripture also makes clear that these two sets of circumstances will synchronize. For, as we have seen, the series of judgments against the Gentile nations, otherwise spoken of as "them that dwell on the earth" (judgments which constitute the wrath of God), cover a considerable period, unfolded from chapters 6 to 19, culminating in the smiting of the nations by the personal intervention of Christ; at the same time the fury of the Gentiles is expended upon Israel (see especially ch. 12.13–17). This is in accordance with Scriptures in the Old Testament, e.g., Psalm 2; Isaiah 42:13, with verse 45, and 43:2; Joel 3.

Inasmuch, then, as "the time of Jacob's trouble," inflicted upon Israel through the human instrumentality of the nations under the Man of Sin, will be at the same time a period in which the wrath of God is poured out directly upon the Gentile powers themselves, it is to be a period from which, according to the specific statements of 1 Thessalonians 1:10 and 5:9, believers living up to the time of the Rapture, members of the Church, the body of Christ, are to be delivered.

THE MODE OF DELIVERANCE

The way in which the deliverance is to come is foretold in the fourth chapter of 1 Thessalonians, verses 16, 17, which describe what has been rightly called the Rapture, a catching away, a word expressive of the statement, "We that are alive, that are left, shall together with them be caught up in the clouds, to meet the Lord in the air." It is not spoken of as a secret Rapture. There is no such word describing its character. It does, however, give a plain statement of facts. The inference drawn by some, that this Rapture is to take place at precisely the time when the Lord is manifested in the culmination of divine judgment to destroy the Beast, to deliver Israel and set up the kingdom, is not only a deduction unsupported by Scripture, but is directly opposed to what Scripture states most explicitly.

To deduce further from such an inference, that the solemn and august tribunal of the Judgment Seat of Christ is to take place simultaneously with the Rapture and the Lord's personal intervention in judgment upon the world, is utterly incompatible with the doctrines of Scripture both concerning the Rapture itself, the *Parousia* of the Lord with the saints, and with what Scripture testifies as to the character of the Judgment Seat of Christ.

BRITTLE EARTHENWARE—A DISTINCTION

With regard to the nation of Israel, while the many, or the mass, make a league with Antichrist, and, as "the clay" (the brittle earthenware), will be ground to powder when "the Stone" pulverizes the Gentile powers, a considerable remnant of the nation will refuse allegiance to the Beast, and, being preserved through the protecting care of the Lord amidst the Great Tribulation, will constitute God's earthly people, when the kingdom is set up. For that deliverance numbers of the Jews will be prepared through the special witness given by the prophet Elijah and other agencies, by means of which they will be converted from their apostate state, and will turn to the Lord in repentance (Mark 9:12, with Mal. 4:6; cp. Rev. 11:3).

As to the preservation of the godly Jews, see Matthew 24:16; Revelation 12:14–16; and Daniel 12:2. "At that time thy people [Daniel's] shall be delivered, everyone that shall be found written in the Book." The Lord has ever had a remnant of faithful ones among His earthly people. As it was in Elijah's day, and as it came to pass in the time of the Lord's first Advent, so in still greater measure will it be at the time of the end. On the contrary, those Jews who remain apostate, are destined to share the wrath of God meted out to the Gentile nations, but that wrath, as we have sought to show, is to be distinguished, in its inescapable retribution, from that which is ministered by God through human agency, constituting "the time of Jacob's trouble," the fiery furnace through which, and from which, the remnant of the Jewish people, converted to their Messiah, will be delivered at His Second Advent.

THE SECOND ADVENT

The circumstances of that Second Advent (quite distinct in character and time from the Rapture of the Church) are described in many parts of the Scriptures.[1] The Lord Jesus will be revealed "from Heaven with the angels of His power in flaming fire, rendering vengeance to them that know not God, and to them that obey not the gospel of our Lord Jesus: who shall suffer punishment, even eternal destruction from the face of the Lord and from the glory of His might" (2 Thess. 1:7–9). That revelation of Christ constitutes the Epiphany (or shining forth) of His *Parousia* (v. 8), which previously will take its inception at the Rapture (1 Thess. 4:15–17).

THE RAPTURE AND THE GREAT TRIBULATION

The closing of the age will be marked by God's wrath. In the past, God has judged His people for their disobedience, bringing many to repentance; but the Scriptures show that the judgments meted out in this period will be

---

1 Many of them are enumerated in the writer's book, "*The Roman Empire, Its Revival and End*."

purely retributive, and will culminate in "the revelation of the Lord Jesus from heaven, with the angels of His power in flaming fire, rendering vengeance to them that know not God, and to them that obey not the gospel of our Lord Jesus." Deliverance for the church comes when the Lord comes into the air (1 Thess. 4:17); deliverance for the Jewish nation takes place when the Lord comes to the earth (Zech. 14:4, 11).

In his discourse to the disciples, as recorded in Matthew 24, the Lord foretold that at a certain time there would be "great tribulation, such as hath not been from the beginning of the world until now, no nor ever shall be" (v. 21). He indicated both the time of its occurrence and that of its termination. It would take place when the "abomination of desolation spoken of by Daniel the prophet" would be seen standing "in the holy place" (v. 15); and immediately after it, He said, "The sun shall be darkened, and the moon shall not give her light, and the stars shall fall from heaven, and the powers of the heavens shall be shaken; and then shall appear the sign of the Son of man in heaven: and then shall all the tribes of the earth mourn, and they shall see the Son of man coming on the clouds of heaven with power and great glory" (vv. 29, 30). That these latter events have never yet been fulfilled is clear.

Turning now to the book of Daniel we find a prediction of the same period, with similar time indications. The closing chapter, the matter of which runs consecutively on from the eleventh, begins with the statement: "And at that time shall Michael stand up, the great prince which standeth for the children of Thy people: and there shall be a time of trouble such as never was since there was a nation even to that same time." As to the termination of the period, the prophecy declares, "at that time thy people shall be delivered, every one that shall be found written in the book. And many of them that sleep in the dust of the earth shall awake, some to [more literally, these shall be for] everlasting life, and some to [those shall be for] shame and everlasting contempt." The latter are set in contrast to the former. "These" are the "many," who are to be raised at that time; "those" are others who do not share in that resurrection, but await a different destiny. The time is to be one of deliverance for the Jewish people, and the intimation is that resurrection will be the portion of many. This deliverance has not yet taken place.

As to the circumstances which are to transpire when this great tribulation takes place, the opening words of the chapter, "At that time," point to what has just been related in the eleventh chapter, which predicts a warfare to take place in Palestine. The unprecedented tribulation cannot therefore be viewed as extending over the long centuries of the present era since A.D. 70. As the time of trouble is connected with a great war and the overthrow of a tyrant, on the one hand, and ends with deliverance and resurrection, on the other, the period must be still future. Again, in the passage in the Gospel of Matthew, the similar time indication, which speaks of the abomination of desolation as standing in the holy place, does not refer to anything which took place in A.D. 70. No warfare has continued all through the centuries. No abomination, or image, or anything of the sort, was set up in the holy place when the Roman armies under Titus besieged Jerusalem and destroyed the temple.

The prophecy in the book of Daniel, concerning the abomination to which Christ referred, is as follows: "and upon the wing [or "pinnacle"] of abomination shall come [or "be"] one that maketh desolate; and even unto the consummation, and that determined, shall wrath be poured out upon the desolator" (9:27; the R.V. rendering is undoubtedly accurate here). Nothing that is mentioned in that passage, as to a covenant with the Jews and the pouring out of divine wrath upon the desolator, was fulfilled in the case of the Roman power in the first century.

That the prediction uttered by the Lord, "when therefore ye see the abomination which was spoken of by Daniel the prophet standing in the holy place," had reference to others than the apostles, is indicated by Matthew's parenthesis, "let him that readeth understand." In similar phraseology Christ said shortly afterwards to Caiaphas and the scribes and elders, "Ye shall see the Son of man sitting at the right hand of power and coming on the clouds of heaven" (26:65). Caiaphas and his fellows personally will not be there to see the event. The Lord's words had reference to the Jewish people who will see it, and who were represented by the high priest and the others on the night of the betrayal. The disciples were not necessarily to be there in person to see the abomination or to flee to the mountains, nor is there any evidence that they were in Jerusalem in A.D. 70, and that they fled therefrom. There have been times of great tribulation in past history, but that to which the prophecies of the book of Daniel and those uttered by the Lord refer was clearly a well defined period, unprecedented in its severity, and of comparatively short duration. Jeremiah speaks of the same time when he says: "Alas! for that day is great, so that none is like it, it is even the time of Jacob's trouble; but he shall be saved out of it" (Jer. 30:7). The whole world will indeed be involved in the Great Tribulation, but what Jeremiah states marks an outstanding feature of it.

Two things stand out clearly, therefore, namely, that the Great Tribulation is destined to take place at the end of the present age, and that it will be terminated by the manifestation of Christ in glory for the deliverance of His earthly people the Jews.

SIMULTANEOUS EVENTS
A Period of Divine Wrath

The closing period of the age is also marked in Scripture as a time of the wrath of God upon the world. Judgments of God have been remedial, and have brought men to repentance; but the Scriptures show that the judgments meted out in the period referred to will be purely retributive, and will culminate in "the revelation of the Lord Jesus from heaven, with the angels of His power in flaming fire, rendering vengeance to them that know not God, and to them that obey not the gospel of our Lord Jesus" (2 Thess. 1:7, 8).[1]

That the divine retribution will extend over a period, and that the period is to be distinct from the present time of God's longsuffering grace and mercy is unmistakably demonstrated as follows. The nineteenth chapter of Revelation describes the culminating act of this closing period, namely, the coming of Christ from heaven in judgment upon the foes of God (vv. 11–21), an event otherwise mentioned in the passage in 2 Thessalonians 1, already referred to. The fifteenth and sixteenth chapters of Revelation describe seven judgments which will precede that event, and the opening statement concerning these is, that "in them is *finished* the wrath of God" (15:1, R.V.). These judgments themselves extend over a period, including the execution of God's retribution upon "Babylon the great," which receives "the cup of the wine of the fierceness of His wrath" (16:19).

Clearly the series of judgments mentioned in chapter sixteen is to fall upon the world before the Second Advent, which is described in chapter 19:11 to 20:3. For under the fifth in that series the kingdom of the Beast is yet in existence (v. 10); under the sixth, the Beast and the False Prophet are still active and are engaged in preparations for "the war of the great day of God Almighty" (v. 14). These passages show, therefore, that this period of wrath will precede the appearing of Christ in glory at His Second Advent, for then it is that the Antichrist will be destroyed by the Lord Himself (2 Thess. 2:8).

That the calamities which will be inflicted in this period are not confined to the Beast and his confederates, is indicated in preceding chapters, for the woes are pronounced upon "them that dwell on the earth" (8:13).

Preceding chapters also describe similar circumstances of divine retribution upon the world (cp. for example, 14:9, 10). In chapter 11:18 the correct rendering is, "the nations were wrath, and Thy wrath came [not "is come"]." The circumstances in these chapters are not those of the display of God's mercy. A distinct period is marked as characterized by the wrath of God.[2]

A Distinctive Assurance

The Scriptures we have considered indicate, then, firstly, that the Great Tribulation will occupy the closing period of this age, and secondly, that the

---

1 That this passage refers to a premillennial event is indicated by the fact that vengeance is rendered to those who obey not "*the gospel of our Lord Jesus.*" A fuller description of the circumstances is given in Revelation 19:11–21, where the Lord is seen coming with the armies of heaven to smite the nations and to tread "the winepress of the fierceness of the wrath of Almighty God" (v. 15).

2 "This wrath is to be understood, then, of the calamities wherewith God will visit men upon the earth when the present period of grace is closed, and which will fall first upon the Jews, then upon the Gentiles (Rom. 2:2, 9). The calamities of the Jews are referred to in Jeremiah 4:7; Zechariah 14:2; Matthew 24:15–21, and those of the Gentiles in Zechariah 14:3; Matthew 24:30; Luke 21:25–29, among many passages. The believer is assured of deliverance from both through the Lord Jesus Christ (cp. 5:9; Rom. 5:9)."—From *"Notes on The Epistles to the Thessalonians,"* by C. F. Hogg and the Writer.

world also is at that time to come under the wrath of God. The two are to be simultaneous.

DELIVERANCE FROM COMING WRATH

In writing to the church at Thessalonica, the apostle Paul reminds them how "they turned unto God from idols to serve the living and true God, and to wait for His Son from Heaven, even Jesus, which delivereth us from the wrath to come" (lit., "the coming wrath") (1 Thess. 1:10). The phrase rendered "which delivereth" consists, in the original, of the article with the present participle. It has been wrongly rendered in the Authorized Version by the past tense. The phrase is, literally, "the One delivering," and is equivalent to a title, "the Deliverer." That indeed is how the same construction of the same word is rightly translated in Romans 11:26. The accurate rendering, then, is "to wait for His Son from heaven, Whom He raised from the dead, even Jesus, our Deliverer from the coming wrath." The wrath referred to is therefore not that which abides now on the unbeliever, as in John 3:36; nor can the phrase be taken to refer to the punishment of the lost in the other world. That the subject with which the apostle is dealing is that of waiting for the Son of God from heaven, is itself an indication that His coming will mean the deliverance of the church from the impending wrath. We know from the epistle itself that the church at Thessalonica had been instructed by Paul orally in matters relating to the Second Advent and the judgments destined to precede it (see ch. 5). The phrase, "the coming wrath," would therefore be familiar to them.

As to the question whether the church is to pass into the period of wrath and be delivered from the midst of it, light is thrown upon this as the epistle proceeds. A categorical statement is given in the fifth chapter. There the apostle says that "God appointed us not unto wrath, but unto the obtaining of salvation through our Lord Jesus Christ" (v. 9). Here again the subject is the Lord's coming. We who are "of the day" are to put on as a helmet "the hope of salvation," and for this reason, that "God appointed us not to wrath." The apostle shows that our deliverance is based on the death of Christ; it is not dependent upon our spiritual condition at the time. He "died for us, that whether we wake or sleep, we should live together with Him." The deliverance referred to is the completion of our salvation—"the redemption of our body."

In this passage, as in the first chapter, the wrath is obviously not that mentioned in John 3:36. Nor is the reference to what will take place in the other world. Even were it possible to conceive that there is any such reference, the statement is categorical, that the saints of the church are not appointed to wrath at any time, and that accordingly they are not appointed to the wrath to be poured out upon the world at the closing period of the present age. They are to obtain salvation when Christ comes to receive them unto Himself. That salvation will be the consummation of the present salvation which they enjoy through the redemptive work of the Cross.

This passage, with that in chapter 1:10, puts the subject in a clear light. The deliverance is not out of the midst of the wrath, but before it is poured out. This truth is confirmed in the second epistle, at the close of the second chapter, where the apostle says: "But we are bound to give thanks to God alway for you, brethren beloved of the Lord, for that God chose you from the beginning unto salvation" (v. 13). That "but" sets the deliverance of the saints in contrast to the state of the world just described in the same chapter as under the power of the Man of Sin, a state which meets with divine retribution.

While these epistles were addressed to the church at Thessalonica, it is necessary to bear in mind that they were indicted by the Spirit of God as part of the inspired Scriptures, and were therefore intended as permanent records for the instruction of churches everywhere. They were designed to abide as truth for the enlightenment and edification of the saints throughout this age. By this time by far the greater portion of the church, is already with the Lord. For those who remain on the earth, whether now, or subsequently, and so until the Rapture, these Scriptures are provided by God, that, inspired by their stimulating hope, the saints may be maintained in a spirit of expectancy, and that, like the Thessalonian saints of old, they may "wait for His Son from heaven."

In support of the view that part of the Church will be here during the Great Tribulation, it is urged that, while there is no penal suffering for believers, any disciplinary stroke on Israel or on the nations before Christ comes, has, in part at least, a corrective character, that it should lead to repentance, and that from this the last Tribulation, though of a very special kind, is not to be excepted. This line of teaching, however, does not adequately regard the fact that the Great Tribulation comes into a period distinctively marked as that of the wrath of God. It also fails to recognize the assurances given to the church in the passages we have just been considering.

The question is asked as to why a promise of deliverance from the wrath to come should be regarded as designed for the church, when there are other saints to whom the assurance has been given of preservation through the period of the Great Tribulation, and who would in that case themselves be present in the world in the period of wrath. In reply to this, Scripture makes a distinction which it is therefore necessary to observe. The promise given in the epistle to the Thessalonians shows that, for the church, deliverance from the wrath to come will be by means of the Rapture (an expression quite Scriptural; see 1 Thess. 4:17), by the power of the Lord, in the resurrection of those who have fallen asleep and the transformation of the living. That assurance is given to the church. Deliverance for the faithful who are preserved in the period that follows will come in a different manner. Theirs is an earthly destiny, and they are to be kept under God's protecting care in a special way. The Jewish nation, as such, is to be preserved for earthly peace and power in the millennium. Gentile peoples will also continue, for such are to enjoy millennial conditions. None of those who have worshiped the Beast and have received his mark will be so kept (Rev. 14:9–11). It follows that Jews and Gentiles who live through the Great

Tribulation into the millennial reign of Christ are such as have not worshiped the Beast and have been preserved from death.

It is important, then, to distinguish between the teaching given, on the one hand, concerning the church, its character, its destiny, and its deliverance, and, on the other hand, concerning God's earthly people the Jews, a large number of which are assured of preservation, a residue of Gentiles also escaping death during the time of wrath, and sharing in the blessedness of Messiah's earthly reign.

As for those who are slain for their faithfulness, and will enjoy resurrection glory, God has His own way of dealing with people, and it is for us to accept what is written in the Scriptures, and to forego reasonings as to why certain people should be dealt with in one manner and certain others in another; why it should be the lot of some people to form part of the church and to be removed from the earth at the Rapture, other people afterwards having their lot with that part of the Jewish nation which is to be kept for millennial blessedness; and why certain people should experience the calamities of that time, and even suffer death, to enjoy resurrection life, apart from actual incorporation in the church. These things lie within the determining counsels of God. Deliverance for the church comes when the Lord comes into the air (1 Thess. 4:17); deliverance for the Jewish nation takes place when the Lord comes to the earth (Zech. 14:4, 11).

THE INTERVAL

The Scriptures already noticed indicate, apart from several similar considerations, that the period of "the wrath of God" marks an interval between the Rapture of the saints and the Second Advent of Christ to the earth for the overthrow of the foes of God and the deliverance of the Jewish nation from their time of trouble. The existence of such an interval is entirely consistent with the meaning of the word Parousia (lit., "being with"), which signifies not only a coming to, but a presence with. This point calls for further attention.

The teaching of the Word of God is always consistent. The plain significance of those Scriptures which we have been considering in the preceding pages is not contradicted by other passages. On the contrary, it is confirmed by them.

OBJECTIONS CONSIDERED

Here the author focuses on key objections and questions that many have delineated over the years. Time is taken to acknowledge and answer differing views with regards to the timing of the Rapture and Tribulation.

We purpose now to notice some of the chief arguments advanced in favor of the view that the Lord will not remove the church until after the Tribulation.

(1) We are told that since Jehovah has said to Christ, "Sit Thou on My right hand, until I make Thine enemies Thy footstool" (Ps. 110:1; Matt. 22:44), the Lord Jesus could not come to receive the saints to Himself, as in

1 Thessalonians 4:16, 17, until the time of the overthrow of His foes, which will not take place till after the Great Tribulation.

This argument presupposes that when Christ comes to receive the church to Himself, He will cease to be at the right hand of God. That is an unwarranted inference. The Lord will not cease to occupy that position when He descends from heaven for the Rapture of the saints. The expression signifies a position of authority and power rather than a physical attitude. A king does not cease to occupy the throne of his country when he pays a visit elsewhere. His occupation of the throne does not depend upon his continuous session in the actual chair of state. Moreover, the martyr Stephen saw the Lord "standing on the right hand of God" (Acts 7:56), yet the Scripture was not broken which said, "Sit Thou on My right hand." An interval between the descent of Christ to the air for the Rapture of the saints and His Second Advent for the overthrow of His foes could not involve any change in His authority.

(2) **The word "apantēsis," "meet," in 1 Thessalonians 4:17, is said to signify that those who go to meet a person, return to their starting place with him, and that therefore when the Lord comes for the church He will come immediately with the church to the earth.**

This idea forces a meaning into the word which it by no means invariably admits. It is true that the word usually suggests that those who go out to meet a person intend to return, in his company, to the place from whence they set out, but the return is not necessarily immediate. If a person leaves Liverpool for London, intending to meet a friend coming from Paris, and to go back with him to Liverpool, not immediately, but after a more or less prolonged stay with him in London, the word *apantēsis* would be quite applicable to describe the meeting, as much as if the return were immediate. Moreover, the form *apantaō*, "to meet," has a wide range of meaning. It is used of meeting a person in argument, and of kings meeting in battle. It is therefore unsafe to base a doctrine on one particular application of the word. We know that the saints are to be caught up to meet Christ, and are coming back with Him in His glory and power to deal with the kingdoms of the world, but to say that the latter event must immediately follow the former, because of a special significance of *apantēsis*, is untenable.

(3) **The apostle Peter testified concerning Christ that the heavens must receive Him "until the times of restoration of all things" spoken of by the prophets (Acts 3:21). The deduction is made from this that Christ cannot come until the Antichrist has run his course; could the rise and power of God's most awful opponent, it is asked, be "the times of restoration"?**

Before considering the phrase itself, it will be well to remark that we have not stated that Christ will come before even the rise of the Antichrist. Again, it is necessary to distinguish between the Rapture and the Second Advent. The Advent of Christ signifies His coming into the world. At His first Advent He was born in Bethlehem; at His Second Advent He will come to the Mount of Olives (Zech. 14:4). At "the Coming [or Parousia] of the Lord" (1 Thess. 4:15) for the Rapture of the saints He will descend to the air (v. 17). The Parousia is not the same as the Second Advent. Nowhere does Scripture state that the Rapture is immediately to be followed by the Second Advent.

As to "the times of restoration of all things," a significance attaches to the fact that it does not say "whom the heavens must receive until the restoration of all things spoken of by the prophets." "The times of the restoration" covers a period. The events which immediately precede the restoration are naturally included in the time relating to it. The wrath of God by which the world suffers retribution for its refusal of Christ and for its reception and worship of the Antichrist, and which will culminate in the destruction of the foes of God, is a necessary preliminary to the setting up of the Kingdom. That period of wrath, therefore, has its place in the times of restoration. In the restoration of a dilapidated building much rubbish has frequently to be cleared out of the way as the first act necessary to the purpose in view. The Rapture of the saints, coming previously to this period of wrath, would consistently be said to introduce "the times of the restoration."

Plainly no doctrine can be built upon this text, as that the Rapture of the saints must be followed in immediate succession by the Advent of the Lord with the saints and with His angels.

(4) It is stated that as the Man of Sin is to be destroyed by the "Coming" of the Lord, according to 2 Thessalonians 2:8, this indicates that His Coming at the Rapture and the destruction of the Man of Sin must be simultaneous.

A careful consideration of what is actually stated in this verse will show that the inference is without foundation. The rendering is as follows: "And then shall be revealed the lawless one, whom the Lord Jesus shall slay with the breath of His mouth, and bring to naught by the manifestation of His coming." The word rendered "manifestation" is *epiphaneia*, and is literally "a shining forth." The word rendered "coming" is *parousia*, and, as has already been pointed out, this (literally, "a being with") signifies the presence of a person with others. Its occurrence in Philippians 2:12, for instance, is a sufficient example, where Paul speaks of his *parousia*, his "presence" at Philippi, in contrast to his *apousia*, his absence from that city. *Parousia* always refers to a period of time, though some particular event in the period may be especially in view. What is here in view, then, is that event, connected with the *parousia* of the Lord with His saints, which will see the destruction of the lawless one. It is called the manifestation, or shining forth, of His *parousia* because, in company with His saints (who will previously have been with Him from the time of the Rapture when His *parousia* began), He will burst in upon the scene of the Man of Sin's activities, and will there and then bring the tyrant to naught, consuming him with the breath of His mouth. That will usher in the millennial reign of righteousness. "The manifestation of His *parousia*" strikingly confirms, then, the teaching that an interval will elapse between the Rapture and the Second Advent.

It will be well here to quote a paragraph or two on the subject of the Parousia, from notes on the epistle to the Thessalonians by C. F. Hogg and the writer. The note is taken from the commentary on the words in 1 Thessalonians 2:19, "*Are not even ye, before our Lord Jesus at* [lit., *in*] *His coming?*"

"*Parousia*, here rendered 'coming,' is a noun formed from the verb *pareimi*—to be present, as in Luke 13:1; John 11:28; Acts 10:33, etc., and hence 'a being present with.' In a papyrus document it is used of a royal visit to a certain district; in another a person states that the care of her property demands her 'presence' in a certain city . . . The usual translation is misleading, because coming is more appropriate to other words, such as *erchomai*, Luke 12:45; 19:23; *eleusis*, Acts 7:52; *eisodos*, 13:24; the difference being that, whereas these words fix the attention on the journey to, and the arrival at, a place, *parousia* fixes it on the stay which follows on the arrival there. It would be preferable, therefore, to transliterate the word rather than translate it, that is, to use 'parousia,' rather than 'coming,' wherever the reference is to the Lord Jesus.

"Where *parousia* is used of the Lord Jesus it refers to a defined period. Thus in 2 Peter 1:16 it describes, not the daily and general companying of the Lord with His disciples among the people, but that limited period during which He was transfigured before them, Matthew 17:1–8. Where it is used prophetically, *parousia* refers to a period beginning with the descent of the Lord from heaven, into the air, 1 Thessalonians 4:16, 17, and ending with His revelation and manifestation to the world.

"During the *parousia* of the Lord in the air with His people, Paul expected to give account of his stewardship before the Judgment Seat of Christ, 1 Corinthians 4:1–5; 2 Corinthians 5:10; the presence there of the Thessalonian converts and their commendation by the Lord, would mean reward to the evangelists who had been the means of their conversion and to the pastors and teachers who had labored among them. For a similar thought see 1 John 2:28, and cp. 1 Peter 5:4. There, too, all would be abundantly compensated for the afflictions they were enduring.

"The *parousia* of the Lord Jesus is thus a period with a beginning, a course, and a conclusion. The beginning is prominent in 4:15; 5:23; 2 Thessalonians 2:1, 1 Corinthians 15:23; James 5:7, 8; 2 Peter 3:4; the course, here and in 3:13; Matthew 24:2, 37, 39; 1 John 2:28; the conclusion, in 2 Thessalonians 2:8; Matthew 24:27."

Again, the passage in Matthew 24:37–39 clearly indicates a period. The Lord says that "as were the days of Noah so shall be the Parousia of the Son of Man." As the days of Noah ended with the coming of the Flood, so the coming period will terminate at the intervention of Christ, in the shining forth, or manifestation, of His Parousia, as in 2 Thessalonians 2:8. At that event He will be accompanied, not only by His angels, but by His saints. He is then coming "to be glorified in His saints, and to be marveled at in all them that believed" (2 Thess. 1:10). That His saints will then come with Him is confirmed by Revelation 19, which describes the same event, for the armies in heaven are seen following Him on white horses, "clothed in fine linen white and pure" (v. 14). The fine linen is defined in verse 8 as "the righteous acts of the saints." The marriage of the Lamb has by that time taken place in heaven, and His wife has made herself ready to come with Him.

As a further illustration of the fact that the Parousia is periodic, and not momentary, the passage in 2 Thessalonians 2 goes on to speak of the *parousia* of the Man of Sin himself. The *parousia* of this despot will be "according to the working of Satan with all power and signs and lying wonders, and with all deceit of unrighteousness." Obviously not merely the occasion of his rise to supremacy is intended by such a description, but his period of supremacy. These things will characterize his presence, his *parousia*, in the world.

Since the Parousia of Christ is a period, the idea that the outshining or manifestation of that Parousia, for the destruction of the Man of Sin, is the same thing as His descent into the air for His saints, is, to say the least, not proven.

(5) In his second epistle to the Thessalonians the apostle says "it is a righteous thing with God to recompense affliction to them that afflict you, and to you that are afflicted rest with us, at the revelation of the Lord Jesus from heaven with the angels of His power, in flaming fire, rendering vengeance to them that know not God, and to them that obey not the gospel of our Lord Jesus" (2 Thess. 1:6–8). It is concluded from this that the Church cannot obtain rest until Christ comes to render this vengeance, and therefore that the Rapture must immediately be followed by the Second Advent.

There is no valid ground in this passage for the inference that the Second Advent, or the coming of the Lord Jesus to render vengeance, is to be immediately preceded by the Rapture. The following note is from *Notes on the Epistle to the Thessalonians*, by C. F. Hogg and the writer.

"The subject immediately before the apostle's mind is not the rest of the saints, but the retribution of God on their persecutors. Hence the words, "and to you that are afflicted rest with us," are an incidental extension of the idea of recompense, and are to be read parenthetically, permitting the words that follow to be connected directly with the close of verse 6, thus: 'affliction to them that afflict you (and to you that are afflicted rest with us), at the revelation of the Lord Jesus.' The time indicated is not that at which the saints will be relieved of persecution, but that at which their persecutors will be punished. The time of relief for the saints had been stated in the earlier letter, 4:15–17; here a passing reference to a fact within the knowledge of the readers was all that was necessary. Such extensions of thought are not uncommon in epistolary writings; cp. v. 10, and 1 Thessalonians 1:6; 2:15, 16.

"Since, then, the rest of the saints begins with the Lord's descent into the air, which marks also the inauguration of the Parousia, the Parousia itself will intervene before the vengeance of God begins to be executed. Whether the period so termed is to be of longer duration—say, extending to years, or shorter—say, limited to hours or even to minutes, is not in question here."

(6) The Lord gave parting promise to the disciples that He would be with them "always [all the days] even unto the end of the world [age]." This is taken

to indicate that the church must be here until the termination of the rule of the Antichrist and therefore also of the Great Tribulation.

The word rendered "end" is not *telos*, which might signify "a termination," but *sunteleia*, "a consummation"; so the R.V. margin accurately renders it. Not the actual termination, therefore, is in view, but the heading up of events which are destined to transpire at the close of the age. A period is connoted in all the five places in this Gospel where the word is found. Until whatsoever time the affairs of the world should arrive at such a consummation the Lord promised to be with His followers. Events might at any time be approaching such a crisis. The removal of the church would at once introduce it. This passage affords no proof that any part of the church must be here until the last day of the age. Other events to follow would be included in "the consummation." Moreover, the absence of the church would not render nugatory the presence of the Lord with any who become faithful during the following period.

(7) In the first epistle to the Corinthians the apostle states that the resurrection of the saints who have fallen asleep, and the transformation of the living saints, will take place "at the last trump" (1 Cor. 15:52). The suggestion is made that this is the last of the series of trumpets mentioned in Revelation 11:15, which introduces a closing scene before the setting up of the millennial kingdom.

The apostle Paul wrote to the church at Corinth long before the apostle John wrote the Apocalypse. The readers of the Corinthian epistle, being Greeks, were quite familiar with the metaphor of the last trumpet. To them it was a military metaphor, and simply indicated the signal given for an army to move. The phrase directed the mind not so much to the series of soundings, but to the fact that an army was to be set in motion. There is no valid reason for supposing a connection between Paul's use of the phrase and the series of trumpets described later in the book of Revelation. Moreover, there is no similarity between the event spoken of by Paul and the events introduced by the series of trumpets in the Apocalypse. The inference that Paul is referring to what was afterwards revealed to John is therefore quite unwarranted.

(8) The apostle states, in Romans 11:25, that "a hardening in part hath befallen Israel, until the fullness of the Gentiles be come in; and so all Israel shall be saved." On the supposition that "the fullness of the Gentiles" is the church, Israel, it is argued, will be saved immediately upon the completion of the church. The inference from this is that people will be brought into the church right up to the time when Israel is to be delivered, and that therefore some members of the church will be here during the Tribulation.

Even if "the fullness of the Gentiles" were coextensive with the church, it would not necessarily follow from the apostle's words that Israel's salvation will be immediately successive to the completion of the church. Certainly the one is conditional upon the accomplishment of the other; but the prediction would be amply fulfilled if there were an interval between the coming in of the fullness of the Gentiles and the deliverance of Israel. It is not necessary to the meaning of the apostle's words that, at the moment the fullness has come in, the hardening of Israel should cease. What he states is that one circumstance must precede the other, and that the latter cannot take place till the former is accomplished.

But it is a questionable interpretation which explains the coming in of the fullness of the Gentiles by the completion of the church. The apostle's subject here is not that of the church, but the dispensational dealings of God with Jew and Gentile, His judicial severity toward the former and His goodness toward the latter. Paul has already used the word "fullness" to signify the promised blessing to the nation of Israel (v. 12), and has shown how God's mercy brought salvation to Gentiles. Again, in this chapter he distinguishes from Gentiles those Jews even who have accepted Christ, and thereby become part of the church; for the converted Jews, members of the church, constitute a spiritual Jewish "remnant" to which the apostle himself belongs (it being true also that in Christ there is neither Jew nor Gentile). The phrase, "the fullness of the Gentiles," would appear therefore to comprehend all Gentiles, as such, who will in any way receive deliverance and blessing previously to Israel's national restoration at the beginning of the Millennium.

(9) It is urged that the word epiphaneia, "appearing," signifies the manifestation of Christ in glory at His Second Advent for the overthrow of the ungodly and the establishment of His kingdom, and that, accordingly, the passages where this word occurs relatively to the subject cannot refer to a Rapture to take place some time beforehand.

Thus to limit the application of this word is an unfounded assumption. Epiphaneia was used among the Greeks in a variety of ways, as, for instance, of the appearance of an enemy to an army in the field, of one of the heathen gods to men, etc. In Scripture it is used of the manifestation of God's power in the help of His people Israel against the Canaanites (2 Sam. 7:23), and of the appearing of the people before Him (Amos 5:22). In the New Testament it is used of the Advent of the Savior at His incarnation (2 Tim. 1:10).

When the apostle exhorts Timothy to keep the commandment, "without spot, without reproach, until the appearing of our Lord Jesus Christ" (1 Tim. 6:14), it is an unwarrantable interpretation which makes it necessary to suppose that the reference is to His manifestation with His saints and angels in flaming fire. The context indicates that the reference is to the descent of the Lord Jesus into the air to the meeting with the saints, as in 1 Thessalonians 4:15–17. That event will certainly constitute an epiphaneia, an appearing, of Christ to His saints.

A similar passage is 2 Timothy 2:1, which is accurately rendered in the R.V., "I charge thee in the sight of God, and of Christ Jesus, who shall judge the quick and the dead, and by His appearing and His kingdom." (This has been wrongly rendered in the A.V., which reads as if the judgment of the living and the dead will be simultaneous.) What we have said above applies here, that there is no ground for the assumption which compels the idea that the appearing and the kingdom are simultaneous or immediately successive. "The appearing" is quite possibly at the descent of Christ for the Rapture of the saints, and "the Kingdom" the subsequent establishment of the earthly rule of Christ when He comes with His saints.

It is true that "*epiphaneia*" is used with reference to this latter event. This is clearly so in Matthew 24:27, which speaks of the shining forth of the glory of the Lord Jesus "as the lightning cometh forth from the east, and is seen even unto the west," but that is immediately consequent upon the unveiling (*apokalupsis*) of His Parousia with His saints. So again in 2 Thessalonians 2:8, the Man of Sin will be brought to naught "by the manifestation [*epiphaneia*] of His coming [*parousia*];" again in Titus 2:13, "looking for the blessed hope and appearing of the glory of our great God and Savior Jesus Christ." (Of this more presently.) But because *epiphaneia* is used, in these three passages, of the later event, that does not afford a ground for limiting every occurrence of the word respecting the future, to that event. Moreover this latter *epiphaneia*, or appearing, of Christ will be with the saints and not by way of His coming to call them to the air to meet Him.

It is necessary to guard against putting an undue limitation to the application of words in Scripture, especially when such words show a variety in their usage. The corresponding verb, *epiphainō*, is used of the stars (Acts 27:20), and of the grace, and kindness and love of God, made manifest in the coming of His Son for the salvation of men (Titus 2:11; 3:4).[1]

What has been said above applies likewise to the word *apokalupsis*, an uncovering, unveiling. This is used in the New Testament with a number of different applications. As regards the future revelation of Christ, the very variety just referred to forbids its being restricted to one event. Clearly in 2 Thessalonians 1:7, which speaks of "the revelation of the Lord Jesus Christ from Heaven with the angels of His power, in flaming fire," the reference is to the Second Advent in judgment upon the world. But this does not justify the conclusion that the word refers to that event in every passage relating to the subject.

For instance, the apostle's commendation of the church at Corinth that they came behind in no gift, "waiting for the revelation of our Lord Jesus Christ" may well point to the time of the Rapture; for when the Lord comes to raise the dead saints and change the living, His act will certainly involve an unveiling of His person to them, and this is quite distinct from His revelation of Himself at His Second Advent, for the overthrow of His foes.

With regard to the trial of our faith, which is to be found "unto praise and glory and honor at the revelation of Jesus Christ," what is referred to here is by some associated with the time of the setting up of the earthly kingdom, by others to what the saints are to enjoy when the Lord comes to receive them unto Himself. So also in regard to their sufferings, in which they are to rejoice, as being partakers of Christ's sufferings, that "at the revelation of His glory also they may rejoice with exceeding joy" (4:13).

---

1 See *The Epistles to the Thessalonians*, by C. F. Hogg and the writer.

Even if the view is correct that this joy is fulfilled at the Second Advent, when the Lord comes to deal with the world in judgment and set up His kingdom, no ground whatever is thereby provided for deducing therefrom that a period does not intervene between the Rapture and the Second Advent, between the removal of His saints to meet the Lord in the air, and His coming with them. For as is pointed out, the latter event is the consummation of the hope of the saints, "the blessed hope," and this would be the time of "exceeding joy" and "praise, honor and glory."

The use of this word *apokalupsis* provides another instance of the need to avoid limiting the meaning and application of the phraseology of Scripture.

(10) From the parable of the tares the deduction is made that, since the tares and the wheat "grow together until the harvest," and the tares are bound in bundles to be burned, and the wheat is gathered into the barn, the church cannot be gathered in until the very end of the age, when the separation takes place, and the righteous shine forth in the kingdom.

This conclusion rests upon the assumption that the wheat represents, and is coextensive with, the church. The assumption will not, however, bear the test of the Scriptures which speak of the Rapture of the saints. Moreover, there is no direct intimation, either in this parable or in our Lord's interpretation of it, that He is speaking of the church in contradistinction to the ungodly. The parable and its interpretation show that the reapers are the angels, and that to them will be committed the work not only of binding the tares in bundles, but also of gathering the wheat into the barn (v. 30). Now there is no Scripture to show that the angels are agents in the Rapture of the saints. On the contrary, the passages which give details of that event state specifically that the Lord Jesus will accomplish the Rapture by His own power. "For the Lord Himself shall descend from heaven with a shout, with the voice of the archangel, and with the trump of God: and the dead in Christ shall rise first; then we that are alive, that are left, shall together with them be caught up on the clouds to meet the Lord in the air" (1 Thess. 4:16, 17). The details of this description, as given in the original, apply to Christ Himself. The article is absent both before "voice" and before "archangel," and this expresses the quality of the shout, its majesty and authority, characterizing it as being uttered by Christ Himself, and not as being the act of an archangel. In other words, the phrase is practically equivalent to "with an archangelic voice." This is confirmed by the preposition *en* (lit., "in," translated "with"), which indicates, not the accompaniment of another being, but the character of the shout itself. So with the phrase "with" (lit., "in") the trump of God. These considerations point to the threefold description as referring to one great signal.

Even if an archangel uttered his voice at the time, there is nothing in this passage to correspond to the gathering in of the wheat by the angels, as mentioned in the parable, or to show that the angels take such a part in the Rapture.

On the other hand, if, as we have endeavored to show, Scripture elsewhere teaches that there is to be a period intervening between the Rapture of the saints and the Second Advent of Christ "with the angels of His power," then the act of the angels mentioned in the parable of the tares (which takes place at Christ's Second Advent to the earth) refers to the separation of the wicked from the multitude of righteous who during that period have dissociated themselves from the evil of the time and have waited for Messiah's return and kingdom.

There is another point in the parable, and its interpretation, suggesting a distinction between that event and what is said of the Rapture. The angel reapers are first to gather up the tares and bind them in bundles to burn them. The Lord interprets this as the gathering out of His Kingdom all things that cause stumbling and them that do iniquity, and the casting of them into the furnace of fire (vv. 41, 43). What happens immediately after that is the shining forth of the righteous as the sun in the kingdom of their Father (v. 43). So again, in the interpretation of the other parable of the net, "the angels shall come forth, and sever the wicked from among the righteous" (v. 49). At the Rapture the righteous will be severed from the wicked. There is nothing to show that the two events are similar or simultaneous. There is much to indicate the contrary.

(11) The argument is advanced that the apostles Peter and Paul expected events to take place before the Rapture; Paul knew that he must stand before Caesar (Acts 27:24), that he would suffer death (2 Tim. 4:6), that certain events must take place at Ephesus (Acts 20:29, 30), that "in later times some would fall away from the faith" (1 Tim. 4:1), and that the time would come when certain believers would not endure the sound doctrine and would turn from the truth (2 Tim. 4:3, 4); Peter knew that he would live to be old and would die for his Lord (John 21:18); again the church at Sardis knew that it was to have tribulation for ten days (Rev. 2:10); accordingly, in contrast to the view that Christ may return at any time, since certain events were destined to take place before that event, it is to be expected that the Rapture of the church will take place after the Great Tribulation.

Let it be noted, firstly, that nowhere have we expressed the view that any apostle expected the Lord to come during his lifetime, or that they taught the churches to anticipate the fulfillment of that event before those which they declared must take place in their lifetime or subsequently. Obviously they did not do so. All these things were long ago fulfilled. It is also true that the expectation of the occurrence of these circumstances did not weaken their hope. No view of the coming of Christ for the meeting of the saints with Him in the air has been expressed in these pages which is inconsistent with the expectation, by the apostles and the churches, of the events mentioned in connection with their lives.

What we have sought to point out from Scripture is that the Great Tribulation is appointed for the end of this age, that simultaneously with this there is to be a period of divine wrath upon the world, that from the wrath of God the church is to be delivered, that therefore no part of the church will be here during the Great Tribulation, and that this involves an interval between the Rapture and the Second Advent, which interval is called again and again in Scripture the Parousia of our Lord with His saints. Nothing concerning the events which were foretold as to take place during the apostle's lifetime and afterwards is contrary to this, nor can it be conceived how it could be so. What the Lord made known to an apostle or to a church, or what the apostles made known to churches, as certain to take place, does not in any way affect the teaching relating to the Rapture as destined to take place before the Great Tribulation. What is clear is that this latter event would not take place in the apostle's time, nor until after the events which the churches were to experience.

As to the apostle Paul's outlook, some have supposed that whereas he had formerly anticipated the Lord's return, in his closing days the knowledge of his impending death impaired that anticipation. On the contrary, his closing epistle, addressed to Timothy, makes clear that Paul was ready not only for death, but for the Rapture, and for winter as well (2 Tim. 4:6, 8, 21).

(12) It has been argued that, since the title "Antichrist" signifies "against Christ," and, further, since the Church which is His body is Christ mystical ("so also is Christ," 1 Cor. 12:12), therefore the title Antichrist must indicate an antagonism on his part against the church; and that as his persecutions take place during the Tribulation, the church (or part of it) must be here at the time.

Such an argument is a sort of special pleading. What is taught concerning the Antichrist shows that he denies the Father and the Son, and the truths relating to Him (1 John 2:22; 4:3), and that he will set himself against the cause of God and the kingdom of Christ (see Rev. 13, etc.). These facts are quite sufficient to account for his title "Antichrist." It is not at all necessary to suppose that his name involves the presence in the world of any part of the church during his satanic activities. There is no Scripture which shows it. If he is against the Father and the Son he is thereby against Christ.

An idea connected with this inference is that, since the apostle John taught his readers (members of the church) concerning the advent and activities of the Antichrist, this, being truth for the churches, indicates that churches will be here under those activities.

This, again, is a gratuitous and unfounded assumption. That an apostle predicted, in writing to a church, that a certain event was to take place, affords no ground for the supposition that churches are to be on the earth when it does take place. Peter, for instance, tells his readers that the heavens are to pass away with a great noise, and that the elements are to be dissolved with fervent heat, that the earth and its works are to be burnt up, and makes these events the basis of an exhortation to the saints to boldness and godliness of life, and to be "earnestly desiring" the coming of the day of God, in which these terrific events are to transpire. But that could not afford any ground for supposing that any part of the church will be here during those events. So neither can predictions concerning the Antichrist afford ground for the conclusion that saints of the Church will be here under his tyranny.

(13) Paul and Barnabas taught the churches that they must "through many tribulations enter into the Kingdom of God" (Acts 14:22). Since, then, the church was to pass through much tribulation, the conclusion is

drawn that it will pass through "the Great Tribulation"; it has even been suggested that the "much tribulation" is practically the same thing as "the Great Tribulation."

This is confounding things that differ. Tribulation is indeed the characteristic lot of faithful followers of Christ in this life, but what is said of the Great Tribulation shows that it is of a distinctive and special character, that it affects the gentile nations as well as the Jewish nation, that it will come as a snare upon "all them that dwell on the face of all the earth" (Luke 21:35); it is to be "the time of Jacob's trouble," and it is to "try them that dwell upon the earth."

To suppose that the Lord's words, "Immediately after the tribulation of those days . . . shall appear the sign of the Son of man in heaven . . . and they shall see the Son of man coming . . . with power and great glory" (Matt. 24:29, 30), refers to the "much tribulation" through which Paul told the churches they must pass, is an utterly unfounded inference. For the Lord specifies the tribulation of which He was speaking, as appointed for a distinct period at the time of the end. It is a tribulation of unprecedented character, and the days will be such that, unless they were shortened, no flesh would be saved.

(14) It is stated that what the Lord Jesus addressed to His disciples on the Mount of Olives He addressed to them as members of His body, the church, and that accordingly members of the church will be here to see "the abomination of desolation," and will flee from Judaea to the mountains (Matt. 24:15, 16).

At the time of the Lord's discourse Peter, Andrew, James and John, and the rest, were simply His disciples, Jews who had become His followers. The building of the church, the body of Christ, was yet future. His words to them were, "I will build My Church" (Matt. 16:18). It is true that in foretelling the events of chapter 24 to the disciples He especially had regard to those to whom His utterances would be applicable in the age in which they would eventually be fulfilled. But to deduce that these who will then be living will be members of the church, is assuming what should be proved.

Taking the facts as they stand in the Gospel record, these disciples were at that time in the same position and category as godly Jews will be in the time to come, Jews who believe in Christ, and await the hope of His kingdom. As we have pointed out, the "ye" was addressed to them representatively in this way, just as the "ye" to Caiaphas and his associates was addressed to them as representatives of those who will actually see the Son of man coming in the clouds of heaven. The sequence of events, as mentioned in verses 21, 29, 30, marks a time at the end of the age and therefore not in the lifetime of the apostles.

(15) The Scriptures which speak of the Second Advent as the hope of the saints, are referred to as demonstrating that the Rapture must take place at the time of the Second Advent, and that therefore there could be no intervening period.

This view presupposes that the Rapture is held to be "the hope" of the saints. Now it is true that some who regard the Rapture as "the hope" argue that to expect the Great Tribulation first would weaken the power of the hope, and they are reasonably met with the answer that the knowledge that certain events must first take place has not had this weakening effect. How needful, then, to have regard to what Scripture states about the hope! While that which is to take place at the Rapture is indicated as a hope "set on Christ" (see 1 John 3:2, 3, R.V.), it is not the consummation of the hope. That will be fulfilled only when Christ comes with His saints in manifested glory, for the overthrow of the foes of God and the establishment of His kingdom. After the Rapture, which will be the initial act of the Parousia, the saints will still eagerly await the Second Advent. That will abide as their hope, until it is realized. Only when Christ is glorified where He was crucified, only when the world is the scene of His millennial glory, can "the hope" receive its complete fulfillment.

In such a hope there is nothing inconsistent or incompatible with the existence of a period between the Rapture and the Second Advent. In view of certain misunderstandings, therefore, it will be well to set this forth somewhat more fully.

When the apostle states that the grace of God has instructed us to live "soberly and righteously and godly in this present world: looking for the blessed hope and appearing of the glory of our great God and Savior Jesus Christ" (Titus 2:13), he is not referring to the Rapture. Believers hope indeed for the Rapture, but it is not "the blessed hope" of that passage. There is a single definite article before the two words "hope" and "appearing," and the *kai*, "and," which joins them makes the second explanatory of the first (as is frequently the case with *kai*). The *kai* is thus equivalent to our English phrase, "that is to say," or "namely." The meaning therefore is, "The blessed hope, namely, the appearing of the glory . . ."

As we have mentioned, the Rapture is also spoken of as a hope. "We know," says the apostle John, "that if He shall be manifested, we shall be like Him; for we shall see Him even as He is. And every one that hath this hope set on Him purifieth himself, even as He is pure" (1 John 3:2, 3). This manifestation is not that of Christ's Second Advent in glory, but His manifestation to His saints at the Rapture, and this is the event spoken of here as "this hope." When that has taken place, then "the blessed hope," the consummation of the hope of the saints will still await fulfillment.

The question as to whether the knowledge that certain events will take place weakens the hope does not therefore affect the subject thus viewed. We know of nothing now that must necessarily take place before the Rapture, but we know that certain events will take place before Christ appears in glory to deliver the Jews and set up His kingdom. This will continue, therefore, to be the hope during the period that intervenes between the Rapture and the Second Advent. There is nothing relating to the subject of the hope which compels the view, or must lead to the conclusion, that the Rapture is to take place after the Tribulation, and is to be followed immediately by the Second Advent. To say that "there is no hope set before the Church prior to the appearing of the Lord in the clouds of heaven" (i.e., when He comes in flaming fire) is a statement unwarranted by the teaching of Scripture.

(16) Upon the occasion of Christ's ascension the assurance was given to the disciples that He would "so come in like manner as they had beheld Him going into Heaven" (Acts 1:11). From the fact that "a cloud received Him out of their sight" (v. 10) the deduction is made that the coming of the Lord to the air for the Rapture of the church is to take place simultaneously with His coming in judgment for the setting up of His kingdom. For does not the prophecy of Daniel 7:13, say, "Behold, one like the Son of man came with the clouds of heaven . . . and there was given Him dominion, and glory, and a kingdom"? And did not Christ say, "They shall see the Son of man coming in the clouds of heaven with power and great glory" (Matt. 24:30)? Did He not testify the same thing to Caiaphas (Matt. 26:64)? And does not the Apocalypse say, "Behold, He cometh with clouds; and every eye shall see Him, and they also which pierced Him; and all the kindreds of the earth shall mourn over Him" (Rev. 1:7)? Moreover the saints of the church are to be caught up "in the clouds, to meet the Lord in the air" (1 Thess. 4:17).

Firstly, it is precarious to draw the conclusion that the two events are to be simultaneous from the fact that clouds are mentioned in connection with both; for clouds are associated with other similar events; see, for instance, Rev. 11:12. That He will come on the clouds at His Second Advent affords no ground for believing that He will not on a previous occasion come to the region of the clouds to receive the saints to Himself.

Secondly, there are several respects in which His Second Advent will differ from the Coming promised in Acts 1:11. At His Second Advent, for instance, He is coming "in flaming fire," coming "with the angels of His power." To conclude that the appearing of the sign of the Son of man in heaven, and the mourning of the tribes of the earth when they see "the Son of man coming on the clouds of heaven," was the expectation of which the apostles were again reminded when He had been taken up from them into heaven, is to put an unwarranted construction upon these Scriptures. It is an effort to enforce the idea of the coincidence of events for the distinction of which, and their separation in point of time, there is ample Scripture evidence.

Thirdly, in the Old Testament, the Gospels and the Acts, broad general statements of fact are made on the subject, which are differentiated in the epistles in point of circumstance. Due regard to this would prevent the confounding of things that differ.

(17) In Revelation 20:4, 5, we read of "the first resurrection." The passage is as follows: "And I saw thrones, and they sat upon them, and judgment was given unto them: and I saw the souls of them that had been beheaded for the testimony of Jesus, and for the Word of God, and such as worshiped not the Beast, neither his image, and received not the mark upon their forehead and upon their hand; and they lived, and reigned with Christ a thousand years. The rest of the dead lived not until the thousand years should be finished.

This is the first resurrection." It is concluded from this that this is the time when the saints of the Church who have fallen asleep are to be raised, and that therefore this is the time of the Rapture. It has even been stated that "there can be no resurrection of the saints till then," and again, that "until the Beast and his persecution are destroyed together there can be no first resurrection" (Tregelles). Appeal in support of this is made to 1 Corinthians 15:22, 23, which states that "in Christ shall all be made alive. But each in his order: Christ the firstfruits, then they that are Christ's at His coming."

The statement, "This is the first resurrection," affords no ground for supposing that all the saints who have part in resurrection are to be raised at that time. For at the death of Christ "the tombs were opened; and many bodies of the saints that had fallen asleep were raised; and, coming forth out of the tombs after His resurrection, they entered into the holy city and appeared unto many" (Matt. 27:52, 53). It cannot be maintained, therefore, that "there can be no resurrection of the saints until the Second Advent."

Again, with regard to the statement, "This is the first resurrection," there is no verb in the original; this of itself suggests, what is borne out by other facts, that the first resurrection is not one summary event, but consists of different parts. It may be rightly understood as "This completes the first resurrection."

Further, the first resurrection began when Christ was raised, for, with reference to the resurrection of the saints, the apostle speaks of Christ as the "Firstfruits" (1 Cor. 15:23). The firstfruits is essentially a part of the first resurrection—"each in His own order; Christ the firstfruits." The clause which follows, "then they that are Christ's at His Parousia," refers to the act of the Lord at the Rapture, which introduces His Parousia with His saints, and not to the Second Advent. There is again, for instance, another resurrection unto life spoken of in the case of the two witnesses (Rev. 11:11).

It seems clear, then, that the first resurrection is made up of various events, beginning with the resurrection of Christ. No one passage describes the whole. Revelation 20:4, 5 gives the completion. The apostle John is there giving in detail, not the whole scene of the first resurrection, but the state of blessedness therein involved for those who, at that closing act, have part in the resurrection.

As regards the various companies mentioned in this passage, Revelation 20, they do not form the whole of the saints who are to enjoy resurrection and to share the reign of Christ, for there are a multitude of others of the saints who are already in glory who are to share the reign of Christ, and to whom the statements concerning the Beast and the image do not apply. Moreover, the undefined "they" at the beginning of the verse, in the statement, "And I saw thrones and they sat upon them," does not necessarily apply to the company of those mentioned at the end of the verse.

(18) "When this corruptible shall have put on incorruption, and this mortal shall have put on immortality, then shall come to pass the saying that is written, Death is swallowed up in victory" (1 Cor. 15:54). This is a quotation from Isaiah 25:8, and since that passage predicts the blessings of restored

Israel (v. 7) and the reign of the Lord "in Mount Sion, and in Jerusalem and before his ancients gloriously" (24:23), it is argued that only at the time of Israel's restoration will the resurrection of those who are Christ's take place. For it is when He destroys "the face of the covering cast over all peoples and the veil that is spread over all nations," that death will be swallowed up in victory. Therefore, "There can be no coming of the Lord (much more no secret coming) until He appears for the accomplishment of His promises to His ancient people Israel" (Tregelles).

It should be noted that the Revised Version rendering is, "He hath swallowed up death." The accuracy of this past tense is confirmed by the quotation in the passage in 1 Corinthians. Again, it is a well-known principle in the apostle's method of quotation, that passages which in the Old Testament primarily refer to Israel are applied to the church, often with a slight variation of meaning. See, for example, Romans 10:6–11 and the Old Testament passages from which the quotations are taken. So with the passage in Isaiah 25:7, 8, when Israel has been restored and the veil is consequently taken away from the nations, death will have been swallowed in victory. The apostle's application of these words to the resurrection and transformation of the saints at the time of the Rapture, by no means implies that this event is to take place "at the time of Israel's restored blessing." To say that "any hope of a previous resurrection must be based, not on Scripture teaching, but upon some thought which has been formed in contradistinction to revealed truth," is quite beside the mark. Scripture does not, by the way, speak of a "secret Rapture."

(19) "After these things I saw, and behold, a great multitude, which no man could number, out of every nation, and of all tribes and peoples and tongues, standing before the throne and before the Lamb, arrayed in white robes, and palms in their hands; and they cry with a great voice, saying, Salvation unto our God which sitteth on the throne, and unto the Lamb. And all the angels were standing round about the throne, and about the elders and the four living creatures; and they fell before the throne on their faces, and worshiped God, saying, Amen: Blessing, and glory, and wisdom, and thanksgiving, and honor, and power, and might be unto our God forever and ever. Amen. And one of the elders answered, saying unto me, These which are arrayed in white robes, who are they, and whence came they? And I said unto him, My Lord, thou knowest. And he said to me, These are they which came out of the great tribulation, and they washed their robes, and made them white in the blood of the Lamb. Therefore are they before the throne of God; and they serve Him day and night in His temple: and He that sitteth on the throne shall spread His tabernacle over them. They shall hunger no more, neither thirst any more; neither shall the sun strike upon them, nor any heat: for the Lamb which is in the midst of the throne shall be their shepherd, and shall guide them unto fountains of water of life: and God shall wipe away every tear from their eyes" (Rev. 7:9–17).

It is stated that those who are thus described as coming out of the Great Tribulation form part of the church, and that therefore the Rapture must be after the Tribulation.

This interpretation is, again, a gratuitous assumption. There is no actual proof that this great multitude consists of people who have been resurrected. Whether this be so or no, their blessings are peculiarly millennial. Their service is "by day and by night" (not heavenly conditions). The closing promise is that "God shall wipe away every tear from their eyes." This is an earthly scene, judging from Isaiah 25:8. Again, the figurative description of the palm branches in their hands receives its interpretation from passages which speak of earthly gladness (cp. Lev. 23:40–42; Ezek. 40:16; 41:18; John 12:13).

Further, there is a distinct company, namely, "the elders," (always elsewhere in Scripture said of human beings), who with the angels and the living creatures are "round about the throne." These elders are themselves on thrones (5:4, not "seats," A.V.) are arrayed in white garments, and have crowns (*stephanoi*, crowns of reward) on their heads—three facts which indicate that they are not spirits. A spirit is not arrayed, nor crowned. Each detail is descriptive of reward. Here then is a company of human beings enjoying resurrection life in heaven, and quite distinct from the great gentile multitude who come out of the Great Tribulation (which, as we have noted, affects Gentiles as well as Jews). The former are blessed with Christ, the latter are blessed under Christ, Who "spreads His tabernacle over them" (7:15, R.V., which gives the accurate rendering; cp. Isa. 4:5, 6).

Realizing what Scripture teaches as to the Rapture, and the fact that at that event Christ will be "our deliverer from the coming wrath," and, again, as to the Lord's Parousia with His saints after the Rapture, there is scriptural justification for the view that this great multitude consists of Gentiles who have refused the worship of the Beast during the interval. There is nothing to show that they form part of the church.

(20) Among other passages quoted in support of the view that the Rapture will take place after the Tribulation, are the following:

Believers are "kept by the power of God through faith unto a salvation ready to be revealed in the last time" (1 Pet. 1:4, 5). Meanwhile such suffer manifold temptations, that the trial of their faith "may be found unto praise and honor and glory at the revelation of Jesus Christ" (v. 7). They are to set their hope perfectly "on the grace that is to be brought unto them at the revelation of Jesus Christ" (v. 13). They are to rejoice in being partakers of Christ's sufferings, "that at the revelation of His glory" they "may rejoice with exceeding joy" (4:12, 13). Again, the faithful elders are assured that "when the Chief Shepherd shall be manifested, they will receive the crown of glory that fadeth not away" (5:4).

Now none of these passages afford any evidence that there is to be no interval between the Rapture and the Second Advent. Even if the fact, that the salvation referred to in chapter 1:5 is "to be revealed in the last time," pointed to the occasion when the Lord comes in flaming fire, that would not show that the

Rapture had not taken place at some time previously. For at the time when the Lord comes in judgment to set up His kingdom, the salvation, already enjoyed by the church in the Parousia of Christ, will be revealed in its consummated glory. Moreover, what has been already pointed out concerning the noun, *apokalupsis*, "a revelation," holds good for the corresponding verb. It could be used with reference to each of the two distinct events, the Rapture and the Second Advent. The coming of Christ for the meeting of the saints with Him in the air will be an *apokalupsis* (or "unveiling") to them, though not to the world; again, the coming of Christ with the angels of His power in flaming fire will be an *apokalupsis* to the world, each revelation having an entirely distinctive event associated with it, and separated the one from the other by an interval.

Verse 7 is understood by some to refer to the second of these events. If that is the meaning, it does not eliminate the occurrence of the interval separating it from the time of the Rapture. When the saints come in resurrection glory with Christ at His Second Advent, the trials experienced by them will certainly be found unto "praise, glory and honor." For Christ is then coming "to be glorified in His saints, and to be marveled at in all them that believed" (2 Thess. 1:10). So with verse 13. The same applies also to the "exceeding Joy" in chapter 4:12, 13.

The passage which speaks of the reward of the crown of glory to be given when the Chief Shepherd appears (*phaneroō*), chapter 5:4 points to the judgment seat which follows upon the Rapture, and not to what will take place when the Lord is revealed in flaming fire, rendering vengeance to the foes of God.

(21) Appeal is made to the Authorized Version of 2 Thessalonians 2:2, 3, which makes the apostle say that the Day of Christ was not at hand, and would not come before the apostasy and the revelation of the Man of Sin.

The Authorized Version is untenable here. The Revised Version, "The Day of the Lord" is abundantly confirmed by manuscript evidence. The rendering, "is now present," is the accurate one. "The Day of the Lord" is a period distinct from the Day of Christ. That is clear from a consideration of all the passages where the phrases occur.

The Day of Christ begins with the Rapture. The Day of the Lord begins subsequently. What the apostle was teaching was that this latter period would not begin until after the apostasy and the revelation of the Man of Sin.[1]

---

1 It has been recently stated that the New Testament "again and again changes 'the day of our Lord' for 'the day of the Lord Jesus' and for 'the day of Jesus Christ,'" and that therefore these varied names are blended into one; further, that "again and again Paul in particular seems to glory in changing the name"; also that when the apostle Peter says of Paul that "in all his epistles" he spoke of these things, he was referring "to the very same day of God" as Peter did.

Such inferences are entirely unfounded, and are contrary to that extreme precision of phraseology which is manifested in the God-breathed writings. The passages relating to "the day of the Lord" refer to that period which is introduced by the Second Advent of Christ, whereas the passages which contain the phrases in which the personal titles, Jesus, or Christ, or both, are found, are all used in quite a different connection and have to do with the circumstances of the Rapture of the saints, their presence with the Lord in His Parousia, and the judgment seat of Christ.

The church at Thessalonica was being taught by errorists that the Day of the Lord had already begun. They might well be apprehensive about the fate of their departed loved ones. For the apostle had instructed them in his first epistle to expect the Rapture first. Now he writes to confirm his teaching and to correct the false doctrines to which they were listening. He makes his appeal "by [*huper*, "in the interests of"] the Parousia of our Lord Jesus Christ, and our gathering together unto Him" (v. 1). It was not to correct a mistake in his first epistle (as some who discredit the divine inspiration of Scripture affirm), it was to confirm what he had there written, that he appeals to his readers on the ground of the Rapture, the gathering to Christ, as distinct from and previous to, the Day of the Lord, which is to be ushered in by vengeance. They are still to wait for the Son of God from heaven, as they had done.

This passage, then, shows the Rapture to be a distinct event, prior to and separated from the revelation of Christ from heaven with His angels to render vengeance to the ungodly.

(22) In writing to the Thessalonian church the apostle says, "But concerning the times and the seasons brethren, ye have no need that aught be written unto you. For yourselves know perfectly that the day of the Lord so cometh as a thief in the night . . . But ye, brethren, are not in darkness that that day should overtake you as a thief" (1 Thess. 5:1, 2, 4). It has been inferred from this that the Day of the Lord will overtake the church, though not as a thief.

It is not necessary to suppose that the apostle's statement suggests that the Day of the Lord is to overtake the church as well as the world, and that the distinction is that it will not overtake the church as a thief. On the contrary, the order of the words and phraseology of the original, as well as the whole context of the passage, shows that the apostle is marking a sharp contrast between the circumstances relating to the Rapture of the saints (4:13–18) and those relating to the world, upon which the Day of the Lord will come with the personal intervention of Christ in judgment. The distinction, which is one in point both of time and character of event becomes clear when we put together the Scriptures which speak of the Day of the Lord. Here in verse 4 the stress which is placed upon the pronoun "ye" and "you" marks the contrast between the destiny of believers and the Day of the Lord which is to come upon the world. Taking the order of the original, the rendering is as follows: "But you, brethren, are not in darkness, that the day you as a thief should overtake." The word "you" is distinctive in its emphasis. The phrase "as a thief" goes closely with "overtake," and has no stress attached to it.

If there were any doubt as to the meaning, it would be necessary to understand the passage according to the teaching of other Scriptures, and this very epistle makes clear what the destiny of the church is.

What the apostle means is, not that the day will overtake the saints though not as a thief, but rather that, with regard to the saints, such is their character and destiny, that what will overtake the world as a thief will not come upon them at all. The saints are "sons of light" and "sons of day." When the Day of the Lord begins, those who have been caught up to meet Him will come with Him. The saints are not to be overtaken by the Rapture, they are to comfort one another in the prospect of it. The Day of the Lord, which will overtake the world as a thief, is entirely distinct from this.

This distinction in verse 4, which may not be clear to the reader of the English version, is confirmed, as we have said, by what the Scripture teaches in relation to the Day of the Lord, as well as in other ways which we have sought to point out. There are two Scriptures, for instance, which, if taken together, show that the Day of the Lord will begin when the Lord Jesus comes on the clouds of heaven, with great glory, for the overthrow of His foes, and the setting up of His kingdom, while Scripture further makes clear that at that Advent the saints will come in glory with Him. Joel's prophecy declares that the Day of the Lord will follow the turning of the sun into darkness and the moon into blood (Joel 2:30, 31). Christ declared that immediately after these calamities in the heavens He Himself would come with power and great glory, and all the tribes of the earth would mourn (Matt. 24:29, 30). The Day of the Lord is therefore to be ushered in by the coming of Christ in this manner.

The Second Advent is likewise described in Revelation 17:14, and in fuller detail in chapter 19:11–21. When Christ comes with power and great glory, as He foretold, He will overthrow the Beast and those who are gathered together under him. That is how the Day of the Lord will be ushered in. Now concerning those foes of God the passage says: "These shall war against the Lamb, and the Lamb shall overcome them, for He is Lord of lords, and King of kings; and they also shall overcome that are with Him, called, and chosen and faithful" (Rev. 17:14). Accordingly the saints are with Christ when He comes in glory, when the foes of God are overthrown and the Day of the Lord begins.

The Day of the Lord cannot have overtaken them as it will the world, for they are among the hosts of the Lord when it begins. It is the saints who are referred to in a similar passage in chapter 19:14, which says that "the armies which are in heaven followed Him upon white horses, clothed in fine linen, white and pure." It is not the angels which are clothed in fine linen. The fine linen belongs to the saints. The Day of the Lord will dispel and replace the world's night; the saints, in resurrection life and glory, are coming with Christ to share in the great event. They will have been previously caught up to meet Him before the Day of the Lord begins.

CONCLUSION

The consideration of these objections in the light of Scripture serves, then, to confirm . . . that the period in which the Great Tribulation will take place is to be likewise a period of the wrath of God in a series of retributive judgments; that from the wrath of God the church is assured of deliverance; and that this deliverance consists, not of preservation through the period of retribution, but of salvation from it at the Rapture.

THE COMING REVIVAL OF THE ROMAN EMPIRE

Here we take a long look at the history and geography of the Roman Empire as it pertains to the prophecies regarding the ten kingdoms that will unite under Antichrist. As this final emperor of the Roman king takes the stage, he will be joined by a False Prophet, and his rule will be imbued with satanic power. Unprecedented social upheaval will lead to a world united under a universal system of commerce and one world religion. After a period of devastating judgments, fierce persecution, and brutal warfare, Christ will return, overthrow His enemies, and establish His everlasting kingdom.

1. THE GEOGRAPHICAL STANDPOINT

The coming revival of the Roman Empire will for our present purpose be best considered from the geographical, political, and religious standpoints.

Geographical Considerations

Any forecast of the exact delimitations of the ten kingdoms constituting the reconstructed empire must necessarily be largely conjectural. That their aggregate area will precisely conform to that of the ancient Roman Empire does not necessarily follow from the fact of its revival, and cannot be definitely concluded from Scripture. An extension of the territories of the empire in its resuscitated form would be quite consistent with the retention of its identity. Moreover, if Roman imperialism may be considered to have continued in the hands of Teutonic monarchs after the fall of the western part of the empire in 476, if, for instance, Charles the Great . . . ruled as a Roman emperor, despite the passing away of the actual empire itself, then the dominions which were under the rule of these later monarchs may yet be found incorporated in the empire, and so form parts of the ten kingdoms. In that case Germany and Holland would be included. Possibly, too, the empire will embrace all the territories which belonged to the three which preceded it, the Grecian, Medo-Persian, and Chaldean. Certainly when the stone fell on the toes of the image, the whole image, representing these former three as well as the fourth, was demolished. Suggestive also in this respect is the fact that the beast in the vision recorded in Revelation 13:2 was possessed of features of the leopard, the bear, and the lion, the same beasts which represented in Daniel's vision the Grecian, Medo-Persian, and Chaldean kingdoms (Dan. 7:4–6), the order in Revelation 13 being inverted. While political characteristics are doubtless chiefly in view in these symbols, there may at the same time be an indication of the eventual incorporation of the first three empires in the fourth. It must be remembered, too, that the authority of the federal head of the ten kingdoms is to be worldwide: "There was given to him authority over every tribe and people and tongue and nation" (Rev. 13:7). It is probable, therefore, that while the ten kingdoms will occupy a well-defined area, their dependencies and the countries which are allied with them will embrace practically the remainder of the world.

If, on the other hand, the Roman Empire is to be reconstructed in exact conformity territorially with its ancient boundaries—such a reconstruction is, of course, not inconceivable—we must consider what period of the conquests of the ancient empire to take, whether under the first emperor, Augustus, or during the apostolic age, or later. We may, perhaps, be helped by the facts already mentioned, that prophecy relating to gentile dominion is focused upon the Jews and Palestine, and has especially in view the presence of the nation in their land. Now, shortly after their overthow, in A.D. 70, their national recognition as possessors of the land ceased. This period, moreover, corresponds broadly to the close of the apostolic age. The dispersion of the Jews among the nations was completed by Adrian in the next century. He desolated the whole of Palestine, expelling all the remaining Jewish inhabitants.

A Review of the Ancient Territories

We will therefore now review the limits of the empire and of some of its provinces at that time, noticing certain circumstances of past and present history suggestive of future issues. In doing so we are not predicting that the boundaries of the revived empire will be those of the ancient.

Commencing with North Africa, it will be observed, on referring to the map, that practically the same strip of territory which belonged to the Roman Empire in the times of the apostles has passed directly under the government of countries which were themselves then within the empire. For Spain rules over Morocco, France over Algeria and Tunis, Italy recently seized Tripoli, and Britain has, since Turkey's entrance into the great war, virtually taken possession of Egypt. It seems not a little significant that no country which was outside the limits of the empire at the time under consideration has been permitted by God to annex these North African territories since the Saracens and the Turks were dispossessed of them.

Passing now to Asia, the territory in that continent which belonged to Rome in the first century is approximately what remained to Turkey immediately prior to the present war. Mesopotamia and most of Armenia were included. The war has already seen Turkey dispossessed of portions of these. The downfall of the Turkish Empire would almost certainly involve territorial rearrangements of deepest import in the light of prophecy, especially as regards Palestine.

Divisions of the Greek Empire: A Possible Renewal

The eighth chapter of Daniel apparently indicates that the Asiatic territories of the empire will be divided much as they were under the Greeks after the death of Alexander the Great. He was obviously symbolized by the great horn (v. 22). The four horns which came up in its place (v. 8) are clearly, too, the four generals who succeeded Alexander, and among whom his dominions were divided, Cassander ruling over Macedonia and Greece, Lysimachus over part of Asia Minor and Thrace (the extent of the latter province was almost exactly what now belongs to Turkey in Europe), Seleucus over most of Syria, Palestine, Mesopotamia, and the east, and Ptolemy over Egypt. Next follows a prediction carrying us to events which are evidently yet future. It is said, for instance, that these events will take place "in the latter time of their kingdom [not, it will be observed, in the time of the four kings themselves who succeeded Alexander, but of the kingdoms over which they ruled], when the transgressors are come to the full" (v. 23). The expressions in this chapter, "the time of the end" (v. 17), "the latter time of the indignation," "the appointed time of the end" (v. 19), and "the latter time of their kingdom" (v. 23), all point to a period still future, namely, to the close of the present age. Again, in reference to the "king of fierce coun-tenance," while much of the prophecy can be applied to Antiochus Epiphanes in the second century B.C., yet no man has hitherto arisen whose character and acts have been precisely those related in verses 9–12 and 23–25. We may also compare what is said of "the transgression that maketh desolate" (v. 13) with the Lord's prophecy concerning the abomination of desolation (Matt. 24:15–22), a prophecy which also manifestly awaits fulfillment.

Possibly, therefore, these Asiatic territories will be similarly divided in the coming time. In regard to the first of the above-mentioned four divisions, the recent extension of Greece to include the ancient province of Macedonia is remarkable. This was an outcome of the Balkan War of 1912. The boundaries of Greece are now approximately what they were under Cassander in the time of the Grecian Empire, what they were also later as the provinces of Macedonia and Achaia in the Roman Empire. There has lately, therefore, been a significant reversion to ancient conditions in this respect.

Other European Territories

Coming now to the dual-monarchy of Austria-Hungary, reference to the map of the Roman Empire in the apostolic age will show that what are now Hungary, Transylvania, Bessarabia, and other states of the present monarchy were with-out the Roman boundaries, while Pannonia, or what is now Austria west of the Danube, was within; even when in the next century Dacia (now Transylvania, Bessarabia, etc.) was annexed, the two parts of the present dual kingdom were separate. The separation of Hungary from Austria has for a considerable time been a practical question of European politics, and may be hastened by present events.

The northern and northeastern boundaries of Italy embraced the Trentino and the peninsula of Istria. Noticeable, therefore, are the present efforts of Italy to acquire these very districts, efforts which seem likely to achieve success. Roman states north of Italy covered what are now Baden, Wurtemberg, Luxemberg, and a large part of Bavaria. The possibility of an eventual severance of these from Prussian domination has been much discussed of late.

The Rhenish provinces of Alsace and Lorraine, originally portions of the Roman province of Gallia (now France), were snatched from France by Germany in the Franco-Prussian war of 1870–71. Their recovery is a supreme object of the efforts of the French in the present war, and not without hope of success.

The British Empire

As to Britain, at the time under consideration the greater part of the island was definitely included in the Roman Empire. Ireland and most of Scotland were never conquered by the Romans. Should Britain form one of the ten kingdoms, there is nothing to show that Ireland or any other part of the British Empire must of necessity be absolutely separated from it. Self-government may yet be possessed by those territories which have not yet received it, and it is significant that Ireland has now practically obtained it. That the lands which are linked with Britain as dependencies, or as in possession of self-government, should remain as integral parts of the empire is but consistent with the coming worldwide authority of the potentate who will be the federal head of the ten kingdoms. And that each state in the British Empire should have its own local government is, on the other hand, consistent with the establishment of a closer and complete confederacy of ten kingdoms, the area of which may correspond largely to that of the ancient Roman Empire. In contrast to the self-government of the other countries of the world at the coming period, the ten united kingdoms will eventually be absolutely under the control of the final emperor just mentioned, for the ten kings over these states, who receive authority as kings with him, will be of one mind to give their power and authority and their kingdom to him (Rev. 17:11, 13, 17).

What has been said of the British Empire may be true also of others of the ten kingdoms which have colonies or dependencies, and thus, while the ten kingdoms will themselves constitute an empire, their alliances and treaties with other countries of the world will apparently involve an extension of the authority of the controlling despot "over every tribe and people and tongue and nation" (Rev. 13:7). If, for instance, the United States of America were at that time in alliance with Britain (quite a possible contingency), their joint influence would probably extend to the whole of the American continents, which would thereby acknowledge his authority.

We may observe, too, the way in which the continent of Africa has come under certain European influences in modern times. The mention of this is simply suggestive. That the Scripture will be absolutely fulfilled is beyond doubt; the exact mode of its accomplishment is known to God.

2. THE POLITICAL STANDPOINT

European Federation

Agencies are already at work for the establishment of a confederacy of European states—not the least significant of the many signs that the end of the age is approaching. The movement toward confederacy is doubtless receiving an impetus from the great upheaval in Europe. A circular issued in December, 1914, and distributed far and wide, announced the formation of a committee of influential men with the object of promoting a "European Federation." The circular says: "In sight of the present situation of ruin it ought to be the general opinion that a firmer economical and political tie is of utmost importance for all nations without exception, and that particularly for Europe the narrower bond of a federation, based on equality and interior independence of all partaking states, is of urgent necessity, which public opinion ought to demand."

A pamphlet published by the Committee recommends that the union of states shall be economical, political, and legal, with an international army as a common guarantee, and that European Federation should become the principal and most urgent political battle-cry for the masses of all European nations, and declares that "when the Governments are willing, when the public opinion of all peoples forces them to be willing, there is no doubt but that a reasonable and practical union of nations will prove to be as possible and natural as is at present a union of provinces, cantons, territories, whose populations often show more difference of race and character than those of nations now at hostilities." The committee calls upon the peoples of Europe to suffer the diplomatists no longer to dispose of them like slaves and by militarism to lash them to fury against each other. It calls upon them to see to it that never and nowhere should a member of any body or government be elected who is not an advocate of the federation, and that the trade union, society, or club to which any individual belongs should express sympathy with the movement in meetings and in votes. "The people," it is said, "have it now in their power, more than ever before, to control the Powers."

Two Possible Ways of Federation

The formation of ten federated states, covering at least the area of the ancient empire at the end of the first century of the present era, may be effected in two ways, either by the peaceful methods of arbitration and treaty, or as a result of strife and confusion. That the present European war will be succeeded by efforts for the creation of permanent international harmony and universal peace is probable, as is also some attempt at such a federation as is proposed by the above-mentioned committee. On the other hand, sinister indications abound today which point to industrial strife and revolution rather than peace. The condition of the industrial world presents a gloomy prospect indeed. There are ominous signs of keener conflict than ever between capital and labor. The forces of Socialism, Syndicalism, Communism, etc., are rapidly increasing in power and in international activity, and their avowed aims presage anything but peace in the near future. We may take, for example, the declared objects of "The Alliance of the Social Democracy"—now incorporated in the International Working Men's Association—"To destroy all States and all Churches with all their institutions and laws, religious, political, juridical, financial, magisterial, academical, economical, and social, and to establish in their place industrial cooperation and collective ownership of land and capital." All this sounds very pretentious, and would probably fail of complete accomplishment, but the agencies at work for it are strong. Attempts on a large scale would certainly lead to unprecedented disorder and chaos.

The Sea Symbolic of National Unrest

Not improbably the ten kingdoms of the reconstructed Roman Empire will arise as a result of political and social confusion. Thus it was in the case of the French Revolution and the consequent uprising of Napoleon. A repetition of such events on a far wider scale in the future is quite conceivable. In the prophetic vision given to the apostle John, the beast was seen "coming up out of the sea" (Rev. 13:1). Now the sea is in Scripture used figuratively of the nations, its characteristic restlessness symbolizing their commotion and strife. Compare the words of Isaiah: "Ah, the uproar of many peoples, which roar like the roaring of the seas; and the rushing of nations, that rush like the rushing of many waters! The nations shall rush like the rushing of many waters: but He shall rebuke them" (Isa. 17:12, 13; see also Ps. 65:7; and Ezek. 26:3). To national unrest the Lord Jesus applied similar language when He foretold to the disciples that there would be "upon the earth distress of nations, in perplexity for the roaring of the sea and the billows; men fainting for fear, and for expectation of the things which are coming on the world" (Luke 21:25, 26). So also the waters which John had seen in his vision are described by the angel as "peoples, and multitudes, and nations, and tongues" (Rev. 17:15). Daniel, too, saw the four great beasts come up from the sea as a result of the breaking forth of the four winds of the heaven upon it, an undoubted representation of a condition of national disturbance (Dan. 7:2, 3). That the beast of Revelation 13:1 was seen coming up out of the sea points, therefore, to the probability that the ten kings who will have brief authority over the revived empire will be raised to their kingdom, not by constitutional methods, but as the result of revolutions and the collapse of present-day governments and institutions.

Revolutions and their Issues

Should any great measure of success attend the syndicalist and communist movements of the day, and especially if they are internationalized, the inevitable revolutions and disorder would almost certainly issue, as revolutions have so frequently issued, in despotism and autocracy, and perhaps in this way the ten kings would arise. The overthrow of the governments in the countries involved would remove what has certainly been the great restraint upon lawlessness[1] from the times of the apostles until now. Everything would be ripe for the appearance

---

1 See *The Epistles to the Thessalonians, with Notes Exegetical and Expository*, by C. F. Hogg and W. E. Vine.

of a universal potentate. The cry would arise for "a man," a controlling organizer to bring order out of chaos. The unstable character of the rule of the ten kings, and the impoverishment of their kingdoms, would lead them, as a matter of diplomacy, to hand over their authority to him.

The Iron and the Clay

The political constitution of the successive empires during "the time of the Gentiles" was indicated in the image of Nebuchadnezzar's vision by the various substances of which the parts of the image were composed. While the regular deterioration in the relative value of these substances is noticeable, we are concerned now with those of the legs and feet. The legs were of iron, and the feet part of iron and part of potter's clay, not moist or miry clay, but "earthenware" (Dan. 2:41, R.V., margin), and consequently brittle (v. 42, margin).

That the iron symbolized militarism seems clear from what is said of the fourth kingdom, that "as iron breaketh in pieces and subdueth all things: and as iron that crusheth all these, shall it break in pieces and crush" (v. 40). Nations are broken and crushed by military power, and thus the nations were treated by the Romans. This was further signified by the iron teeth of the fourth beast, as is definitely stated in Daniel 7:19, 23: "And shall devour the whole earth, and shall tread it down, and break it in pieces."

The supposition that the clay represents democracy is gratuitous and arbitrary. The early Roman Empire, symbolized by the legs of the image, was built up under democratic rule. When republicanism was superseded by imperialism, democratic principles still prevailed. Democracy, therefore, played its part from the very commencement of the fourth kingdom, and had it been symbolized by the clay, not only the feet and toes but the legs themselves would have consisted of mingled iron and clay. Moreover, democracy in the generally accepted sense of the term has not always been found to be of an unstable or brittle character; witness the republicanism of the United States. Democracies, too, may be established on strictly constitutional principles.

Another explanation, therefore, of the symbolism of the clay must be sought, and it is not unlikely to be found in those revolutionary principles to which we have already referred, which were evidenced at the time of the French Revolution, and are finding expression, though in greater variety today, in such projects as those of the International Working Men's Association. Certainly the masses of the people of Europe are being permeated both by militarism and by the revolutionary doctrines of which we have spoken. Should these principles spread among the civil services and forces, everything would be in a complete state of preparedness for

Unprecedented Political and Social Upheaval

which would effect the overthrow of present forms of government. From the world's point of view the situation would require a consummate genius with powers of worldwide organization. Doubtless Satan's masterpiece of infidel ingenuity would be at hand for the occasion.

We are not predicting that this is to be the manner of the revival of the empire and of the advent of its imperial head. We have merely suggested possible circumstances in the light of Scripture and present-day movements. The actual circumstances attending the rise of the ten kings and their emperor must for the time remain conjectural. Certainly these kings will receive authority with him for one hour (Rev. 17:12), a phrase which may be translated "at the same time"; and certainly they will agree to give their power and authority to him (v. 13).

3. THE RELIGIOUS STANDPOINT

We will now note the religious conditions which are to prevail for a time upon the resuscitation of the empire. These are plainly indicated for us in Revelation 17. The apostle sees a woman sitting on the seven-headed and ten-horned beast. The woman is gorgeously arrayed, holds in her hand a golden cup full of abominations, and is drunken with the blood of the saints. Her name, written on her forehead, is

"Mystery, Babylon the Great,"

"the mother of the harlots and of the abominations of the earth" (vv. 3–6). The woman is symbolically described as the city of Rome (v. 18), and that leads on to a second mention of Babylon, in chapter eighteen, and a new description. Now to the description of the woman in chapter seventeen nothing more closely corresponds than the papacy. But if the Babylon of chapter seventeen is to be identified with that of chapter eighteen, the Papacy answers to the whole description only to a limited extent. While, however, there is much in common in the two descriptions in these chapters, yet the two Babylons are possibly to be distinguished. The Babylon of chapter seventeen is a "mystery," not so that of chapter eighteen. Again, the destruction of the one is different from that of the other. The first will be destroyed by the ten kings and their emperor (17:16), the second by the direct judgment of God (18:5, 8, 20); the first as the result of human antagonism, the second by famine, fire and earthquake. We are perhaps, therefore, justified in taking the more limited view in connection with the circumstances of chapter seventeen. Even so the woman may be regarded as representing the apostate sacerdotal systems which have sprung from the papacy as well as that system itself.

The position of the woman indicates an exercise of power which is voluntarily supported by the beast. That she sits upon the waters implies her religious dominion over the nations; that she is carried by the beast, who rules over the nations politically, implies that there will be a complete alliance between her and the ten kings with their chief, and that the sphere of her influence will be coextensive with the dominions of the beast.

The Papacy: Its Present Power

Now though the papacy lost its temporal power in 1870, it is far from having lost its political influence. Ecclesiastically, too, though it has received various setbacks, it is manifestly gaining power. This is especially observable, for example, in Britain, the overthrow of which as a Protestant power is undoubtedly the object of the persistent aggressiveness of Romanism. This aggressiveness is manifest in all the dominions of the British Empire, as well as in other lands.

Again, while certain governments have of late shaken off the ecclesiastical yoke, and infidelity has spread among the people of Roman Catholic lands, the number of Roman Catholics has increased with great rapidity. They were estimated at somewhat over 200,000,000 twenty years ago, they are now said to number about 300,000,000.

Indications are not wanting of a tendency toward

A Reunion of Christendom,

which would be facilitated by a willingness on the part of the papacy to adapt itself to the impulse of the time.

Present events, therefore, point to a great renewal of papal power involving the fulfillment of the prophecy relating to the woman and the beast that carries her. This renewed alliance between the political and the ecclesiastical powers will, however, be of brief duration. The successful efforts of governments in recent times to liberate themselves from papal authority, as in the case of France and Portugal, are but foreshadowings of the eventual entire destruction of ecclesiasticism and sacerdotalism under the revived Roman Empire. "The ten horns . . . and the beast, these shall hate the harlot, and shall make her desolate and naked, and shall eat her flesh, and shall burn her utterly with fire" (Rev. 17:16). Thus it would seem that, when at the very zenith of its power and ambition, the papacy, at the head of amalgamated Christendom, will suddenly meet its doom.

The Doom of Religious Babylon

Its accumulated wealth would probably be an incentive in determining the ten kings to take this step, owing possibly to the impoverishment of their kingdoms as a result of wars and political and social upheavals. An additional cause will doubtless be the widespread spirit of antagonism against all religion.

Submission to the papal yoke has invariably had an aftermath of infidelity; similarly the temporary subservience of the beast to the woman will issue in the casting off of all religious restraint and in the universal acknowledgment of the presumptuous claims of the world ruler.

Satanic Authority of the Emperor

The authority of this final emperor of the Roman kingdom will be satanic. "The dragon gave him his power, and his throne, and great authority" (Rev. 13:2);

"the beast . . . was, and is not; and is about to come up out of the abyss, and to go into perdition" (Rev. 17:8). This implies that he has been on the earth in the past. The same thing is indicated in the interpretation of the seven heads. Topographically they are described as seven mountains, personally as seven kings (v. 9). Of these, five had fallen, the sixth was in power in John's time, the seventh had not then come (v. 10). The beast (clearly here symbolizing, not a kingdom, but a person) would be an eighth, and yet would be of the seven (v. 11). These heads have been regarded by some as forms of government, by others as empires, or again, as emperors. There seems to be no reason why they are not to be regarded as emperors, though doubtless their empires are in view, as being associated with them. Accordingly, the fact that the eighth is also one of the seven indicates his reappearance on the scene. Various suggestions have been made as to his identification, but this must remain uncertain until his advent. With him the ten kings for a time receive authority (v. 12), subsequently handing it over to him with their kingdom (v. 17), but not before they have together with him crushed the great religious system symbolized by the woman (v. 16). His stupendous power and brilliant abilities, the evidence of his superhuman origin, his phenomenal capacity for organization, and the consolidation of the empire under his absolute control will cause the whole world to marvel at him (Rev. 13:3; 17:8). To the world, in its divinely inflicted and therefore retributive delusion, he will appear like a god who has come to deliver from woe, and to introduce the long-looked-for age of peace and prosperity. Wonder will be succeeded by worship, both of the man and of Satan. "They worshiped the dragon, because he gave his authority unto the beast; and they worshiped the beast, saying, Who is like unto the beast? and who is able to war with him?" (13:4).

The world is now in course of rapid preparation for all this:

The "Superman"

has of late become a much-discussed topic in various classes of society and in the press, and the idea is supported by the theories of evolution which are receiving increasingly wide acceptance. A spirit of expectancy is being thus aroused which will undoubtedly facilitate the recognition of the man himself at his advent, and the acknowledgment of his claims to divine honor. But this will involve the worship of Satan, and to this end the effective agency of

Spiritism

has been long at work. Spiritism leads to devil worship. It must do so; its energizing power is Satan himself. Both spiritism and theosophy, and similar forms of error, all of which are rapidly on the increase today, are paving the way for worldwide worship of the dragon.

The imperial power and worship of this emperor will be promoted by another potentate similarly energized by Satan. This latter is the second beast, described in Revelation 13:11–end. Later on in the book he is called

The False Prophet

(Rev. 16:13; 19:20; 20:10), indicating that his activities are chiefly of a religious character, and perhaps that he will be more closely connected with Jewish affairs. He will make "the earth and them that dwell therein worship the beast," the emperor of the ten kingdoms (13:11), deceiving the world by supernatural signs wrought in the presence of the first beast (v. 12), and enforcing the worship of his image (v. 15), the abomination of desolation set up in the temple at Jerusalem (Matt. 24:15). With the worship of an image the times of the Gentiles began (Dan. 3:1), and with similar idolatry they will end. In the days of the early Roman emperors their deification was celebrated by the adoration of their images. Then, as formerly under Nebuchadnezzar, those who refused to worship suffered death. So will it be under the final emperor and his colleague.

Various opinions are held regarding these two beasts of Revelation 13, as to which is the Man of Sin spoken of by Paul in 2 Thessalonians 2, which the Antichrist mentioned in John's epistles, and which of the two is the willful king described in Daniel 11. Limitations of space preclude our entering into the subject in detail here. The present writer holds the view that all three are the same person, and that they are also the same as the horn in Daniel 7:8, 11, and as the first beast of Revelation 13, and that these are all different descriptions of the final head of the revived empire. The Old Testament passages somewhat briefly announce the arising of this worldwide ruler; the New Testament passages unfold and expand the preceding predictions concerning him, among the additional details given in the New Testament being the fact that he is to have a prophet who will assiduously support his claim to deity and his administration. It is the world emperor, and not his prophet, who is to be worshiped, and who therefore proclaims himself as God (2 Thess. 2:4). His prophet, the second beast of Revelation 13, in the exercise of all the power of the first, will cause the world to worship him (13:12). As his prophet and prime minister he would not himself endeavor to usurp the position of him whose avowed deity he seeks to support.

The similarity of the details in the above-mentioned passages indicates that the same person is in view in each case. His blasphemies, for instance, and his assumption of deity are mentioned in Daniel 7:25; 11:36, 37; 2 Thessalonians 2:3, 4, and Revelation 13:5, 6, and his war with the saints in Daniel 7:21, 25 and Revelation 13:7. Further, the blasphemous proclamation of himself as God is consistent with what is said in John's epistles concerning the Antichrist. For in his self-deification he is directly "antagonistic to Christ," he denies that Jesus is the Christ, and therefore denies the Father and the Son (1 John 2:22).

The two potentates will establish not only a universal religion, but also a

Universal System of Commerce

The second beast "causeth all, the small and the great, and the rich and the poor, and the free and the bond, that there be given them a mark on their hand, or upon their forehead; and that no man should be able to buy or to sell, save he that hath the mark, even the name of the beast or the number of his name" (Rev. 13:16, 17). This indicates a worldwide protectionist system, such a system as, for instance, might conceivably be established under some form of syndicalism. Undeniably, circumstances in the industrial world today manifest an increasing tendency in this direction. The principles previously mentioned, as now making for industrial and international revolution, and the present stupendous movements toward amalgamation, are clearly preparing for the fulfillment of this prophecy by facilitating the eventual establishment of the unrighteous commercial system of the reconstituted empire.

THE EVERLASTING KINGDOM

We have now to consider the dealings of the two beasts, the final Roman emperor and his false prophet, with

THE JEWS

With the Romans the Jews joined in the death of Christ, and with the rulers of this fourth empire they will be in agreement for a time at the close of their long course of apostasy. This was especially made known to Daniel in the prophecy of

THE SEVENTY WEEKS

(Dan. 9). These weeks (lit., *hebdomads*, or periods of seven, i.e., seven years each) had been divinely decreed (or "cut off," i.e., from the period of "the times of the Gentiles") upon his people and his city. From the going forth of the commandment to restore and to build Jerusalem unto the Anointed One (the Messiah), the Prince, would be seven weeks and threescore and two weeks. After this the Anointed One would be cut off, and would have nothing (Dan. 9:24–26). This period is 69 times 7, or 483 years, and to the very day this was the period commencing with the command of Artaxerxes Longimanus, King of Persia, for the restoration of Jerusalem (Neh. 2:1–9), and ending with the triumphal entry of Christ into the city (Matt. 21:1–11).[1] Four days later He was crucified, "the Anointed One was cut off and had nothing," i.e., He did not enter then upon His messianic kingdom. The prophecy predicted that the people of the prince (lit., "a prince") that would come would destroy the city and the sanctuary. That took place in A.D. 70, under Titus Vespasianus. But Titus is not "the prince that shall come." This, apart from other considerations, is clear from what follows: "And his [the prince's] end shall be with a flood [or rather, "in the overflowing," i.e., of the wrath of God]," a prediction at once inapplicable to Titus. The mention of

---

1 See *The Coming Prince*, by Sir Robert Anderson.

The Last "Week"

is deferred, indicating an interval between the sixty-ninth and the seventieth. Now the events predicted for the seventieth had no historical fulfillment immediately after the sixty-ninth. The one, therefore, did not follow the other consecutively. At the commencement of the intervening period the Jews were scattered from their land. At the seventieth they will have been restored, and the events of that week concern "the prince that shall come," the last world emperor, and his dealings with them. "He shall make a firm covenant with many [lit., "the many," i.e., the great majority of the nation] for one week" (v. 27). This covenant is described in Isaiah's prophecies as a "covenant with death" and an "agreement with Hell." The covenant, he says, "shall be disannulled," and the agreement "shall not stand; when the overflowing scourge shall pass through, then ye shall be trodden down by it" (Isa. 28:18). That this refers to a time yet future and not to past Israelitic history may be gathered from verse 22, where the theme and the language are similar to those of the passage in Daniel now under consideration. Daniel tells us the mode of the disannulling. "In the midst of the week [R.V., margin] he shall cause the sacrifice and oblation to cease." Accordingly after three and a half years the Antichrist, manifesting his real character, will prove himself a traitor and break the covenant, and thus Isaiah's prediction will be fulfilled.

Apparently at the very time when he thus breaks his league with the Jews the Antichrist will determine upon his public deification and the establishment of his worship in the temple. For he it is who "opposeth and exalteth himself above all that is called God, or that is worshiped; so that he as God sitteth in the temple of God, showing himself that he is God" (2 Thess. 2:4). This, with the setting up of his image, will doubtless be the fulfillment of the prophecies recorded by Daniel, that "upon the wing [or pinnacle] of abominations shall come one that maketh desolate" (Dan. 9:27, cp. 11:31 and 12:11), and "they shall profane the sanctuary, even the fortress, and shall take away the continual burnt offering, and they shall set up the abomination that maketh desolate" (11:31, cp. 12:11); a fulfillment also of the Lord's prediction that "the abomination of desolation, which was spoken of by Daniel the prophet," will "stand in the holy place" (Matt. 24:15). In the establishment of this blasphemous worship of the emperor, the false prophet will play a prominent part, as we have seen from the latter part of Revelation 13.

The many references to the desolator and the desolations are indicative of the

FIERCE PERSECUTION

which will follow. This will be at first directed against "the remnant," the large numbers of Jews who will repudiate allegiance to the beast and to the false prophet, many doubtless having been converted to their coming Messiah through the testimony of two witnesses who will be sent from God to the nation. "They shall prophesy a thousand two hundred and three-score days, clothed in sackcloth"

(Rev. 11:3–13). The success of their ministry will apparently arouse the bitter antagonism of Satan and his human instruments. The breaking of the covenant with the people as a whole indicates that an effort will also be made to crush the entire nation. Thus the latter half of the seventieth week will be the time of "Jacob's trouble," "a time of trouble, such as never was since there was a nation even to that same time" (Dan. 12:1), though the unprecedented tribulation will not be confined to the Jews only.

ARMAGEDDON AND AFTER

The bitter antagonism of the Man of Sin, and his colleague, the False Prophet, against God and His people will culminate in the gathering together of all the forces of the empire in Palestine in final conflict for the complete domination of the world. This tremendous event is thus indicated by the apostle John: "And I saw coming out of the mouth of the dragon, and out of the mouth of the beast, and out of the mouth of the false prophet, three unclean spirits, as it were frogs: for they are the spirits of devils [correctly, "demons"], working signs; which go forth unto the kings of the whole world, to gather them together unto the war of the great day of God, the Almighty" (Rev. 16:13, 14).

In reality the issue at stake will be the supremacy of Christ or of Satan in the earth. The objective will be neither territorial conquest nor naval supremacy, nor commercial predominance. The war of the beast and the ten kings under him is against the Lamb (Rev. 17:14). This the second Psalm had foretold: "Why do the nations rage, and the peoples imagine a vain thing? The kings of the earth set themselves, and the rulers take counsel together against the Lord, and against His Anointed, saying, let us break their bands asunder, and cast away their cords from us." The issue is not uncertain: "He that sitteth in the heavens shall laugh: the Lord shall have them in derision."

The Scene of the Conflict

in Har-Magedon, commonly known as Armageddon (Rev. 16:16). The name, which is associated with Megiddo, a locality famed in Old Testament history for its decisive battles (Judg. 5:19; 2 Kings 23), doubtless stands here for a wider area, stretching, as we shall see, from the north to the south of the land.

The combatants, the conflict and its conclusion, are described by John in vivid language of terrible grandeur in Revelation 19:11–21: "And I saw the heaven opened: and behold, a white horse, and He that sat thereon, called Faithful and True; and in righteousness He doth judge and make war. And His eyes are a flame of fire, and upon His head are many diadems; and He hath a name written, which no one knoweth but He Himself. And He is arrayed in a garment sprinkled with blood: and His name is called the Word of God. And the armies which are in heaven followed Him upon white horses, clothed in fine linen, white and pure. And out of His mouth proceedeth a sharp sword, that with it He should smite the nations: and He shall rule them with a rod of iron: and He treadeth the winepress of the fierceness of the wrath of Almighty God. And He hath on His garment and on His thigh a name written, King of Kings, and Lord of Lords.

"And I saw an angel standing in the sun; and he cried with a loud voice, saying to all the birds that fly in mid heaven, Come and be gathered together unto the great supper of God; that ye may eat the flesh of kings, and the flesh of captains, and the flesh of mighty men, and the flesh of horses and of them that sit thereon, and the flesh of all men, both free and bond, and small and great.

"And I saw the beast, and the kings of the earth, and their armies, gathered together to make war against Him that sat upon the horse, and against His army. And the beast was taken, and with him the false prophet that wrought the signs in his sight, wherewith he deceived them that had received the mark of the beast, and them that worshiped his image: they twain were cast alive into the lake of fire that burneth with brimstone: and the rest were killed with the sword of Him that sat upon the horse, even the sword which came forth out of His mouth: and all the birds were filled with their flesh" (Rev. 19:11–21). Ezekiel similarly describes the scene in his prophecy in chapter 30:17–21.

Thus it is that the climax of the world's rebellion against God is to meet its doom. This is the manner of the overthrow of the ten-kingdomed empire, the fourth of Daniel's visions. Accordingly, what we have now read from Revelation 19 is identical with (1) the falling of the stone upon the feet of the image in Nebuchadnezzar's vision, the annihilation of all gentile government (Dan. 2:45); (2) the consuming of the dominion of the fourth beast in Daniel's subsequent vision (Dan. 7:26); (3) the pouring out of God's wrath upon the Antichrist, the desolator (Dan 9:27); and (4) the coming of the Son of man on the clouds of heaven with power and great glory (Matt. 24:30). The great emperor, the Man of Sin, is to be crushed by the Lord Jesus, "with the breath of His mouth," and brought to nought "by the manifestation of His coming" (2 Thess. 2:8).

Now this "manifestation of His coming" is, to transliterate the Greek words,

THE EPIPHANY OF HIS PAROUSIA

An epiphany is, literally, the "shining forth" of that which has been hidden; and the word Parousia is, literally, "presence" (see margin of R.V. and Phil. 2:12). This latter word is used of the coming of Christ to the air for His saints, "to receive them unto Himself," and of their consequent presence with Him (1 Thess. 2:19). They are thus to be "ever with the Lord" (1 Thess. 4:17), and with Him they will come when He descends at His revelation "from heaven with the angels of His power in flaming fire, rendering vengeance to them that know not God, and to them that obey not the gospel of our Lord Jesus" (2 Thess. 1:7, 8). The sudden bursting forth of His glory thus "to execute judgment" (Jude 15) will be the "Epiphany, or shining forth, of His Parousia," and by it the Man of Sin is to be brought to nought and his empire demolished. He and his False Prophet will be "cast alive into the lake of fire," and his armies will perish (Rev. 19:20, 21).

This is to be the issue of the world's attempts to establish a millennium of its own by schemes of federation and amalgamation. This is the upshot of its fancied progress and improvement without God and His Christ.

We must now see what other Scriptures have to say concerning this scene. The instrument which the Lord uses for the destruction of His foes is a sword which proceeds *out of His mouth*; the destruction is described as the treading of the winepress.

THE VOICE OF THE LORD

First, as to the instrument. The sword is symbolic of the utterance of the Lord's voice. No material instrument is needed, a word is enough. This is clear from many passages. In the second Psalm the overthrow of the foe is thus described: "Then shall He *speak* unto them in His wrath, and vex them in His sore displeasure" (v. 5). Joel prophesies of the same event: "The sun and the moon are darkened, and the stars withdraw their shining: and the Lord *uttereth His voice* before His army; for His camp is very great; for He is strong that executeth His word: for the day of the Lord is great and very terrible; and who can abide it?" (Joel 2:10, 11; and see 3:16. With this compare Isa. 11:4 and 30:30–33.) The same voice of judgment is implied in Paul's prediction of the doom of the lawless one, that "the Lord Jesus will slay him *with the breath of His mouth*" (2 Thess. 2:8). In the same connection we are doubtless to read Psalm 29, the psalm which describes the terrible majesty and effect of the *voice of the Lord*.

We must presently dwell more fully upon this psalm in order to observe its application to the circumstances under consideration, and its connection with the passages which describe the judgment of the foe as

THE TREADING OF THE WINEPRESS

These passages are Isaiah 63:1–6; Joel 3:16; Revelation 14:17–20, and the one already quoted in Revelation 19. It is observable, too, that in the first of these the voice of the Lord is mentioned again, for the Deliverer describes Himself as "I that *speak in righteousness.*"

We shall first refer to Revelation 14:17–20. Two angels appear coming forth, the one from the temple in heaven with a sickle in his hand, the other from the altar. The latter calls to the one with the sickle to gather "the clusters of the vine of the earth," symbolic of the Man of Sin and his gathered armies. The angel then casts his sickle into the earth, gathers the vintage, and casts it into the winepress of the wrath of God. The winepress is "trodden without the city," and "there came out blood from the winepress, even unto the bridles of the horses, as far as a thousand and six hundred furlongs" (i.e., 200 miles). The great emperor and his prophet, and their vast forces, will thus be gathered in dense battle array throughout the length of Palestine, Jerusalem being their objective. Joel calls the scene of the battle "the Valley of Decision." "Come, tread ye," says the prophet, "for the winepress is full, the vats overflow; for their wickedness is great. Multitudes,

multitudes in the valley of decision! for the day of the Lord is near in the valley of decision" (Joel 3:13, 14). The multitudes are the forces of the Man of Sin.

The first six verses of Isaiah 63 narrate in the form of a dialogue

THE OVERTHROW OF THE MAN OF SIN

and his forces. The dialogue is between Messiah the Deliverer and the Jews. Having just overthrown the foe in the treading of the winepress, and the armies of the empire being destroyed throughout the battle line from the north of the land to the south, the Messiah, in the fruits of His victory, reveals Himself to His astonished earthly people. In wondering admiration they exclaim: "Who is this that cometh from Edom, with dyed garments from Bozrah? this that is glorious, marching in the greatness of His strength?" To this their Deliverer answers, "I that *speak in righteousness*, mighty to save." The significance of this is at once apparent to the reader who calls to mind the various passages mentioned above in reference to the voice of the Lord. "I that speak in righteousness"—this is the voice uttered before His army (Joel 2:10), "the sword that proceedeth out of His mouth" (Rev. 19:15); the "breath of His mouth," by which the Man of Sin is crushed (2 Thess. 2:8), and the "voice" of Psalm 29.

The people, struck by the appearance of the victor, next ask: "Wherefore art Thou red in Thine apparel, and Thy garments like him that treadeth in the winefat?" The language is doubtless symbolic. Messiah explains in reply how the threatening foes have been crushed: "I have trodden the winepress alone; and of the peoples there was no man with Me: yea, I trod them in Mine anger, and trampled them in My fury; and their lifeblood is sprinkled upon My garments, and I have stained all My raiment. For the day of vengeance was in Mine heart, and the year of My redeemed is come. And I looked, and there was none to help; and I wondered that there was none to uphold: therefore Mine own arm brought salvation unto Me; and My fury, it upheld Me. And I trod down the peoples in Mine anger, and made them drunk in My fury, and I poured out their lifeblood on the earth" (vv. 3–6). The words of a previous prophecy express the joyful recognition of the delivered nation: "And it shall be said in that day, Lo, this is our God; we have waited for Him, and He will save us: this is the Lord; we have waited for Him, we will be glad and rejoice in His salvation" (Isa. 25:9).

Turning now to Psalm 29 we find

THE SCENE OF JUDGMENT

strikingly depicted; the very length of the battle line is indicated, in agreement with the later and clearer description in Revelation 20:14. Indeed, the passages which foretell the events of this coming terrible day afford a remarkable illustration of the progressive character of the revelations of Scripture. The psalm is divided into three parts: (1) The first three verses are a call to the saints in heaven, the "sons of the mighty," to worship the Lord in view of the judgment He is just about to execute for the deliverance of His people the Jews, their land

and their city. (2) The second part, verses 3–9, describes the actual judgment by means of "the voice of the Lord." The psalmist was doubtless thinking of a thunderstorm. The Spirit of God was giving prophetic utterance concerning a more terrible scene, and the geographical limitations of the psalm are of prophetic import. The first place mentioned is Lebanon, in the north, with its mountain-spur Sirion (vv. 5, 6). The last place is the wilderness of Kadesh, in the south, the center of which is Bozrah, in Edom (v. 8), a point of connection with Isaiah 63:1. Now the distance from Sirion to Bozrah, in the wilderness of Kadesh, is 200 miles, and this is the 1600 furlongs of Revelation 14:20. Here, then, in one fell stroke of divine wrath the Man of Sin and his forces are overthrown, and the Jews are delivered. The later revelations of Scripture thus enable us to pass from the natural and physical setting of the psalm to the veiled reality. Thus this portion of the psalm is to be read in connection with the passage from Revelation 19 quoted above. (3) The last two verses describe the results of the conquest.

THE JEWS IN THEIR EXTREMITY

were threatened with annihilation. But man's extremity is God's opportunity. The people now see their Deliverer in person, they "look on Him whom they pierced." They realize that their enemies were destroyed because "the Lord sat as King at the flood." And now "the Lord sitteth as King forever." He whose right it is to reign has come to Zion. Hence the psalmist can next say: "The Lord will give strength unto His people; the Lord will bless His people with peace." Armageddon is over, the winepress of God's wrath has been trodden, and the war against the Lamb is ended. Psalm 30 follows on with the people's song of praise for deliverance.

The judgments of God in the earth will be accompanied by

SEISMIC DISTURBANCES

including "a great earthquake such as was not since there were men upon the earth," the overthrow of the cities of the nations, and the displacement of islands and mountains (Rev. 16:18–21). Then doubtless will be fulfilled the prophecy of Zechariah, that in the day when the Lord goes forth to fight against the nations that are gathered against Jerusalem, His feet will stand upon the Mount of Olives, and the mountain will be divided, leaving a very great valley east of the city (Zech. 14:1–5).

THE EVERLASTING KINGDOM

In this tremendous intervention in the affairs of the world for the termination of gentile dominion the Son of God will be accompanied by all His saints. He will come "to be glorified in His saints, and to be marveled at in all them that believed" (2 Thess. 1:10). So from earliest times Enoch had prophesied: "Behold, the Lord came with His holy myriads, to execute judgment upon all" (Jude 14, 15, margin). And Zechariah: "The Lord my God shall come, and all the saints with Thee" (14:5). They are to take an active part in the inauguration of His kingdom, and in its government. For "the saints of the Most High shall receive the kingdom, and possess the kingdom forever, even forever and ever" (Dan. 7:18). "The kingdom and the dominion, and the greatness of the kingdoms under the whole heaven, shall be given to the people of the saints of the Most High" (v. 27).

Then shall the Lord "be King over all the earth" (Zech. 14:9). God's claims will be vindicated. His Christ will reign as King of Righteousness, and King of Peace, the center of His government being the very place where once He was despised and rejected, and men cast Him out and crucified Him. Of the increase of His government and of peace there shall be no end, upon the throne of David, and upon His kingdom, to establish it, and to uphold it with judgment and with righteousness from henceforth even forever. The zeal of the Lord of hosts shall perform this (Isa. 9:7). His saints "shall be priests of God and of Christ, and shall reign with Him a thousand years" (Rev. 20:6). Then will be fulfilled the words of the Lord, "I am returned unto Zion, and will dwell in the midst of Jerusalem: and Jerusalem shall be called the city of truth; and the mountain of the Lord of hosts the holy mountain" (Zech. 8:3). The days of Israel's mourning will be ended, the nation will be a "crown of beauty in the hand of the Lord, and a royal diadem in the hand of her God," and Jerusalem will be a praise in the earth (Isa. 61:3; 62:3, 7). "The heavens shall rejoice and the earth be glad," and "the earth shall be full of the knowledge of the Lord, as the waters cover the sea" (Ps. 96:11; Isa. 11:9). According to God's eternal counsel the despised Nazarene will yet be manifested and acknowledged by all as King of kings and Lord of lords.

"To Him be glory forever and ever, Amen."

THE FOUR WOMEN OF THE APOCALYPSE

Of the four women mentioned in the book of the Revelation two symbolize agencies that have spread corruption, while the other two are symbolic of the two great communities which God has formed to bear witness for Him, and to act as His instruments of government in the ages that are to come. The first woman is described in the letter to the church in Thyatira. She is the corruptress of the Lord's servants there, and the Lord remonstrates with that church for allowing her presence and influence. He says: "I have this against thee, that thou sufferest the woman Jezebel, which calleth herself a prophetess; and she teacheth and seduceth My servants to commit fornication, and to eat things sacrificed to idols" (2:20).

THYATIRA TRADE GUILDS

Thyatira was situated northeast of Smyrna, in a fertile valley in the Province of Asia. Its inhabitants were possessed of considerable commercial advantages. At the same time they were grossly immoral. The citizens were formed into several trade guilds. Membership of these was essential to worldly success. Guild feasts were held at appointed times, and the proceedings on these occasions were characterized by the utmost licentiousness. "The bond which held a guild together lay always in the common religion in which all united, and in the common sacrificial meal of which all partook; the members ate and drank fellowship and brotherhood in virtue of the pagan deity whom they served. In the existing state of society it was impossible to dissociate membership of a guild from idolatry, and the idolatry was a kind that by its symbolism and its efficacy exerted great influence on its adherents, making them members of a unity which was essentially non-Christian and anti-Christian. In the second place, the common banquets were celebrated amid circumstances of revelry and enjoyment that were far from conducive to strict morality."[1]

"To hold aloof from the clubs was to set oneself down as a mean-spirited, grudging, ill-conditioned person, hostile to existing society, devoid of generous impulse and kindly neighborly feeling, an enemy of mankind."[2]

This shows the danger to which the converts in Thyatira were exposed. The woman spoken of as Jezebel, posing as a prophetess, as the advocate of broad-mindedness and enlightenment, would easily seduce the careless believer to go in for membership of a guild, or to return to it if it had been abandoned at conversion. The advantages would be great. Ridicule and persecution would be avoided. Prosperity in business would be practically ensured. Personal prestige in the city would be enhanced. And why not bring a healthy influence into society by joining the guild? These and other arguments, with which Christians who are tempted by the worldly minded are so familiar today, would be used to entice believers from their faithfulness to Christ.

Whether Jezebel was actually the woman's name or not, we may take it that there was such a woman in Thyatira, and that she inculcated doctrines in the church by which she successfully allured some of the believers to partake in the licentious and idolatrous practices referred to. Here, then, in the early days of church history antinomianism became rife, and immorality was practiced under the fair garb of the Christian faith; there was a form of godliness, but a denial of the power thereof.

JEZEBEL AND AHAB

We cannot dissociate this woman's name from the Jezebel of 1 Kings. She was the daughter of Ethbaal, a Sidonian. Her father was priest to Astarte, the vile goddess

---

1 Prof. W. M. Ramsay, in the article "Thyatira" in *Hasting's Dictionary of the Bible*.

2 Prof. W. M. Ramsay. *The Letters to the Seven Churches*, p. 348.

of the Syrians, the religion of whom was derived immediately from Babylon. Jezebel, whose name signifies a "dung heap," came into the midst of Israel as the wife of Ahab, and was the dominating influence amongst God's people. Her husband was practically her subordinate. The story of her pollution of the nation, her slaughter of the prophets of God, and her substitution for them of the prophets of Baal, is well-known. Through her instrumentality Ahab "did yet more to provoke the Lord, the God of Israel, to anger than all the kings of Israel that were before him." The gorgeous ritual of the worship of Astarte replaced that of Jehovah. Jezebel's baneful influence continued during the reigns of her two sons, Ahaziah and Jehoram, and, through the marriage of her daughter Athaliah to Jehoram, the son of Jehoshaphat, King of Judah, it extended to the tribe of Judah. Athaliah had a house of Baal erected in Jerusalem and her sons "broke up the house of God; and also all the dedicated things of the Lord did they bestow upon the Baalim" (2 Chron. 24:7).

THE SEVEN LETTERS

In the letters to the seven churches there is every indication of a wider scope of teaching than what was immediately applicable to those churches. Clearly there is a great deal to be said for the view that the churches are, in the two chapters which contain the letters addressed to them, purposely arranged in an order which represents anticipatively the whole course of what is called Christendom during the present era. We notice, for instance, in connection with the subject we are considering, the immediate sequence of Thyatira after Pergamos. There were false teachers present in Pergamos but Thyatira suffered them. Pergamos was indifferent to the evil; Thyatira became associated with it. These two succeed Smyrna, which was appointed to endure persecution. Correspondingly in early church history, after the persecutions which took place in the period from the Emperor Domitian to Constantine, i.e., from about A.D. 170 to the beginning of the fourth century, the churches experienced a time of immunity from opposition and cruelty, and rapidly became possessed of worldly influence and authority. Departing from the path of simple allegiance to Christ, the church sought a power and affluence for which her founder had not destined her, and eventually placed herself under the ready patronage of the emperor. The weakening of paganism, and the self-aggrandizement of the churches, provided Constantine with an opportunity for acquiring supreme political power which his ability and energy were not slow to seize.

A PARALLEL

Under his prestige the union of the church with the world proceeded apace. The conditions represented by the letters to Pergamos and Thyatira rapidly took shape. As in the days of Israel under Ahab and Jezebel, the faithful ministers of God's Word, the true prophets of the Lord in the churches, were expelled, and pagan priests, advocates of the religion of the Egyptian goddess Isis, were brought into the house of God to act as the spiritual guides of His people. This diabolical amalgamation of Christianity with paganism was completed by Pope Damasus at the end of the fourth century. The apostate Church had become heathenized. Damasus was not only made the leading ecclesiastic in the church; he was also elected Pontifex Maximus, or Chief Pontiff, of the heathen world. Nothing could be more striking than the comparison between the idolatrous decadence of Israel under Jezebel and that of the church under the Roman prelacy. The corruptions which were spread by the symbolical Jezebel amidst the churches were of the same sort as those by which the pagan queen poisoned the life of God's earthly people Israel. Damasus vauntingly acted on the principle that the end justified the means. No matter how glaring the enormity, how unrighteous the deed, everything was justified so long as the cause of the church's religious and political power was advanced. The abominations of heathendom were admitted into the churches under the cloak of the Christian faith.

THE DOOM PRONOUNCED

Thus what took place in the narrower sphere of Thyatira transpired subsequently in the broad realm of Christendom. Whether those who were guilty of yielding to Jezebel's seductions in Thyatira actually repented of their deeds, or whether the Lord's threat was carried out, we cannot definitely say. We may gather that it was so, however, from the fact that the Lord says, "I will kill her children with death; and all the churches shall know that I am He which searcheth the reins and the hearts: and I will give unto each one of you according to your works" (v. 23). Probably what took place in the slaughter of the children of Ahab and Jezebel in Israel (2 Kings 10:11) had its counterpart in the case of Jezebel's children in the church in Thyatira. So, again, in the broader view of the subject, when the Babylonish ecclesiastical system of Christendom in its final form is hereafter overthrown by the anti-Christian federacy of nations (Rev. 17:16), then this threat against the evil in Thyatira will receive its fulfillment in the wider sphere of Christendom.

MYSTERY, BABYLON THE GREAT

The second of the two evil women described in the Apocalypse is the subject of a vision given to John and recorded in the seventeenth chapter. There came to him one of the seven angels that had the seven bowls of the wrath of God, and talked with him, saying, "Come hither, I will show thee the judgment of the great harlot that sitteth upon many waters; with whom the kings of the earth committed fornication,[1] and they that dwell in the earth were made drunken with the wine of her fornication."

---

1 The reason why these events are described as already having taken place, though they were actually future to the apostle's time, is because they are viewed from the time when the judgment is to be executed.

The apostle was carried away in the spirit into a wilderness, a place suggestive of destitution and apparently symbolizing a condition barren of all that is fruitful for God, void of that which could delight His eye; a striking contrast, as we shall see, to the place from which the apostle was afterwards called to see the fair heavenly woman, the bride, the Lamb's wife. He now sees a woman "sitting upon a scarlet-colored beast, full of names of blasphemy, having seven heads and ten horns. And the woman was arrayed in purple and scarlet, and decked with gold and precious stones and pearls, having in her hand a golden cup full of abominations, even the unclean things of her fornication, and upon her forehead a name written, MYSTERY, BABYLON THE GREAT, THE MOTHER OF THE HARLOTS AND OF THE ABOMINATIONS OF THE EARTH."

WHY "MYSTERY"?

That the woman is called "Babylon the Great" indicates her association with the ancient city of the East. That the word "Mystery" is annexed to the title implies that the appellation has a spiritual significance, that facts relating to the woman have something more than a mere geographical and historical connection with the city. A mystery in Scripture is not calculated to convey to the mind of the believer the obscurity attached to what is mysterious. It comprises facts which he is intended to understand, the truths relating to which are to shape his conduct according to the will of God, whether preventatively or formatively, and thus to direct his loyalty to Christ. A mystery lies outside the ken of the natural mind, for "the natural man understandeth not the things of the Spirit . . . they are spiritually discerned."

The last phrase of the woman's title, "the mother of the harlots and of the abominations of the earth," intimates that Babylon is the source both of unholy unions of the people of God with the world, whether in Israelitic history or in Christendom, for such associations are described in Scripture as spiritual fornication (Jer. 3:6, 8, 9; Ezek. 16:32, e.g.), and of all systematized idolatry in the world, for whatever is set before men as an object of worship other than God is, in the language of Scripture, an abomination. The language is also suggestive of the immorality and unchastity which accompanies idolatry.

BABYLON THE SOURCE OF IDOLATRY

Idolatry, in an organized form, originated with Babylon, under the rule of Nimrod, son of Cush. The name of the ancient god, Bacchus, denotes "Son of Cush," and is therefore to be identified with Nimrod, who was deified after his death. The most ancient pagan religions of the world, though varying in details, have certain features in common which are distinctly traceable to the primal system of idolatry known to have been established by Nimrod and his queen Semiramis in Chaldea after Nimrod had made Babel the beginning of his kingdom (Gen. 10:10). The Baal and Astarte worship to which we have made reference in connection with Jezebel, sprang from the ancient Chaldean system. The nations had drunk of the wine of Babylon and had become intoxicated (Jer. 51:7). It was in this original Babel cult that the worship of a trinity of father, mother and son was initiated, the mother being regarded as the queen of heaven. That place she retained among the nations under such names as Astarte, among the Syrians; Diana, among the Ephesians; Aphrodite, among the Greeks; Venus, among the Romans; Isis, among the Egyptians. Israel itself was corrupted into worshiping the queen of heaven (Jer. 7:18; 44:17–25), and later the same Eastern source affected Christianity in the establishment of the worship of the Virgin Mary.

FROM BABYLON TO ROME

The Chaldean religion was transferred to Rome in the following way. After the capture of Babylon by the Medo-Persians, under Cyrus, in 539 B.C., the tonsured priests of the Chaldean cult, still unchanged in its character from the time of its inception in the days of Nimrod and Semiramis, were expelled. They fled to what is now Asia Minor, where they were welcomed by the Lydian king and established with all their ritual at his capital, Pergamos. Satan thus transferred thither the seat of his power ("Satan's throne," Rev. 2:13, R.V.). In 133 B.C., on the death of Attalus III, the last of the Lydian kings, his kingdom, and the Chaldean hierarchy with it, passed under the dominion the Romans. In the next century Julius Caesar removed the priests and all their ritualistic equipment to Rome, so as to enhance the glory of the office he already held as Pontifex Maximus, or "Chief Pontiff," of the pagan religion of Rome. Combining in himself political and religious authority, as both Imperator and Pontifex, he was now not only dictator of the republic, but also the recognized head of the Romanized oriental priesthood. Thus Rome became the seat of the Babylonish abominations. This was the satanic preparation for the corruption of the Christian religion when, having already declined from its apostolic purity, it found its ecclesiastical center in Rome. In this manner Rome became "Mystery Babylon." The vast political power of Rome had thus been mounted by the Babylonish woman before Christ appeared, and, at her instigation, the whole machinery of the empire was eventually set in motion to crush His true church.

What has been said above, then, provides the explanation of the fact that not only is the woman named "Mystery, Babylon the Great, the Mother of the Harlots and of the abominations of the earth," but also, in the interpretation at the end of the chapter, is identified with Rome, "the great city which reigneth over the kings of the earth" (v. 18).

HER INTOXICATION

The apostle saw the woman "drunken with the blood of the martyrs of Jesus" (v. 6). Everything that has been and is represented by mystic Babylon is chargeable with the slaughter of saints of God. The same spirit that leads men to the spiritual abominations of setting up any other object of worship than the true God, likewise instigates them to the persecution of His people. While the political rulers of the earth, allured by the woman's pomp and grandeur, are intoxicated by the wine of the cup of her abominations, she herself is intoxicated by the blood of the true followers of Christ.

THE WOMAN AND THE BEAST

Again, the woman was seen sitting on a scarlet-colored, seven-headed, ten-horned beast. It will be beyond the scope of our immediate subject to go fully into the details of the latter.[1]

In the interpretation the beast is indicated as the ultimate federal head of the ten-kingdomed league of nations. A comparison of the details of this seventeenth chapter with the thirteenth, and with Daniel 7, shows that the term "beast" is symbolic both of the monarch and of his dominion (cp. Dan. 7, v. 17 with v. 23), and that his dominion will consist of the resuscitated Roman power in this altered form. That the woman is seen riding the beast clearly sets forth the domination of the ecclesiastical system centering in Rome over the political federation of nations. The ecclesiastical power has dominated the civil in separate kingdoms in past history, but at no time has it exercised its power over a league of federated nations. The fulfillment of the vision is yet future. It is true that the Romish religion has received severe checks and setbacks in the past, but it is nowhere decadent or dying today. Its converts are multiplying in almost every country, and its power is far from being on the wane. The woman will yet occupy, though only for a brief time, a position of religious and political domination over the nations comprised in what was the ancient empire. She not only rides the beast, she sits "upon many waters," which are interpreted as "peoples and multitudes and nations and tongues." That is to say, besides controlling the ten-kingdomed league with its rulers, she exercises her influence over the masses of the people.

HER DESTRUCTION

Her doom, however, is sealed. Her destruction is destined to take place at the hands of the very potentates who will have supported her. The change in the situation is dramatic. "The ten horns which thou sawest, and the beast [not "upon" the beast as in A.V.], these shall hate the harlot, and shall make her desolate and naked, and shall eat her flesh, and shall burn her utterly with fire" (v. 16). How this will actually transpire is made clear in the thirteenth chapter. The two beasts, the confederate world rulers there mentioned, will establish a religion coextensive with their universal dominion. Its creed will be simple but absolute. The emperor must be acknowledged as God. Refusal will be punished by death. "And he deceiveth them that dwell on the earth by reason of the signs which it was given him to do in the sight of the beast; saying to them that dwell on the earth, that they should make an image to the beast, who hath the stroke of the sword, and lived. And it was given unto him to give breath to it, even to

---

1 See "The Roman Empire in Prophecy," and "The Mysteries of Scripture," by the same writer.

the image of the beast, that the image of the beast should both speak, and cause that as many as should not worship the image of the beast should be killed" (Rev. 13:14, 15, R.V.). The power at the disposal of these two potentates will be sufficient for the enforcement of this worship. Every other religion must be crushed, Romanism included.

Various movements amidst humanity are today directly preparing for this. A striking illustration of the manner in which the woman is to be destroyed has taken place in Russia. Atheistic Communism is spreading its influence rapidly throughout the world. Its institutions are working in practically every nation. The idea of God and the Christian religion are to be overthrown. Man is to be his own savior and master. Within the pale of Christendom, in the congregations of those who dissent from Rome, rationalism and modernism are playing their part toward the same end. The issue of it all is clear from Scripture. The ruling potentates of the ten-kingdomed league, having committed their power to the Antichrist, will with him destroy popery and everything else that is associated with mystic Babylon. Its ecclesiastical possessions, with all its vast wealth and treasures, will be confiscated, its ritualistic paraphernalia given to destruction, its cathedrals, churches, and other idolatrous fanes demolished, and those who refuse to acknowledge the new worship slaughtered. The woman will be made "desolate," stripped of her wealth; "and naked," stripped of her finery; they will "eat her flesh," she will be deprived of her power; "and shall burn her utterly with fire," she will be reduced to utter social and political ruin. The divine decree has gone forth. The human instruments will be ready at the appointed time; "for God did put in their hearts to do His mind, and to come to one mind, and to give their kingdom unto the beast, until the words of God should be accomplished" (v. 17, R.V.).

THE WOMAN ARRAYED WITH THE SUN

We are now to consider the two other women depicted in the Apocalypse. Their character is entirely different from those which have been before us in the preceding pages. The first is described in the twelfth chapter. This chapter really has its beginning in the last verse of chapter eleven. "The temple of God was opened in heaven, and the ark of His covenant was seen therein," details which, taken with the context, indicate that what follows has to do with the nation of Israel. Indeed the twelfth, thirteenth and fourteenth chapters are to be taken together, and carry us through affairs connected with that nation from the time of the birth of Christ till the end of the Great Tribulation and the overthrow of Antichrist by the Son of man.

The apostle was shown a great sign in heaven, "a woman arrayed with the sun, and the moon under her feet, and upon her head a crown of twelve stars; and she was with child, and she crieth out, travailing in birth, and in pain to be delivered. And there was seen another sign in heaven; and behold, a great red dragon, having seven heads and ten horns, and upon his head seven diadems.

And his tail draweth the third part of the stars of heaven, and did cast them to the earth: and the dragon stood before the woman which was about to be delivered, that when she was delivered, he might devour her child. And she was delivered of a son, a man-child, who is to rule all the nations with a rod of iron: and her child was caught up unto God, and unto His throne" (Rev. 12:1–5, R.V.).

THE SUN, MOON, AND STARS

That she was arrayed with the sun, possibly points to the nation's being under the protecting power of God; that is directly set forth subsequently in the chapter. That the moon (an emblem of derived authority) is seen under her feet, indicates that the power she might have exercised under God has gone from her, and that at the time in view in the vision she is in a position of subjection to her foes. At the same time there is a suggestion that she is yet to be possessed of supreme authority on the earth. The first mention of the sun, moon and stars in the Bible is in connection with the government of the earth (Gen. 1:16). The crown of twelve stars indicates the glory and universality of the administration which God has determined for His chosen nation. He has said, "I will make . . . her that was cast far off a strong nation, and the Lord shall reign over them in Mount Zion from henceforth even forever, and thou, O tower of the flock, the hill of the daughter of Zion, unto thee shall it come; yea, the former dominion shall come, the kingdom of the daughter of Jerusalem" (Mic. 4:7, 8).

THE GREAT TRIBULATION

Using the analogy of childbirth, Isaiah uttered a prediction concerning Israel which provides a key to the present passage. In connection with the birth of Christ in the nation, and the still future time of the Great Tribulation, "the time of Jacob's trouble," the prophet foretold that the historical order would be the reverse of the natural process of generation. Of Israel he says: "Before she travailed, she brought forth; before her pain came, she was delivered of a man-child. Who hath heard such a thing? Who hath seen such a thing?" Then as to the fact that a remnant of the nation will be preserved through the time of trouble and brought into millennial glory, he continues: "Shall a land be born in one day? Shall a nation be brought forth at once? For as soon as Zion travailed she brought forth her children. Shall I bring to the birth, and not cause to bring forth? saith the Lord. Shall I that cause to bring forth shut the womb? saith thy God." The Lord thus assures His people Israel that they shall be completely and suddenly delivered from their relentless foes, and that, though the nation will be largely depopulated, "a remnant shall be saved." That the time is millennial is clear from the joyous predictions that follow: "Rejoice ye with Jerusalem, and be glad for her, all ye that love her . . . rejoice for joy with her, all ye that mourn over her. . . . For thus saith the Lord, Behold I will extend peace to her like a river, and the glory of the nations like an overflowing stream . . . as one whom his mother comforteth, so will I comfort you, and ye shall be comforted in Jerusalem . . .

and the hand of the Lord shall be known toward His servants, and He will have indignation against His enemies" (Isa. 66:7–14).

THE MAN-CHILD

As to the man-child, the same prophet had given the divine assurance to the nation that it should give birth to the One who would break the yoke of its enemies and be its deliverer: "For unto us a Child is born, unto us a Son is given; and the government shall be upon His shoulder: and His name shall be called Wonderful, Counselor, Mighty God, Everlasting Father, the Prince of Peace. Of the increase of His government and peace there shall be no end, upon the throne of David, and upon His kingdom, to establish it, and to uphold it with judgment and with righteousness from henceforth and even forever. The zeal of the Lord of hosts shall perform this" (Isa. 9:6, 7, R.V.). Micah speaks of the same events without referring to the inversion of the natural process in the analogy. He specifies the tribe into which the man-child would be born, and the place of His birth: "But thou, Bethlehem Ephratah, which art little to be among the thousands of Judah, unto thee shall One come forth unto me that is to be Ruler in Israel; Whose goings forth are from of old, from everlasting. Therefore will He give them up, until the time that she which travaileth hath brought forth: then the residue of His brethren shall return unto the children of Israel" (Mic. 5:2, 3).

The woman, then, seen in the vision given to the apostle, is Israel, and the man-child of whom she was delivered is Christ. So the apostle Paul, speaking of his own nation, says: "Of whom is Christ as concerning the flesh" (Rom. 9:5). He was not brought forth by the Church, be it noted, for the church springs from Him. The woman "was delivered of a Son, a Man-Child" (v. 5, R.V.), when Christ was born in Bethlehem—long anterior to the time of her travail, for that is yet to take place at the close of the present age. He it is who "is to rule all the nations with a rod of iron," as Jehovah had declared in the second Psalm: "Yet I have set My King upon My holy hill of Zion. I will tell of the decree: the Lord said unto Me, Thou art My Son; this day have I begotten Thee. Ask of Me, and I will give Thee the nations for Thine inheritance, and the uttermost parts of the earth for Thy possession. Thou shalt break them with a rod of iron; Thou shalt dash them in pieces like a potter's vessel" (Ps. 2:6–9)[1] The description given of Him as a "man-child" is suggestive of His perfect humanity, in virtue of which, or, to use His own words, "because He is the Son of man," "the Father gave Him authority to execute judgment" (John 5:27).

THE DRAGON

The vision next reveals the arch-adversary of God and His people. "And there was seen another sign in heaven; and behold, a great red dragon, having seven

---

1 Some would associate the church with Christ in the interpretation of the man-child. While several details are true of the church as well as of Christ, there is no direct indication that the symbolism refers here to more than Christ Himself.

heads and ten horns, and upon his heads seven diadems. And his tail draweth the third part of the stars of heaven, and did cast them to the earth." These details are symbolic of his control over, and its effects upon, the Roman Empire, especially in its final and yet future phases, under the power of which, at his instigation, the Jewish nation is to suffer its last woes. The consideration of these details lies beyond our present subject.

"And the dragon stood before the woman which was about to be delivered, that when she was delivered, he might devour her child." The failure of his effort, intimated here by the absence of any further reference to it, is recorded in the Gospel of Matthew, in the account of the futile attempt of Herod to destroy the infant Christ. Instead, after all things concerning the days of His flesh and His resurrection were accomplished, "her child was caught up to God and unto His throne." This statement, actually fulfilled when Christ ascended, is reminiscent of His own words, "I also overcame, and sat down with My Father in His throne" (3:21).[1]

THE FLIGHT OF THE WOMAN

The vision now carries us, in point of time, from that event to the efforts of the devil against the Jewish people at the end of this age. He had been unable, in spite of numerous attempts, to prevent the Son of God from accomplishing his irremediable defeat at Calvary, and thereby, potentially, his everlasting destruction; his final premillennial effort will be against the nation, through the instrumentality of which Christ became the man-child.

"The woman fled into the wilderness, where she hath a place prepared of God, that there they may nourish her a thousand two hundred and threescore days" (v. 6). The subject of her flight and of the effort of the dragon against her is continued in verse 13. The parenthetic passage, from verses 7 to 12, indicates the time of these events. That passage describes the casting out of Satan the dragon from the heavenly places, a sphere in which his activities are as yet partly carried on (Eph. 6:12). Since his energies will then be confined to the earth, its godless inhabitants will be given over to the last premillennial woes, and a great voice in heaven declares that the time of the kingdom of God and the authority of His Christ has come. That proclamation is a time-indicator. The flight of the woman is to take place during the Great Tribulation. At that time, that which nationally corresponds to the symbolism of the woman will consist of the godly remnant of Israel, who are to be preserved alive through the time of extreme national distress and peril under the dragon's persecution. Then it is that the woman flees to the wilderness, as previously mentioned in verse 6. "There were given to her the two wings of the great eagle." God had borne His people "on eagle's wings" when they fled from Pharaoh into the wilderness of Sinai (Exod. 19:4; Deut. 32:12). So now the same metaphor describes His care in preserving them from the final fury of Satan. The eagle's wings are suggestive of swift escape and certain deliverance.

---

1 When the church is caught up it will not be to His Father's throne; see 1 Thessalonians 4:17.

She is nourished "for a time, and times, and half a time," a period identical with the 1260 days of verse 6. For this period the Great Tribulation is destined to last (Dan. 7:25; 12:7). The time is the same as the latter part of the 70th week, or period of seven years, in Daniel 9. That the "times" are years is clear by comparison with Daniel 4:23. The one description views the period in its smaller divisions of days, the other in its broader divisions. God, who views things in their whole scope, takes into His view at the same time the minutest details.

THE PLACE OF HER REFUGE

God has a place prepared as a temporary refuge for the Jewish remnant, "a shelter in the time of storm." That the locality is a wilderness suggests the absence of natural resources. Scripture has given intimation as to the region. East of Judaea, on the far side of Jordan and the Dead Sea, there lies a remarkable district occupied in ancient times by the nations of Edom, Moab and Ammon. The territory contains mountain fastnesses of an extraordinary character, hollowed out by gigantic gorges and chasms, occasionally broadening out into areas of considerable size, though still surrounded by lofty perpendicular cliffs. In some of these wide hollows lie the ruins of famous ancient cities, the most famous of which was Petra. Along the sides of the gorges there are caverns and tombs of enormous size, many of them artistically constructed, the whole of these gorges and recesses being sufficient altogether to provide accommodation for hundreds of thousands of inhabitants. The ornamentation and sculpture give evidence of an attainment to a high degree of art, and suggest that the population, while secure from foes, lived in comparative ease and luxury. The nature of the locality is such that people could today take shelter there in immunity from the power of modern implements of war, safe even from the mightiest guns and the deadliest gases.

Now it is significant that the prophecies in the eleventh chapter of Daniel relating to the warfare of the end of the present age, the time of the Great Tribulation, predict that this very region is to be delivered from the attacks of the king of the north. "These shall be delivered out of his hand, even Edom and Moab, and the chief of the children of Ammon" (Dan. 11:41). Again, coincidentally with this, our Lord, foretelling events of the same period, and predicting the tyrannical acts of the Antichrist, gave warning that the people of Judaea should then flee to the same district. "When therefore," He says, "ye see the abomination of desolation, which was spoken of by Daniel the prophet, standing in the holy place (let him that readeth understand), then let them that are in Judaea flee unto the mountains" (Matt. 24:15, 16)—obviously the mountains lying to the east and southeast.

It has been pointed out that an army, attempting to cross from Judaea to this district, would have to traverse a sandy plain several miles wide, frequently the scene of sudden and terrific sandstorms of such violence as to render military movements impossible. It is not difficult to conceive how comparatively simple would be the fulfillment of that part of John's vision recorded in Revelation

12:15, 16, following upon the flight of the woman into the wilderness from the face of the serpent: "and the serpent cast out of his mouth after the woman water as a river, that he might cause her to be carried away by the stream. And the earth helped the woman, and the earth opened her mouth, and swallowed up the river which the dragon cast out of his mouth." The language is of course symbolic. The actual fulfillment, political and military, is known to God.

To whatever these details may actually refer, the godly remnant of the Jews, so frequently spoken of in the Psalms and the prophets, would be able to dwell in this region, under the care of Jehovah, literally, "in the secret place of the Most High," passing the night of the Great Tribulation "under the shadow of the Almighty" (Ps. 91:1). Their defense would be "the munitions of rocks." God's people would find here "a stronghold to the needy in his distress, a refuge from the storm, a shadow from the heat, when the blast of the terrible ones is as a storm against the wall" (Isa. 25:4). The whole of this passage, from Isaiah 24:16 to the end of chapter 25, should be read in this connection. It speaks of the judgment which immediately precedes the Millennium and of the deliverance of God's people at that time.

There are numerous passages in the Old Testament which foretell, in language confirmatory of what we have been setting forth, the circumstances relating to God's protection of His people in the manner indicated. There may indeed be a prophetic import, relative to these events, in the fact that here David hid his father and mother while being pursued by King Saul (1 Sam. 22:3, 4). Cp. Isaiah 16:4, "Let Mine outcasts dwell with thee, Moab; be thou a covert to them from the face of the spoiler."

THE REST OF THE JEWS

Baffled in his attempt to destroy the woman, the dragon, with increased wrath, goes away to make war "with the rest of her seed, which keep the commandments of God and hold the testimony of Jesus" (v. 17). Judging from the Lord's prophecies as recorded in Matthew 24:15–22, there will be a considerable number in the nation who are not included amongst those who flee to the mountains. Comparing this passage with what is set forth in Revelation 11 concerning the testimony of the two witnesses, we may gather that a multitude of Jews will by this time have turned to God as a result of their ministry and will be expectantly anticipating the appearing of Christ in glory. They would, therefore, properly be described as those "who keep the commandments of God and hold the testimony of Jesus," in contradistinction to those people who will own allegiance to, and obey the commands of, the Antichrist. The "testimony [or witness] of Jesus" is to be put into connection with verses 3–7 of the preceding chapter. It is especially a testimony given to the two witnesses there mentioned, of whom it is said that, when they had finished their testimony, "the beast that cometh up out of the abyss shall make war with them, and overcome them and kill them." We may reasonably conclude that these two witnesses are amongst "the rest of her seed" spoken of in chapter 12:17, and that the objects of Satan's malignity will be all God-fearing Jews in whatever part of the world they are found.

The vision passes. No more is seen of the woman. We do not even find in the remainder of the book of Revelation the definite mention of the establishment of the children of Israel in the land of Palestine, for it is not the specific object of the Apocalypse to describe this. The millennial blessedness of the nation as symbolized by the woman is there by implication. That God has determined to deliver His people Israel, and restore them to communion with Himself, with their Messiah reigning over them in peace and righteousness, and associating them with Himself in His sovereignty over the nations, is clearly foretold in many other Scriptures. Michael, who is spoken of in this twelfth chapter as defeating Satan and his angels, and driving them out of heaven (vv. 7–9), was described in the book of Daniel as "the great prince which standeth for the children of thy people" (Dan. 12:1), and the divine promise made to that prophet was "at that time [the time of unprecedented trouble, v. 1] thy people shall be delivered, every one that shall be found written in the book." The number of the children of Israel shall yet be "as the sand of the sea, which cannot be measured nor numbered; and it shall come to pass that, in the place where it was said unto them, Ye are not My people, it shall be said unto them, Ye are the sons of the Living God" (Hos. 1:10).

THE BRIDE THE LAMB'S WIFE

We now turn to consider the last of the women mentioned in this book. The vision is one of undimmed glory. No adverse power is present. There is no dark background of suffering and persecution. Here we are brought to the closing presentation of one of the greatest subjects of Scripture. Previously it has been set forth in various ways, by illustration and type, by prophecy and doctrine; now it constitutes the final vision given to the beloved apostle. Here Christ is seen with His bride in all her beauty and glory. It is His glory that shines in her. His enemy who had assiduously sought to prevent her very existence and to thwart the divine purposes of Him who died to make her His own and hereafter to consummate her union with Himself, has been hurled to his doom. His subtlety and fierce antagonism have only served to enhance the glory and increase the blessedness of this union, and to show forth the power and grace of God who designed it.

A CHANGE OF VISION

It must have been a great relief to the apostle, after all that he had seen in prophetic vision, of upheaval and disaster, of fearful conflict and divine judgments, consequent upon the breaking of the Seven Seals, now to survey the scene of unclouded glory, which he describes in the latter part of chapter twenty-one and the beginning of chapter twenty-two. One of the seven angels who had taken his part in emptying the bowls of divine wrath at the last premillennial judgment on the foes of God, comes to give a message of joy and cheer to the wondering seer. It was one of those same angels that had shown him the vision of the other woman, the corruptress of the world (17:1–3). Then the invitation was, "Come hither, I will show thee the judgment of the great harlot"; now it is, "Come hither, I will show thee the bride, the wife of the Lamb" (21:9). Then the apostle was carried away in the Spirit into a wilderness, an appropriate locality for that vision of evil; now he is carried away to a great and high mountain, suggestive of strength, stability and permanency. We must mount to lofty heights to see the glory of God. It was when Moses and the elders of Israel had come up into the mount that they saw the glory of the Lord. The dazzling splendor of Christ's transfiguration was to be seen, not down on the plains of earth, but on the mountain's height. John was invited to behold the bride; the angel showed him a city, "that great city, the holy Jerusalem." How striking is the parallel to the vision of the evil woman! She, too, was presented as a city, "the great city which reigneth over the kings of the earth." That was Satan's anticipative imitation of the pure and virtuous woman, the bride of the Lamb, the heavenly city.

CONCERNING CHRIST AND THE CHURCH

We have to go back to the beginnings of human history to see the first intimation of this combination of symbols. Let us see what the Genesis record states about the formation of Eve in this respect. In the Hebrew of Genesis 2:22, the word which means "to make" is purposely set aside and a word denoting "to build" is chosen instead: "the rib which the Lord God had taken from the man builded He into a woman, and brought her unto the man" (see R.V. margin). Here then is the application of the metaphor of building to the formation of her who was created to be a helpmeet for Adam, language anticipative of the words of Christ Himself long after: "I will build My Church" (Matt. 16:18). In the epistle which especially sets forth the union of the church with Christ, the same two figures are employed. The apostle Paul, in the epistle to the Ephesians, uses the metaphor of the city in reference to the church, in chapter 2:19, and then depicts it, in chapter 5, as the bride of Christ, the object of His love. For her He "gave Himself up . . . that He might present the Church to Himself a glorious Church, not having spot or wrinkle or any such thing." The apostle dwells upon the union of husband and wife (5:25–32) to complete his illustration of the union between Christ and the church.

Here then, in Revelation 21, the bride, the Lamb's wife, a symbolism suggestive of the closest relationship and the most intimate love, is also seen as "the Holy City, Jerusalem, coming down out of heaven from God, having the glory of God" (v. 10), an organized community, enjoying fellowship and association under the authority of the Lord. The next words have frequently been understood as if they referred directly to the light of the city; that is because the word *phōstēr*, which means "light-giver," has been translated "light." The margin of the Revised Version "luminary," gives the correct rendering. Christ Himself is in view. He it is who is described in the statement, "her Light [-giver] was like unto a Stone most precious, as it were a jasper stone, clear as crystal." He is the source of her light. The city owes all her glory to Him. He is the precious stone. The jasper sets forth the various traits of His character in their perfect combination.

The words "clear as crystal" represent one verb in the original, and may be translated more literally "crystallizing": that is to say, the stone is described not merely as clear as crystal itself, it has a crystallizing power. Christ imparts beauty to His redeemed, He makes His church resplendent with His own glory. In shining out upon creation she reflects His light, setting forth His character and attributes.

THE LAMB AND THE STONE

The association of the figurative use of the Lamb and the stone, in reference to Christ, is frequent in Scripture. All that in His relationship to the church He is as the stone, emblematic of strength and stability as a foundation, as well as of ornamental splendor, is due to His sacrifice at Calvary as the Lamb of God. The reader will find profit in comparing in this respect the following Scriptures, which are but few among many: 1 Samuel 7:9, 12, which narrates how Samuel first took a sucking lamb for the whole burnt offering, as a preparation for victory over the Philistines, and then, after the conflict, a stone, to which he gave the name Ebenezer, as a celebration of victory accomplished; Psalm 118:22–27, where the psalmist sings both of the sacrifice to be bound to the altar and of the stone which is become the Head of the corner. So in 1 Peter 1:19, with 2:4–7, where the apostle first speaks of the value of the precious blood of Christ as of a Lamb without blemish and without spot, and then of His preciousness as the chief cornerstone. Again, the apostle Paul, in Ephesians 2:13, 20, speaks of the union of believers both Jew and Gentile in being made nigh together by the blood of Christ, and then represents them as being builded together upon the same foundation, "Christ Jesus Himself being the Chief Cornerstone."

THE WALL AND THE GATES

The twelfth verse of Revelation 21 continues the description of the city, and the words, "having a wall great and high," are to be connected with the beginning of verse 11. The wall is emblematic of defense and security. There are twelve gates with twelve angels standing at them. The angels are associated with the church, though they never could form part of it. They have, for almost two thousand years, been learning by means of the church the wisdom and grace of God (Eph. 3:10 with 1 Cor. 11:10), and throughout the Millennium they will rejoice in witnessing the glories of the completed union between Christ and His bride.

On the gates are written the names of the twelve tribes of Israel. In Eastern cities the gate was the place where the elders sat to administer judgment. The name on the gate was not descriptive of the city itself, but of a locality outside it, suggesting that the said locality was under the influence of the city. Thus in the earthly Jerusalem, for example, there are the Jaffa Gate and the Damascus Gate. That the names of the tribes of Israel are on the gates of the heavenly city signifies that judgment over Israel will be administered by some who form part of the church. This is just what our Lord told His apostles. "When the Son of man," He said, "shall sit on the throne of His glory, ye also shall sit upon twelve thrones, judging the twelve tribes of Israel" (Matt. 19:28). The thrones of the apostles will not be literally and materially set up on the earth in the Millennium, for they themselves are part of the church. Their authority will therefore be exercised from the heavenlies.

There are three gates on each of the four sides of the city, for in the Millennium with Israel ruling over the whole world, the influence of the church will proceed in every direction. Again, the wall has twelve foundation stones, and on them are the names of the twelve apostles. This is not a matter of the administration of judgment, but of the foundation of the city itself, for the church is built upon the foundation of the apostles and prophets; that is to say, on the foundations of divine truth laid by them (Eph. 2:20). These foundations are adorned with all manner of precious stones, symbolic of the glories of the Lord Jesus and of the church in association with Him, as set forth in other Scriptures.

The adornment is not something additional to the foundation stones, as in the case of ordinary buildings, but forms an essential part of the foundation itself. The glories of the Lord, made known by the truths of Holy Scripture, will be revealed in perfection in the very church herself as well as through her instrumentality.

THE MEASUREMENT

The city, the gates, and the wall were measured with a golden reed, indicative of a righteous and infallible judgment. But more than this, the very fact of the measurement indicates the preciousness to God of that which is measured. Compare chapter 11:1, which describes the measurement of the temple of God in Jerusalem, and the altar and the worshipers, all as being precious to God and set apart for His service and glory amidst the confusion of earth at that time. See again Psalm 16, where Christ, speaking of the saints as His "goodly heritage," says that "the measuring lines are fallen unto Him in pleasant places," a statement expressive of the infinite value to Him of His redeemed people (v. 6).

The angel measured the city "as far as twelve thousand furlongs." It is not necessary to understand by the preposition *epi*, "as far as," that the measurement is incomplete, though that may possibly be so, especially if the suggestion is that an angel cannot comprehend all the glories of the church. The preposition may, however, simply serve to emphasize the enormous dimensions of the city. The length and breadth and height of it are equal. Probably, in the vision given to John, the city was in the shape of a pyramid. In verse 17, which describes the height of the wall as 144 cubits, and this as being "the measure of a man, that is, of an angel," there is perhaps a suggestion that an angel can comprehend all that is conveyed by the wall, the protective outworks of the city, in contrast to the infinite wonders of God's grace as set forth in the structure of the city itself. A finite mind, whether of man or angel, can grasp the one, the other is comprehended only by God.

ITS TEMPLE

The city itself is "of pure gold, like unto pure glass" (v. 18, R.V.), while the street of the city is "like unto pure gold, as it were transparent glass." The gold exhibits the glory of divine righteousness. The city and the street are not only free from defilement, but therein are seen all the perfections of God's character as exhibited in Christ. There is no temple in the city, "for the Lord God Almighty and the Lamb are the temple thereof." There is no need to enter a sanctuary, for there God is publicly seen in Christ. For this reason no created light, as of the sun or moon, is required; the uncreated light of God irradiates the city. "The lamp thereof is the Lamb." That is to say, the light that shines does so as the outcome of the sacrifice of Calvary. The nations of earth will walk by the light of it (R.V., margin), and the kings of the earth will bring their glory into it. They cannot bring their material wealth into it, for it is heavenly, but they will acknowledge its glory, submit to its rule, and pay homage to Him whose city it is.

ENTRANCE INTO IT

All who have resurrection bodies, apart from those who constitute the church itself, will have free entry into the city; that is to say, there will be complete fellowship between those who symbolically constitute the city itself and those who have access to it. To use the somewhat imperfect illustration of an earthly city, there are those who, as its permanent residents, constitute its citizenship, and those who, as visitors, enjoy association with and the privileges of the citizens themselves. Those who have the right to enter into the heavenly city, that is to say, those who in resurrection life enjoy fellowship with the church, have their names written in the Lamb's Book of Life (v. 27).

THE RIVER AND THE TREE

It is a pity that a break was made by introducing chapter twenty-two here. The first five verses of the twenty-second chapter are a completion of the twenty-first. The apostle is now shown "a river of water of life, bright as crystal," which proceeds from the throne of God and of the Lamb. This is apparently symbolical of all the blessings that come from the Father and the Son by the Holy Spirit. Where God's throne is from thence flow streams of water, for He who is universally sovereign is the source of every blessing (see Ezek. 47:1; Joel 3:18; Zech. 14:8). "There is a river the streams whereof make glad the city of God, the Holy Place of the tabernacles of the Most High" (Ps. 46:4). Wherever the sovereignty of God is acknowledged, and wherever God Himself is worshiped, there His worshipers receive blessing. The river refreshes the city itself. Jesus said, "The water that I shall give him shall become in him a well of water springing up unto everlasting life" (John 4:14). The river also flows on to minister refreshment to others, and so it will be the joy of the church to be the channel of blessing to all the subjects of the wide kingdom of God.

On both sides of the river is the Tree of Life yielding fruit every month. All spiritual fruit comes from Christ. He is the Tree of Life. There will be no cherubim to guard the way. The tree will be of free access to all—it grows on either side of the river. The divine restrictions necessarily laid down in Eden, and the curse pronounced when man fell, will be forever removed. The fruit of the tree will impart delight and refreshment to all those who constitute the city, and to all who have access to it, for Christ will forever continue to minister of Himself to all His saints in glory. The leaves of the tree will be for the healing of the nations, so that from Christ Himself, through the instrumentality of the heavenly city, the nations of earth will not only receive their administration and their light, but also the undoing of the works of the devil and all the havoc he has wrought among them.

HIS NAME IN THEIR FOREHEADS

The servants of God and of the Lamb "shall do Him service and see His face, and His name shall be in their foreheads." Their capacity to serve then will depend upon their faithfulness now, and their sphere of service then will be determined by their rewards for service rendered now. There will be unbroken communion between Him and them, and they will unfailingly show forth His glory, presenting in perfection all the traits of His character. Those who look upon them will at once recognize Christ in them. Finally, those who constitute the city will reign with Christ forever and ever.

This beautiful city, then, with all that is set forth in the symbolism of this passage, is "the bride, the Lamb's wife." She it is who is to share His sovereign power. How striking the contrast in this closing prophecy of her reign with Him forever and ever, to what is set forth in the case of the woman in chapter seventeen, who sought to reign, and so successfully for a time, in her self-assumed pride and glory, over the kings and the inhabitants of the earth! May the wonders of our soon-to-be-realized glory in union with our blessed Lord and Redeemer, as set forth so vividly in this final vision of Holy Scripture, stimulate us the more earnestly to look for, and the more ardently to love, His appearing, and the more devotedly to present ourselves to Him for the service here of Him who loved us and gave Himself for us, that He might hereafter present us to Himself, "without spot or wrinkle, or any such thing."

THE SEALED BOOK OF THE APOCALYPSE

Who is worthy to open the sealed scroll? Only Jesus, the Lamb. This name for our Savior highlights the twofold significance of His role. He is the sacrifice that provides salvation from sin, but He is also the One who unleashes judgment upon all who trample upon the blood of Christ. Death unto death. Life unto life. He who is the Lamb is also the Lion, and He is fearsome to His foes. This article details the many seals and judgments that devastate the earth during the last days. They are the Wrath of the Lamb.

SCRIPTURE

"And I saw in the right hand of Him that sat on the throne a book written within and on the back, close sealed with seven seals. And I saw a strong angel proclaiming with a great voice, Who is worthy to open the book, and to loose the seals thereof; And no one in the heaven, or on the earth, was able to open the book, or to look thereon. And I wept much, because no one was found worthy to open the book, or to look thereon: and one of the elders saith unto me, Weep not: behold, the Lion that is of the tribe of Judah, the Root of David, hath overcome, to open the book and the seven seals thereof. And I saw in the midst of the throne and of the four living creatures, and in the midst of the elders, a Lamb standing as though it had been slain, having seven horns, and seven eyes, which are the seven Spirits of God, sent forth into all the earth. And He came, and He taketh it out of the right hand of him that sat on the throne. And when He had taken the book, the four living creatures and the four and twenty elders fell down before the Lamb, having each one a harp, and golden bowls full of incense, which are the prayers of the saints. And they sing a new song, saying, Worthy art Thou to take the book, and to open the seals thereof: for Thou wast slain, and didst purchase unto God with Thy blood men of every tribe, and tongue, and people, and nation, and madest them to be unto our God a kingdom and priests; and they reign upon the earth" (Rev. 5:1–10. R.V.).

THE JUDGE AND HIS GLORY

The Gospel of John presents the Son of God as the world's Savior; the book of the Revelation presents Him as the universal Judge. The first chapter gives a description of Him in that capacity, depicting His perfect righteousness and the unerring character of His estimation. In the second and third chapters He is seen engaged in His work as the Judge of His saints. Judgment begins at the house of God, and consequently these preliminary chapters reveal Him discerning the ways of His servants in the churches with a view to the apportionment of rewards at His judgment seat.

The fourth chapter begins that portion of the book which deals with His judgment of the world. This is to be distinguished entirely from what has preceded.

The fourth and fifth chapters describe a scene in heaven preparatory to the execution of judgment in the earth. The fourth presents a graphic and awe-inspiring description of the throne, its occupant, the symbols of the judgment about to issue from it, and the attendant worshipers and their worship. The fifth chapter, continuing the scene, brings Christ into view as the only person qualified to act as the judge of the world. At first, however, the book is seen in the right hand of God, close sealed with its seven seals, and there appears to be no possibility of the disclosure of its contents. The mention of the apparent absence of anyone worthy to open it prepares the way for the revelation of Him who alone is worthy. His glories are thrown into all the stronger light by the loud proclamation of the angel, "Who is worthy to open the book, and to loose the seals thereof"; and by the statement that no one in the wide universe was able to do so, or even to look on the book. The effect of this on the apostle was to fill him with grief. His sorrow, however, was soon turned to joy.

THE LION AND THE LAMB

It was one of the elders who said to him, "Weep not! behold, the Lion that is of the tribe of Judah, the Root of David, hath overcome, to open the book and the seven seals thereof." The elders are representative of those, both of this and former ages, who have a knowledge of the ways of God in Christ. That Christ is here called "the Lion that is of the tribe of Judah" and "the Root of David" indicates that the contents of the sealed book have to do particularly with the Jews, and this we find to be the case as we peruse the subsequent chapters. All that is mentioned of the affairs of the world centers in and around that nation and its city and temple.

The apostle beholds, in the midst of the throne, a Lamb. There is a solemn significance attaching to this title in view of the impending judgment. The sacrifice which was provided for the expiation of sins, and which forms the basis of the gospel of God's grace, must hereafter prove the doom of those who trample upon the blood of Christ. The gospel which proclaims the atoning character of His sacrifice is a savor of death unto death when it does not become a savor of life unto life. The combination of the figurative title, "Lion of Judah," with that of a lamb is very suggestive. The lamb is the emblem of meekness. The wrath of one who is meek is far more terrible than that of a passionate man. Now while Christ is essentially "meek and lowly," He is also essentially full of majesty and strength; He who is the Lamb is also the Lion. How fearful for His foes will be the exercise of His attribute in the latter respect, when divine justice demands that He carry out His "strange work"! The scene depicted in this chapter is a confirmation of the statement of Christ Himself in the days of His flesh, that the Father judgeth no man, but "He hath given all judgment unto the Son, and He gave Him authority to execute judgment, because He is the Son of man," (John 5:22, 27, R.V.).

THE GOD-MAN

We should notice that the Revisers have rightly put a comma after the word "overcome." In the original this verb is widely separated from the verb "to open." Emphasis is thus given to the victory of the Cross. There it was that Christ overcame. His Cross was the determining factor in the judgment of the world. "Now," He said, "is the judgment of this world; now shall the prince of this world be cast out" (John 12:31). The Lord stated, as the reason why the Father had committed all judgment into His hands, that He is the Son of man. He it is who through His incarnation combines in Himself the two natures of Godhead and manhood. He is thereby uniquely qualified to act as the judge. Being one in the Godhead with the Father, He has perfect knowledge of the character and the requirements of God; and being perfect man, having passed through human experiences, with all human temptations, sin apart, He has complete knowledge of man. On this account He alone could look on the book and open its seals. By Him and Him only the judgments contained therein can be executed.

His infinite knowledge and power, and all the glory and majesty of His being and position, are seen in the latter part of the fifth chapter to produce the worship not only of the heavenly host but of the whole creation. As the creation has been defiled by sin and brought thereby into the bondage of corruption, so it is to be delivered by the power of the Son of God, in virtue of His atoning work.

THE DAYS OF THE SON OF MAN

The sixth chapter introduces the execution of the judgments contained in the sealed book. The period in which these events will transpire is the same as that described by the Lord as "the days of the Son of man" (Luke 17:22), the days, that is to say, when Christ will intervene in the affairs of the world, first by preliminary judgments and then in personal presence. "As it came to pass," He said, "in the days of Noah, even so shall it be also in the days of the Son of man. They ate, they drank, they married, they were given in marriage, until the day that Noah entered into the ark, and the flood came, and destroyed them all. Likewise even as it came to pass in the days of Lot; they ate, they drank, they bought, they sold, they planted, they builded; but in the day that Lot went out from Sodom it rained fire and brimstone from heaven and destroyed them all: after the same manner shall it be in the day that the Son of man is revealed" (vv. 26–30).

Note that He first speaks of "days of the Son of man" and then of "the day that the Son of man shall be revealed." "The days of the Son of man," corresponding to the days of Noah, form the period immediately preceding His appearing in glory, and therefore the time of the judgments spoken of in Revelation 6 and subsequent chapters.

THE CHURCH REMOVED

That the church will be removed prior to the execution of these judgments seems to be indicated by the following considerations:

1. The time referred to is that in which the world will be subject to the wrath of God. The period will therefore differ entirely in character from the present era, which is a time of unparalleled grace and the long-suffering of God. The Church is taught to wait for the Son of God from heaven as the one who "delivereth us from the wrath to come" (1 Thess. 1:10, R.V.). Again, "God hath not appointed us to wrath, but unto the obtaining of salvation through our Lord Jesus Christ" (5:9), a passage which also refers to the Lord's second coming. Further, "We shall be saved from the wrath of God through Him" (Rom. 5:9). These Scriptures clearly show that the church cannot be here during the time when the wrath of God is being executed upon the world in its rebellion under the Antichrist. There have been calamities during the present era which are recognizable as of a divinely retributive character. We must distinguish, however, between these occasional catastrophes and those recorded in the Apocalypse. The latter belong to a period characterized as a time of the wrath of God. The further the judgments proceed the more determined is man's resistance against God (see 9:20).

THE ELDERS

2. In the fourth chapter those who are described as elders (the number 24 is undoubtedly symbolic) are clothed and crowned with crowns of reward (*stephanoi*). They cannot therefore be in their present spirit-condition. Rewards for faithfulness have been assigned to them. They cannot then be merely the saints of Old Testament times, for the writer of the epistle to the Hebrews says that "apart from us [i.e., the saints of this age] they [the Old Testament saints] are not to be perfected" (Heb. 11:40). They would not therefore be clothed and crowned before those who belong to the church had similarly been clothed and crowned. We conclude accordingly that the fourth chapter describes a scene in which the church is present in the glory with the Lord, the saints who constitute it having received their rewards at the judgment seat of Christ.

Moreover, the company represented by the elders is seen in association with the Son of God in anticipation of the execution of His judgments and the establishment of His kingdom on earth. Their rewards having been given them, they now worship Him in view of His impending interference in the affairs of the world, and His personal intervention for the establishment of His kingdom. They will then come with Him in glory. They are to be identified as those who, in the description of the great event given in chapter nineteen, are seen accompanying Him "clothed in fine linen, white and pure," when He comes in His glorious Advent with the hosts of heaven (19:14). The same event is described by Paul when he says that the Lord Jesus will come "in flaming fire, rendering vengeance to them that know not God, and to them that obey not the gospel . . . when He shall come to be glorified in His saints, and to be marveled at in all them that believed" (2 Thess. 2:8, 10). They are seen "clothed in white raiment" both in chapter 4:4 and in chapter 19:14. They are around the throne in heaven in the former passage before the sealed book is opened, and they come forth with

Him when the events recorded under the opening of the seals have transpired on earth. The church is therefore seen to be in heaven after the third chapter.

THE THREE PARTS OF THE APOCALYPSE

3. That this is the position of the church in the fourth chapter is confirmed by the arrangement of the whole of the Apocalypse. When John was commissioned to pen the book he was told to write it in three parts "The things which thou sawest, and the things which are, and the things which shall come to pass hereafter [lit., "the things which shall come to pass after these things"]" (1:19).

(a) The things which he had seen he describes in the first chapter;

(b) Plainly, "the things which are" are given in the second chapter and the third. That they were not limited merely to the seven churches as existent in John's time is abundantly evident. The exhortation, "He that hath an ear, let him hear what the Spirit saith to the churches," which accompanies each letter, is given to all believers. The message given to one of the churches is "Hold fast till I come" (2:25), and to another, "I come quickly: hold fast that which thou hast, that no one take thy crown" (3:11), words which apply to, and are needful for, all churches throughout this era. The return of the Lord, an event yet future, was the *terminus ad quem* to which the churches were directed, the consummating event which would bring to a close their present testimony and service on earth. "The things which are" must therefore relate to the earthly witness and experiences of churches throughout the whole of the era. There are other evidences of this in these two chapters, which we need not here enumerate.

(c) We get at the beginning of chapter four a clear indication of the third portion of the book, containing "the things that shall come to pass after these things." After the completion of the letters to the churches, John heard a voice saying, "Come up hither, and I will show thee *the things which must come to pass after these things*"; the last clause is practically word for word the same as in chapter 1:19. "After these things," in chapter 4:1, repeated both at the beginning and at the end of the verse, undoubtedly refers to the things recorded in the second and third chapters. Church testimony on the earth has then ceased, and the next part of the book, from chapter four onward, relates to the subsequent affairs in the world.

DISTINGUISHING FEATURES OF THE THIRD PART

4. Again, there are several features which characterize the section of the Apocalypse beginning at chapter four, which distinguish it from Scriptures relating to the gospel and the church.

(a) The names of God are those by which He was known in ages previous to the gospel age, as in covenant relation with His earthly people. The title Father does not occur after chapter three, save in chapter 14:1, where it is "His Father"; nowhere is such a phrase found as "our Father," or "our God and Father." This is the more noticeable since to John was committed to unfold, in his gospel and epistles, the Father's name and character.

(b) The throne of God is seen in a very different light in these chapters from that elsewhere in the New Testament. It is not now a throne of grace to which believers draw near to obtain mercy. They are seen around it as worshipers. It is a throne of judgment exercised in vindication of the rights of the Son of God and against rebellious humanity. It is true that the throne has a rainbow around it, but that is a sign of God's covenant with the earth, and is indicative of ultimate mercy in the Millennium.

(c) The way in which Christ is spoken of as a Lamb differs from the way in which He is so represented elsewhere. Nowhere else do we read of "the wrath of the Lamb" (6:16). In chapter 17:14 the Lamb is seen overcoming His foes. The period indicated in these chapters, 4 to 19, must not be confounded with the present time of God's long-suffering mercy, and of gospel testimony by the church. The very word rendered Lamb in the Apocalypse is different from that used elsewhere of the sacrifice of Christ. In other passages it is *amnos*, here it is always *arnion*; this diminutive, expressive of the lowliness and humiliation of the Lord Jesus in His death, serves to set forth in greater contrast the statements of His majesty and power. It is when, as the Lamb, He takes the sealed book that He is also described as the Lion of Judah, and the opening of each seal is an act preparatory to judgment.

(d) This portion of the Apocalypse, since it relates to divine interposition in the affairs of the world, and since prophecy in this respect centers in the nation of Israel, is Jewish in its subject matter and its features. In the sixth chapter those who have been slain are heard crying for vengeance on their persecutors. This is entirely foreign to the attitude of the church, but is consistent with Old Testament history and prophecy relating to Israel and with the so-called imprecatory psalms. In the seventh chapter the 144,000 who are sealed are all of the nation of Israel. The prophecies which follow chapter ten are distinctly said to be "over [i.e., concerning] many peoples and nations, and tongues and kings" (10:11, R.V.), and Jerusalem and its temple immediately come into view, and the two witnesses who are to bear testimony in the Jewish nation during the close of this age. Chapter twelve presents Israel (not the church) under the symbol of a woman arrayed with the sun, and exhibits Satan's antagonism against the nation at the time of the end. The thirteenth chapter shows the human instruments of this satanic malignity, and the conditions of the world under them. Chapter fourteen predicts seven events relating, not to the church, but to the eschatological events of the same period respecting the faithful saints of the time, the nations of the world and the adherents of the Beast. The chapter begins with Mount Zion and ends with the city of Jerusalem. The fifteenth gives another scene in heaven preparatory to the final series of judgments in the earth. These are mentioned in chapters sixteen and nineteen, chapters seventeen and eighteen being parenthetic, relatively to the abominations of Babylon and the kings and leaders of the world. In all this any mention of the church as being on the earth is conspicuous by its absence. It has been rightly said that "the only place in which the church is seen from chapter 4:10 to chapter 19:4 is in heaven."

THE SEVENTIETH WEEK OF DANIEL 9

A comparison of the prophecies of the book of Daniel and this portion of the Apocalypse shows that what is predicted as about to take place under the breaking of the seven seals belongs to the same period as what is called "The Seventieth Week" of Daniel 9. That "week" is really a *hepdomad*, or period of seven years, and is severed off (a literal rendering of the word translated "decreed"—or determined, A.V.—in Dan. 9:24) from the preceding sixty-nine. That prophecy has to do with the Jews and Jerusalem—"thy people and thy city"—and that which relates to the seventieth week is a brief outline beforehand of the events which will transpire under the rule of the Antichrist.

The outline is filled up by other Scriptures, and nowhere in greater detail than in the Apocalypse. A large proportion of the sacred volume concentrates upon the period under consideration, a fact which is suggestive of its extreme importance, as being the culmination of so much that has transpired in human history, and as immediately preceding the millennial reign of Christ. The week, or seven-years' period at the end, is marked by three outstanding events: (a) it begins with the covenant between the Antichrist and the Jews, after their complete political restoration, an agreement which Isaiah calls a "Covenant with Hell"; (b) halfway through the period the covenant will be broken by the Antichrist himself, and this will be followed by the Great Tribulation, a time spoken of in the Daniel 9 passage as one of desolation, and in Jeremiah 30:7 as the "time of Jacob's trouble," the policy of the world powers being the destruction of the Jewish race; (c) these efforts will issue in the overthrow of Antichrist and his colleague, and the forces under him, through the personal intervention of Christ for the deliverance of the nation and the establishment of His kingdom on earth. The prophetic scheme of Revelation 6 to 19 runs parallel to it.

THE OPENING OF THE FIRST SEAL

Turning now to the sixth chapter we notice that the period is ushered in by the opening of the first seal and the accompanying voice of one of the living ones, saying, "Come"—not "Come and see," as in the A.V. The utterance is not an invitation to John, but a challenging command calling forth that which has been destined for the occasion. The immediate response is the appearance of a rider on a white horse.

We must distinguish this rider from the one in chapter 19:11. The rider in the latter case is Christ at His Second Advent. The one in chapter six is apparently a satanic anticipatory imitation of Christ, and represents the Antichrist at his accession to power. Whatever revolutionary upheavals or national wars may have given rise to his advent, he himself begins the period of his power in a different way. He wields not a sword, indicative of the carnage of warfare, but a bow, suggestive of conquest carried on at a distance and by the removal of individual opponents. He rides to power by an easily gained series of successes, and, as a satanically endued genius, he attains to leadership over the nations by his attractive personality and by his unprecedented powers of organization.

A TIME OF STRONG DELUSION

It would seem from other Scriptures that prior to his advent the world will be in a considerable amount of chaos and confusion owing to revolutions and social and international disturbances.[1] Gifted with capacities for the rectification of these troubles, he will introduce a brief period of peace, and men will be deceived into thinking that a golden age of permanent prosperity has begun. The days spoken of by the Lord, and referred to above as resembling those of Noah and the times of Lot, will have begun, and people will be planting, building, buying, selling, and marrying and given in marriage, in utter disregard of God. As a result of the covenant between Antichrist and the Jews, that nation, though in utter apostasy from God, will enjoy temporary affluence and power, and their position of completed political restoration will provide a key to international conditions in general.

We are told by the apostle Paul that the world will be given over by God to strong delusion (2 Thess. 2:11). The great potentate who is destined to control the affairs of the world for a brief time, through whom Satan will challenge the claims of the Son of God, will have power to deceive men into thinking that the age of universal peace and safety has been brought in at last. He might explain away even the Rapture of the church by some form of spiritist teaching. Whether or no, the fact that those who belong to the true Church have gone will only lead to the concentration of satanic efforts in the world. Even now the devil is persuading multitudes of religious people in Christendom into thinking that the Second Coming of Christ has already taken place, and that many of the prophecies of this part of the Apocalypse have been fulfilled.

THE OTHER THREE HORSEMEN

In this connection we may briefly refer to the other three horsemen, who appear on the opening of the second and third and fourth seals respectively. It is generally admitted that the significance of the appearance of the rider on the red horse, who wields a great sword, and takes peace from the earth, is that the world is plunged into war; and that the circumstances following the appearance of the rider on the black horse indicate conditions of famine: food is at famine prices, according to verse 6. The opening of the fourth seal, and the appearance of death as the rider on the pale horse, are followed by bloodshed, famine, pestilence, and destruction by wild beasts. All this reveals how, in a preliminary way, God will suddenly interfere with the state of peace and safety brought about by the advent

---

1 See *The Roman Empire in Light of Prophecy*, by the Author (written in 1915).

of the Antichrist: "When they are saying peace and safety, then sudden destruction cometh upon them."

We are being told today that these events have already transpired; that the opening of the seals of the book has already begun; that the conditions referred to above have taken place in connection with the Great War, and are still in course of procedure. This is being taught with the aid of a widely advertised film entitled, *The Four Horsemen of the Apocalypse*. We need to be on our guard against this misapplication of Scripture, lest we be led away by the error of the evil one. By causing people to think that the judgments predicted for the coming period under the rule of the Man of Sin have already taken place, Satan is, as we have pointed out, preparing for the deception, the "strong delusion" referred to above.

RUSSELLITE ERROR

The teachings of the so-called International Bible Students' Association, which is another name for Millennial Dawn or Russellite teachings, are that Christ, who is blasphemously said to be only a Spirit, came in 1914, and that the calamities which have occurred, and are occurring, through the recent war and its effects, are the judgments which will issue in the Millennium. The time of universal regeneration is thus said to be near at hand, and therefore "millions now living will never die." There are other teachings by which an attempt is made to show that these prophecies in the book of Revelation have had their fulfillment in past history. It is not our purpose to enter into these doctrines now, as they are not so insidious and dangerous as the Millennial Dawn teaching just mentioned.

How easy, when the Rapture of the church takes place, to persuade people that, as Christ (being a Spirit as Russellites say) is here, though unseen, so the thousands who have been suddenly removed are spirits, still here in the world! What an opportunity for Spiritists to advance their cause, and to persuade people that they can communicate through mediums with those who have been removed! Spiritism, Millennial Dawnism, and other forms of error will play their part in explaining the Rapture to satisfy their theories. The great event will seem far less startling to the world than we might at first suppose. Deny that Christ "cometh in the flesh" (see 2 John 7, R.V.), deny bodily resurrection, and the way is open for all sorts of satanic delusion.

Let Christians beware. The period of final judgments spoken of in Revelation 6 to 19 has not yet been ushered in. The time is undoubtedly near. But the disastrous events of the Great War, and the famines, pestilences, and earthquakes which have followed, are not the fulfillment itself. They are premonitory symptoms of what is impending.

THE FIFTH SEAL OPENED

After the breaking of the fifth seal the apostle sees underneath the altar the souls of them that had been slain for the Word of God and for the testimony which they held. They are heard crying out for vengeance. As we have mentioned this could not be applied to the church. When read in connection with other Scriptures relating to the period under Antichrist, we get a true view of what is here set forth. It would seem from the seventeenth chapter that the papal system will have acquired an unprecedented measure of world power by the time of the advent of Antichrist. The present indications of this are numerous. In the chapter referred to the woman is seen riding the beast until he and his ten-kingdomed confederacy overthrow and destroy her. The great ecclesiastical system, the travesty of the church of the living God, is doomed to destruction at the hands of combined anti-Christianity. Those mentioned after the opening of the fifth seal will have suffered death under one or other of those two systems, either during their association or after the overthrow of the ecclesiastical. The divine retribution upon the latter is to be meted out at the hands of man; Antichrist will be dealt with by the Son of God Himself.

THE SIXTH AND SEVENTH SEALS

The opening of the sixth seal introduces catastrophes of a still more terrible nature than those which have preceded. Some think that what is here mentioned at the close of the sixth chapter will transpire at the end of the whole period. This is possible. The opening of the seventh seal, however, introduces the events indicated under the blowing of the trumpets and the outpouring of the vials or bowls. The culmination of this is recorded in the nineteenth and twentieth chapters, after the parenthetic chapters seventeen and eighteen, which give the two aspects of Babylon, mystic and literal, and her judgments. The Son of God, invested with His own sovereign rights over the world, comes to overthrow the Beast and the False Prophet, and their assembled armies. Thus "the days of the Son of man," during which He has been acting in judgment from heaven, issue in "The Day." The Jews are delivered, the earth is rid of its anti-God tyrants. The usurper, Satan, whose instruments they were, is bound and shut down in the abyss, and the reign of the King of kings and Lord of lords begins.

The remaining contents of the sealed book disclose the final scene of the Millennium, when Satan is loosed for a season, and man is shown that not even the presence of Christ in sovereign power is sufficient to regenerate the heart; only repentance and faith and the efficacy of His sacrifice can effect that. The last and brief effort of mankind against God under the instigation of the evil one meets with immediate retribution. Satan is cast into the lake of fire. The earth and the heaven flee away. The tribunal of the great white throne is set, the dead are judged thereat, and the new heavens and earth, wherein dwelleth righteousness, are brought into being.

"Here, Babel and corruption,
    Man boasting in his shame;
But there, God's holy city
    His glory shall proclaim.

Here, those who follow Jesus,
    Reproach and shame must bear;
But there, enthroned, the meanest
    A diadem shall wear.

Here, down before his idol
    The heathen bends his knee;
But there, unveiled the glory
    Of God his eyes shall see.

The light of God shall cover
    The earth's wide fields, as spread
The tractless wastes of water
    O'er ocean's spacious bed.

O keep us, Holy Father,
    Keep us for that blest day,
When Jesus' royal scepter
    Holds undisputed sway.

Come, then, all-glorious Savior!
    Thy day bring swiftly nigh,
With foot that doth for fleetness
    The winds of Heaven defy.

Come! End the night of weeping,
    Bring in eternal day;
Come, Thou Bright Star of Morning!
    For this Thy people pray."
        —J. Boyd

APPENDIX

NOTE A

John 5:29 and Acts 24:15 are the only places in the New Testament in which there is specific reference to the resurrection of others than those who have trusted in Christ. In John 12:48, and a few other passages, their resurrection is implied.

That "the Last Day" is a period covering more than a thousand years, is clear from Revelation 20:4–12. Neither in John 5:29, nor in the passages in which the phrase occurs, is there any indication of this interval. "The Last Day" opens with the resurrection and rapture of believers, G-F, and closes with the resurrection and judgment of those who have not accepted Christ, and includes the millennium which intervenes, J-B. (See diagram, p. 156.) It is not "the end of the world," vulgarly so called, but the last day, or period, of man's accountability to God in his condition as a fallen being.

The "hour" of John 5:24, "The hour cometh, and now is, when the dead shall hear the voice of the Son of God and they that hear shall live," has already extended to nearly two thousand years, C-G. The "hour" of verse 28, "the hour cometh in which all that are in the tombs shall hear His voice, and shall come forth; they that have done good, unto the resurrection of life; they that have practiced ill, unto the resurrection of judgment," must be understood in the same way, G-B. "Day" and "hour," both used in an extended sense, are interchanged in John 16:25, 26.

Intervals between events are not always marked in the predictions of Scripture. Things that are foretold in the same sentence may yet be separated by long periods of time in the fulfillment. In Genesis 3:15, for example, three distinct things are predicted. Enmity between the woman and the serpent sprang up immediately; the serpent bruised the heel of the woman's Seed at the Cross, four thousand years later; after six thousand years the bruising of the serpent's head is still awaited.

Of the prophecy of Isaiah 11, verses 1–3 were fulfilled at the First Advent of Christ; the rest of the chapter refers to the effects of the Second Advent. "The acceptable year of the Lord" was ushered in when He came the first time, and continues unto this day. "The day of vengeance of our God" arrives when the Lord Jesus is revealed "from heaven with the angels of His power in naming fire," H-J. No interval is suggested in the words as they are recorded in Isaiah 61:2, yet the Lord ceased His reading at the end of the former phrase, and said, "Today hath this Scripture been fulfilled in your ears." The rest awaits. (See Luke 4:21; 2 Thess 1:7, 8.) The words of the Lord in John 5:29 present the same feature.

NOTE B

That John 5:25 does not refer to the resurrection but to the spiritual quickening, which is a present experience of each believer, seems plain enough. First, the addition of the words "and now is" which are absent from verse 28, is to be noted.

Second, the Lord speaks of "all that are in the tombs" to describe those whose bodies have ceased to discharge the functions of life and passed into corruption, reserving the word "dead" for the spiritual condition of all men in virtue of their descent from Adam. (See Eph. 2:1.) Third, these words are explanatory of verse 24, where those who believe are said to have passed out of death into life, obviously not an event to happen to the body in the future, but a present experience of the believing soul.

NOTE C

A different deduction is sometimes drawn from certain Scriptures, such as Revelation 14:4, which speaks of "firstfruits unto God and unto the Lamb." The firstfruits of the harvest is that portion which is earliest garnered. The word is used in the Old Testament only in a literal sense, in the New Testament only in a figurative. Believers of the apostolic age were "a kind of firstfruits of His [God's] creatures," that is, the beginning of the great and varied harvest of the Cross (James 1:18).

The Thessalonian converts had been chosen of God "as firstfruits unto salvation" (2 Thess. 2:13, marg.), which is probably the correct reading. Salvation is defined in the following verse as "the obtaining of the glory of our Lord Jesus Christ." Many among them had deserved the apostle's censure, but exclusion of such is not suggested by the apostle. Not some of the believers at Thessalonica, but the whole of them, are thus described as "firstfruits unto salvation."

This principle must be borne in mind throughout. Epaenetus did not differ from the converts that followed him in Asia Minor (Rom. 16:5). The household of Stephanus were not more faithful than those in Achaia who were converted later (1 Cor. 16:15).

In 1 Corinthians 15:20, 23 Christ is said to be "the firstfruits of them that are asleep." That is Christ personal, not Christ mystical, as though any of those who believe on Him were contemplated as included with Him. This is clear from verse 20, for it was Christ alone who was raised from the dead. Moreover the word firstfruits is a singular noun, notwithstanding the final s. In the general statement of Romans 11:16 "firstfruit" is used, but the Greek word is singular throughout.

The only remaining occurrence of the word is Revelation 14:4, where it is applied to a company of 144,000 persons (possibly the number is symbolic), who are seen with the Lamb on Mount Zion. An exposition of the passage would be beyond the limits prescribed for these chapters. The following suggestions may, however, be offered. The preceding chapter describes the condition of the world under the first beast, the false prince of peace, who attempts, by mingled fraud and force, by diabolic and by human power, to establish a universal empire. Chapter fourteen presents the contrast. Here is the true universal monarch, set by God on His holy hill. With Him are associated a host who are described as "purchased out of the earth." This is the sole ground of their presence with the

Lamb. There is no suggestion that by peculiar faithfulness or watchfulness they had earned the right to be there. It is possible they may be those who refused the mark of the beast. But there is no warrant for identifying them with an hypothetical company of faithful Christians who are to be caught away before the Great Tribulation, while the mass of then living members of the body of Christ pass through it. It is from the epistles of Paul that we learn of "the Church which is His Body," and of the resurrection and rapture of its members at the beginning of the Parousia, G-F. These epistles know nothing of a rapture earlier than that of 1 Thessalonians 4:13–17, which is to include all who belong to Christ (1 Cor. 15:23). Nor do they know anything of a firstfruits from the Church, though they do of a firstfruits from the world, as we have seen.

NOTE D

The words "we that are alive, that are left unto the Parousia of the Lord," do not commit the apostle to the belief that the Lord Jesus would return during his lifetime. Shortly afterward we find him using the same language concerning resurrection (2 Cor. 4:14), "shall raise up us also"; but that did not commit him to the belief that he would die before the Lord had come.

When the Lord Jesus returns, believers will be as they are now, and indeed as they were at Thessalonica, divided into two classes, the living and the dead. But the time of that return has not been revealed, it is among the secret things concerning which God has kept His own counsel. (See Deut. 29:29; Mark 13:32; Acts 1:7.) Consequently, in speaking of the return of the Lord Jesus, the apostle sometimes associates himself with the one class, looking forward to resurrection, as in 2 Corinthians 4:14, sometimes with the other, looking forward to change, as in 1 Thessalonians 4:13–17, and 1 Corinthians 15:51. His sympathy with those who were anxious about their dead leads him to associate himself with the mourners at Thessalonica; his sense of failing physical powers leads him to associate himself with those who had died at Corinth.

The second epistle to the Corinthians, moreover, in which he associates himself with those lying asleep, was written at no greater interval than three or four years after that to the Thessalonians, in which he associates himself with the living, at the Parousia.

It contains a passage, 5:1–10, expressing his own attitude toward the alternative possibilities, death and the coming of the Lord, and in it also he uses "we." In verses 2–4 he expresses his longing for that which cannot take place until the Lord comes, to be clothed with "our habitation which is from heaven," the "building from God," the "house not made with hands." In verse 6 he asserts that he is of good courage in the face of death, and in verse 8 repeats the assertion, adding that he is "willing rather to be absent from the body and to be at home with the Lord," i.e., to die. Longing for the Parousia of Christ, which is certain to come, yet not afraid of death, which may possibly come first, is, then, the characteristic attitude of each generation of Christians.

In the epistle to the Philippians, written perhaps seven years later still, while he describes his own attitude toward death, 1:21–24, in language akin to that used to the Corinthians, and suggests that it is no very remote contingency, 2:17, he yet uses "we" and "our" in describing the characteristic attitude of Christians to the coming of the Lord. His advancing years and the threatening nature of his circumstances, while they brought before his mind increasingly the possibility that he might die before the Parousia, did not prevent his saying, "heaven, from whence also we wait for a Savior" (Phil. 3:20).

And in the pastoral epistles, latest of all, whereas he uses language only explicable on the suggestion that he knew his own death to be imminent, he still speaks of the reward awaiting those who have loved the appearing of Christ (2 Tim. 4:6–8), and of the grace of God "instructing us, to the intent that . . . we should live . . . looking for the blessed hope" (Titus 2:11–13). Indeed, before he closes the epistle in which he says, "I am already being offered," he urges Timothy to come to him "before winter," a season presumably still some distance away, and to bring with him Mark as well as some articles of which he anticipated he would be in need. As always, so now when there seemed to be no escape from death, the apostle stood ready either for suffering or for service, or for the rapture of the saints that would deliver him from the one and bring the other to an end.

It seems clear, therefore, that no conclusion can be drawn from the apostle's language as to his personal expectations. He shared in what should be the attitude of each generation of Christians, the desire for, and the expectation of, the Parousia of the Lord, but there is no reason to suppose that he knew more on the subject than he taught (cp. 1 Cor. 13:12). Neither is there any evidence that the statements of the later epistles are intended to correct those written earlier. On the contrary, as we have seen, they supplement, but in no case do they contradict, previous declarations. Moreover, these words to the Thessalonians claim to be a revelation from the Lord Himself, and, while they might be expanded or explained by later revelation, they would not be set aside, much less could they be attributed to a mistaken apprehension on the part of the apostle. Throughout his life, as it is reflected in his epistles, he maintains the same attitude toward the great alternatives. There is no inconsistency. His example and his words alike teach us to be prepared to meet death with unflinching courage, but, above all things, to look for the Parousia of the Lord.

Hosea 12:4; Romans 13:13; Hebrews 12:25 may be compared for examples of this use of "us" and "we."

It is true of each man at all times, as it was true of David pursued by Saul, "there is but a step between [us] and death." And yet true as the apostle knew this to be of himself, he knew also that the Lord might come first. Experience has taught men that death is the one thing which can be really reckoned upon as an ever-present possibility. In the gospel it is revealed that to the Christian the Lord may possibly come first. If wise men thus reckon with death, how much more should the believer count upon the Parousia of the Lord!

NOTE E

Too often, it is to be feared, the word "rapture" is taken to refer to the peculiar joy of the redeemed when they meet the Lord. But the idea of ecstasy which arises from the conception of being carried out of oneself with joy, is entirely absent from the New Testament use of the word *harpazō*. Nor is the word "secret" ever attached to it there. In view of unhappy controversies it is well to confine ourselves to Scriptural phraseology as far as possible. As to the fact, this much may be said, that what is to happen "in the twinkling of an eye," cannot be witnessed and therefore must, insofar, be secret. But the removal of even a "little flock" from among men could not long remain a secret, if it was ever a secret at all. See *Notes on Thessalonians*.

NOTE F

Neither soul nor spirit is said to sleep at death; the word of 1 Thessalonians 4:13 (*koimaomai*) is used only of the body of the believer. This is clear from such a passage as Acts 13:36, for example: "David fell on sleep . . . and saw corruption." That part of David which fell on sleep was the part that saw corruption. At death the unclothed spirit (a condition in itself distasteful to the apostle, as may be seen from a comparison of 2 Cor. 5, v. 3 with v. 8) is "at home with the Lord." It is in view of this that he is ready even to die, for, he writes elsewhere, "to die is gain . . . to depart and to be with Christ . . . is very far better" (Phil. 1:21–23). To suggest that the otiose state, quiescence, if not unconsciousness, of spirit would commend itself to the apostle as preferable to his life of activity in service here betrays a curious misconception of his character.

Moreover, the preposition translated "with" (*pros*) in 2 Corinthians 5:8, denotes not merely to be in the same place with another, it means to be in communication with, to be receiving impressions from and imparting impressions to, another. The preposition would be inappropriate were the souls or spirits of the dead in Christ to be conceived of as in a state of unconsciousness.

NOTE G

"The Last Trump." It is hardly possible that the reference is to the last of the seven trumpets of the Apocalypse. These are figures, not actual trumpets; like the seals and the bowls they are part of the symbology under which the future was unfolded to John. To suppose that Paul refers to the seventh of John's series is to mistake the character of the Revelation, and to assume that what John saw and heard were the actual things that are yet to be seen and heard when the fulfillment comes, and not symbols, or figures, of those things. Moreover, there is no hint in his writings that Paul had any knowledge of the form under which the developments of human history were revealed to John, or, indeed, that he was acquainted with the Apocalypse at all. Moreover, he is not describing a vision; he is imparting information, describing things that are to occur. All the rest of the passage is to be understood literally; so also must this according to any sound canon of interpretation. The figure is that of any army receiving the signal to march; the "shout" of 1 Thessalonians 4:16 is also a military word with a like significance. It is possible the apostle may have in mind the trumpets by which the Israelites were summoned. The first and second blasts gathered them, the third was the signal to march (Num. 10:2–6).

NOTE H

Like "resurrection," "mortal" is applicable only to the body, and, indeed, only to the bodies of the living. The word immortality of necessity follows it; that is, it also is applicable only to the bodies of living believers as these will be affected by the change which is to take place in them at the Parousia of the Lord. "The immortality of the soul" is a purely pagan conception, arising out of the mistaken notion that evil is inherent in matter, and that, therefore, the body is the seat of sin and the source of all the ills of life. The only other New Testament occurrence of the word (athanasia) is 1 Timothy 6:16. The common use of immortal as equivalent to continuously existing is not found in the Bible at all. Immortality is not used of the unregenerate there, but neither is countenance given to the notion that any man will ever cease to be.

NOTE J

Zōopoieō, "to make alive," in the New Testament invariably means to impart life to what is dead. God raises the dead, that is, the bodies of the dead, and imparts life to them; so also does the Son (John 5:24; 1 Cor. 15:22). Romans 8:11 is to be understood in the same way; God will impart life to this mortal body; it shall put on immortality. There is no other passage of Scripture in which zōopoieō means a reinforcement of vigor, spiritual, mental or physical. There is no reason for the introduction of this idea here, since it is unwarranted either by the usage of the word or by the context.